Peace Education Around the World
Learning from the Past for the Future

Edited by
Robin Burns & Magnus Haavelsrud

Peace Knowledge Press

Peace Education Around the World: Learning from the Past for the Future
Editors: Robin Burns & Magnus Haavelsrud

Copyright © 2025 Peace Knowledge Press

Published by
Peace Knowledge Press
South Euclid, OH
peaceknowledgepress.com

ISBN: 978-1-7329622-4-8 (print edition)
ISBN: 978-1-7329622-5-5 (ebook)

The **cover photo** was taken by Palestinian journalist Aisha Zakzouk. It shows children with traditional handmade kites at the annual Dar il-Hikma (Nomura Center) Palestine kite festival in Gaza 2023.

Peace Knowledge Press book series editor: Tony Jenkins

Peace Knowledge Press is an imprint of the International Institute on Peace Education (IIPE) in partnership with the Global Campaign for Peace Education (GCPE). Net proceeds benefit these two global peace education initiatives. For this special volume, proceeds will also be shared with the Peace Education Commission of the International Peace Research Association.

Contents

Part III: Peace Education in Formal Education

Part IV: Informal and Non-formal Education, Communication and Cognitive Justice Initiatives

Introduction

Robin Burns

When I originally authored this introduction the Gaza ceasefire held precariously. Amid the scenes of joyous reunions on both sides, there was the terrible devastation of massive areas including whole cities in Gaza, and images of the injured, many of them children. We don't see the effects of strikes in Israel. The ceasefire, as this chapter was written, did not hold nor is there a new one. The terrible devastation of massive areas including whole cities in Gaza continues, with images of the injured and now starving, many of them children. And in Ukraine and Russia? In the West we see images of foreign soldiers captured, injured and worse, serving the Russian side, against Ukraine. The war in Ukraine and in the Middle East, and internal conflicts in Sudan, the Democratic Republic of the Congo and Myanmar are but the more prominent cases of direct violence in the world today, on a national and international scale. A reported 50% increase in incidents of assault in the public schools in the state of Victoria was recent front-page news here. Reports multiply of increased religious hate, domestic violence, growing rich-poor gaps and insidious extremism. And we read that yet another native animal or plant has become endangered by climate change, loss of habitat and land clearance for human activities. The media rarely reports the structural and cultural violence of ongoing, indeed growing inequalities, denigration of indigenous knowledges or human rights abuses but they exist.

Against a media bombardment with direct violence, some friends have asked, as I talk enthusiastically about this book, what use is peace education? And why am I involved with it? To answer that, as we have asked the contributors to this volume, I would have to go back to family experiences and attitudes in my childhood in post-World War II Australia, to the associations I joined at University advocating for independence of former colonies, involvement in their development, and in the disarmament movement. One issue led to another and in 1974 to the Peace Education Commission (PEC), some lasting friendships and my establishment of peace education within teacher education. The peace education anthology *Three Decades of Peace Education around the World* (Burns & Aspeslagh, 1996) focused on the work of members of PEC.

The 1975 *Global Strategy for Communication and Consciousness-raising*, the product of peace educators meeting at an International Peace Research Association (IPRA) Summer School (Burns & Aspeslagh, 1996, p. 17) was the starting point for the contributions to that anthology. An overview of the background, concepts and theoretical issues involved with peace education was its starting point, followed by perspectives on the substance and impact of peace education, and finally a range of approaches to the process of peace education. The overall aim in this volume is to consider what is happening in the field since that time. In his concluding chapter, Haavelsrud raises some challenging conceptual issues especially concerning the formation of a person's consciousness in particular contexts and, where violence or conflict is involved, what should be changed, the goals, and the means for this. Chapter after chapter addresses these issues and while some authors aim for a universal culture or cultures of peace, Haavelsrud and Wulf in particular propose the pluriverse as the critical context. This in turn necessitates empowering the individual to interrogate their position within power structures and work for change.

Three decades ago some peace educators moved the goal from structural peace to personal peace. But in the move from the global to the local, the link to the global was often lost. Personal peace may be one desired consequence for some peace work, as part of the creation of community peacefulness, for example Amada's account of indigenous knowledge as "the good life", for the group as well as the individual. The psychological/biological level may empower learners to exercise agency but does not stop at the personal. Bajaj (2018) distinguishes between agency leading to resistance and change of educational structures from unequal outcomes for learners, and one that can lead to transformative change beyond the educational institution. Zembylas and

Bekerman (2013) question the possibility for formal education to reform in order to adopt, and to prepare teachers to instill, the 'appropriate' knowledge and skills in students for "the implementation of peace, tolerance, justice, equality, and recognition values for all" (p. 5).

Some current authors do indeed challenge educational institutions as a medium for transformative peace education; half of the contributions detail work in the non-formal or informal sectors. Formal The scope of the learning activities has broadened, and whereas indigenous knowledges and equal partnership in the natural world were tentatively mentioned in 1996, they recur in the current chapters. Respect for the other, both in dialogic encounters in violent situations, and as a principle in peace work, are also prominent now. There is less discussion of pedagogy as such in the descriptions of peace work. Nevertheless, there is large and varied range of approaches described.

Before discussion of the actual chapters here, how we have gone about obtaining them will be presented.

The Origins of this Book

For the 50th anniversary of the founding of the Peace Education Committee in 1972, Betty Reardon, co-founder with Christoph Wulf, and with Magnus, first executive secretary of the Peace Education Commission, wrote a message for current PEC members. The anniversary was celebrated at the 2023 Trinidad General IPRA conference. Magnus and Betty's account is reprinted here. The authors used it to set a course for PEC's future. Magnus has continued to be involved with peace education since that time and through this book has offered me an invaluable opportunity for involvement and re-connection with peace educators internationally.

I ceased my formal involvement with PEC when my term as executive secretary ended in 1987, friendship with Magnus and with Robert Aspeslagh continued. When Robert sadly died of cancer in 2016, I wrote an obituary for the *Journal of Peace Education*. They advised that they did not publish such accounts. A journal Board member subsequently suggested a new book on peace educators. By its 50th anniversary in 2022 PEC was already missing some leading peace educators: Mario Borrelli (Italy), Robert Aspeslagh (The Netherlands), Sanàa Osseiran (Lebanon) and Anita Wenden (Canada) come to mind. The numbers continue to mount and we have now lost Johan Galtung (Norway), Betty Reardon (US), Ian M. Harris (US) and Olga Vorkunova (Russian Federation). As we go to press, the sad news of Kazuyo Yamane's (Japan: ch. 23) passing reached us.

Magnus and I decided it was time for another anthology as it was 28 years since the publication of *Three Decades of Peace Education around the World*. Our first thoughts were to review pioneering work by PEC members in the field. As we discussed contributions in the PEC-initiated *Journal of Peace Education* more names were added. Then as we identified contextual, geo-political and pedagogical gaps, networking has resulted in nearly 30 chapters from around the world. For example, friends would ask me, "Have you got someone from Ukraine?" remembering World University Service-Austria worked extensively with Balkan institutions so I asked our Austrian contributor for a suggestion. He introduced us to our contributor in Ukraine. One Israeli writer was introduced by a former university colleague, while a former diplomatic colleague introduced me to our British Quaker contributor. Magnus has a much wider knowledge of the field as he has been active for more than half a century, with conference attendance, visiting positions, membership of the board of the *Journal of Peace Education* and friendships. He has suggested most of the names. As a reflection of his concern with the importance of context in designing peace education initiatives, we increasingly looked to find writers in a range of violent, conflicted situations as well as from different worldviews (see his chapter for an extended discussion of this).

Contributors were tasked as follows: We wish you to write about your personal 'journey' into peace educational practice and then move on to discuss the context, values and pedagogical practices that have been central to your work for peace. It is not intended as a strictly academic book but rather a record of the different approaches to peace education that have been formed and the details of your particular work for peace through education.

Behind each person's involvement with peace education is a unique journey, but recounting it suggests the contextual factors that motivate a person to become involved with peace education, advocacy and peace building. Those contexts may be very local, or extend to the global; change, interact, and as some authors point out, include those internal to the individual through interaction with their external world. In one way or another all want the transformation of a context steeped not only in direct violence but structural and cultural violence, to one where equality, respect and justice prevail. And to work between the local and what can now be termed the pluriversal. Education alone cannot achieve this, but failure to address the issues in lifelong formal, informal and non-formal learning settings is to perpetuate the current status quo.

Over the year we have been working together with contributors, a rich and varied tapestry of issues, approaches and ways of writing has emerged.

We have contributions from Palestine and Israel, Ukraine and Russia writing about ongoing peace research and educational forms and initiatives in their war-torn countries, and from Myanmar and South Korea. One chapter briefly mentions Sudan but we have been unable to locate someone to write from there. In addition to Ukraine, I have been asked: "What about Afghanistan?" I was given a book by an Australian volunteer who first visited Afghanistan in 2016 (Isaacs, 2019, p. ix). There he was introduced to a Pakistani doctor who with a group of volunteers had established a multi-ethnic share house. Inspired by Peace House, Isaacs returned a year later. Through interviews with participants in the Peace House, he wrestles with the historical complexities of the ethnic composition of Afghanistan, its tribal nature, and cultural and religious obstacles to dialogue and shared action for peace. There were brave female volunteers at the Peace House and he explains the particular barriers they have faced.

That was in the relative calm before the return of the Taliban. Akbari (an Afghani academic at Monash University, Australia) and True (2024) outline four peace and conflict phases in Afghanistan in the past 20 years. Their study examined the attempted embedment of the UN policy framework Women, Peace and Security. This policy framework recognises that peace and security is more sustainable when women are equal partners in the prevention of violent conflict, the delivery of relief and recovery efforts, and in the forging of lasting peace. They concluded that the program in Afghanistan lacked a grounded understanding of gendered constraints in a conflict transition, as well as a political strategy. This points to a more generalised issue with attempts to connect an international normative framework to local voices who understand the context-specific, patriarchal power dynamics. Respect for local knowledge is crucial for effective action for change. Both of the foregoing studies underline the importance of analysis of the local context as a basis for this, a theme that appears in many of the chapters here.

While we have not been prompted to consider Lebanon or Syria, or the general uncertainties in the Middle East but readers should be apprised of the work undertaken by the late Sanàa Osseiran (see Epilogue). Both Magnus and Robert were each involved with her initiatives.

Directions for Content, and Resulting Contribution

With the obituary for Robert Aspeslagh as the starting point, and the increasing number of publications, particularly the contributions to debate, research, theorising and ideas for programs found in the *Journal of Peace Education*, we took a different approach to the 1996 anthology. There have been earlier accounts of peace education 'journeys' (Toh, 1991; Zuber, 1994). Where are they leading now? We therefore asked contributors to outline how they became involved in peace education and then to write about their ideas and activities. Some have explicitly traced this, in several cases using their journey as the key organising principle for their contribution as they recount people and situations they have encountered and the way these have formed their peace activities (see especially Borrelli as recounted by Desideri, Italy; Kumar, India; Sheliazhenko, Ukraine; Toh, Malaysia/Canada, and Cawagas, Philippines/Canada; Wintersteiner, Austria; Zuber, US). Odora Hoppers (Uganda) takes readers along her intellectual journey.

Those working in formal, especially tertiary institutions, their framework for their peace education work is a conceptual journey. Sergunin presents this for the late Vorkunova. Köylü presents his analysis of peace in Islam and its use in formal education and presumably also in his theological teaching. In collaboration with the late Betty Reardon, Snauwaert's tertiary courses arise from and incorporate their detailed philosophy for peace education. And while less prominent in their accounts, a conceptual rationale is integral to the varied peace education and related activities in the non-formal and informal spheres presented here.

One factor leading contributors to concern for peace has been early learning of the negative experience of family members with war or the military, as told by Amal Amara Takkash (Palestine), Yurii Sheliazhenko (Ukraine), Kazuyo Yamane (Japan), and Soon-Won Kang (South Korea). Ela Gandhi continues the work at the South African settlement her grandfather Mahatma Gandi established in 1904. For some the underpinning is religious beliefs especially Quakerism (Diana Francis, UK; Yurii Sheliazhenko, and Celina Garcia of Costa Rica) and Roman Catholicism (Virginia Cawagas, Philippines/Canada and Mario Borrelli, Italy, though he left the priesthood to better serve the people and challenge authorities). The practice of his faith is foundational for Bob Zuber (US). On the other hand, Maung Zarni (Burma/Myanmar) is critical of the active support of Burmese Buddhism for the militaristic regime. He has had to overcome a long history of family connections with and support for the military. Both Yurii's father, in the Soviet Army, and Hillel Schenker (Israel) were repulsed by experience in the military. These and other pathways to involvement with active peace work are found here. The range of work is wide, from explicit teaching, to grass-roots activism, the media, advocacy and research.

Minorities, the 'Other' and Different Voices

Since post-modernism and subsequently post-colonialism appeared especially in social and cultural studies, there are vexed questions for researchers concerning who we choose to speak with and the power relationships with those we seek to study. The anthropologist Clifford Geertz (1988) raised the additional issue of what happens in the process of writing about other people's lives. How we choose with whom to speak has been criticized by minority group people for decades. At a development education conference I attended in 1973 a participant from the then Southern Rhodesia questioned the criteria for participation and dramatically walked out of the conference. Geography and context as well as known peace work but not ethnicity were used in our invitations to contribute. The issue of coloniality however has been raised by several authors here (Odora Hoppers, Wintersteiner) in addition to consideration of examples of indigenous knowledges for better living (Benavides de Perez). There is also criticism of the impact of western materialism and greed, science, technology on the survivability of the planet (e.g.

Gandhi, Kaneko, Qumsiyeh).

Gender Inclusivity Within Peace Research, Education and Action

Thus, inclusivity has emerged as a theme by many contributors, and we have tried to be inclusive both of gender and context. As a female academic and former diplomat who commenced her working life in 1965, I have always been in the minority in the workplace and related circles. This has often been apparent to me at conferences, especially international conferences. In 1966 there were only four women at the World University Service general assembly in Tanzania and I was the only woman at a subsequent international workcamp in Burundi, the only woman in the Department of Psychology when I undertook post-graduate work, then again, the only woman in the Centre for Comparative and International Education where I remained alone for 27 years. In the early 1980s I became the first female president of the Australia and New Zealand Comparative and International Education Society and the first female executive secretary of PEC. I am happy that my successor (Celina Garcia), Candice Carter and other women have subsequently held that position, most recently Olga Vorkunova. Education, at least at the formal pre- and school levels, is largely conducted by women, though the occupants of senior positions in schools have only slowly reflected this. Betty Reardon pointed out decades ago that "few women and fewer feminists, have been read or heard, much less attended to, in research and policy discourse" (1975, p. 72). She further argues that this had consequences for the way that peace research was defined and studied.

Women have had a public role in peace work from the Women's International League for Peace and Freedom founded in 1915 (Bussey & Tims, 1980). Women's actions, especially directed against nuclear arms, were prominent during the first International Women's Decade (1975-1985), most notably: the Greenham Common Women's Peace Camp in the UK (1981 -2000 after the American missiles and base were evacuated), and cross-national Peace Walks (e.g. Copenhagen to Paris, 1981; Stockholm to Minsk, 1982). Women have always been involved in war, as producers and 'servicers' of soldiers (male) and on the other hand, as symbols of values such as peace and nurturance, with an interest as mothers, in conflict resolution (Boulding, 1975, p. 167; Burns, 1996,

p. 45). But to consider all women predisposed towards peace is to anchor values in gender, not the culture in which attitudes, values and behaviour are formed (Eglin, 1984).

We have not specifically sought to select or analysed our contributions on the basis of gender or gender-based concepts, values and programs. Odora Hoppers clearly raises gender as an issue in her chapter and elsewhere gender issues are now included as context and/or content for peace education (e.g. Francis, Kumar, Richardson, Wintersteiner). You the readers can decide if women (and these days members of the LGBTQI community) have different approaches to key concepts and the promotion of a culture of peace, and if so the implications for peace building. This in turn has implications for both the ways to approach that culture and its very nature. Respect for the other and their knowledge and contextual experience is now central in peace education for many of the contributions here – see in particular chapters by Bekerman (Israel), Benevidas de Perez (Colombia), Soudien (South Africa), Kaneko and Yamane (both Japan), Snauwaert including his reflections on Betty Reardon's work (both US).

Contextual Considerations in Selection of Contributors: Geography and Demography

As noted above, we have contributions from authors involved in well-recognised situations where conflict and violence are common experiences: Palestine, Israel, Ukraine, Myanmar and also South Africa. The latter then segues into many further situations where violence is at least an underlying threat. In the present decade extremism is fueling social division that spills into violence, and structural factors can underlie family violence in its many forms from physical to psychological and economic. And as a number of contributors also argue, violence is also wreaked on nature; its repair through recognition that we are a part is vital for the planetary future (see especially Wulf, Germany; Kaneko, Japan, and Qumsiyeh, Jarrar & Sadar, Palestine).

Borrelli (Italy), Kumar (India) and Zuber (US) have worked in disadvantaged communities. For Borrelli, designing interventions in order to weaken the political manipulation of the marginal and excluded sub-proletariat involved them in the quest for improving public and social services (Borrelli, 1975).

There are echoes of this work in other chapters. It could be argued that wherever peace education starts with those outside the 'mainstream', with violent black youth in South Africa (Soudien) or prisoners in Costa Rican jails (Garcia & Romero), refugee children (Takkash, Palestine and Egypt), children of ethnic minorities in British schools (Richardson) or supporting local leaders and activists in conflict situations (Francis), disadvantage is being addressed. This flows directly in most accounts from Johan Galtung's distinction between direct, structural and cultural violence (Galtung, 1971, 1981).

Contributors come from every inhabited continent.

We briefly discussed trying to include China. It is the second most powerful economy, is especially present in the South China Sea and building infrastructure such as ports particularly in Africa and the Pacific. In the world today, and with rivalry shaping up between China and the US in 2025, it is unfortunate we do not have a contribution from or about China.

I received one comment on the perceived senior years of contributors. Yes, most are in the later stages of their working lives though most who have officially 'retired' are still intellectually and socially active. Nor did we consider age as such in our search. We hope that through presenting a range including more experienced peace educators we are able to show both continuities and changes in the field. At least one contributor has critically evaluated his work over a number of decades (Werner Wintersteiner).

Other than requesting they write about their journey to and with peace education, and their main ideas and activities, we have given very little direction to authors and this has resulted in a rich tapestry of approaches and accounts.

The Chapters: An Overview

There is ongoing engagement in these pages with key concepts, their development and critique. Some contributions are academic, others more personal. Some deal mainly with underlying theoretical considerations, while others provide inspiring examples of peace building work. There is not only an interesting variety of 'stories' and examples of peace-building and education in a large range of contexts, but an underlying sense that peace IS possible and that it is a goal towards which we can aspire. Opening each chapter, I have often been tearful not just with what the author has experienced, but the hope and determination they express, and the underlying humanity and love they share. We hope that you who read this book will find it too.

No chapter deals with one theme or issue only so it is difficult to attempt to organise them in that way. That is particularly the case in the extended peace journeys of Toh & Cawagas (Malaysia/Philippines), Wintersteiner (Austria), Ukraine (Sheliazhenko) and South Africa (Soudien). They move between formal educational institutions and community organisations. Toh & Cawagas include work with army recruits and Celina with prisoners. Key concepts will be subsumed here within the discussion of themes, First, however, is the issue of for whom peace education is intended.

Intended Participants in Peace Education

Perhaps the most basic distinction is between peace education directed at learners in formal education and those intended for nonformal and informal settings. Kölyü analyses the religious and moral knowledge curriculum in Turkey for links with peace-related issues, thus affirming the formal system. In an historical overview, Richardson outlines the development of World Studies in the UK as issues relevant to a more peaceful culture have been included. The courses established by Sheliazhenko (Ukraine, within Law) and Vorkunova, Russian Federation (international relations and security studies) are detailed, though the underlying theme of Sheliazhenko's chapter is a critique of the normative, militaristic basis of Ukrainian institutions. Kang & Kwon critique unification education in schools in South Korea, suggesting a different orientation to the issue of reunification of the two Koreas (Kang & Kwon, South Korea). Formal education is the assumed base though non-formal is mentioned in Snauwaert's contribution; both were certainly important for his mentor and collaborator Betty Reardon. Many different participants are intended in the large number of chapters dealing with informal and non-formal teaching and learning. The activities include the production of printed media (Zarni, Burma/Myanmar; Hillel, Israel). Direct resistance (Borrelli, Zarni, Sheliazhenko, Wintersteiner) has been to government and its instrumentalities. On the other hand, demonstrations and boycotts usually target the public in general though media attention is often the clearest achievement, even objective (Douglas, 2004, ch.1).

Content

Writing of her early education in Uganda, Odora Hoppers tells how she recited a chapter of "Rip van Winkle" at a school concert to an uncomprehending audience most of whom did not speak English, and had to learn songs about English meadows and Canadian woods which were foreign even to their teachers. It reminds me of being told how the stories of the "Little red engine that could" were widely found in schools in Papua New Guinea which still has no railways. Although old examples, there are doubtless still equivalents in appropriate materials and tasks, for instance for recently arrived migrant and refugee children at their new schools. For Kaneko government war museums in Japan do not show a critical side of Japan's performance in war while Yumiko's criticism is especially of western science and religion claiming dominance over nature contrary to Japanese Shinto religion. Bekerman (Israel) is not only critical of basic concepts in education but includes academic research in his critique. Some deplore the ignorance of indigenous knowledges and their absence from formal institutions. Further, Benavides de Perez in Colombia demonstrates the loss of the value base of other types of knowledge in academic-western Cartesian research and consequent formal education

Since the Burns & Aspeslagh anthology, there is a broadening of discussion of content. While 'other educations' were described as 'confusing' in that anthology (p.13), where mentioned now, most authors include peace, conflict, development, human rights, gender and other forms of discrimination, and the environment. This enables the construction of discourses that identify the forms violence takes in a particular context, and therefore possible paths to transformation of the violence towards a just, respectful, peaceful world. Education alone will not achieve this, but if the causes of violence are not addressed, there is little hope for change. And while no program addresses all the issues at once, it is a larger palette from which to sketch action here, in this place and at this time. The current anthology is rich with examples.

Context

This is fundamental to most of the current authors' work (see especially chapter 30 by Magnus Haavelsrud). I am reminded of his question at a PEC meeting in the late 1970s, when we had been discussing the final struggles for independence especially in Africa. As we wrestled with this question, Magnus asked: "What would peace education look like in a liberation movement?" I think the closest we come to some consideration of related contexts here is Crain Soudien's in South Africa, dealing with post-apartheid conflict, and Amal Takkash's work with children's identity through learning about history and culture in war-torn Palestine. In both examples, changing or developing identity in which the person gains respect for themselves is primary. On that basis it is possible to enter into a dialectical relationship with others and extend to them mutual respect. In turn, respect in our engagement with the environment enables the discovery of the bases of conflict there and possibilities to address them. The work of the South African Research Chair Initiative (SARCHI), developed by Odora Hoppers, involving Soudien, Haavelsrud and others offers practical examples. Zarni engaged in dialogue with the 'enemy' in Myanmar though even with advocacy from Johan Galtung it was short-lived. On the other hand, in the context of the Philippines Toh and Cawagas engaged especially using creative tasks, with new soldiers, while Young worked with militia brigadiers disarming and disbanding after the Northern Ireland Easter Peace Agreement.

Education in all its forms, from socialisation in the family onwards, is critical for the formation of identity, in turn critical for our ways of perceiving and acting with the layers of context within which we live. Bekerman maintains that the notion that peace education can exist separately from primary learning theories or perspectives on human development is fundamentally flawed and undermines the integrity of educational research. How identity is formed will affect the way the individual behaves in the world. For example, Soudien investigates how a violent youth identity is formed among marginal black youth in South African schools.

The largest canvas is painted by Christoph Wulf using the concept of the Anthropocene to create a global – or rather, pluriversal - context, acknowledging diversity and all that implies for the way we work. Based on UNESCO's promotion of global citizenship he proposes three dimensions for peace education: the cognitive, the socio-emotional and the behavioural, thus bringing together knowing, feeling and acting. He urges planetary awareness of a common natural and cultural heritage as an important ingredient for people's self-image and for the development of a global citizenship oriented towards sustainability and peace. Such an awareness is vital for the comprehensive transformations that lie ahead in the Anthropocene. He does not suggest here how we convince people to participate. However, others are more detailed about the pedagogies that are to be employed.

How Teaching-learning Communication Takes Place

Linking content, context and pedagogy, Wulf suggests that the approach he has taken to thinking about building understanding between and amongst ourselves as human beings – not just making peace but *keeping* it - is that we have to prioritise the critical procedure of sense-making. This, however, is easier said than done. What sense-making procedures do we have at our disposal? And given the strong associations between formal educational and the concept of pedagogy and the much wider range of examples in this volume, it is suggested that 'communication' is a more accurate basic concept.

As a basic approach to communication, Odora Hopper stresses the importance of 'cognitive justice'. Applying this, the university was mandated "to link with other stakeholders, particularly those at the margins who are the holders of other epistemologies and producers of knowledge in other systems, and together, work out protocols, terms and conditions for the integration of the different traditions of knowledge" (see her chapter here). Benavides de Perez, Kumar and Borrelli's work illustrates how this can be undertaken.

The question of communication and cognitive justice is linked to critiques of formal educational systems that are based on the dominant western paradigm. Bekerman, Odora Hoppers and Soudien tease out the disempowering effects of the suppression of local culture and histories, for example those that underlie conflict. All three contributors, through different examples, have used dialogue among stakeholders as a basis for learning different behaviours and attitudes. Paulo Freire, the Brazilian educator, is mentioned by several contributors and seems still to be the provider of a learning methodology to enable the learners to examine their context, identify the bases for their concerns especially the role of powerlessness, and work towards transformation.

Critical dialogue, with acknowledgment and inclusion of different, especially indigenous knowledge systems, emerges as a basic necessity in creating a transformative path to positive peace. And several authors give a variety of examples of experiential learning as a key to changing perceptions of self and other (Benevides de Perez, Toh & Cawagas, Takkash, Yumiko). Haavelsrud has written of the way novels and short stories can facilitate learning about the other (2023). Kumar's contribution uses poetic form to bring us into a different psychological state for considering key issues.

The most extensive examples of informal education are found in Udayakumar's account of protest movements against nuclearisation in India. He argues persuasively that protest IS peace education and shows the connections that the nuclear issue has with violence against the human and the natural world justice, inclusion and giving the silenced people voice.

Now read on and discover the riches, the contentious issues, the questions and the resources our contributors offer.

References

Akbari, F. & True, J. (2024). Bargaining with patriarchy in peacemaking: The failure of women, peace, and security in Afghanistan. *Global Studies Quarterly* 4. Available at: https://doi.org/10.1093/isagsq/ksac004.

Bajaj, M. (2018). Conceptualizing transformative agency in education for peace, human rights, and social justice. *International Journal of Human Rights Education* 2(1). Retrieved from https://repository.usfca.edu/ijhr/vol2/iss1/13.

Boulding, E. (1975). *Women in the twentieth century world*. Sage.

Burns, R. (1996). Is peace a feminist issue? Outline for a tertiary course based on evidence from women's involvement in peace education, research and action. *Pacifica Review* 8(2), 45-79.

Burns, R. J., & Aspeslagh, R. (Eds.). (1996). *Three decades of peace education around the world*. Garland.

Bussey, G. & Tims, M. (1980 re-issue). *Pioneers for peace. Women's International League for Peace and Freedom 1915-1965.* WILPF British Section.

Douglas, R. (2004). *Dealing with demonstrations: The law of public protest and its enforcement.* The Federation Press.

Eglin, J. (1984). Women and Nonviolence. *Social Alternatives* 4(1), 21-5.

Freire, P. (1972). *Pedagogy of the oppressed.* Penguin.

Galtung, J. (1971). A structural theory of imperialism. *Journal of Peace Research* 8, 81-117.

Galtung, J. (1990). Cultural violence. *Journal of Peace Research* 27(3), 291 – 305.

Geertz, C. (1988). *The anthropologist as author.* Stanford University Press.

Haavelsrud, M. (2023). How novels and short stories are resources for learning about the other. *The Journal of Social Encounters.* 7(2), 186-202. Available at: https://digitalcommons.csbsju.edu/social_encounters/vol7/iss2/13.

Isaacs, M. (2019). *The Kabul Peace House.* Hardie Grant Books.

Reardon, B. A. (1985). *Sexism and the war system.* Teachers College Press.

Toh, Swee-Hin (Ed.). (1991). *Journeys in peace education: Critical reflections from Australia.* EARTH.

Zembylas, M. & Bekerman, Z. (2013). Peace education in the present: dismantling and reconstructing some fundamental theoretical premises. *Journal of Peace Education,* DOI:10.1080/17400201.2013.790253.

Zuber, R, (1994). *Journeys in peace education: critical reflection and personal witness.* Malmö: School of Education Peace Education Report no. 14.

Chapter 1

IPRA-PEC – Projecting a Next Phase: Reflections on Its Roots, Processes and Purposes

Magnus Haavelsrud and Betty A. Reardon

Reviewing PEC's Past to Project its Preferred Future [1]

In observation of the 50th anniversary of the establishment of the Peace Education Commission (PEC) of the International Peace Research Association, two of its founding members reflect on its roots as they look to its future. Magnus Haavlesrud and Betty Reardon (also founding members of the Global Campaign for Peace Education) invite current members to reflect on the present and the existential threats to human and planetary survival that now challenge peace education to project a significantly revised future for PEC and its role in taking up the challenge.

A Message to Present Members of the Peace Education Commission (PEC) of IPRA From Magnus Haavelsrud and Betty A. Reardon, Founding Members

Introduction: Setting a Course for PEC's Future

The 2023 Trinidad General Conference is an appropriate venue in which to observe the 50th anniversary of the Peace Education Commission of the International Peace Research Association, to review its goals and methods and to set a course for its future. The foundation was laid in Bled, Yugoslavia at the 1972 General Conference when Saul Mendlovitz, Christoph Wulf and Betty Reardon proposed it to the IPRA Council which set up a Peace Education Committee with Christoph Wulf as chair. The Commission was officially founded in 1974 at the IPRA General Conference in Varanasi, India where Magnus Haavelsrud was elected PEC's first Executive Secretary. From its inception PEC was conceptually clear, normatively guided and structured its organization for normative consistency in fulfilling its purposes. Its founding documents, its strategy and bylaws appear in Appendices 1 and 2.

Circumstances and Contexts of PEC's Beginnings

From the beginning, PEC was purposeful and systematic, and more than a biennial gathering of peace educators. The young PEC was a vital learning community whose members had a strong sense of solidarity, a profound commitment to making education a significant instrument for peace, a fierce loyalty to each other and a shared vision of a transformed world that they had commonly conceived. It was focused, purposeful and intentionally organized as can be seen in "A Global Strategy for Communication and Consciousness Raising in Various Local Settings" (Burns & Aspeslagh, 1996) developed in 1975 at IPRA's Summer School in Västerhaninge, near Stockholm, Sweden (full text in Appendix 1).

The conceptual and communal cohesion of PEC's early days were the consequence of these IPRA Summer Schools which provided, over several consecutive years, a venue for intensive exchanges and formative learning as members from all world regions grappled with the commonalities and differences of professional contexts, perspectives and problem priorities. Working through and learning from these differences and engaging in analysis of commonalities enabled PEC as a learning community to produce "A Global Strategy...," influenced by the structural analyses of peace research and the critical pedagogy, newly introduced by Paolo Freire. The document, a product of a fully participatory and open process, articulates a purpose well worth reviewing today to assess not only the relevance of its substance, but to understand the importance of process and context to determining and articulating common purposes.

In those early days, following the end of the Vietnam War, in the midst of neo-colonial struggles, peace researchers and peace educators, becoming awakened to the structural violence of the world system, began to learn from each other, building a common body of learning. Those common learnings became the foundation of peace education as it developed over the last third of the 20th century through liberation struggles, the Cold War, the rise of the anti-nuclear movement and their waning. That foundation remained relevant until the first years of the 21st century challenged it with the "War on Terror."

Throughout its first decades, members of the PEC learning community brought this foundation to their involvement in landmark events and developments in the field, continuing to learn from all available sources, as its members provided conceptual frameworks and guiding values to the work of others in the field. Among the events and programs influenced by PEC members were: the First World Conference of the World Council for Curriculum and Instruction in 1974; UNESCO's World Conference on Disarmament Education in 1980; the founding of the first graduate program in peace education at Teachers College Columbia University and the first International Institute on Peace Education in 1982: a UNESCO project of producing a Handbook on Disarmament Education; and The Global Campaign for Peace Education, established in 2000, among others.

PEC has also been a significant influence on IPRA itself, having introduced to the association gender and ecology as essential substance for peace research. Issues raised by an emerging women and peace movement were addressed within PEC until they were assumed by a separate IPRA commission. It has been the most consistently organized and purposeful of all the commissions. It is the only commission to be governed by bylaws drafted at its founding, guided by the common purpose and shared vision of global strategy, and the only one to publish its own journal.

These events and developments were parallel to on-going collaborative efforts among members that produced a body of literature on the theory and practice of the field that facilitated its worldwide development and dissemination. While specifics of the field varied from region to region and country to country, those developments in which PEC members were involved continued to be infused by the vision of the Global Strategy. In recognition of these achievements, IPRA was awarded the 1989 UNESCO Prize for peace education.

All of this developmental history culminated in the founding in 2004 of the *Journal of Peace Education* more or less simultaneously with the emergence of the challenges of a new historic context.[2] The journal is evidence of a firmly established field, but it could also become the medium for what we believe to be the need for a new vision, purpose and strategy that responds to the peace challenges of the mid decades of the 21st century. For these reasons we encourage close attention to reviewing PEC's founding statement of purpose with a view to the formulation of one for its next phase. The work of PEC has been seminal in the evolution of the contemporary fields of peace knowledge; and we believe it can play a similar role in the present and future.

"A Global Strategy for Communication and Consciousness Raising in Various Local Settings": A Statement of Founding Purposes [3]

A reflection of the emerging structural analyses that peace research was then bringing to a growing awareness of the injustices of global economic and political structures, "A Global Strategy..." is also a statement of anti-imperialism. It was based on a belief that peace education must be formed to the particular types of violence integral to those structures as they are manifest in the various locales in which it is practiced. With a view toward learning to transcend and transform those forms of violence, the strategy asserts a pedagogical preference for dialogue (i.e. "communication") and for challenging dominant modes of thinking (i.e. "consciousness raising.") These assertions reinforce PEC's predilection toward contextual design and practice, recognizing the integral relationship between the local and the global in its context. and embracing critical dialogic reflection as the preferred pedagogy.

The strategy is intended to strengthen the formation of a peaceful movement towards a new reality based on values of a just peace. Communication and consciousness raising in this movement relates to all parts of the world system, thus it is global. Participation of all parts of the system is necessary for achieving changes towards peace values through the development of a new reality. Strengthening links and cooperation among all parts of the world system, such as that which characterized the young PEC was held to promise a greater impact. We believe it is imperative that PEC continue to involve members from diverse contexts and all world regions on such consideration of education´s role in the transformation of the global systems and structures that still deprive and oppress too many.

In 1974, the purpose of peace learning was seen as the transformation of contextual conditions that cause direct, structural and cultural violence. Learning peace, the drafters believed, is not limited to critical reflection. It requires the experiential learning of action toward the desired transformation. Actions should be judged on their potential to change both structures and cultures – at various levels from persons and communities to the macro structures that comprise the world system.

We have learned that peace learning supports and initiates developments towards more peace (i.e. less violence) and evidence of this may be found in all places and times, ranging from individual experiences in everyday life to movements at the global level. The cultural voice of education, we now argue, is therefore of political relevance to illuminate the need for transformation of problematic – sometimes violent – contextual conditions. When problematic circumstances prevail, pedagogic activity may respond by adapting to the status quo – or resist it with the intention of change. If such resistance is not possible within formal education, it is always possible, as historical experience has demonstrated (to varying degrees of difficulty – and danger) in informal and/or non-formal education. Clearly, PEC's founders recognized that the integrity of peace education is directly related to the moral courage of its practitioners. This we learned from our colleagues "on the ground" in non-formal programs confronting structural oppression as actually experienced. Education in developments towards nonviolent conflict transformation, liberating and democratic learning in opposition to oppressive political authorities, is a different challenge from education provided by the dominant powers of societies.

Within such a libratory ethos there is need for agreed orders of procedures to assure normative consistency and effective, focused action. The Bylaws were our attempt to establish such guidelines for the organization of the Commission.

The Bylaws of PEC:
Assuring that the Process Serves the Purpose[4]

PEC's founders agreed that the continuity and effectiveness of our common work must be assured by clearly stated guidelines for governance of the endeavors of our diverse group bound together by our common purpose. Toward this end Bylaws were adopted that – although fallen from practice – are still in force. We structured them within the larger structure of IPRA, hoping to assure that education would remain an integral part of the Association's mission.

Believing that the interest of developing present and future peace building and peace learning requires participation of all parts of the present world system, the Bylaws are meant to ensure such participation and may still serve as a tool towards this purpose.

Conclusions and Suggestions for Projecting
PEC's Future

With a view toward honoring the efforts of the late PEC Executive Secretary, Olga Vorkunova, who saw the possibility of a vital future for the field; assuming that PEC's membership continues to be a diverse community of peace educators representing all world regions; and with hope that members will work together in such a manner as to effectively advance the substance and practice of peace education, we offer the following suggestions for consideration by both the general membership of IPRA and the present members of PEC.

Re Bylaws: Establishing Procedures
to Achieve Purposes

At the next IPRA General Conference in Trinidad-Tobago elections of Executive Secretary, Executive Committee and Council as prescribed in the appended Bylaws may take place. As the Bylaws do not stipulate how nominations are made, we suggest that the present Executive Secretary of PEC in cooperation with the Secretary General invite the membership of PEC and IPRA to nominate candidates for the various positions in PEC. Additional nominations may be made at the administrative meeting of the General Conference, followed by elections. We also suggest that the 2022 General Conference of IPRA invite the new PEC leadership to submit a proposal to the next General Conference of IPRA on updating the Bylaws on

1. how nominations are to be made
2. including the agreement with Taylor and Francis on PEC sponsorship of the Journal of Peace Education
3. any other changes in the Bylaws of PEC.

Re: Strategy: Setting a New Course within a Vision for Change of the Present Reality

We believe that PEC's present and ongoing mission would be well served by a review of its purposes within the context of today's peace problematic. We suggest that time be given in the upcoming Commission sessions for reflection and discussion of the following contextual queries:

How do the existential planetary threats of climate catastrophe and nuclear holocaust affect our respective local contexts? Do these fundamental problems manifest in particular forms of violence that should be addressed by peace education?

How has the "War on Terror," the rise of authoritarianism and the backlash against the human rights of women and the marginalized affected the problematic of positive peace?

In what ways should international standards promulgated in the last 20 years such as UN Security Council Resolution 1325 on Women, Peace and Security, The Paris Accords on Climate and the Treaty on the Prohibition of Nuclear Weapons be integrated into a statement of purpose and the actual practice of peace education?

In what ways should the growing role of international civil society in confronting the existential threats and working to overcome the multiple and increasing problems of war, climate change, deprivation, oppression, displacement and the refugee crises and multiple human rights violations be addressed in defining the context of peace education and setting goals for that area of the field referred to as global citizenship education?

How should changes in context affect the use and relevance of the foundations of peace education? What current realms of peace research might be useful in assessment of the relevance of the foundations?

A drafting committee might be set up to summarize the responses to these queries or similar ones to propose a new strategy or statement of purpose for PEC. Yours is the task of setting the future for the unique global learning community that is IPRA's Peace Education Commission.

We wish you the best as you take up the challenge.

Magnus Haavelsrud
Betty Reardon
September, 2022

Endnotes

1) This article was originally published by the Global Campaign for Peace Education and is reprinted here with permission. See: Magnus Haavelsrud and Betty Reardon, "IPRA-Pec - Projecting a next Phase: Reflections on Its Roots, Processes and Purposes." Global Campaign for Peace Education, September 21, 2022. https://www.peace-ed-campaign.org/ipra-pec-projecting-a-next-phase

2) Documentation of PEC activities since the beginning are available in the authors' archives on peace education at the University of Toledo: https://hdl.handle.net/20.500.14324/90; and the Norwegian University of Science and Technology https://arkivportalen.no/entity/no-NTNU_arkiv000000037626 (especially items Fb 0003-0008; G 0012 and 0034-0035)

3) Originally published in the IPRA Newsletter available in archive on peace education https://arkivportalen.no/entity/no-NTNU_arkiv000000037626 and also included as chapter 3 in Robin J. Burns and Robert Aspeslagh (1996). *Three Decades of Peace Education around the World: An Anthology*. New York: Garland. See Appendix 1 for full text.

4) Found in Percival (1989). See Appendix 2 for full text.

References

Burns, R. J. & Aspeslagh, R. (1996). *Three decades of peace education around the world*. Garland Press.

Haavelsrud, M. & Reardon, B.A. (2022, September 21). *IPRA-Pec - Projecting a next phase: Reflections on its roots, processes and purposes.* Global Campaign for Peace Education. https://www.peace-ed-campaign.org/ipra-pec-projecting-a-next-phase

Percival, M.A. (1989). *An intellectual history of the Peace Education Commission of the International Peace Research Association.* [Doctoral dissertation, Teachers College, Columbia University]

Part I: Missing Colleagues

Chapter 2
Johan Galtung: A Lifetime for Peace

Magnus Haavelsrud and Syed Sikander Mehdi

Part 1: Magnus Haavelsrud

Voices from all corners of the world join in a chorus of honoring and remembering Johan Galtung. I have selected a few voices below. Part 2 is an account of his life for peace by Syed Sikander Mehdi, professor at Karachi University. Appendix 3 presents the text of the last nomination for the Nobel Peace Prize only weeks before Johan died. First, my personal reflections.

In the mid-60ies after completing military service and enrolled as a student of education at the University of Oslo, one of my teachers, Eva Nordland, recommended me to get in touch with Johan Galtung. She told that two of his students were already doing research on children's and youngster's "thinking about war and peace" – a topic I was interested in. Inspired and supported by Johan, I planned a comparative study with samples from East and West Berlin, but the Minister für Volksbildung, Margot Honecker, refused my application in East Berlin as she knew already – as I understood her - that all the children in the German Democratic Republic (GDR) were for peace and against war. West Berlin contacts recommended by Johan welcomed my research.

This first meeting with Johan led to many more in years to come, not least my work with the Chair of Conflict and Peace Research at the University of Oslo in 1973-74; our work in IPRA over many years; when he was directing the Global Indicators Program in Geneva; intensive seminar days in Honolulu including free use of his apartment there when I was on a sabbatical; his work as adjunct professor at my university in Tromsø where in a course for doctoral students he shared the contents of the classic book he later published entitled *Peace By Peaceful Means* (1996); celebrating New Years Millennium Eve in 1999 in his and Fumi´s house in Bois Chatton, France where we put what we called a big *millennium* log on the fire watching French TV posing the question of who so far had been the most influential academician (I was surprised when he suggested Sigmund Freud). Upon receiving the news from Yeltsin that he had resigned and Vladimir Putin was chosen to be his successor - Johan commented how clever Yeltsin was to select exactly that timing as the concern over the Year 2000 bug (Y2K bug) was worldwide; and finally walking in Beijing on the occasion of the World Futures Studies Federation Conference in 1988 chatting about our very different backgrounds as the son of a doctor / vice mayor of Oslo and a farmer in a mountain valley, respectively – and his concluding that he came from Norway 1 and I from Norway 2! Participating in the Founding Panel of the Global Campaign on Peace Education, Hague Appeal for Peace Conference in 1999, he inspired hundreds of participants who applauded his call for learning transcending conflict transformation whether in everyday life or in international conflicts (Galtung, 2000).[1] Rasmussen (2016, pp. 87-92) has a great expose of his practical SortingMat tool in learning conflict transformation. Let me finally mention the conference I attended at the Madrid Complutense University honoring Johan with splendid papers by academicians from many countries in 2022 (Pedro-Caranana & Carrasco-Campos, 2023). Considering also voices I have included below it was with disappointment we received the decision that our nominations for a Royal Appreciation from the King of Norway were turned down.[2]

Those of us who were fortunate to meet and work with Galtung were inspired, sometimes in awe, but also in friendship that is not to be forgotten. I agree with Gleditsch who wrote in an obituary: "For those of us who were young in the 1960s and entered the social sciences, and especially peace research, Johan Galtung was an unusually inspiring mentor. He was generous with his time and supplied endless scholarly guidance and encouragement. When something did not go well, he would take the time to explain why."[3]

Maybe his welcoming of us young students was just a follow-up of what he as a 21-year-old had written in his application for status as conscientious objector that he intended researching for peace. When he was 25 he wrote "It is human and valuable to be able to dream about a world free of the many of its horrors and shortcomings. In our time the dream is rather projected into the future instead of the hereafter – in order to form a utopia for happy people" (quoted in Borrelli & Haavelsrud, 1993, p. 33).

Udayakumar[4] writes that Galtung was not only a researcher and scholar but also very much of a doer and quotes the opening sentence of his 2008 book, *50 Years: 100 Peace and Conflict Perspectives* where he puts it tersely: "The Big Point justifying this book –and the considerable amount of work behind it— is solution orientation" (Galtung, 2008).

In a personal tribute Maung Zarni writes[5]: "Galtung exuded eternal optimism and bubbling energy, 'eternal sunshine', to put it poetically. A situation as dire and seemingly intractable as Palestine, Galtung would talk about his positive vision wherein all the Arabs and the Israelis can live in peace and equality. Not only was Galtung intellectually towering, but he was also a physically towering figure, with characteristic disarming laughs and smiles.

The last time I saw him was when he was holding the Tun Mahathir Global Peace Chair at the International Islamic University in Kuala Lumpur in 2014. Alongside the moral and intellectual giants, including Gideon Levy of Israel, Denis Halliday of Ireland (who resigned from his position as UN Coordinator in Saddam's Iraq, to protest the US sanctions that resulted in the death of hundreds of thousands of Iraqi children), Galtung spoke at the Conference which the former Prime Minister Mahathir Mohamad organized and hosted designed to mobilize public opinion to "criminalize war" – all wars.

We were in Rangoon together in the fall of 2005. It was during my short-lived, unsuccessful attempt at Track II mediation in my country of birth where we had reached a stalemate between Aung San Suu Kyi leadership and the ruling military regime. I arranged a one-on-one meeting for him to talk to the 3rd ranking Burmese general, who headed the country's military intelligence services, about the possibilities of peace from TRANSCEND perspective.

The then British Ambassador Vicky Bowman put the Galtungs up in the ambassador's residence colonially named "Balmoral" across the old War Office on Shwedagon Pagoda Road. At her arrangement, Galtung was also meeting with the country's peace NGOs, run by a group of national minority representatives. The Burmese military junta wanted to know if "the professor is our friend?" But Galtung was no friend of any party in conflict, little did they know. He was there to help mediate the conflict. The generals were seriously disturbed that Galtung would go and talk to the ethnic equality rights advocates. His mission was to talk with everyone in the conflict. So, he naturally spent a day with those who wanted to rebuild the post-independence Burma of multiple ethnic nations as a 'federalist' entity where every group had equal representation and an equal say in the way the country was governed. Paying lip service to 'federalism', the junta viewed any version of Burma other than effectively 'unitary state', as a formula for its disintegration."

Richard Falk nominated Galtung for the Nobel Peace Prize several times (at least 2008, 2016 and 2020) and I include the following from his 2016 nomination here:

> I am writing in support of the nomination of Johan Galtung as candidate for the 2016 Nobel Peace Prize. I write as a professor of international law who taught at Princeton University for 40 years before retiring there in 2001, and since then have been associated with the Global Studies Program at the University of California on its Santa Barbara campus. I have known Johan Galtung for more than 40 years, and followed his work intimately.

> Johan Galtung has been the sort of dedicated warrior for peace that it seems to me the Nobel Prize was created to honor and by so doing raise public consciousness of what must happen if we are to overcome the war system and enjoy the material, political, and spiritual benefits of living in a world of peace premised on the nonviolent resolution of disputes among sovereign states and respect for the authority of international law.

> For decades Johan Galtung has been an inspirational and tireless presence in the field of peace studies broadly conceived. His exceptional vitality and mobility have brought this message of understanding and insight into peace with justice to the four corners of the planet in a remarkable fashion that is truly unique in the weight of its educational

and activist impact. It is no exaggeration to write that he invented and established the field of peace studies as a respected subject of study in institutions of higher learning throughout the world. As a consequence of his charismatic speaking ability and seminal writing Johan Galtung has reached the hearts and minds of thousands of people throughout the world, conveying the belief above all that peace is possible through the dedicated efforts of ordinary people if they work to change the political climate sufficiently to educate and exert pressure on the political leaders of the world as well as on global media.

With all due respect, the time is long overdue to honor those who through thought and deed have brought Alfred Nobel's vision to life for thousands of students and activists of all civilizational backgrounds. It is only by creating this global peace consciousness and peace literacy at the grassroots level that we can have any realistic hope of overcoming the entrenched militarism that remains so dominant in governmental bureaucracies throughout the world. Giving Johan Galtung the kind of platform that the Nobel Prize affords would itself be an enormous contribution to the realization of a peaceful world, and the fact the he is a Norwegian son would have a special resonance in the country and beyond.

It is with conviction and my own commitment to the ideals of the Nobel Prize as envisioned by Alfred Nobel that I encourage the Committee to give the utmost attention to the nomination of Johan Galtung who has for so long been deserving of this supreme recognition of his extraordinary contributions to the study and achievement of peace. (Falk, 2016)

Part 2: Syed Sikander Mehdi

(This is a shorter version of Professor Mehdi´s publication entitled *Henry Kissinger, Johan Galtung and the Nobel Peace Prize*, Mehdi, 2024[6])

Galtung was born on 24 October 1930 in Oslo, Norway. The Second World War itself and the experiences and memories of the war had considerably influenced his understanding of war and peace from an early age. His father, an ear, nose and throat surgeon, worked day and night to save the life of as many soldiers from the occupiers as possible. When the young Johan asked his father if he wasn't sometimes tempted to let his "scalpel slip a little", the father's reply was this: "Absolutely not! The most essential duty of a physician is to save lives, anyone's life, without distinction." (Galtung & Fischer, 2013, p. 3)

The humanitarian approach of his father had a deep impact on young Galtung. He learnt more about war when he witnessed the destruction of Norway because of German invasion and occupation, and when his father along with other prominent Norwegians were taken to a Nazi concentration camp in Norway in 1944. The father returned home only a month before the end of the war, but his forced separation from the family and the fears and the uncertainties significantly impacted the mind, memory, and thinking of the teenager. When he was only 17, he learnt about the assassination of Gandhi and he cried. By that time, he was already beginning to hold a vague idea that alternatives to war and violence were there (Urdal, 2019).

Galtung was already a peace activist when the 1950s unfolded. He refused to join the military service which was mandatory, declared himself a conscientious objector and opted to serve 18 months of social service in place of military service. After a year, he sought the permission of the government to spend the remaining six months doing peace related work. His request was turned down and he was sent to prison. While in prison, he wrote his first book together with his mentor Arne Naess: *Gandhi's Political Ethics.* It was published in 1955.

Galtung's passion for peace and firm belief that peace is possible for all societies never dwindled. He obtained a degree equivalent to PhD in Mathematics from the University of Oslo in 1956. Next year in 1957, he obtained the same degree in Sociology from the same university. At the age of 27, he joined Columbia University in New York as Assistant Professor for Mathematical Sociology. After five semesters he was offered a tenure post there, but his passion for peace studies brought him back to Oslo, where he established the International Peace Research Institute (PRIO) – the world's first academic research centre focusing on peace. He became the first Director of the Institute. Later he helped establish dozens of peace research institutes around the world. He founded two high quality and influential research journals -

Journal of Peace Research in 1964 and *Bulletin of Peace Proposals* in 1969 (now *Security Dialogue*). Furthermore, he helped founding the International Peace Research Association (IPRA) in 1964. IPRA has now grown into the largest and most established global professional organization in the field of peace research.

Galtung left the directorship of PRIO in 1969 and joined the University of Oslo as Professor of Peace and Conflict Studies, another world. He held this position till 1978. Over the course of his seven-decade career, he worked as visiting professor of peace studies in 30 different universities in different cities and continents, including Berlin, Belgrade, Paris, Santiago, Buenos Aires, Cairo, Ritsumeikan (in Kyoto), Princeton, Tromso, New Delhi, and Bern. As a teacher, researcher and colleague working in different institutions, he inspired thousands of students and researchers from all over the world and encouraged them to study peace studies and do serious peace research work. He also induced them to get actively involved in a series of peace movements, including the anti-nuclear movement, pro-democracy movement, movement against violence to women and children, and movements against economic and cultural exploitation, human rights violations, slavery of all kinds, extremism and racism. It is not an exaggeration to say that the history of these movements and several other movements for peace and change are incomplete without referring to Galtung's ground-breaking studies on peace and change.

The peace teacher, peace scholar, a globe-trotter and conference and seminar frequenter was also a prolific writer. He was author or co-author of over 150 books - sole author of 96 of them. He also authored more than 1700 articles published in research journals and popular magazines and as book chapters. His works have been translated into 30 languages. The knowledge world and especially the peace knowledge world is immensely indebted to him for his original research and insights in many areas of intellectual inquiry. The areas covered include peace studies, peaceful conflict transformation, reconciliation, education, macro-history, theory of civilization, human rights, basic needs, life-sustaining economy, future studies, deep culture as well as non - offensive defense, religion and peace, ecology, sociology and health sciences. Besides earning a worldwide reputation as a founder of the discipline of peace studies, he is highly rated in the leading academic and research circles

as an exceptional thought leader who gave a new perspective - a peace perspective - to various academic disciplines including mathematics, physics,
medical sciences, sociology, psychology, international relations, political science, history, journalism, anthropology, gender studies and so on.

In so many ways and directly or indirectly, many of his studies revolve
around wars, conflicts and violence and attempt to offer solutions for peaceful resolution of conflicts. According to Bishnu Pathak, a leading South Asia
peace scholar, some of Galtung's major ideas include: "Direct, Structural and
Cultural Violence; Conflict Transformation by Peaceful Means (Transcend
Method), Transcend Method in Conflict Mediation Across Levels, Mahatma
Gandhi as the Master of Masters, Peace Journalism, and from a 20th Century
of War to a 21st Century of Peace'. Pathak adds that 'Democracy for Peace
and Development, Peace Studies and Conflict Resolution, the Six and Fifteen
Contradictions of USSR and USA respectively, and Reconciliation are some of
the other key parts of Galtung's findings", and also points out that "Galtung
frequently refers to the negative vs. positive peace and peace-conflict lifecy-
cle and their structural and institutional, individual, procedural, and political
levels of relations." (Pathak, 2016)

Galtung – almost always - put forward very persuasive arguments to stress
the point that wars can be avoided, conflicts can be resolved peacefully and a
better future can be built for all. It is said that the medical profession was the
main profession of all his ancestors for several generations. He turned out to
be a social scientist. However, he also emerged as a physician, but of a different type. His patients were not individuals but entire societies with their
pathologies. He adopted the terminology of medicine, developed diagnosis
(source of suffering), prognosis (what is likely to happen if not attended to)
and therapy (what possibly can be done to reduce violence and sufferings).
At a later stage, he added "therapy of the past" or counterfactual history:
how could violence have been prevented if different courses of action had
been taken at a given point in the past (Galtung, 2000). Explaining the parallel
between disease/health and violence/peace in an excellent study published
by the UN, Galtung observed:

> Peace can be defined as the capacity to handle conflict autonomously,
> nonviolently, creatively, with participation of everybody, just as health

can be defined as 'the capacity to handle disease oneself, without doing violence to the body' (like surgery, chemotherapy, radiotherapy). Sometime we may have to use a minimum of violence for the greater good of health/peace. But we should not idealize those means; they are stop-gap measures, and nonviolent means should always be tried first. (Galtung. 2000, p. 2)

In 1993, Galtung founded Transcend International, a global network for peace through peaceful means. It comprised both peace scholars and peace activists. Ever since its establishment, the network has made its presence felt in the knowledge world as well as in policy making centres. Since 2000, it has run the Transcend Peace University - the world's first online peace studies university. It has pooled together the peace teachers and scholars and dispute resolvers from all over the world. It offers dozens of online courses on peace and peace related themes and issues to students drawn from different parts of the world. In addition, Galtung founded the Transcend University Press in 2008. It encouraged online publication of important works of peace scholars, and facilitated translation and their online publication in different languages. A media wing was also established to emphasize the importance of peace journalism and project its role in helping resolve conflicts at local, national and international level. While the creation of an innovative institutional support system to pave the way for the resolution of conflicts and dissemination of peace ideas is itself a significant contribution of Galtung to peacebuilding, no less significant is his novel transcend approach to peaceful conflict resolution (Fischer, 2013).

Clearly Galtung was not only a theorist of peace or a prolific writer of peace; nor was he only a major social science academic establishing peace studies as a social science discipline. He was also a practitioner and proponent of peace diplomacy and peace action. He was a peace visionary, who helped peace studies transform into an applied social science as well. His exceptionally busy life was therefore not only dedicated to theorizing peace and strategizing peace, but also dedicated to the practical application of his peacebuilding methodologies. He, in fact, offered concrete evidence to show that peace through peaceful means is possible. He mediated in over 150 conflicts between states, nations, religions, civilizations, communities and persons since 1957.

For example, the territorial dispute between Peru and Ecuador originated in the 16th century. By 1995 following further aggression retreat from their rigid positions remained unlikely despite the costs to both countries becoming unbearable. At this stage the Ecuadorian ex-President met Galtung and requested him to suggest a viable solution. "How do we draw the border", he said and added: "We're fighting. We've had four wars. We have sacrificed lots of young men's lives." Galtung asked him what he thought of the idea of not drawing a border and converting the disputed territory into a jointly administered "binational zone with a natural park", which would also attract lots of tourists and bring additional income to both countries. The ex-President was shocked and flabbergasted. However out of curiosity, he proposed it to Peru and was surprised to receive a positive response. The war-weary countries could see the light at the end of the tunnel. They reached an agreement with some minor modifications, and resolved the centuries old territorial dispute peacefully with a joint economic zone which was established in 1998. Later Galtung observed proudly: "It is now a blossoming zone and most people have even forgotten the wars."

Galtung's contribution to peace studies and peacebuilding is huge, and his contribution is gratefully acknowledged by the peace academic and peace research circles around the world. He was awarded more than ten honorary doctorate degrees from different universities and numerous other honors like the Right Livelihood Award (aka the Alternative Nobel Peace Prize), the Norwegian Humanist Prize, the Socrates Prize for Adult Education, the Bajaj International Award for Promoting Gandhian Values and the Alo'ha International Award, First Morton Deutsch Conflict Resolution Award, Augsburg Golden Book of Peace. However, he was never considered worthy enough to be awarded a Nobel Prize for Peace by the Norwegian Nobel Committee. Denying the Peace Prize to Galtung was a gross injustice to him.

It is true that the selection of the Norwegian Nobel Committee to award the Nobel Peace Prize have been severally criticized on different occasions. Likewise, the challenges the Committee faces every year in making the final decision for the award is understandable.

The likelihood of a decision being controversial is always there. However, the decision like not awarding the Prize to Mahatma Gandhi will always be remembered, criticized and condemned. It will always be remembered not only as a gross injustice to Gandhi but also a gross injustice to the Prize itself and the founder of the Prize: Alfred Nobel.

Even a cursory review of the list of recipients of the Nobel Peace Prize from when it was first awarded in 1901 reveals that a number of very deserving candidates were ignored by the Norwegian Nobel Committee. The Late Fredrik Heffermehl, Norwegian lawyer and Vice President of both the International Peace Bureau and the International Association of Lawyers against Nuclear Arms, published a study in 2023 on the Nobel Peace Prize, with chapters on the Nobel laureates who received the Prize from 1901 to 2022 and on *those who should have won*. In this scathing study on the Prize, he mentions several peace educators, peace researchers and public intellectuals and explains why they should have been given the award in different years. This list of *those who should have won* includes Alfred de Zayer (professor at the Geneva School of Diplomacy for 2022), Klaus Schlichtmann (peace academic and peace intellectual for 2019), David Swanson (author and a dedicated anti-militarist peace organizer, for 2016), Jan Oberg (peace educator and researcher for 2012), Glenn Paige (professor and pioneer of nonkilling social science for 2004), E.P. Thompson (historian for 1982), Ruth Leger Sivard (economist and author for 1981), Gene Sharp (leading theorist on nonviolent political struggle for 1978), Edward Zinn (professor of history for 1975) (Heffermehl, 2023).

It is interesting to note that the Nobel Peace Prize was awarded to the International Labour Organization in 1969, but Heffermehl says that the award should have been shared between three outstanding peace scholars: Elise Boulding, Kenneth Boulding and Johan Galtung. In fact, Galtung was a very deserving formidable candidate for the award from late 1960s on till his death on 17 February 2024. He was nominated for the award a number of times, but he was not considered by the Norwegian Nobel Committee to be deserving enough to be awarded the Nobel Peace Prize.

Perhaps it wasn't so important for Galtung to have received the Nobel Peace Prize as it was for the Norwegian Nobel Committee to have presented this award to Galtung. This 'Champion of Peace' has now joined the distinguished company of Mahatma Gandhi, who was nominated for the prize a number of times but never awarded the prize. However, the credibility of the prize has been severely diminished because of the award not given to Galtung. He will be celebrated all over the world, year after year, for his contribution to building a global human society, and the Norwegian Nobel Committee will carry the stigma for ever for denying the Nobel Peace Prize to several most deserving candidates including Gandhi and Galtung.

Endnotes

1) Talk recorded and archived in www.arkivportalen.no UBIT/A-0303/F/Fb/0003 Peace Education

2) Nomination for a Royal Appreciation by the King of Norway was submittet by Randi Rønning Balsvik, Knut Holtedahl, Magnus Haavelsrud and Vidar Vambheim March 30, 2022. It was turned down. The nomination for a different Royal Appreciation Award in 2023 was also turned down (Holtedahl died on July 15th, 2022 and was not part of the nominating group for this second nomination). These nominations included all orders and medals as explained in www.kongehuset.no. Documents archived in www.arkivportalen.no UBIT/A-0303 Peace Education

3) Nils Petter Gleditsch https://www.prio.org/news/3505

4) Personal communication

5) Zarni March 11, 2024 on www.transcend.org entitled A Personal Tribute to Johan Galtung (24 Oct 1930 – 17 Feb 2024): The Man for Just Peace

6) Permission to reprint this short version has been obtained from the Pakistan Institute for International Affairs' journal *Pakistan Horizon Quarterly*.

References

Borrelli, M., & Haavelsrud, M. (1993). *Peace education within the archipelago of peace research, 1945-1964*. Arena.

Falk, R. (2016, February 1). *Nomination of Johan Galtung as candidate for the*

2016 Nobel Peace Prize. Letter to the Norwegian Nobel Committee. https://web. archive.org/web/20210426055549/http://www.nobelwill.org/galtung_ falk_nomination2016.pdf

Fischer, D. (2013, November 13). *A brief history of Transcend.* Transcend. https://www.transcend.org/history/, November.

Galtung , J. & Naess , A. (1955). *Gandhis politiske etikk.* Tanum.

Galtung, J. (1996). *Peace by peaceful means : peace and conflict, development and civilization.* Sage Publications.

Galtung, J. (2000). *Conflict transformation by peaceful means (the Transcend Method).* United Nations Disaster Management Training Programme.

Galtung, J. (2008). *50 Years: 100 peace & conflict perspectives.* Transcend University Press.

Galtung, J. & Fischer, D. (2013). *Johan Galtung: The pioneer of peace research,* Springer.

Heffermehl, F. (2023). *The real Nobel Peace Prize: A squandered opportunity to abolish war.* realnobelpeace.org.

Mehdi, S. S. (2024). Henry Kissinger, Johan Galtung and the Nobel Peace Prize. *Pakistan Horizon, a quarterly Journal of Pakistan Institute of International Affairs, 77*(2-3), 55-70.

Pathak, B. (2016, August 29). *Johan Galtung's conflict transformation theory for peaceful world: Top and ceiling of traditional peacemaking.* Transcend. https:// www.transcend.org/tms/2016/08/johan-galtungs-conflict-transforma- tion-theory-for-peaceful-world-top-and-ceiling-of-traditional-peacemaking/

Pedro-Caranana, J., & Carrasco-Campos, Á. (2023). Presentación del núme- ro: Comunicación y paz: Homenaje a Johan Galtung. *CIC. Cuadernos de Información y Comunicación, 28,* 11-14. https://doi.org/https//:dx.doi. org/10.5209/ciyc/89289

Rasmussen, A. J. (2018). *Colonialism, peace and sustainable social cohesion in the Barents Region - Creating theoretical and conceptual platforms for peace building and restorative action.* [Doctoral dissertation, University of South Africa]. UNISA.

Setreng, S. K. (2010). With Johan Galtung to India – on the road. In Johansen, J. & Jones, J. Y. (Eds.). *Experiments with peace: A book celebrating peace on Johan Galtung's 80th birthday.* Pambazuka Press.

Urdal, H. (2019, May 15). *Inspiration from a father: Johan Galtung interviewed by Henrik Urdal.* Prio. https://www.galtung-institut.de/en/home/johan-galtung/

Chapter 3
The Moral Point of View of Humanity: Reardon's Vision of Sustainable World Peace

Dale T. Snauwaert

Betty A. Reardon was a world-renown pioneer in the development of peace education and human rights. Her groundbreaking work as a teacher, activist, researcher, author, and consultant laid the foundation for a cross-disciplinary field that integrates peace, justice, and human rights education within a normative, gender-conscious, holistic perspective. In recognition of her many contributions, awards, and achievements, including the founding of the International Institute on Peace Education, she was nominated by the International Peace Bureau in 2013 for the Nobel Peace Prize.

My association with Betty Reardon spanned over three decades. Our mutual interest and dedication to the formulation of peace, justice, and human rights education gave rise to meaningful collaboration over the years, enriching my own perspective in countless, invaluable ways. A number of Reardon's original lines of inquiry and foundational ideas have significantly influenced my work and potentially the future of peace education. These ideas include peace as the presence of justice; the ideals of universal human dignity and universal moral inclusion; human rights as the ethical core of peace education; political efficacy as the primary goal of peace education, and a pedagogy of reflective inquiry as a key component of peace education.

The purpose of this chapter is to elaborate upon Reardon's foundational ideas outlined above, reflect on their meaningful influence within my own perspective, and explore their legacy for the future of peace education. It is my hope that readers will find their understanding of Reardon's perspective on peace education and its transformative value to cultivate human potential and political efficacy enhanced. It was Reardon's vision that a society that recognizes and values dignity and moral inclusion through universal actualization of human rights can secure an enduring foundation for a just and sustainable world peace.

The Normative Foundations of Reardon's Conception of Peace Education

At the foundation of Reardon's conception of peace education are two normative, that is, ethical and moral claims, of what *should* be: universal human dignity and moral inclusion (Reardon & Snauwaert, 2015a; Reardon & Snauwaert, 2015b; Snauwaert, 2019b; Snauwaert & Reardon, 2022). Universal human dignity is the ethical claim that all human beings possess an equal, intrinsic value and dignity that invokes the basic duty of respect for persons. In turn, dignity entitles every person to *equal standing* in the moral community; all persons should be recognized and morally included as equal members of the moral community as a matter of basic respect for persons. These normative imperatives assert that we have a basic duty to recognize the humanity of all persons and thereby to entitle them to equal moral consideration. Reardon maintains that dignity and inclusion are essential requirements of peace. She asserts, "A sustainable world peace can only be assured through the universal actualization of human dignity." (Reardon, 2009, p. 46)

Reardon articulates this perspective in terms of human rights. Human rights are justified demands for the societal protection and enjoyment of basic social goods that persons have reason to value. These social goods include various freedoms, such as political self-determination, and substantive goods, such as economic opportunity, education, and health care, among others. As such, human rights are the ethical core of peace education. Reardon (2009) writes:

> As a political framework for the actualization of human dignity, human rights are the ethical core of peace education, not a complement, or a particular component, and certainly not an alternative or an ed-

ucationally equivalent substitute for peace education. Human rights
are integral to peace education, that is, without human rights peace
education lacks a primary component of its core and essential substance. (p. 47)

From within this perspective, "Human rights study provides us with tools of
definition and diagnosis of what comprises violence, experientially as well
as conceptually . . ." (2009, p. 3). This diagnosis is of especial importance for
Reardon in the analysis of gender discrimination, which she holds as the paradigm case of injustice (Reardon, 1996; Reardon & Snauwaert, 2015b). Reardon conceives peace in terms of the protection of human rights: "Human
rights standards are the specific indicators and particular measures of progress toward and the realization of peace. Human rights put flesh on the bones
of the abstraction of peace and provide the details of how to bring the flesh
to life" (2009, p. 47). Given that peace is defined in terms of the protection of
human rights, peace entails justice. (Snauwaert & Reardon, 2022) She writes:
"justice, in the sense of the full enjoyment of the entire range of human rights
by all people, is what constitutes positive peace" (Reardon, 2021 [1988], p.
31). This rights/justice-based conception of peace is clearly expressed by, and
grounded in, Article 28 of the *United Nations Universal Declaration of Human
rights* which states that "Everyone is entitled to a social and international order in which the rights and freedoms set forth in this Declaration can be fully
realized" (UN, 1948).

The conception of peace as the presence of justice, in turn, is the defining element of peace education. Reardon (2021 [1988]) maintains: "Most ... agree
that there is no neutral education. Education is a social enterprise conducted for the realization of social values. The question is what values are to be
realized through education, and how." (p. 23) Education is situated within,
and driven by, the values and principles of a society's "normative order".
The normative order of a society is based upon the values and principles of
a normatively justifiable conception of justice. (Forst, 2024) The theory, and
in turn the practice of education rests upon the foundation of this normative
order. If the overarching goal of peace education is peace, then the conception
of a peaceful society in terms of justice as the realization of human rights, is
determinative. Establishing and sustaining peace within all levels of societies
is a basic and urgent imperative of justice.

Political Efficacy as the Primary Goal of Peace Education

From within this perspective, Reardon argues that the basic goal of peace education should be the development of the political efficacy of future citizens (Reardon & Snauwaert, 2011; Reardon & Snauwaert, 2015a). In general, political efficacy is a basic capacity to engage in transformative political action, which is necessary for the transformation of society toward a just peace. As I discuss below, an important element of political efficacy is the capacity for moral reasoning and judgment. As Reardon (2023) suggests: "The development of the capacity for moral/ethical reasoning is the most promising route out of the amoral and immoral morass into which many world polities have sunk. Indeed, without a citizenry that has achieved and applied these capacities, I fear that we have little chance of surviving as a species, and certainly not as the reflective reasoning individuals and communities that produced human civilization" (p. xiii).

Reardon's Pedagogy of Reflective Inquiry

Reardon argues that developing basic capacities for engaging in effective political efficacy involves learning, the development and practice of complex skills that in turn require pedagogies of reflective inquiry. She articulates three forms of reflective inquiry: critical/analytic; moral/ethical; and contemplative/ruminative (Reardon, 2010; Reardon & Snauwaert, 2011; Reardon & Snauwaert, 2015a). Critical/analytic inquiry reflects on the nature of power and explores questions of justice surrounding social institutions, the structural dimensions of social life, and the political/economic origins of violence. Moral/ethical inquiry reflects on questions of justice guided by principles of a human-rights framework and explores the application of principled moral reasoning to questions of justice. Reardon emphasizes principled moral reasoning as fundamental to developing political efficacy. Contemplative/ruminative inquiry is a wider sphere of reflection focusing on what is meaningful and valuable and expands moral reasoning to include affect and intuition. It cultivates the self-recognition of being a moral and political agent of justice through which citizens become agents of social and political justice.

Reardon maintains that these forms of reflective inquiry comprise a pedagogy that can develop political efficacy, or the human capacities of political self-empowerment and abilities to engage in transformative action. What a pedagogy of reflective inquiry discloses is that these capacities of political efficacy, including reasoning and judgment, are most effectively developed through learning, exercise, and practice or in a Deweyan sense, reflective experience (Dewey, 1916).

Reardon's Influence and Legacy

Reardon's conceptualization of these foundational ideas of peace education have significantly influenced my work. Following Reardon I believe that peace is best conceived as the *presence of justice* (Snauwaert, 2023) and is contingent upon the informed political participation of citizens, based in their capacity for political efficacy. Current citizens have a *civic duty* to provide future citizens with a political education that is devoted to the development of their political efficacy (Snauwaert, 2020), hence the significance of inquiry into the normative, ethical and moral, foundations of peace education (Snauwaert, 2023). In this sense my work is informed by, and addressed to persons who aspire to, democracy. I explore moral reasoning concerning justice as intimately linked to the sociopolitical context of democracy and democratic processes of deliberation (Baier, 1958; Forst, 2014; Habermas, 1996; Rawls, 1971, 1993, 2001; Sen, 2009). A core part of my philosophical research has been inquiry into the nature of justice and moral reasoning as *normative justification* of principles of justice. Specifically, inquiry into the basic ethical and moral criteria that can serve as *reasons* for the *justification,* or consensual validity, of values and principles of justice, as well as the normative source of those criteria, are a central aspect of my work (Snauwaert, 2011; Snauwaert, 2020; Snauwaert, 2021; Snauwaert, 2023; Snauwaert, 2024). Furthermore, I situate Reardon's two moral imperatives of universal human dignity and inclusion within the normative philosophical tradition that rests upon and follows from Immanuel Kant's imperative of universal respect for persons as ends as it has been developed by John Rawls, Jürgen Habermas, Thomas Scanlon, and Rainer Forst, among many others. The claim of universal dignity and inclusion find their normative source in Kant's formulation of the 2nd and 3rd formulations of the categorical imperative—to always treat persons as ends and not only as means and to recognize them as equal members of the human moral community respectively. This reading is Kantian in the sense that it is grounded in the imperative of respect for persons, while deviating from Kant's original formulation in terms of its justificatory basis as both dialogical and post-metaphysical as opposed to being monological and asserting a metaphysical foundation (Snauwaert, 2019a; Snauwaert, 2023; Snauwaert, 2024).

Conceptualizing Justice

My inquiry into the nature of justice and its principles is based upon the important distinction between the 'concept of justice' *and* "conceptions of justice" (Rawls, 1993, pp. 76-77; Rawls, 1971). A 'concept' refers to the basic, core meaning of an idea, while a "conception" pertains to a specific conceptualization of a concept. The *concept* of justice refers to the common elements that define the core meaning of justice, which is analogous to the primary, constitutive rules of a game that define the game. At the core of the concept of justice is the idea that the normative principles of justice that define and regulate the basic institutional structure of society *should avoid being morally arbitrary* (Hart, 1961; Rawls, 1971). More specifically, social institutions are just (in a basic sense) when "no arbitrary distinctions are made between persons in the assigning of basic rights and duties and when the rules determine a proper balance between competing claims to the advantages of social life" (Rawls, 1971, p. 5). In other words, the concept of justice entails "accepting that the institutions [citizens] share must be based on norms that all can share as equals and do not simply codify the (contestable) values of one group and declare them as the law" (Forst 2024, p. 107).

Arbitrary distinctions are, therefore, those that are based in invalid reasons of justification (for example, the distribution of political power or educational opportunity based upon ancestral heredity or inherited wealth). This means that principles of justice must not merely be accepted; their acceptability should be justifiable in terms of valid normative reasons. This element of the concept of justice refers to the second-order metanormative criteria for the justification of first-order principles of justice. The concept of justice so defined suggests the idea of *justice as justification* (Forst, 2024).

Conceptions of justice, on the other hand, are *specific formulations of principles of justice* that specify what each person is due *and* what we owe each other consistent with the concept of justice. As Rawls puts the distinction between a concept and conception of justice:

> Roughly, the concept is the meaning of a term, while a particular conception includes, as well, the principles required to apply it. To illustrate: the concept of justice applied to an institution means, say, that the institution makes no arbitrary distinctions between persons in assigning basic rights and duties, and that its rules establish a proper balance between competing claims. Whereas a conception includes, besides this, principles and criteria for deciding which distinctions are arbitrary and when a balance between competing claims is proper. People can agree on the meaning of the concept of justice and still be at odds, since they affirm different principles and standards for deciding those matters. To develop a concept of justice into a conception of it is to elaborate these requisite principles and standards. (Rawls, 1993, p. 14, footnote 15)

The work of theorizing justice is "to work out from easily agreed upon concepts to particular detailed conceptions" (Dreben, 2003, p. 330). *Conceptions of justice* are specific articulations of principles of justice that are normatively justifiable in terms of consistency with the concept of justice. In general, given human freedom and fallibility, a plurality of reasonable, normatively justifiable conceptions of justice that meet the basic requirements of the concept of justice are possible (Cohen, 2003). Furthermore, working out a particular conception of justice entails reflection on a plurality of spheres or domains of justice expressed in terms of basic questions that every society faces, and needs to answer (Snauwaert, 2023). Specific principled answers to these basic questions of justice comprise a *conception of justice*.

In general, the *basic questions of justice* include:

1. *Whose Security?* Who should have an equal right to security of person?
2. *Who Belongs?* Who should be considered an equal citizen and thus a full participant in the society? (Mettler & Lieberman, 2020)
3. *Whose Truth?* What conception of truth and thereby reality should be affirmed? What is the valid basis of determining truth and knowledge?
4. *Who Gets What?* What constitutes a just distribution of the basic goods, rewards, opportunities, and resources of a society?
5. *Who Decides?* What constitutes a just distribution of political (collective

decision-making) power?

6. *Whose Resistance?* Is there a right and duty to resist and redress injustice? If so, what principles of corrective justice should guide that resistance? Who should bear this duty to resist? (Snauwaert, 2023)

In formulating a conception of justice, principled answers to these basic questions need to be articulated and justified.

Regarding inquiry into moral reasoning and justification, knowledge claims, as well as normative claims require *supporting reasons of justification*. Justification is the offering of reasons that support the validity of one's claim. The claim that a principle's acceptability is justifiable presupposes that we have *non-arbitrary, valid* reasons to affirm that principle. Normative justification entails *offering valid reasons* that support the justifiability of the principles of justice.

As Thomas Scanlon demonstrates, "thinking about right and wrong is, at the most basic level, thinking about what could be justified to others on grounds that they, if appropriately motivated, could not reasonably reject" (Scanlon, 1998, p. 5). The justification of principles of justice thus presupposes criteria for the validation of that justifiability. In considering a just society, we need to inquire into not only what principles of justice we should accept and in turn teach (that is, what conception of justice should be affirmed) but we also need to ask on what normative basis are the validity of those principles grounded; in other words, to what normative criteria can we appeal in order to confirm the justifiability of principles of justice.

The Moral Point of View of Humanity

I understand Reardon's ethical values of equal human dignity and universal moral inclusion as constituting the moral point of view of a shared humanity which can be understood in terms of the elements of fairness (Snauwaert, 2024). For example, in a telegram to prominent Americans on May 23rd, 1946, Albert Einstein made the following statement: "The unleashed power of the atom has changed everything save our modes of thinking, and we thus drift toward unparalleled catastrophe. We shall require a substantially new manner of thinking if mankind is to survive" (cited in Ionno Butcher, 2005, p.

12; Times, 1946). Building on Einstein's plea, the subsequent Russell-Einstein Manifesto (signed by a group of prominent scientists), stated the following: "We are speaking ... not as members of this or that nation, continent, or creed, but as human beings ... We appeal, as human beings to human beings: Remember your humanity, and forget the rest ..." (Russell & Einstein, 1955).

This point of view is a call for mutual respect for persons as foundational to a just and peaceful world. Reardon's work points us to the moral point of view of humanity. It calls for the perspective of a global citizen, exploring the possibilities of a shared normative perspective from within the principles of equality, reciprocity, and impartiality which are presupposed within the idea of mutual respect for persons based in our shared humanity. A conception of peace education for democratic citizenship grounded in the moral point of view of humanity is a possible long-term means for supporting a just world.

Shared ethical values and moral principles allow for the recognition of a common humanity among diverse individuals and peoples, which reduces the hostility and bias between them (Mason 2018). By affirming shared values, a common civic identity can be the basis of membership and standing among citizens with a plurality of beliefs, values, and social identities. The moral point of view of respect for persons anchored in our shared humanity offers a common perspective as the basis of our civic identity. It places one in the perspective of a citizen free from the constraints of in-group bias and sorted political identity.

What does this point of view entail? I have argued that the Russell-Einstein perspective articulates a moral point of view that is based in the elements that comprise fairness - equality, recognition, impartiality, and reciprocity (Snauwacrt, 2023; Snauwaert, 2024). *Equality* presupposes that every human being be considered as inherently of equal value and standing, ensuring the equal consideration of their interests (Singer, 2011; Kymlicka, 1990). Through this equal recognition persons cease to be regarded as objects and can more easily come to intersubjectively affirm each other as coauthors of shared norms (Honneth, 2021). When we engage in normative justification, we necessarily presuppose that the addressee is morally equal. Impartiality refers to the presupposition that the reasons we offer others to justify our claims be free of the bias of exclusive self-interest. Fairness demands that we impartially consider the claims and interests of others, expressed by the axiom that no one should be a judge in his own case (Amar, 2012). Reciprocity demands that one cannot rightly claim for oneself what one would deny others. Furthermore, mutual respect invokes a duty to offer reasons of normative justification that can be accepted and affirmed by others; that they do not have valid reason to reject (Scanlon, 1998). Reciprocity, moreover, has a universal scope, extending moral consideration to all persons (Gutmann, 1999). If all persons share an equal, inherent dignity and are recognized as equal, then each person is due to be treated fairly, equally, reciprocally, and impartially.

I argue that we can appeal to these elements of fairness as metanormative criteria of justification (Snauwaert, 2023; Snauwaert, 2024; Snauwaert, 2025: accepted). The elements of fairness follow from equal human dignity. I spell out the nature of these metanormative criteria in detail in my recent book, *Teaching Peace as a Matter of Justice* (Snauwaert, 2023).

Moral reasoning and judgment entail a process of reflection on the metanormative criteria of justification, the consistency between those normative criteria and principles and values of justice that define a just society, and in turn, the *application* of justifiable principles of justice to the justifiability of laws, public policies, institutional rules, structures, policies, and practices. The justifiability of laws and policies is based in their consistency with the principles of justice upon due reflection.

Furthermore, and in alignment with Reardon's critical reflective inquiry, unjust social structures and practices are sustained by invalid justifications. An important part of judgment, therefore, is the critical analysis of invalid, ideological justifications. Critical analysis requires that everyone submit their normative judgments of justice to critical scrutiny (Forst, 2024). In my work, research into this critical dimension of moral judgment has involved inquiries into, and applications of, both the moral traditions of just war theory and the philosophy and strategy of nonviolence (Gerson & Snauwaert, 2021; Snauwaert, 2004; Snauwaert, 2023).

The Peace Constitution Project

The presuppositions of equality, recognition, impartiality, and reciprocity are not tied to a particular nation or political point of view but are understood to reflect a foundational call for mutual respect for persons. The centrality of moral reasoning and judgment points toward the important question of how to develop reflective and analytic capacities. What can be considered as the best pedagogical approach to this development? Following Reardon, my approach is grounded in the insight that these capacities can only be developed through exercise and practice. In this regard, I have proposed a 'peace constitution project' as an approach to the pedagogy of reflective inquiry (Snauwaert, 2023).

This pedagogy is intended to engage students in reasoning and deliberation to construct a *constitution of a just society* comprised of basic principles of justice, justified by the normative criteria of the elements of fairness, and in turn the application of those principles to more specific laws and policies. The constitution is framed in terms of principled answers to what I have identified as the basic questions of justice alluded to above. As noted, principled answers to these questions comprise the fabric of a *peace constitution*. A "constitution" is a statement of principles of justice that articulates fair terms for the regulation of the basic institutional structure of society; it is a declaration of what a just society should be in principle. Moral reasoning concerns the normative justifiability of those principles of justice grounded in the elements of fairness (equality, recognition, reciprocity, and impartiality).

The *peace constitution project* is designed as a pedagogical means for the development of reflective and analytic capacities of students as well as their abilities to engage in moral reasoning and judgement, which are central to gaining political efficacy. The affirmation, teaching, and enactment of this global perspective, this new way of thinking, would go a long way towards creating the necessary conditions and the means for the continuing realization of a just society. In order for persons to be dynamic agents of justice, the development of the reflective and analytic capacities of all citizens is paramount (Snauwaert, 2023). This pedagogical process can be employed in both formal and informal educational settings.

Conclusion

Human reason is fallible, often inconclusive and burdened with conflicts arising within a plurality of socio-cultural, philosophical, and religious perspectives. Also, our basic human tendencies to categorize and order the social world in terms of an us vs. them dichotomy gives rise to in-group bias and out-group hostility (Klein, 2020; Mason, 2018; Sherif *et al.*, 1988; Tajfel *et al.*, 1971); we are all prone to positional confinement and insulated points of view (Sen, 2009). This challenge is exacerbated by mounting local, regional, and global political polarization which fosters anger-driven political activism and breakdowns of civil discourse, instead of reason-driven public participation (Mason, 2018).

Addressing this destabilizing positional confinement and political polarization with perspectival broadening that includes shared ethical values and moral principles can bring about a transformative recognition of our common humanity. Perspectival broadening, which reduces hostilities and bias, can allow for a sense of global citizenship to emerge within a common normative perspective based on mutual respect for persons, our shared humanity, and our planet.

One of Reardon's' most significant and enduring legacies to the future of peace education is her life-affirming vision that realization of universal human dignity and universal moral inclusion are essential for creating a sustainable world peace. For Reardon, the moral point of view of humanity is integral to a transformational pedagogy of peace that endeavors to cultivate a global civic identity through developing respect for all persons. Given that human reason is fallible, often inconclusive, and burdened with conflicts, *truth-claims* arising within the plurality of our socio-cultural, philosophical, and religious perspectives are rationally unresolvable, posing a serious challenge to democratic stability (Forst, 2024; Forst, 2013). Moreover, there exists a basic human tendency to categorize and order the social world in terms of an *us vs. them* dichotomy, which presents as in-group bias and out-group hostility (Coleman, 2021; Mason, 2018; Klein, 2020; Sherif et al.,1988; Tajfel, 1970; Tajfel et al., 1971). We are all prone toward positional confinement within insulated points of view (Sen 2009).

This challenge is exacerbated by the advent of political polarization. Political polarization occurs when individuals with diverse ethnic, racial and cultural identities are sorted *and* aligned with a political faction and/or ideology

(Mason, 2018). The result is that the individual becomes positionally confined and identified with an insulated and narrow political point of view. In-group victory becomes the sole priority, leading to the decline of the legitimacy of, and often disdain for, the opposition. Civil discourse and reasonable public deliberation break down into divisive rhetoric. The potential of cooperation, reasonable disagreement, compromise, and toleration sharply decline. The result is anger-driven political activism instead of reason-driven participation (Mason, 2018).

The way to transcend positional confinement, and thus political polarization, is to comparatively broaden the perspective of persons on both sides of the polarization (Sen, 2019). Regarding this perspectival broadening, shared ethical values and moral principles allow for the recognition of a common humanity among culturally diverse individuals, which reduces the hostility and bias between social groups (Mason, 2018). By affirming shared values, a common civic identity can be the basis of membership and standing among citizens with a plurality of beliefs, values, and social identities. This identity can be cultivated through developing the disposition and value of mutual respect for persons.

To live in peace in our world with an expanded sense of human identity that prioritizes awareness of our fundamental interconnectedness may sound utopian. However, it seems that new, transformative ways of thinking, grounded in our moral obligation to one another and to the planet must take root in the interest of affirming and preserving our democracy, and in a larger sense, the complex web of all planetary life. The potentials for increased political division and conflict urgently calls for the education of citizens with a global perspective that cultivates reflective inquiry, political efficacy, and capabilities to morally reason from the perspective of humanity as a whole.

References

Amar, A.R. (2012). *America's unwritten constitution: The precedents and principles we live by.* Basic Books.

Baier, K. (1958). *The moral point of view: A rational basis of ethics.* Cornell University Press.

Cohen, J. (2003). For a Democratic Society. In S. Freeman (Ed.), *The Cambridge companion to Rawls* (pp. 86-138). Cambridge University Press.

Coleman, P.T. (2021). *The way out: How to overcome toxic polarization.* Columbia University Press.

Dewey, J. (1916). *Democracy and education: An introduction to the philosophy of education. Text-book series in education* The Macmillan company.

Dreben, B. (2003).On Rawls and political liberalism. In S. Freeman (Ed.), *The Cambridge companion to Rawls* (pp. 316-346). Cambridge University Press.

Forst, R. (2013). *Toleration in conflict: Past and present.* Cambridge University Press.

Forst, R. (2014). *Justice, democracy and the right to justification: Rainer Forst in dialogue.* Bloomsbury Academic.

Forst, R. (2024). *The noumenal Republic: Critical constructivism after Kant.* Polity.

Gerson, J. & Snauwaert, D.T. (2021). *Reclaimative post-conflict justice: democratizing justice in the world tribunal of Iraq.* Cambridge Scholars Publishing.

Gutmann, A. (1999). *Democratic education.* revised edition. Princeton University Press.

Habermas, J. (1996). *Between facts and norms: contributions to a discourse theory of law and democracy. Studies in contemporary German social thought.* MIT Press.

Hart, H.L.A. (1961). *The concept of law.* The Clarendon Press.

Honneth, A. (2021). *Recognition: A chapter in the history of European ideas. The Seely Lectures.* Cambridge University Press, trans. J. Ganahl.

Ionno Butcher, S. (2005). *The origins of the Russell-Einstein Manifesto. Pugwash Conferences on Science and World Affairs* Pugwash, Nova Scotia: Cardinal Press. Available at: https://pugwash.org/2005/05/01/report-the-origins-of-the-russell-einstein-manifesto/.

Klein, E. (2020). *Why we're polarized.* Avid Reader Press.

Kymlicka, W. (1990). *Contemporary political philosophy.* Oxford University Press.

Mason, L. (2018). *Uncivil agreement: How politics became our identity.* University of Chicago Press.

Mettler, S.& Lieberman, R.C. (2020). *Four threats: The recurring crisis of American democracy.* St. Martin's Press.

Rawls, J. (1971). *A theory of justice.* Belknap Press of Harvard University Press.

Rawls, J. (1993). *Political liberalism.* Columbia University Press.

Rawls, J. (2001). *Justice as fairness: A restatement.* Harvard University Press.

Reardon, B. (1996). *Sexism and the war system.* Syracuse University Press.

Reardon, B.A. (2009). Human rights learning: Pedagogies and politics of peace. *UNESCO Chair for Peace Education Master Conference,* University of Puerto Rico.

Reardon, B.A. (2010). Meditating on the barricades: Concerns, cautions and possibilities for peace education for political efficacy. In P. Trifonas & B.L. Wright (Eds.), *Critical peace education: Difficult dialogues.* Springer.

Reardon, B.A. (2021 [1988]). *Comprehensive peace education: Educating for global responsibility.* Peace Knowledge Press.

Reardon, B.A. (2023) Preface. In. D.T. Snauwaert (Ed.) *Teaching peace as a matter of justice: Toward a pedagogy of moral reasoning.* Cambridge Scholars Publishing.

Reardon, B.A. & Snauwaert, D.T. (2011). Reflective pedagogy, cosmopolitanism, and critical peace education for political efficacy: A discussion of Betty A. Reardon's assessment of the field. *Factis Pax: Journal of Peace Education and Social Justice,* 5(1), 1-14.

Reardon, B.A. & Snauwaert, D.T. (Eds.). (2015a). *Betty A. Reardon: A pioneer in education for peace and human rights.* Springer.

Reardon, B. A. & Snauwaert, D.T. (Eds.). (2015b). *Betty A. Reardon: Key texts in gender and peace*. SpringerPress.

Russell, B. & Einstein, A. (1955). *The Russell-Einstein Manifesto*. Pugwash Conferences on Science and World Affairs. Available at: https://pugwash.org/1955/07/09/statement-manifesto/ 2024).

Scanlon, T. (1998). *What we owe to each other*. Harvard University Press.

Sen, A. (2009). *The idea of justice*. The Belknap Press of Harvard University Press.

Sherif, M., Harvey, O.J. , White, J.B., Hood, W.R. & Sherif , C.W. (1988). *The robbers cave experiment: Intergroup conflict and cooperation*. Wesleyan University Press.

Singer, P. (2011). *The expanding circle: Ethics, evolution, and moral progress*. Princeton University Press.

Snauwaert, D.T. (2004). The Bush Doctrine and just war theory. *OJPCR: Online Journal of Peace and Conflict Resolution -- http://www.trinstitute.org/ojpcr/6_1snau.htm*, 6(1), 121-135.

Snauwaert, D.T. (2011). Social justice and the philosophical foundations of critical peace education: Exploring Nussbaum, Sen, and Freire. *Journal of Peace Education*, 8(3), 315-331.

Snauwaert, D.T. (2019a). The dialogical turn in normative political theory and the pedagogy of human rights education. *Education Sciences*, 9(52). https://doi.org/10.3390/educsci9010052

Snauwaert, D.T., ed. (2019b). *Exploring Betty A. Reardon's perspective on peace education: Looking back, looking forward*. Springer.

Snauwaert, D.T. (2020). The peace education imperative: A democratic rationale for peace education as a civic duty'. *Journal of Peace Education*, 17(1), 48-60.

Snauwaert, D.T. (2021). The two moral powers and the purpose of peace education. *Samyukta: A Journal of Gender and Culture*, 6(2). Doi:10.53007/SJGC.2021.V6.I2.26.

Snauwaert, D.T. (2023). *Teaching peace as a matter of justice: Toward a pedagogy of moral reasoning.* Cambridge Scholars Publishing.

Snauwaert, D.T. (2024) The moral point of view of humanity and nuclear risk."*Peace Review,* 36(4), pp. 571-580.

Snauwaert, D.T. (2025: accepted). Theorizing social justice in education: A conceptual framework. In Polat, F. & Hick, P. (Eds.). *Handbook of social justice in education.* Edward Elgar Publishing.

Snauwaert, D.T. & Reardon, B.A. (2022). Dialogue on peace as the presence of justice: Ethical reasoning as an essential learning goal of peace education—An invitation to peace educators. *In Factis Pax: Journal of Peace Education and Social Justice,* 16(2), 105-128.

Tajfel, H. (1970). Experiments in intergroup discrimination. *Scientific American,* 223(5), 96-103.

Tajfel, H., Billig, M.G., Bundy, R.P. & Flament, C. (1971). Social categorization and intergroup behavior. *European Journal of Social Psychology,* 1(2), 149-178.

Times, N.Y. (1946). Atomic education urged by Einstein." *New York Times* Available at: https://timesmachine.nytimes.com/timesmachine/1946/05/25/100998236.pdf?pdf_redirect=true&ip=0.

UN, General Assembly. (1948) *Universal declaration of human rights.* United Nations.

Chapter 4
Mario Borrelli: Peace Education and Educating the Downtrodden [as the main aims of his work]

Giuseppe Desideri
(translated by Mirna Cicioni)

The name Mario Borrelli immediately comes to mind whenever we speak of inadequate education, social disadvantage, peace and peace education. The charismatic 'Don Vesuvio', as he was called when he was an ordained priest, and then just Mario, after he left the priesthood, chose peace education and educating the most vulnerable members of societies as the cornerstones of his teaching and all his activities. His teaching, aimed at the downtrodden, the *ultimi*[(1)], and his work with *scugnizzi*[(2)] have been constants in all his life, from the end of World War II to his death.

The dazzling relevance of his activity and research on peace and peace education is particularly evident now, as we look at the images we receive every day from the media, that show the small or large wars being fought all over the world, with the weakest and most vulnerable suffering the worst traumas.

Borrelli had experienced these issues first-hand in the period following the end of World War II, together with the *scugnizzi* he cared for. Later on, as time went by, similar traumas were experienced, in different ways, by many children and young adults who found, and still find, themselves in situations of socio-economic-cultural deprivation. As a consequence, they often become not only victims of war, but often, in our society, victims of violence, and may in turn themselves become perpetrators of violence and bullying.

The valuable action of practical support and rehabilitation developed by Borrelli in his main achievement, the Casa dello Scugnizzo (Street Kids' Home), did not end with his death: it is still a living reality, and Borrelli's heart is still beating strongly in the centre of Naples as his mission is being carried out.

His exceptional contribution to many areas is widely known and recognised not only in Italy but on a world-wide level. First came his social work activities in Naples in the years immediately following the end of World War II, aimed at *scugnizzi* and other disadvantaged people. Then came work as an educator and a sociologist. In 1977, with Antonino Drago and Giuliana Martirani, he founded IPRI (Italian Peace Research Institute), which aimed to promote peace research initiatives. Chaired by Borrelli until 1988, the Institute was affiliated with IPRA (International Peace Research Association), founded in 1964 by Johan Galtung.

After the near-total oblivion that followed his death, interest in Mario Borrelli finally grew again in 2020 and then in December 2023. In 2023 his work was discussed in depth at the conclusion of the initiatives celebrating the hundredth anniversary of his birth, part of an international research conference entitled "Education Between Courage and Responsibility. A Journey Into the Theory and Practice of Education in the Work of Mario Borrelli (1922-2007)." The conference was held in Naples and was organised by the non-profit foundation Casa dello Scugnizzo, the Mario Borrelli Study and Research Centre, the Università Federico II in Naples, the Università Suor Orsola Benincasa, the AIMC (Associazione Italiana Maestri Cattolici, Italian Association of Catholic Teachers) and the World Union of Catholic Teachers. It was sponsored by the City of Naples, SIPED (Società Italiana di Pedagogia, Italian Education Society) and SIPeGeS (Società Italiana di Pedagogia Generale e Sociale, Italian Society of General and Social Education).

The conference consisted of six sessions and round table discussions on the following topics: Forms of Community Education; Peace Education; The Experience of the Casa dello Scugnizzo: An Educational/Social Reading. The discussions emphasised that Mario Borrelli's education project – which may have been considered unrealistic for the period when it was conceived – included among its main purposes also peace education, understood as recognition of the other.

Participants analysed Borrelli's activity and initiatives, which at first targeted people emerging from war and despair, and subsequently expanded to assist all the most vulnerable people.

Focusing on Borrelli's work of care and support for the most basic needs (such as a roof over one's head and a hot meal) of the neediest people, cast aside by institutions, may however, have a problematic consequence: that his emphasis on education, fundamental in his work, may be downplayed and almost forgotten. Mario Borrelli did, in fact, set up an effective educational project for *scugnizzi*, who belonged to a fairly wide age range that went from childhood to late teens. They all lived by their wits, because, obviously, they were marginalised by a society that was itself marginalised as a consequence of the material and spiritual destruction caused by war.

Scugnizzi – organised into small groups, which often became criminal 'bands' – were mostly boys who had been orphaned by war or who had been abandoned by, or had run away from, families or communities. They were on the very bottom rung of society, they were homeless and – due to the dramatic general situation – went unnoticed by adults and institutions. Borrelli not only tried to give them a home, but formed an education-based relationship with them. First of all, he did not judge them; this is the primary, fundamental element of his educational approach. *Scugnizzi*, the 'children of war', were children who fought to survive under hostile circumstances, in a dog-eat-dog adult world, unfit for growing children. They were on the bottom rung of society, they did not get special attention because of their age, but rather competed against adults for a mouthful of food, a blanket, a safe, warm place to sleep.

They are quite different from the street kids we hear about today from the crime reports in the news. Both groups are downtrodden and are produced by disadvantage and indifference, but, while the boys of the 1940s and 50s formed gangs to help one another cope under difficult circumstances, today's boys form gangs – which Italian journalists call 'baby gangs' – to claim hero status, however negative, in spite of their disadvantaged status.

Mario Borrelli was not judgemental and did not, unlike many other charity workers and most priests in the Neapolitan church hierarchy, have a patronising approach towards these kids. 'Don Vesuvio' chose not to pass judgement, and his choice was motivated by his strong sense of ethics and founded on his awareness of the boys' deprivation and hand-to-mouth existence. First of all, he decided to live with the boys: he plunged into their life and circumstances, and did not judge them because he shared their daily hardships. He lived their life with them, slept rough as they did, suffered just like them as he struggled beside them, and this led him to identify with them and their life. Mario Borrelli's pedagogy was not top-down, it was 'immersion education' arising from the real needs of these boys.

Scugnizzi are not 'only' delinquents, not 'only' marginalised young people – they are human beings who deserve human dignity and respect. These are also fundamental elements of any project of peace education.

This educational theory is part of a trend that, not coincidentally, originated in Catholic circles, and that produced other leading figures during and after World War II. The best known of them, the one most often mentioned in the media, is Don Lorenzo Milani, the founder of the School of Barbiana.[3] Other important figures were Father Ernesto Balducci, a well-known anti-war campaigner, and Don Zeno Saltini and Father David Maria Turoldo, who founded the town of Nomadelfia, based on utopian educational principles. The British Monsignor John Patrick Carroll-Abbing founded the *Città dei Ragazzi* (Boys' Town) in Rome, providing vocational education for homeless boys. Don Salvatore D'Angelo founded the *Villaggio dei Ragazzi* (Boys' Village) in Maddaloni, not far from Naples, which provided educational and vocational training. Many priests and clerics focused on young people living in social disadvantage in big cities, where it is easy to be marginalised. It is perhaps not surprising that most of these priests were mistrusted and that some were, in turn, marginalised by their own church hierarchies.

The similar, but also profoundly different, experiences of all these men shared one aspect: they all believed that being close to the most disadvantaged children was the fundamental aim of their existence and mission. We could say that the meaning of Mario Borrelli's action foreshadows, many decades before our time, what Pope Francis has been saying – that we need to serve our neighbour with words, but first and foremost with action.

Disadvantage is a feature of a person's social context, not of that person, and the focus of Mario Borrelli was the person. He focused on the rich life of *scugnizzi*, boys who were real, genuine, full, lively people, and who gradually developed a sense of brotherhood and solidarity even though their social context put them into competition with one another and encouraged selfishness. 'Don Vesuvio' managed to get them to work together to recover their dignity, and this is the true essence of his educational practice. The young priest became a teacher almost spontaneously, almost unwillingly. He became an 'educator' in his daily practice; at first, he did not envisage his work as teaching or instruction, and in fact his way of relating to these boys went beyond traditional educational frameworks. It was practical training in life skills, and it was enormously effective: it attracted, in spite of real problems, a great many marginalised people, young men and women as well as children.

The Casa dello Scugnizzo faced serious problems. Borrelli was not popular with the Curia, with conservatives, and with the very boys he worked with, who were suspicious of anyone wearing a cassock. He managed to overcome their mistrust and, with his daily, practical work, managed to create, from scratch, a teaching and educational project that was based on sharing and mutual help. This developed into a solidarity network, first locally and later internationally.

The work of the Casa dello Scugnizzo, not widely recognised in Italy, was greatly appreciated outside Italy, especially in the United States. Borrelli – as, some years later, in Barbiana, did Don Lorenzo Milani as a consequence of the conflicts between his community and the Florence Curia – came into conflict with the church hierarchy in Naples. He decided that, in order to be able to teach his boys to be free, he needed first of all to be free himself, and he decided to leave the priesthood. He did that mainly because he wanted an open-minded, secular relationship with the *scugnizzi* and the other downtrodden people who trusted him.

Although their historical circumstances are different, yesterday's *scugnizzi* are similar to today's *scugnizzi* because both experience marginalisation. Clearly today's circumstances are different from those of post-World War II Italy, but many young people are still being pushed out of mainstream society due to social, economic and above all cultural reasons. These young people do not believe that they can make decisions about their future, in fact they cannot even envisage a future life where they can make decisions.

This is extreme educational disadvantage, and Mario Borrelli's example and work are still relevant and necessary to face it, because his example is real, practical, concrete testimony of *education aiming to recover personal dignity*. It is along the lines of Paulo Freire's "Pedagogy of the Oppressed", (1970) which is fully relevant to the educational emergency that we are experiencing today.

Borrelli's ideas are also clearly relevant when he talks about peace and peace education. As was mentioned previously, he founded IPRI (Italian Peace Research Institute), which promoted research into non-violent defence strategies, peace education and non-violent economics. The Institute's activity contributed to making known several highly important works of peace research which were being published in other countries. Borrelli also became a member of PEC (*Peace Education Commission*) within IPRA (*International Peace Research Association*). He published many essays and research papers on peace education; his aim was to find and present a frame of reference that could view peace education as an independent science, just like peace research.

Among his many publications there is one of his best-known essays: *Integrazione tra Ricerca sulla Pace, Educazione alla Pace e Azione per la Pace* ([Integrating Peace Research, Peace Education and Peace Action] (1979), presented at the General Conference of IPRA, held at Oaxtapec, in Mexico, in 1977. This essay is still essential reading for researchers interested in peace education. Borrelli also devised some practical experiments, which he developed and carried out in the Centro Comunitario Materdei (Materdei Community Centre) within the Casa dello Scugnizzo.

Analyses of Borrelli, his educational activities and constant work in peace studies and peace education, most of which were written outside Italy, have helped to make known his life and work.

Peace studies are closely linked to twentieth-century history. Between the two world wars it became known as a *bona fide* research area, whose aim was to prevent further wars. It became known as a formal academic discipline only after World War II.

Several Italian educators, including Maria Montessori, had already spoken about peace and peace education. *Educazione e pace* [Education and Peace], published in 1949, is a collection of several lectures about peace given by Montessori, from the lecture given at the *Bureau International d'Éducation* in Geneva in 1932 to the speech she gave in London, at the *World Fellowship of Faiths*, in 1939.

"Everyone talks about peace, but nobody educates for peace" Montessori said in the twentieth century. In Italy, with and after her, several others became involved in education for peace and non-violence: Don Lorenzo Milani, Don Primo Mazzolari, Don Zeno Saltini, Father Ernesto Balducci, Father David Maria Turoldo, Aldo Capitini, Danilo Dolci, Don Tonino Bello, Aldo Visalberghi and others. As well as theories, they tried, in their daily field work, to formulate practical projects that might contribute to the education and training of the younger generations.

In Italy the process of establishing peace studies as a legitimate research area began in 1998, after Law 230 ("New Regulations Regarding Conscientious Objection") was passed on 8 July 1998. Subsequently, universities established inter-departmental centres and degree courses in Science for Peace and Peace Studies centres. A separate centre was the Centro Studi Sereno Regis, which, after Naples hosted IPRI until 2006. Then IPRI disbanded in order to join the Rete Corpi Civili di Pace [Network of Civilian Peace Corps] and to form a new association, Istituto Italiano per la Ricerca della Pace – Rete Corpi Civili di Pace (IPRI-RETE CCP), still based at the premises of the Centro Studi.

Throughout the twentieth century debates developed both in the United States and in Europe, and numerous new research centres opened. In the 1980s the international scientific community could count on between 2,000 and 3,000 peace studies scholars and practitioners. The 1990s were characterised by greater intellectual receptiveness and greater opportunities for research and applied research. In the 2000s peace research tried to respond to the new challenges presented by the global situation: it was necessary to move beyond the theories developed by Galtung, who no longer was the only peace studies expert, as he had been in the Sixties and Seventies.

Mario Borrelli also took an active interest in these discussions and, due to his hands-on experience as a scholar, sociologist and educationalist, was able to provide important contributions to this very important topic. His work was recognised also by people who later on would work in close contact with him.

Antonino Drago writes that "until the Eighties, academic work towards peace was carried out by individuals working alone" (Drago, 2001). He also recollects that "the most striking feature in Italian academia in those years was not only that hardly any peace research was carried out in universities, but there were no institutes for peace research, whereas in Northern Europe these institutes were set up soon after the end of World War II and subsequently proliferated". The person who told Drago about peace research was, as Drago recalls, "an intellectual who was not an academic, Mario Borrelli, who had a number of international connections because of his work of social welfare and development in Naples" (Drago, 2001).

Borrelli was one of the forerunners of peace studies in Italy. As his research progressed, he analysed scholars and theories in depth, and eventually he himself became one of the internationally recognised leading authors within peace research and peace education.

Mario contributed to discussions with other scholars and collaborated, sharing ideas and research, not only with Antonino Drago, but also with Magnus Haavelsrud, Robin Burns, Johan Galtung, Giovanni Salio and others.

In *Concetti di violenza, pace ed educare alla pace* [*Notions of Violence, Peace and Peace Education*] Borrelli writes: "The notions of violence, peace and peace education are related to our *Weltanschaaung* – the way we visualise the physical and social world in which we are immersed – and to the relationships we build with the *continuum* around us" (Borrelli 1984a, p. 11). The notions he refers to "change whenever our intellectual approach to reality changes." In his research he narrows the field of his analysis down to peace research in his time, which is "more directly connected with peace education" (Borrelli 1984a, p. 11).

His thorough analysis has its starting point in a distinction made by economist Kenneth Boulding, one of the first to initiate peace studies and research. Boulding outlines three intellectual approaches: structural, dialectical and evolutionist. Then he makes a further subdivision, according to whether each approach contains or does not immediately reject violence from the very start. This produces six different perspectives, which Borrelli analyses in detail. He also looks at other authors within the three main perspectives, and proceeds to make a methodological suggestion which "might open up a dialogue" between the various ideological standpoints. His aim is "to discover possible common elements of at least some features that are not in conflict, that may form a common framework for an all-embracing, more effective methodology" (Borrelli, 1984a, p. 19).

Let us see what idea that arises from this new formulation:

> My proposal aims to achieve this because it suggests starting from the analyses typical of the structural perspective, organising them more systematically, and expanding them into normative science. At the same time the dialectical perspective is also used, provided that it does not imply violence as a means of changing the present structures of society. The behavioural perspective will also not be neglected, as a contribution parallel to structural modifications. (Borrelli, 1984a, p. 19)

Borrelli clarifies this notion further:

> When we talk about normative science, in connection with the structural method, we mean an interdisciplinary kind of knowledge, that can use biology, anthropology, psychology and sociology in the process of discovering a series of inalienable needs which are specifically human, which have been proven to be valid, and which have been universally accepted as human values. Therefore such values could become the objective towards which the dialectical and behavioural perspectives should aim in their work, in order to help society and each of its members to become more peace-oriented. (Borelli 1984a, p. 20)

It goes without saying that creating such a system is anything but easy. Borrelli acknowledges this, stressing that it is necessary to rethink existing notions or to create new ones that need to be compatible and to "underpin a social relationship that rules out violence". Therefore he believes that it is essential to work in order to "decode notions such as democracy, representation, self-determination, non-interference, self-reliance, nationalism, nation, defence, etc." if the aim is "to embark on a patient work of synthesis, from which a set of alternative values can be drawn". These alternative values cannot be forced on people, because this too would generate violence. "Experimentation is the only concrete means to transform basic alternative values into alternative social reality (Borelli 1984a, p. 20).

Borrelli's conclusion is:

> Let us re-affirm the importance of a new way of facing the problems of peace in its three inseparable dimensions (research, education and action for peace), using anything that is positive and constructive in each of the afore-mentioned intellectual perspectives, and discarding anything that can be stereotypical and mechanical in each perspective. That is the only way intellectual research can really be employed to build an alternative society, freed from violence and founded on values of peace. (Borelli 1984a, p. 20)

In *Diritti umani e metodologia per la pace* [*Human Rights and Methodology for Peace*] (Borrelli 1984b, p. 33), Borrelli provides a definition of peace education: "It is a learning process, through which we become aware of how human rights can be won, protected and respected. Peace education implies a global project for a society where power and resources are shared fairly, both at macro- and micro-level." This education is for everyone, especially those sections of the population that most suffer from violence.

In Borrelli's opinion, peace education "transmits knowledge that is dynamic rather than neutral, that allows those who receive it to know their position in the hierarchy of their world, so that they can connect this position to the wider world of which their world is a part, and so that they can discover what strategies can be used to stop violence at their level, in a way that creates an imbalance in the relationship between local violence and violence at a higher level" (Borrelli 1984b, p. 33). Thus peace education is not only an educational issue, it is also a political experience. It is not only education, but also "consciousness raising" – and Borrelli quotes Paulo Freire, the most important thinker and experimenter in this area.

Borrelli also stresses that "action for peace is the natural outcome of peace research and peace education" (Borrelli 1984b, p. 34).

In our time, just as in Mario Borrelli's time, peace education is central in our society. Teachers and education scholars must be increasingly aware of their duty and responsibility towards the next generations, and of the efforts they need to make during teaching and training so that education will contribute to social progress, inclusion, respect for differences and diversity, respect for one another, multiculturalism.

The recent "Recommendation on Education for Peace and Human Rights, International Understanding, Cooperation, Fundamental Freedoms, Global Citizenship and Sustainable Development" (UNESCO, 2023), passed during the forty-second General Conference of UNESCO in 2023, which replaces the 1974 recommendation, acknowledges that:

Peace requires not only the absence of war or armed conflicts, but also an inclusive, democratic and participatory process promoting

- Human security;
- Respect for state sovereignty and territorial integrity;
- Dialogue and solidarity;
- Resolution of internal and international conflicts through mutual understanding and cooperation;
- Achievement of sustainable development in all its dimensions;
- Guarantees of universal access to life-wide education in all situations, including emergency and conflict;
- Elimination of poverty in all its forms and dimensions, including extreme poverty;
- Upholding all human rights and freedoms of all persons, without any exception;
- Promotion of active global citizenship.

The Recommendation also reaffirms "the important link between education and the achievement of peace, human rights and fundamental freedoms, international understanding, cooperation, democracy, the rule of law, global citizenship and sustainable development."

A significant document for nations and individuals, because it defines the notions of education, peace, culture of peace, fundamental human rights and freedoms, education for human rights, education for sustainable development, education for global citizenship, inclusion, life-changing education.

Mario Borrelli's Working Methods for Assisting Participation in Structural Change

Editorial Addendum

Mario Borrelli was the prime mover in designing interventions in the problematic conditions existing in the Neapolitan subproletariat. His work became a model for many in the involvement of non-violent popular participation in community development. His intervention strategies were firmly grounded in a thorough analysis of the sub-proletarian mentality as a product of contextual conditions. Borrelli gave a new meaning to community development as a result of designing interventions in order to weaken the political manipulation of the marginal and excluded sub-proletariat by involving them in the quest for improving public and social services (Borrelli, 1975).

His purpose was not to assist in adapting individuals and groups to existing structures but to actually assist people in effecting structural changes by strengthening their capacity to participate in transformation. His research found that direct violence often was a product of structural violence. Therefore, he saw it as a major strategy to resist structural violence in order to foster non-violent behaviours. In this understanding, non-violence became the product of policies towards social justice and fair sharing, i.e. an invitation to political authorities to assist in contributing towards non-violence through non-violent policies. He saw the improvement of public and social services as a most important and realistic goal to work towards when inviting the participation of the marginalised and excluded. This action for change had the two-sided function of returning resources to the marginalized at the same time, as it was important in changing their understanding of their exclusion. Sub-proletarian mentality is analysed in terms of socio-economic facts documenting that a third of the population in the city belonged to the sub-proletarian category living on a minimum of resources and excluded from the productive process. The local power is analysed in terms of a long-standing aristocracy, a political oligarchy, a pseudo middle class, a rather small working class and the large sub-proletarian mass making it possible for local po-litical bosses to adopt modern 'democratic' parameters in combination with social mechanisms of a feudal type.

The manipulative feudality in the political system would not have been pos-sible without the mentality of the sub-proletarian clan culture: The individ-ual was sunk into the clan and acted through it, never taking any decision without its approval (and gratification). His only strength was in the clan and anyone who betrayed it was eliminated. The only world which the individual accepted was that of the clan. Even the physical orbit of the clan coincided with the world in which they felt at home. The outside world was perceived as strange and hostile and whoever ventured into it without a 'protection' or a 'recommendation' of a 'friend' was likely to perish because the clan could no longer defend him (Borrelli 1975). This mentality of the sub-proletarian constitutes an important contextual condition for the selected intervention methodology. Education is not seen as preparation for action but as a reflec-tion after the action to be utilized in the next action for survival. Hence the schooling system cannot be utilized as it is an instrument of the powerful. Non-formal education as part of the action for improving social and public services is therefore the most appropriate option and selected as the venue for the intervention strategy.

Endnotes

1) The word *ultimi*, literally *the last*, has been used since the 1950s in the dis-course of socially radical Catholics to refer to the marginalised, the down-trodden, society's rejects. (Translator's Note)

2) *Scugnizzi* are street kids in the slums of Naples. The word has been used in Italy since the nineteenth century. (Translator's Note)

3) The experiences of the School of Barbiana have been narrated in the influ-ential, collectively-written book *Lettera a una professoressa* (*Letter to a Teacher*), first published in 1967. (Translator's Note)

References

Borrelli, M. (1967). *Un prete nelle baracche*. La Locusta.

Borrelli, M. (1975). *Communication and consciousness raising: A strategy for the socio-economically marginal and excluded*. Unpublished Paper presented to the Working Group on Communication and Consciousness Raising at the Summer School of the International Peace Research Association on "Europe and Africa: Exploitation or Development", Available in Box 31-32 Private Archive No. 303, University Library, Norwegian University of Science and Technology, Västerhaninge, Sweden, 18.

Borrelli, M. (1979). Integration of peace research, peace education, and peace action. *Bulletin of Peace Proposals*, 10(4), 389–395. http://www.jstor.org/stable/44480726

Borrelli, M. (1984a). Concetti di violenza, pace ed educare alla pace. In: Borrelli, M., Drago, A. & Salio, G. (Eds.). *Se vuoi la pace educa alla pace*. I.P.R.I., Gruppo Abele.

Borrelli, M. (1984b). Diritti umani e metodologia per la pace. In Borrelli, M., Drago, A. & Salio, G. (Eds.). *Se vuoi la pace educa alla pace*. I.P.R.I., Gruppo Abele.

Borrelli, M. (1995). *Marciapiedi*. Edizioni La Meridiana.

Borrelli, M. & Thorne, A. (1963). *A street lamp and the stars*. Peter Davies.

Drago, A. (2001). La ricerca per la pace in una società di transizione. Una prospettiva storica. In: Licata, A. (Ed.). *Università per la pace. Il ruolo dell'università nell'analisi e nell'impegno a favore della pace*. I.S.I.G. - Istituto di Sociologia Internazionale, Università degli Studi di Trieste.

Freire, P. (1970). *Pedagogy of the oppressed*. Seabury Press.

Hargreaves, P. (1973). *Mario Borrelli*. El Alamein Press.

Montessori, M. (1949). *Educazione e pace*. Garzanti Editore.

UNESCO (2023). *Recommendation on education for peace and human rights, international understanding, cooperation, fundamental freedoms, global citizenship and sustainable development.* (Ref CL/4487). https://unesdoc.unesco.org/ark:/48223/pf0000391686_eng/PDF/391686eng.pdf.multi.page=3

West, M. (1957). *Children of the sun.* Heinemann.

Chapter 5
Robert Aspeslagh

Robin Burns

The death in late 2016 of Robert (Rob) Aspeslagh, while a sad occasion and one which leaves a large hole in many people's lives around the world, is also an opportunity to celebrate the life of someone who spent many decades exploring peace through research, writing, speaking, painting and practice. Born in 1940 in the Dutch East Indies at Tanjung Pinang, Riau Islands, young Robert and his parents became Japanese prisoners-of-war. In later years he speculated that his experiences in the camp as a victim of war may have stimulated his concern for peace-making. Further, his visits to his birthplace in his last decade, and his ongoing close relationship with his 'second mother' and 'camp brother' from those times, show the deep marks those early years left. He was able to talk about them, and to visit the site of his and his mother's prison camp. And eventually he worked through his flinch reaction when he heard loud commanding voices, to work with Japanese peace education colleagues, and to attend the International Peace Research Association conference in Japan in 1992.

An Educator First and Foremost

Education always played a major role in anything Robert did. I suspect this was even the case during his compulsory military service where he refused any role involving weapons, spending most of his time on naval paperwork. He began to train as an elementary teacher, though found that training disappointing and at the suggestion of one of his teachers, took up a position as history and geography teacher at an unusual secondary school. Based on the principles of the Dutch educational reformer Kees Boeke, the IVO school is run by the Kindergemeenschap [Children's community]. The school emphasised individualised learning, freedom through self-discipline, equality between teachers and pupils, and a concern for others and for the environment. Robert described its basis in a 1993 interview as "pacifist, non-violent, anti-militaristic ideas, which were translated into pedagogy" (Bjerstedt, 1993, p. 5). While he didn't know at the time that "it was peace education that I was doing" (Bjerstedt, 1993, p. 5), these ideas came to underpin his subsequent work and thought about peace education and international relations.

An influential experience at the school was an opportunity to "work with Language and Image, trying to find a connection between what is written or said and the expression through arts" (Bjerstedt, 1993, p. 8). Not only did Robert love both literature and art, but combined both when he retired and became a full-time painter. The two came together in his books entitled *Pictures and Poems* [schilderijen en gedichten], finally brought together as *Poems Painted* [Gedichten Geschilderd] (Aspeslagh, 2016). At the school, he worked with Theo Vesseur, the poet, and artist Joop Willems.

His decade teaching at the IVO Kindergemeenschap had a profound effect on Robert professionally and personally, and in turn he clearly influenced those he taught. He continued to meet former students and colleagues throughout his life, the last reunion occurring shortly before his death. This happened in every job and association with which he became involved, with treasured reunions and meetings right up to his last weeks. The importance of people to Robert is expressed in both a complex mosaic of miniature paintings of family members and friends, and this accompanying poem:

Sublime life

By war, I remained an
only child; others came
into my life and stayed,
some remained only for
a moment, then they were gone,
for good…
…Family comes to you

for life, friends you've got
for long or for a time.
Together they made my life
sublime. (2016, 62)

He loved children, his daughters, his grandchildren and many many more, and he has left a legacy not just of relationships and positive pedagogical experiences, though there was often a didactic intent in his interactions, but of very practical assistance to disadvantaged youth in Indonesia, South India and South Africa. Travelling with him, you were aware how he noticed children, made contact, and was concerned in particular for their safety.

A Developing Peace Educator

Not wanting to become stale, in 1975 he reluctantly left the IVO school after ten happy years there, for a position as education staff member at the *Nederlands Instituut voor Vredesvraatstukken* [Netherlands Institute for Studies on Peace and Security]. His new focus was on peace education, which he reflected he had been doing at the school without realising it. His new tasks included both research and curriculum development. As a pedagogue, Robert liked to be provocative, true to his firm belief that learners should be allowed to discover issues and solutions for themselves. He would question rather than give answers, and this includes his own conception of peace education which he maintained was not a single entity but "a step-by-step process in education, aiming at a concept or idea of peace that people develop together" (Bjerstedt, 1993, p. 6). Always there was the goal to aim for the "creation of responsibility for and contribution to a more liveable and human world society, which is non-violent and just"(Bjerstedt, 1993, p. 6).

Tension between the individual and the world, one's own group and others, and the common polarities East-West and North-South continued to weave through his work. While he did not explicitly reject these bipolar conceptualisations of issues, he sought ways around them, especially through the recognition that education exists within a socio-economic, political and cultural framework and that will determine peace education priorities. He saw the goal of peace education as work towards a more just and less violent society, both local and global. Working with this, he espoused internationalism and rejected extreme relativism, wrestling with the issues of education for plural-ist societies including his own, minorities and intercultural conflict. A survey of peace education in different countries undertaken by Swedish educator Åke Bjerstedt concluded that central to the debate and work in The Nether-lands was the concept of *'mondiale vorming'* [global education] "referring to an integrated global political education, focusing on disarmament, ecology and underdevelopment" (Bjerstedt, 1988, p. 57). Robert espoused the global objective, care for the environment and for developing countries; he saw dis-armament education as only a part of peace education (Aspeslagh & Weise, 1981) and something that unfortunately could be presented in a way that approached indoctrination rather than enabling learners to make their own discoveries.

Underlying all his work in peace education there is a dual concern with ped-agogy and content. At the time Robert was working explicitly in peace educa-tion, he was a member and for four years international executive secretary of the Peace Education Commission (PEC) of the International Peace Research Association (IPRA). The debate about the task of peace educators was lively within IPRA, many of the researchers considering that the only role of the educators was to package their findings for transmission especially to learn-ers within formal education settings. Within PEC, however, "peace educators also saw the need to integrate research, education and action, rather than just posing an alternative solution to war or a separate approach to peace" (As-peslagh & Burns, 1996, p. 42). And while PEC paid less attention especially in the 1970s and 1980s to pedagogy and didactics *per se*, the recognition that education must include research into the issues, and the possibility to take action as a result of findings, combined to form a basis for peace education and one that was integral to Robert Aspeslagh's work. Essential as the basis of peace education was the recognition that violence is the most over-arch-ing concept. War is a significant example but not the only one (Aspeslagh & Burns, 1996, p. 43). 'Positive peace' then becomes the goal, implying the absence of both overt and covert violence. Through the recognition that the way in which learning takes place may in itself be violent and reflect such relations outside the classroom, creating a culture of peace can be seen as the over-arching task of peace educators. Creating a peace culture at the interna-tional level is one aspect; creating it within the classroom in relations between learners and between learners and teacher, shows the vital relationship between pedagogy and substance for effective peace education.

In order to delineate the broad scope needed for peace education, Robert summarised his view of its scope as five different domains of interests: the international system, peace, development, human rights and the environment. It should also "create an awareness of the relationships between the different levels of human existence and presence, namely the personal, the structural, the cultural, the regional, the national, sub-global and the global level, and add a global dimension to all these levels through education" (Aspeslagh, 1996, p. 334). How these could be taught, both the setting and the methods, can be seen in his curriculum development work.

Robert's principles were realised through his work. It is difficult now to find his name on peace education materials which he was instrumental in creating during the 11 years when that was his primary task. One curriculum dealt with power, titled "Who's afraid of the lion?" [*Wie es bang voor de Leeuw?*] and used that image with a cartoon presentation for classroom application. "They and us: how groups face each other" [*Zij en wij: hoe groepen tenenover elkaan stan*] is another, Robert having prepared the teacher workbook (1985). The realities of both pupils and teachers were the starting points for these courses. Working with teachers and trialling in the classroom was the method to develop materials and curricula, and for Robert to maintain close connection with those involved in peace learning. Reflection on those experiences continued to inform his approaches to classroom learning and to widen his perception of the huge scope and variability of peace education around the world.

Executive Secretary of the Peace Education Commission

Following Magnus Haavelsrud of Norway as PEC executive secretary in 1979 opened up that wider world for Robert. It was a time when the international political climate stimulated UNESCO's work in first promoting education for international understanding (1974) and then disarmament education (1980). Robert represented PEC/IPRA at the 1981 informal consultation on disarmament education at Unesco headquarters in Paris. In a critical report of that meeting, he noted that there was a danger that an interest in peace is moving from the North-South relationship towards the relationships between East and West. By that one emphasizes the danger of armament and the prevailing ideas on the prevention of war instead of the unjust relations in the world as the main focus of peace education for disarmament and education for peace go hand in hand and are both necessary in the quest for social justice.

During his time as PEC executive secretary Robert, like Magnus Haavelsrud (and myself as his successor as executive secretary) worked hard to spread the PEC network both East and South. The support of local initiatives, and his work to enable greater representation at the IPRA international conferences contributed to the development and strengthening of his desire for inclusiveness and diversity. He saw the complexity and diversity of peace education and its main direction in different socio-economic and politico-cultural contexts. While there was an inevitable Euro-centric hub for his work, given the limited opportunities to travel as executive secretary, he responded to the ongoing challenge of a flourishing of diverse inputs to peace education and their dissemination. And bearing in mind his early background in Indonesia, and his strong sense of the nature of power and the need for social justice, in his work for PEC he was particularly concerned to encourage dialogue with colleagues in Latin America, Africa, and South and Southeast Asia. From this emerged a firm conviction that there could be no single peace education. Rather, as we expressed in an attempt to chart what was happening in PEC from its inception, it is possible to discern:

> ...a core set of values [that] provides a basis for constructing models which can be used to clarify education aims and their human, social and ecological consequences. It also provides a basis for charting one's way through the maze of educations which are all in some way concerned with the future, and with shaping it to more 'desirable' moulds. Appropriate pedagogical and didactic techniques follow from the values which define the models; in many instances we lack tried versions of these, and the models therefore present a challenge to educators, and perhaps a new way of thinking about the tasks of education itself. (Aspeslagh & Burns, 1996, p. 59)

In the process of envisioning preferred futures, culture became a central issue in Robert's work, not just its conceptualisation as 'intercultural understanding' as promoted by Unesco, though that he considered as part of the continuum. Striving for a peaceful global culture was his ultimate goal. His pedagogy focussed on peaceful relations within the classroom as a key component of peace education, and he did implicitly espouse psychological approaches especially in his curriculum work, from political socialisation through fear of war, enemy images and conflict resolution. However, he rejected any focus on 'personal peace' as either a starting point or end point for peace education. Rather, for Robert the work of Brazilian Paulo Freire was central to conceptualising the pedagogical relationship between 'learner' and 'teacher', research/theory and action/practice, and the importance of the learners' reality as the starting point of the educational process.

Peace education has a firm basis in The Netherlands, with schools established in the 1930s based on the peace-oriented ideals of educators Montessori, Freinet and Boeke (Bjerstedt, 1993, p. 7). Peace education was first promoted by a working party in 1968, following the formation of an institutional peace research institute in Groningen in 1962 (Bjerstedt, 1988, p.57). Robert became an integral part of the ongoing development of the field in The Netherlands. However, through PEC opportunities arose for him to participate in very different situations. In particular, from 1988 to 1993 he was involved in a project on peacebuilding in Lebanon. The project was undertaken by IPRA in collaboration with UNESCO and resulted, after several drafts and many meetings, in a *Handbook Resource and Teaching Material in Conflict Resolution, Education for Human Rights, Peace and Democracy* (1994; see Aspeslagh 1994).

Robert contributed a section on "Education for a pluralist society, peace, culture and human rights" which can be read as a summary of his approach to peace making and peace education. He begins with the assertion that "Education cannot be separated from society. The society of a given nation cannot be seceded from the region or the continent to which it belongs, and they all form part of the world." Education itself is "a mirror of society" (Aspeslagh, 1994, p.11). While applying it specifically to Lebanon at that time, he stated that all society is now heterogeneous, in other words, pluralist. However, pluralism does not simply occur because of heterogeneity, it is "an attitude through which people are reckoning with the opinions, experiences and actions of others when making their own judgements or their own action" (Aspeslagh, 1994, p.11).

His analysis of the situation in Lebanon suggested that "Communities can obtain peace by acting for the establishment of a pluralist society, which is built on the idea of co-operation and seeking for a common overarching framework on the one hand, and strengthening of each separate framework on the other hand" (Aspeslagh, 1994, p.13). This would not guarantee the absence of conflicts but promote compromise and the finding of ways and means to achieve peace. Towards this, education should start with the learners' reality, paying attention to what is shared rather than what differentiates people. Ideally, he considered NGOs the best organisations to implement education for pluralism, human rights, peace and democracy, and went on to list 20 issues to be addressed in selecting materials for such education.

From Education to Research and Diplomacy

The Netherlands Institute for Studies of Peace and Security merged with four other institutes in 1983 to form the Netherlands Institute for International Relations Clingendael, "a think tank and diplomatic academy which combines research, training and public debate whereby it aims to inspire and equip governments, businesses, and civil society to contribute to a secure, sustainable and just world" (Clingendael, n.d.). Robert came with the smaller institute. His position was 'scientific worker' in a unit that covered education and information, but soon realised that peace education was not a high priority for the new institute, at least not for schools and not as a specific field.

He was able to continue some of his prior educational work and in 1984 proposed an East-West co-operative project which the Dutch National Committee of UNESCO was prepared to co-sponsor once approval was obtained from the Foreign and Education Ministries. It appears not to have gone ahead but with colleagues outside the Institute he developed a plan for a peace education project between Hungary and The Netherlands. The project was to run from the start of the 1987-1988 school year through to 1991-1992. In order to enhance communication with participants in Hungary Robert studied the Hungarian language, and developed a strong bond with his Hungarian counterpart, who sadly died before the project concluded (personal communications). I cannot locate a formal report of the project.

With no colleagues in the Institute working in the field of education, Robert was under pressure to place more emphasis on information, including the preparation of brochures and booklets on international issues for the public in general, which raised for him the issue referred to previously of peace researcher - peace educator roles. Perhaps the only outcome of informational work by Robert was a controversial booklet on drugs and the law (1987b). The only formal education task Robert had was to organise an annual United Nations Day for Teachers, in part because the institute received some funding from UN agencies. The 1985 theme he chose for the day was the way the United Nations was treated in Dutch history textbooks (1986a). He subsequently undertook research on the way nuclear issues were handled in Dutch history textbooks (1986b) and we both presented papers on nuclear issues in school history books at the 1986 IPRA conference in Brighton, England, including a discussion of the different content analysis methods we used (Aspeslagh, 1986b; Burns & Bampton, 1986).

During the 1980s Robert continued his involvement with the Peace Education Commission, which included editing one issue of the international journals *Gandhi Marg* and the *Bulletin of Peace Proposals*. He also published a book on the tension between wholeness and diversity in education about world issues (1987a).

Towards a Pluralist, More Just and Humane Future

Culture came increasingly to play a key role in his research. This was seen in the Lebanon project, above, and in work he undertook on the situation of minorities in Eastern Europe. He was one of seven contributors assessing the opportunities for democracy and tolerance in the region. His over-arching concern was always the reduction of violence and conflict, acknowledgment of how people perceived the issues, and the creation of opportunities for action towards a more just and humane future society, whether at the local, national or international level. This desire is clearly the over-arching concern and the key to all his work.

His final major project at Clingendael was research on the attitudes of Dutch youth to Germany and Germans which led to a focus on Dutch-German relations, and collaboration especially with Henk Dekker of Leiden University. He became scientific secretary of the Dutch Foundation for the Promotion of German Studies in The Netherlands and of Platform Germany. Clingendael includes a large diplomatic academy and diplomacy was clearly Robert's major *modus operandi* during this final period at Clingendael. Through the institute's courses, consultations, public presentations and program of interns, as well as through ongoing contact with those with whom and for whom he worked, his educational outreach continued.

Yet another strand in Robert's life work was his interest in and concern for Indonesia, his birthplace. He was involved in discussions with Indonesian officials during his time at Clingendael, and he wrestled with post-colonial relations between the two countries. One act was to participate in discussions in 2000 concerning a monument in Amsterdam to Van Heutsz, the Dutch general who became governor-general of the Dutch East Indies in 1904 after successfully ending the war in Aceh, where he was military governor. The monument had been defaced a number of times. Robert argued that it should remain in place as it was part of Dutch history which should not just be swept away (it was re-named as a Dutch East Indies memorial in 2004, omitting van Heutsz's name). And he visited Indonesia a number of times in his final decade, alone and with family or friends, searching for old connections and forging new ones, especially with the Batak Sialagan family.

Robert retired from Clingendael in 2002, in order to spend time painting, travelling and with his grandchildren. This did not mean loss of interest in the essential task of peace education, however, as he continued to put it into practice in his personal relations, his work with the other artists in the studio complex where he painted, his support for young artists to find a place to work, involvement in local government issues, ongoing interest in former pupils and interns, and with his friends around the world. Many of his paintings reflect this concern, as he strove to express his worldview through his art. His many papers, books and research reports are testimony to the development and refinement of this view. This short poem, to accompany a painting from a bushwalk in Tasmania, Australia, is a succinct and subtle summary:

Steps take us
beyond the rock
of today
to an unknown
future of hope (2016)

That "future of hope" is spelt out in his many publications, friendships and actions over the decades, through dialogue between the local and the global, and for peace educators, through an attempt to "integrate research, education and action, a desire to communicate across the present structural, cultural and situational barriers, justice throughout and between societies."

References

Aspeslagh, R. (1985). *Zij en wij: hoe groepen tegenover elkaan stan: werkboek voor ondervijs* [They and us: how groups face each other: workbook for education]. Vredesopbouw.

Aspeslagh, R. (1986a). De Verenigde Naties: ist daar nog wel les over te geven? [The United Nations: are there still lessons to be uncovered?] (no details available)

Aspeslagh, R. (1986b). *The nuclear issues in Dutch history textbooks* [Conference presentation]. International Peace Research Association conference, Brighton, Sussex UK.

Aspeslagh, R. (1987a). *Een olifant in het onderwijs: over de spanning tussen eenheid en versheidenheid bij opvoeding en onderwijs over wereldproblemen* [An elephant in education. About the tension between wholeness and diversity in education about world issues]. International Peace Information Service (IPIS) Dossier 9.

Aspeslagh, R. (Ed.). (1987b). *Een wereld vol drugs?* [A world full of drugs?] Netherlands Institute for International Relations.

Aspeslagh, R. (1994). Education for a pluralist society, peace, culture and human rights. In International Peace Research Association (Ed.), *Handbook*

Resource and teaching material in conflict resolution, education for human rights, peace and democracy (appendix IV, pp. 11-13). International Peace Research Association (IPRA) in collaboration with UNESCO

Aspeslagh, R. (2016). *Poems painted*. Blurb.

Aspeslagh, R. & Burns, R.J. (1996). Approaching Peace through Education. Background, concepts and theoretical issues. In Burns, R.J. & Aspeslagh, R. (Eds.). *Three decades of peace education around the world. An anthology* (pp. 25-69). Garland.

Aspeslagh, R. & Wiese, V. (1981). Recent discussion on disarmament education. In Haavelsrud, M. (Ed.). *Towards disarmament education* (pp.1-7). Westbury House.

Bjerstedt, Å. (1988). *Peace education in different countries*. Malmö School of Education Educational Information and Debate 81.

Bjerstedt, Å. (Ed.). (1993). *Visions of peace education*. Malmö: School of Educational and Psychological Research, School of Education, Educational Information and Debate 99.

Burns, R.J. & Aspeslagh, R. (1996). *Three decades of peace education around the world*. Garland.

Burns, R.J. & Bampton, M. (1986) *Conflict and mass destruction: a content analysis of Australian history textbooks* [Conference presentation]. International Peace Research Association conference, Brighton, Sussex UK.

Clingendael. (n.d.). *About us*. https://www.clingendael.org/about-us

Chapter 6
Olga Vorkunova

Alexander Sergunin

Short Bio-Note

Olga Vorkunova was born in Moscow (1951). In 1974, she graduated from the Faculty of History, Moscow State University. The same year, she joined the Institute of World Economy and International Relations (IMEMO), Soviet Academy of Sciences. Olga earned her PhD from IMEMO in 1985. The title of her PhD dissertation was "Scandinavia and the developing countries in the mid-1970 - mid-1980s". In recent years, she was a Senior Researcher at the Caucasian Project, IMEMO Center for Post-Soviet Studies. Since 2017 Olga was also an Associate Professor in the Department of Area Studies Theory, Moscow State Linguistic University (Paczynska, 2021).

In October 2021, Olga was infected by the COVID-19 virus and passed away on 25 October. It was a heavy blow for her relatives, friends and colleagues who loved and respected Olga and who will cherish fond memories of her.

Social Activities

Olga was not an armchair scientist. She was very active in the profession and a real institution builder. She was Convener of TRANSCEND (A Peace and Development Network for Conflict Transformation by Peaceful Means); a member of the European Peace Research Association (EuPRA) Board and of the International Peace Research Association (IPRA) Board and Convener of the Peace Education Commission of IPRA. Olga also contributed to the activities of the Steering Committee of the Conflict Early Warning Systems Research Project of the International Social Science Council and Expert Group of the Cultural Policy and Action Department of the Council of Europe. She was a member from Russia of the Black Sea Peace-Building Network, Crisis Management Initiative, Martti Ahtisaari Center, International Expert of the project "Peacebuilding in South Caucasus," Austrian Study Center for Peace and Conflict Resolution, Stadtschlaining, Austria, the Caucasus Institute of Peace, Democracy and Development, Gudauri, Georgia and participated with Johan Galtung in the peacebuilding mission in Nagorny Karabakh (Meyer, 2022; Vambheim, 2021).

Olga managed to bring the peace research problematique to the International Studies Association (ISA). She was a member of ISA since 1999 and was elected one of the Non-North American Members at-Large of the ISA Governing Council 2013 – 2015. In 2020 she was elected to the Executive Committee of ISA's Peace Studies Section and was active in the intellectual life of the Section (Paczynska, 2021).

In 2003, Olga established the Center for Peace Research and Development 'Forum', which was effectively used as a platform for coordination of peace and conflict resolution studies among Russian NGOs, as well as for cooperation with foreign peace researchers. A series of conferences, expert seminars and workshops were held under the Forum's auspices.

In 2005, Olga founded the Russian Peace Academy which focused on peace education and promotion of a culture of peace and non-violence. As the Academy's President Olga contributed to peace research, connecting the peace researchers from Russia and CIS countries to international organizations dealing with peace studies (including IPRA, EuPRA, ISA, etc.) and expanding channels of communication and collaboration in peacebuilding and conflict resolution.

Research Interests

As far as Olga's scholarly activities are concerned, she was an expert on ethnic conflicts, early warning systems, peacebuilding, theory of peace studies and peace education. She conducted her research on the basis of numerous case studies, including Caucasus, the Black and Caspian Seas region, Central

Asia, Sino-Russian relations and South Asia.

Concerning ethnic conflicts, in the early 1990s, Olga together with Kumar Rupesinghe and Peter King coedited a path-breaking work titled "Ethnicity and conflict in a post-Communist world: the Soviet Union, Eastern Europe, and China" (1992). This edited volume consisted of revised papers presented at the 1990 IPRA Conference. The book demonstrated that the post-Communist world has seen a dramatic revival of ethnicity and nationalism. Many of these societies were facing a multidimensional crisis, since the movement towards full democracy also had to cope with widespread demands for self-determination and minority protection as well as the consequences of dismantling the totalitarian state.

The volume explored the sources, scope and intensity of nationality conflicts in the post-Communist world. The authors studied the resurgence of ethnicity and nationalism, after *perestroika* and *glasnost*, within a disintegrating Soviet Union. They examined the consequences and effects of ethnic conflicts within the various regions of the former USSR. This study explored identity formation, the nature and implications of internal conflicts and possible paths toward conflict resolution in these societies. The interlink between the processes of democratization and generation of new conflicts was also examined based on the cases of East European countries and China. In her chapter, Olga focused on management of inter-ethnic conflicts in the former Soviet Union, specifically during the most dramatic period of national conflicts, 1988–1990.

Along with many other Russian peace researchers, Olga used Johan Galtung's structural and cultural violence theory to explain the sources of conflicts within societies and between the states (Vorkunova, 2019, p.27). She believed that structural violence as a sociopolitical phenomenon is deeply rooted in capitalist society and economy and constantly reproduced by the capitalist mode of production. She also believed that the forms of contemporary exploitation are different from those depicted by Karl Marx, Friedrich Engels, and Vladimir Lenin, but the essence of this phenomenon is still the same, and it will continue to generate violence and conflicts both domestically and internationally.

Olga emphasized that along with structural violence, its cultural variation should be also taken into account (Vorkunova, 2019, p. 33). She noted that in the era of global communications, cultural violence can be even more effective than its direct or structural versions. She believed that the so-called color revolutions in the post-Soviet space and Arab countries were often generated or at least facilitated by the West with the help of public diplomacy based on the cultivation of liberal-democratic values among the local youth and political opposition. Olga agreed with Galtung that cultural violence can be even more dangerous than other forms of violence because it not only reinforces other 'angles' of the 'conflict triangle', but it can also have long-term negative and unexpected effects (Galtung & Jacobsen, 2000).

Concerning Olga's positions on conflict resolution and peacebuilding, they are very close to the so-called sociological approach to conflict studies (Vorkunova, 2019, pp.30-31). She put emphasis on the need to identify the causes of the conflict and eliminate them. She also paid greater attention to conflict prevention and post-conflict peacebuilding rather than to conflict management, peacekeeping, and peace enforcement, which were seen as technical/instrumentalist in nature and of secondary importance.

Olga noted that different causes generate different types of conflicts. Some wars have their origin in domestic political weakness, others in a secure domestic political domination that allows free rein to an adventurous leader. Some are fought to establish domination over a weaker neighboring country, others to establish widespread hegemony, and others to defend themselves or to defend one's existing hegemony over others against a vigorous challenge.

Over the post-Cold War era, Olga produced numerous case studies on ethnic conflicts. The North and South Caucasus was Olga's priority: she produced a series of case studies on the Nagorny Karabakh, Abkhazia and South Ossetia conflicts (Vorkunova, 1999, 2020a). She also examined the cases of other conflicts in the post-Soviet space (Vorkunova, 1999), Balkans (Vorkunova, 2020a) and even in Sri-Lanka. (Vorkunova, 2021b).

Over time, Olga moved from case studies to theoretical generalizations in the field of conflict studies. For example, in one of her last publications, she tried to give a typology of conflicts in Eurasia, summarize their causes and ways to resolve them (Vorkunova, 2020b). She arrived at the conclusion that numerous internal conflicts in Eurasia stem from socioeconomic and political problems, the struggle for power, disputes over natural resources and territorial claims, interethnic and interreligious differences – all this provokes the use of extremist and terrorist methods by the conflicting parties. Olga believed that peaceful transformation of the Eurasian continent should include methods related to both "hard" counteraction to international terrorism and "soft" methods of peacebuilding.

In the late period of her research activity, Olga came to the conclusion that it is not enough to focus only on conflict prevention, management and resolution and even post-conflict peacebuilding. The most effective means of a region's peaceful transformation is the creation of a reliable security system there. In this regard, Olga was a follower of Johan Galtung's ideas, who back in the 1970s believed that enduring peace could be established through the formation of appropriate regional and functional international relations systems. Such systems are designed to support the internal local potential for conflict management and resolution. At the same time, the emphasis should be placed on mobilizing efforts of the 'bottom-up' type – from local initiatives to the central government's level, which provides for decentralization of social and economic structures and the transition from structural and cultural violence to a culture of peace. Conflict resolution mechanisms should be integrated into the structure of society in order to transform it and resolve conflicts by peaceful means. These mechanisms can be activated as needed, similar to how antibodies in a healthy body are activated in response to the threat of disease (Vorkunova, 2017, p. 13).

Olga believed that regional security systems can be created only with solid institutional support. In particular, she noted the special role of such global governance institutions as the International Bank for Reconstruction and Development, the International Monetary Fund, the World Trade Organization, as well as regional institutions, primarily the EU, ASEAN, Asia Pacific Economic Cooperation, Eurasian Economic Union, etc.

The United Nations and its specialized organizations, which now act as the main bearers of the spirit of cooperation and partnership, are important tools for creating regional security systems as well. The UN structures expand the capabilities of weaker states, including small countries, to implement independent policies in the field of peaceful transformation. The creation of regional security systems, in turn, depends on shifts in the socioeconomic and political structures of the international relations actors, the development of practices and technologies for peaceful conflict resolution, as well as the participation of non-state actors in this process (Vorkunova, 2017, p.20).

Olga noted that in general usage 'peace' conveys the notion of 'the absence of war' and not any particular ideal condition of society (Vorkunova, 2019, p.33). However, this broad consensus view of peace was unsatisfactory from Olga's (and other peace researchers') point of view since we need to know more about the nature of a possible world without armed conflict. According to Galtung (1985, 2006), peace seen merely as the absence of war is considered to be 'negative peace', and the concept of 'positive peace' has been used to describe a situation in which there is neither physical violence nor legalized repression. Under conditions of positive peace, war is not only absent but also unanticipated and essentially unthinkable. A state of positive peace involves large elements of reciprocity, equality, and joint problem-solving capabilities.

Olga underlined that there have been many different proposals for the positive definitions: integration, justice, harmony, equity, and freedom, all of which call for further conceptualization. Analytically, peace was conceptualized by some Russian scholars in a series of discrete categories ranging from various degrees and states of conflict to various states of cooperation and integration. According to Olga, the dominant trend in the Russian peace research of 1990s and 2000s was to interpret peace as synonymous with the category of sustainable development (Samarin, 2008; Stepanov, 2014).

Olga herself believed that 'positive' peace can be seen as a sort of a social order where not only violence, exploitation, and major security threats are absent but also the favorable conditions for human creativity are provided (Vorkunova, 2019, p.33).

In an article by Olga shortly before her fatal illness and published after she passed away, she tried to analyze the challenges to peacebuilding in the post-COVID era. Particularly, the paper addressed the questions of what is new about complex identity and what it means for peacebuilding. She believed that scales and identity must be considered in their totality, as part of a complex bundle of technological, economic, and socio-cultural forces. Olga also pointed out that peacebuilding is a process that gradually evolves and not a thing that suddenly appears. While every new age holds marked change, it also contains elements of continuity. Peacebuilding was then defined by Olga as holding five essential components: (1) building self-sustainable peaceful societies, (2) democratic transition processes, (3) economic reform and development, (4) institution-building, and (5) structural adjustment. Olga also identified both the positive and negative implications that the post-COVID world portends for peacebuilding. Olga noted that the good news included rising prosperity, development cooperation and aid, and increased democracy. The bad news consisted of sharpening imbalances, increased social disorder, and greater people's expectations. Finally, Olga suggested some ways of coping with these prospects, such as the development of horizontal, network-type peacebuilding regimes and institutions at the local and regional levels (Vorkunova, 2022b).

Promotion of Peace Education and Peace Culture

As mentioned above, along with conflict resolution and peacebuilding studies, Olga paid great attention to the promotion of peace education and peace culture.

In a special chapter on models and strategies of peace education published in an edited volume, Olga described different approaches to peace education and made their historical overview (Vorkunova, 2016). Her analysis provided deeper insights into the philosophy and the roots of contemporary peace education programs. She tried to explain that it is useful to employ all methods of analysis dealt with in peace research, each of which allows us to see only a part of reality of the phenomenon being studied, but which when taken all together in their interrelations and complementarily can help us to understand the object of our study, in this case peace education, more deeply. The chapter had an ambition to give an idea of how different methods and techniques of observation can be used differently according to how a teacher has set up his or her methodology, and how these tools can be freed from the excessive weight of some particular school or view, which tends to deprive the tool of any validity.

Following traditions of the Western peace research school, Olga argued that the interest of peace education is emancipatory. She believed that political violence, the threat of violence and the preparation for violence first and foremost define the subject of peace education. However, peace education should not focus only on avoiding war and violence, but also on the conditions of positive peace. Moreover, peace researchers and educators should not assume the ideal of harmony but allow for conflicts and dramatic changes.

Olga noted that the field of peace education has significantly developed over the past decades from the training courses in nonviolence to constructive learning about human rights, cooperative values, active communication, conflict resolution, disarmament and peacebuilding. At the same time, she underlined that after 9/11 peace educators must address issues such as radical Islamism and other forms of extremism, understanding both fundamentalist and aggressive practices.

Olga believed that all the existing approaches to and methodologies of peace education have contributed to the development of this field. However, the strength of the US and European peace education schools is that they sought to approach the problem of peace by way of a creative encounter between the third-party roles and parties that are directly involved in conflicts. Moreover, they developed diagnosis and prognosis strategies based on a method of dialogue.

Iin this chapter, Olga tried to make some proposals to improve peace education tools, based on critical and comparative approaches to both its theory and practice. Particularly, she believed that the effectiveness of peace education programs can be increased by focusing on issues such as combating global inequalities and center-periphery divisions on different axes, strengthening social cohesion based on the notions of pluralism, equality and inclusion (Vorkunova, 2016).

In 2020, in the midst of the COVID-19 epidemic, Olga worked on a textbook on peacebuilding, which, after its publication in 2021, she planned to use for her teaching at the Russian Peace Academy and the Moscow State Linguistic University. I was lucky enough to be one of the reviewers of this textbook at the stage of preparing the manuscript for publication. Unfortunately, her illness and premature death did not allow her to use this textbook in the educational process herself. But other Russian teachers still use this textbook with great success to teach disciplines on conflict resolution and peacebuilding.

The textbook consists of two parts. The first part analyzes the origins of international conflicts; positions, values, goals, problems, interests and needs of conflict participants; the structure and process of conflict development; main stages and types of conflicts; post-conflict settlement; forecasting and conflict prevention. The second part of the textbook examines the role of the time factor in the conflict development and resolution, as well as peculiarities of peacebuilding strategies in Eurasia (Vorkunova, 2021a).

In the first issue of the *Peace and Change* journal in 2022 Olga's paper on peace education was published. This article, a work in progress at the time of the author's passing in October 2021, explained how knowledge, organizational forms, and societal institutions interact to shape peace education and innovative learning capabilities (Vorkunova, 2022). It focused on peace education and training systems, and types of organizations as key societal institutions shaping work organization and the knowledge base of the universities. Olga used a tacit (implicit) knowledge concept introduced by Michael Polanyi as opposed to formalized, codified or explicit knowledge that is difficult to express or extract. Therefore, it is more difficult to transfer it to others by means of writing it down or verbalizing it.

The article's central premise is that tacit knowledge, which is difficult to create and transfer in the absence of social interaction and people's mobility during pandemic circumstances, constitutes a most important source of learning and sustainable competitive advantage in the knowledge society. Institutions that can harness tacit knowledge as a source of learning are more likely to produce strong innovative capabilities. The analysis suggests that there are two alternative models of competence-building, which are especially favorable to learning and innovation, and examines cases of peace education as illustrative examples. It argues that societies with different institutional arrangements will continue to develop a variety of organizational forms and learning strategies that privilege some sectors and discourage others. Institutionalized variation in patterns of learning and innovation therefore reproduces distinctive regional or national patterns of specialization.

Impact on the Russian Peace Research School

Our cooperation with Olga began with the fact that we both shared many ideas of the Scandinavian peace research school and especially the concepts of Johan Galtung. Olga, during her work on her PhD thesis in the first half of the 1980s, familiarized herself with the works of Scandinavian peace researchers. In the 1990s, when Russian scientists got the opportunity to travel abroad and work in research and educational centers there, Olga could personally communicate with representatives of the Scandinavian peace research school. It should be noted that among European academic institutions, peace research centers were most interested in cooperating with social scientists from former socialist countries and offered them good working conditions. Olga was one of the first Russian scholars to take advantage of this opportunity and establish strong ties with her Nordic colleagues.

At about the same time, I, like Olga and some other Russian scientists, began collaborating with Nordic peace research centers. Since 1993, I have implemented several projects with the Copenhagen Peace Research Institute on Russian security policies in Europe, including Nordic Europe. I also had good cooperation with SIPRI, PRIO, TAPRI, etc. Since then, the problems of Nordic Europe and the Arctic, as well as peaceful conflict resolution in this region, have become the subject of my research (Heininen, Sergunin & Yarovoy, 2015a, 2015b, 2015c; Sergunin, 2019; Sergunin & Konyshev, 2016 and 2019). Along with the ideas of Peter Wallensteen, Håkan Wiberg, Jan Oberg, Raimo Vayrynen and Pertti Joenniemi, I, like Olga, was also particularly attracted to Galtung's theories, which seemed to me the most capable of explaining the origin of conflicts and suggesting ways out of various international crises.

Of all the Scandinavian peace researchers, Galtung's ideas impressed Olga the most, as they offered a systematic vision of both the origins of conflicts and methods of their resolution and post-conflict peace building. Olga paid special attention to popularizing Galtung's ideas about positive security and positive peace in the Russian peace research community. With the help of her European colleagues from EuPRA and IPRA, she organized numerous conferences, seminars and training on the basis of first IMEMO, and then the Forum and the Russian Peace Academy, designed for established scientists and especially for young researchers who had problems finding theoretical foundations for their research.

Due to Olga's efforts Russian peace research was able to challenge the dominant realist and liberal IR paradigms concerning understanding of conflict. Olga and other Russian peace researchers offered an approach based on the assumption that conflicts are a natural product of various contradictory processes in the society. They did not reduce the causes of conflict to the legal ones (as, for example, the liberals did); among the sources of conflict peace researchers identified the economic, social, identity, political, military, environmental, cultural, ideological, religious and other factors (Vorkunova, 2019, 2020b, 2021a). Thereafter, the Russian peace researchers did not limit the conflict resolution methods and techniques to the legal instruments and procedures. Under Olga's and other like-minded scholars' influence the Russian peace research school realized that to resolve a conflict and preclude its reemergence, its causes should be eliminated first and foremost. For this reason, already in the 1990s and early 2000s this school's conflict resolution arsenal was much richer and more complex. In addition to the instruments that the 'legalists' suggested (e.g. negotiations, cease-fire, truce and peace agreements, peacekeeping and peace enforcement mechanisms, etc.), peace researchers offered a broad agenda for post-conflict peacebuilding and development that envisaged a radical transformation of the society and its institutions with the aim to eradicate the causes of the conflict (2021a).

Olga was one of the first Russian peace researchers who told that to prevent new conflicts an early warning/monitoring mechanism should be created in the conflict-prone areas. The latter should be based on a system of indicators that should monitor dangerous developments and identify problematic areas. Such a system could be helpful in detecting and preventing conflicts at an early phase. In contrast with the legalist approach which related the conflict resolution activities basically to the state and statist instruments, Olga believed that conflicts can be resolved and lasting peace is possible if not only governments but also societies talk to each other and develop non-hierarchical, horizontal contacts. That's why peace researchers welcomed an active participation of non-state actors in the conflict-resolution activities: people-to-people, NGO-to-NGO, company-to-company contacts, the so-called 'people's' or 'civil diplomacy' (Vorkunova, 2017, 2021a).

Despite its marginal positions in the Russian expert-analytical community, due to Olga's and her colleagues' activities the Russian peace research school continues to provide Russian scholarship with innovative approaches and useful insights into basic IR issues such as causes of war and conflict, nature, sources and manifestations of violence, essence and ways of achieving both 'negative' and 'positive peace', transformation of the international relations system in the post-Cold War era and so on. In addition, this type of research continues to challenge Russia's predominant IR paradigms, thus forcing them to develop their concepts, argumentation and research techniques.

To sum up, it should be noted that it is difficult to overestimate Olga's contribution to the development of the Russian peace research school and IR studies in general. Despite the fact that a number of Russian peace researchers criticized Olga for her orientation to the Western peace theories and concepts, as well as for her attempts to apply Western methods of conflict resolution and peacebuilding to Eurasia, all the members of the Russian peace study community, without exception, loved and respected her for her sincere commitment to the cause of peace and her titanic efforts to promote peace education and a culture of peace. Both the Russian and international peace research communities are grateful to her for all her contributions and will miss her presence and insights.

References

Galtung, J. (1985). Twenty-five years of peace research: Ten challenges and some responses. *Journal of Peace Research*. 22(2), 141–158.

Galtung, J. (2006). Peace by peaceful means: Peace and conflict, development and civilization. In Global Marshall Plan Initiative (Ed.), *Towards a world in balance: A virtual congress for a better balanced world* (pp.119-123). Global Marshall Plan Initiative.

Galtung J. & Jacobsen, C. (2000). *Searching for peace: The road to TRANSCEND*. Pluto Press.

Heininen, L., Sergunin, A. & Yarovoy, G. (2015a). Norway-Russia: the Barents Sea. In Brunet-Jailly, E. (Ed.), *Border Disputes, Vol. 1* (pp. 385-393). ABC-CLIO.

Heininen, L., Sergunin, A. & Yarovoy, G. (2015b). Russia-United States: the Bering Sea. In Brunet-Jailly, E. (Ed.), *Border Disputes, Vol. 2.* (pp.661-669). ABC-CLIO.

Heininen, L., Sergunin, A. & Yarovoy, G. (2015c). Russia-United States: the Northern Sea Route. In Brunet-Jailly, E. (Ed.), *Border Disputes, Vol. 3* (pp. 819-826). ABC-CLIO.

Meyer, M. (2022). Olga Vorkunova (1961–2021): Memories and Memorials. *Peace and Change.* 47(1), 72-73. DOI: 10.1111/pech.12514

Moscow State Linguistic University (2021, October 26). *In Memory of Olga Alekseevna Vorkunova.* Retrieved from: https://linguanet.ru/fakultety-i-instituty/institut-mezhdunarodnykh-otnosheniy-i-sotsialno-politicheskikh-nauk-fakultet/novosti-instituta/?ELEMENT_ID=9848&ysclid=ltv4wshs-rx349764366 (in Russian).

Paczynska, A. (2021, November 4). *In Memoriam: Olga A. Vorkunova.* International Studies Association. https://www.isanet.org/News/ID/6190/In-Memoriam-Olga-A-Vorkunova

Rupesinghe K., King, P. & Vorkunova, O. (Eds.). (1992). *Ethnicity and conflict in a post-Communist world: the Soviet Union, Eastern Europe, and China.* St. Martin's Press.

Samarin, A. (2008). *Peace Culture as an Open Interdisciplinary Project.* Retrieved from: http://www.confstud.ru/content/view/28/2/ (in Russian).

Sergunin, A. (2019). Russian approaches to international peace, security and institutions: Debating within IR schools. In Kulnazarova, A. & Popovski, V. (Eds.), *The Palgrave handbook of global approaches to peace* (pp.215-242). Springer Nature.

Sergunin, A. & Konyshev, V. (2016). *Russia in the Arctic. Hard or soft power?* Ibidem-Verlag.

Konyshev, V. & Sergunin, A. (2019). In search for peace in the Arctic. In Kulnazarova, A. & Popovski, V. (Eds.), *The Palgrave handbook of global approaches to peace* (pp.685-716). Springer Nature.

Stepanov, Y. (2014). Ensuring modernization in the context of ongoing globalization. *Conflict Studies* 9(1), 9–27 (in Russian).

Vambheim, N.V. (2021, December 3). *In Memory of Olga Vorkunova, Exec. Secretary of IPRA'S Peace Education Commission.* Global Campaign for Peace Education. https://www.peace-ed-campaign.org/in-memory-of-olga-vorkunova-exec-secretary-of-ipras-peace-education-commission/

Vorkunova, O., (Ed.). (1997). *North Caucasus – Trans-Caucasus: problems of stability and prospects for the development.* Grif-F (in Russian).

Vorkunova, O. (Ed.) (1999). *Regional security and cooperation in Central Asia and Caucasus.* The Center for Peace Research and Development "Forum" (in Russian).

Vorkunova, O. (2016). Models and strategies of peace education. In: K. Pandey, (Ed.), *Promoting global peace and civic engagement through education* (pp. 52-65). IGI Global.

Vorkunova, O. (2017). Peacebuilding in the regional security system. *Occasional Papers of the Moscow State Linguistic University. Series "Social Sciences".* Issue 3 (787), 9-27 (in Russian).

Vorkunova, O. (2019). Theoretical and methodological problems of peace research. *Occasional Papers of the Moscow State Linguistic University. Series "Social Sciences".* Issue 4 (837), 24-40 (in Russian).

Vorkunova, O. (2020a). The Balkans and Caucasus: phenomenon of geopolitical transformation. *Occasional Papers of the Moscow State Linguistic University. Series "Social Sciences".* Issue 1 (838), 9-21 (in Russian).

Vorkunova, O. (2020b). Conflicts in Eurasia: problems of peaceful transformation of the Eurasian space. *Occasional Papers of the Moscow State Linguistic University. Series "Social Sciences".* Issue 4 (841), 25-35 (in Russian).

Vorkunova, O. (2021a). *Conflict resolution in Eurasia: the textbook on methods of analysis and conflict resolution.* Direct-Media (in Russian).

Vorkunova, O. (2021b). Peacebuilding in Sri Lanka. *Oriens* 1, 93–105. DOI: 10.31857/S086919080013556-8 (in Russian).

Vorkunova, O. (2022a). Alternative societal models of peace education and innovation in the knowledge society. *Peace and Change* 47(1), 57-61. DOI: 10.1111/pech.12517

Vorkunova, O. (2022b). Toward a culture of peacebuilding and complex identity in the post-COVID world. *Peace and Change* 47(1), 62-71. DOI: 10.1111/pech.12524

Part II: Critical Issues in Peace Education

Thinking Beyond Peace Education: Challenging Conceptual Rigidities. A Personal Note

Zvi Bekerman

Though some of my colleagues recognize me as deeply involved in peace education, I admit that this description came as a surprise to me. Generally speaking, I was a latecomer to academia and even later to the field of peace education—if indeed I've ever truly been a part of it. My focus is anthropology of education, which broadly involves examining what happens in any context dedicated to learning or teaching. This could mean almost any human situation, though to avoid making it too broad, we can narrow it down to what we consider formal or informal education settings.

More specifically, my interest lies in how humans learn, which, in my view, is synonymous with the very act of living. Suddenly, and for reasons too complex to delve into here, I found myself at the School of Education at the Hebrew University of Jerusalem. Around the same time, a colleague of mine was invited by an NGO to evaluate Israel's first integrated Palestinian-Jewish school. Thinking that an anthropologist's perspective might be beneficial, my colleague invited me to join the project. The experience was exhilarating, and a year later, I continued the work independently, thanks to a grant that allowed me to deepen and broaden the research into a full-fledged ethnography of the schools.

I never saw myself as conducting peace education research until I began publishing my findings and receiving invitations to conferences. It was these conferences that made me aware of a field I never knew existed. Even after realizing that my work fell within a recognized area of study, I struggled to understand how or why. I have similar reservations about other specialized fields like cognitive studies or civic education. To me, these academic divisions often seem arbitrary and more about territorial academic politics than about meaningful learning distinctions. Peace, democracy, or computation—these aren't just concepts; they're activities that can lead to varied results but on a human (activity) level are quite similar, thus enriching our understanding of human behavior and learning across disciplines.

This might sound like a plea for interdisciplinarity, but my issue with this term is that it still acknowledges the existence of separate disciplines, which are, after all, constructs shaped by political negotiations rather than reflections of the real world. Ian Hacking (2011, 2004) once suggested that instead of falling into the trap of interdisciplinarity, we should view knowledge as an archipelago where lowering the sea of ignorance reveals that all islands of knowledge are connected. Conducting ethnography at the integrated bilingual schools was precisely this for me—an opportunity to explore how people learn in a context that, while unique, did not fundamentally change my broad approach to observation.

It took me a year or two to realize that I like many before me, had approached the school with preconceived notions that Palestinians and Jews were distinct analytical categories, rather than understanding them as ideological and normative constructs. This realization underscored that viewing these identities as fixed obscures the necessary exploration of their constructed nature—a process essential for identifying and addressing the root causes of conflict.

It took me time to realize I had taken for granted what I was told by teachers and other stakeholders. They indicated without difficulty which of the children was Palestinian (Arab as they usually called them) and which were Jews and I followed their lead in my observations. If I would have continued, I would have never reached the details which I did when I finally started asking myself how are Palestinians and Jews organized / created / constructed in the school. What is most embarrassing is that I already knew at the start of my fieldwork that Jew and Palestinian are not traits of individual minds but these theories I knew from my studies melted as if they did not exist when abandoning the flatness of written texts and entering the depth of the realities of reality.

This perspective should not be mistaken for an opposition to categorization per se—whether ethnic, national, religious, or other. I acknowledge that while these categories are constructed and consequential, recognizing their artificiality is crucial. Only by unveiling the constructed nature of these identifications can we begin to seek genuine solutions and understand the underlying forces that sustain conflicts.

I recognize that addressing issues, as I do, in broad strokes can lead to debatable generalizations, yet this approach is sometimes necessary. Although aware of the potential pitfalls, I assert that the issues discussed in the following are relevant even for initiatives that might not completely align with the patterns described. Clearly, my insights are informed by my observations in the Israeli Jewish-Palestinian context. However, through numerous formal and informal interactions with colleagues working in similarly conflicted settings across various regions—Bosnia, Northern Ireland, South Africa—it has become evident that these observations could be instrumental in critically reevaluating educational efforts in multiple societies experiencing conflict.

Regrettably, I must confess that I have grown increasingly impatient with educational research. Despite its long history - over a century - educational research appears to have achieved little in terms of improving the plight of those who suffer. It seems that education, despite its redemptive aspirations, cannot rescue the world from its misery as hoped (maybe because hope is the problem – Spinoza (Gatens et al., 2020) and Nietzsche (Holte, 2020) would not engage with it). Perhaps some forms of education do assist individuals with their daily struggles in the marketplace, but institutionalized education primarily serves to support governmental ideologies. Governments often utilize institutionalized education as a placebo, giving the impression of genuine interest in the development and well-being of their citizens, though this is frequently (to say the least) not the case.

This might explain why recent research consistently shows that educational reforms implemented in Western societies over the past half-century have done little to improve the fortunes of the destitute. Often, when education fails to meet its proclaimed objectives – the advancement of that which is human - it is the teachers and their purported lack of preparation who are blamed by mainstream politicians and media. This should not be surprising, particularly when reflecting on the traditional roles assigned to universal education within nation-states - shaping national 'consciousness' and ideologies and supporting human advancement only in as much as it serves the rulers' market.

Among others, the problems I outline are part of a broader set of issues within the social sciences and the organization of higher education. There is a persistent trend towards further compartmentalizing knowledge, which seems to serve narrower academic and political interests rather than the pursuit of knowledge itself. It is crucial to understand that while specializations are necessary, they should not be confused with artificial boundaries around supposed subject matters. Instead, these should reflect the intricate interconnections within which chosen topics are embedded.

Specializations like peace education often abandon critical educational foundations - namely, the processes of learning and human understanding - to other disciplines, typically the psychological sciences, which may not have all the answers. Worse still is the assumption that these disciplines have found the correct answers, thereby going unchecked and shaping educational policy based on potentially flawed premises.

The notion that peace education can exist separately from primary learning theories or perspectives on human development is fundamentally flawed and undermines the integrity of educational research. Moreover, educational interests and research are increasingly driven by trends, such as the latest in leadership education or well-being, rather than solid empirical findings while the methodologies applied have little connection to practical, empirical outcomes, focusing instead on narrow experimental designs that yield results with little relevance to actual educational practice.

There seems to be a neglect of the primary goal of educational sciences, which is to enhance the welfare of learners, similar to how medical sciences aim to improve our health. Unfortunately, much of the educational research, even that which is considered relevant and successful, fails to significantly affect the very individuals it targets – teachers, students, and educational systems. My experience in Israel with the long-standing research projects on integrated Palestinian-Jewish schools is pertinent here.

In my research projects, I made concerted efforts to involve all relevant parties - teachers, parents, principals, and officials from the Ministry of Education. I was quite successful in engaging these groups, securing funding, and developing accredited workshops to ensure participants felt their involvement was valued and integral to the project's development. I also supported school authorities in their publicity efforts and more. I believe the relationships I developed with what were sometimes colleagues and sometimes research subjects were trustful and respectful. Judging by their reactions to my work and the data I presented, which we often analyzed together, they seemed to find the insights gained relevant to their roles. I was frequently asked to share my published papers on the NGO's website, and during workshops, teachers created curriculum items that addressed serious issues identified by the research. These efforts were a source of pride for both the teachers and me.

Most of what I thought I had discovered turned out to be already known by the teachers and parents I engaged with in a trustful environment for sharing perspectives. This was a humbling (though not surprising) revelation. The difference between us researchers and the shareholders were their deeper understanding of why the good analyses of current educational challenges couldn't be addressed. It wasn't due to a lack of ideas on how to make improvements, but rather a keen awareness of the risks such changes might pose for the school.

These shareholders, often criticized by researchers for lacking a critical perspective or not taking enough responsibility for their educational goals, actually had a deep understanding of the constraints within which these schools operate, given the sociopolitical context. They were not intellectually deficient or lacking in criticality. Very early in the process, they recognized, without vested interests in the research outcomes (as researchers have), that the research itself was problematic—not due to any methodological flaws, but because it often ignored the sociopolitical context in which it needed to be implemented.

An example may illustrate one aspect of what we just discussed. After almost a year of continuously observing and recording activities in the third-grade class from early morning until everyone went home, I had an enlightening interaction with the Palestinian teacher of the class. I sensed she pitied me for focusing so intensely on recording classroom activities without considering what she thought were central issues. One day, she called me over with a mix of respect and disdain, pointed to a book, and asked if I had ever paid attention to it. Admitting I hadn't (enough), she suggested that it might offer some answers to the issues I was interested in, even if just by examining its cover.

All teachers in the school recognized one of the main challenges of the integrated initiative was the lack of suitable curricular materials. The standard curricular development directed by the Ministry of Education primarily catered to the population of Jewish schools. Although the Ministry likely recognized the need for curricular variations, adaptations were mostly confined to religious Jewish schools, which sometimes developed materials that addressed value-laden issues. These adaptations were not without controversy but generally took place. In contrast, for the regular "Arab" schools, there was scant allowance for incorporating Palestinian culture or historical perspectives into their curriculum, largely due to fears that this might foster dissent.

Jewish teachers were aware of and supportive of the need for change and were involved in the NGO's efforts to develop appropriate curricular materials for the integrated schools. However, they were generally less attuned than their Palestinian colleagues to the subtle implications of using standard Ministry of Education materials in "Arab" schools, which made these materials particularly problematic.

When I finally looked at the cover of the book the teacher pointed out - a book on social and personal issues available in both Hebrew (the original edition) and Arabic (translated edition) - I was struck by a detail I had previously overlooked. The book, titled "Each One and His/Her Family", featured a cover illustration that, while maintaining the same family structure in both versions, had been "culturally adapted" for the Arabic edition. The family on the Hebrew cover—parents with two boys, dressed in typical modern Western attire—appeared on the Arabic cover with darker skin, thicker eyebrows, and curlier hair. The parents' attire was changed to resemble villagers', and the boys' clothing was altered to what could be described as a type of rap attire.

As for using the book, the teachers who used it were well aware of the problems its design might raise. They knew it was not worthwhile doing noise about something that though important they felt could be easily ignored while other issues needed taking care of and by themselves were truly much more difficult, e.g., the Nakba.

This moment made me acutely aware of my own limitations and biases as a member of the privileged Jewish group, realizing that racism was indeed pervasive, especially visible to those who suffer from it. Teachers share our critical approaches and are attentive, very attentive, to their surroundings, each focusing on what his experience has trained her to be attentive to; in a sense they are very similar to researchers.

I need, now, to revisit my initial acceptance of the ethnic and national identities of participants in the integrated initiative to address broader issues that have traditionally been overlooked in peace education research. Recent years have seen some improvement, but peace education often continues to operate under assumptions that do not adequately consider contextual and historical factors. This oversight can simplify complex issues, making them seem more manageable and less daunting - a tendency driven by research that is often influenced by political and economic pressures to provide policy solutions or so-called practical educational guidance, areas where much of social research is admittedly lacking.

There is a prevailing belief that many conflicts could be resolved if those involved simply understood certain basic facts or had a better grasp of their adversaries or their own psychological workings. This perspective suggests that conflicts arise primarily from a lack of knowledge or from flawed psychologies. Such assumptions align with the trajectory of Western intellectual history, from Plato through Descartes to Kant, who developed their philosophies under specific socio-political tensions – at times willing to be kings and at others to safeguard the sciences. In any case these assumptions lack serious empirical basis and, in this sense, evolved independently of the benefits brought by the scientific revolution—a revolution to which I am committed, as should be all scientific endeavors, with their emphasis on empirical evidence as that which is measurable and accessible to the senses.

However, these cognitive perspectives have bequeathed us a worldview that does not necessarily benefit us or our ecosystems. People are not merely the sum of their knowledge, identities, or cultural backgrounds (if such things are at all real). We are not solipsistic beings detached from our context and the passage of time. Therefore, conflicts should not be addressed solely at individual levels, epistemological depths, or abstracted frameworks. Discussions on identities and cultures, particularly when they are essentialized (and they usually are), are unlikely to lead to meaningful outcomes. We are, indeed, beings constantly emerging in context. While certain organic activities like eating, walking, and breathing must be performed individually - as articulated by H. Maturana's (Maturana & Varela, 1991; Maturana & Valera, 1987) concept of autopoiesis - beyond these essential actions, we are the products of our interactions within our contexts, and so too are our knowledge, belongings, and cultures.

Any attempt to individualize and essentialize these aspects of our existence is an ideological assault on our humanity, aiming to embroil us in conflicts. It should not be surprising, then, that nation-states and their current neoliberal agendas have harnessed individualism, identity, and culture to further their colonial globalizing goals.

For the community to be envisioned as a unified nation, borders had to be expanded and diverse groups needed to be amalgamated through homogenizing effort; culture had to be solidified into a set form, and the relationship between the individual and the sovereign had to be strengthened to dilute the influence of smaller communal belongings. Hidden behind the facade of universal (in)equality was the sovereign's demand for allegiance from individuals devoid of any group affiliation.

The conceptual framework of nation-states has grown so influential that, akin to language as described in the Sapir-Whorf hypothesis (Jessel, 1978; Sapir, 2023), nationalism shapes and directs our fundamental ideas about society and individual identity. When these influences are not considered in peace education efforts, there's a risk of reinforcing the very issues such efforts aim to resolve.

Our research in the social sciences appears to have become ensnared by methodological nationalism - the assimilation of the global regime of nation-states into our analytical frameworks, transforming folkloristic or political concepts into analytical categories, a practice that stands in stark contrast to any critical approach.

This methodological nationalism, when combined with Western epistemological colonialism, constructs a web of imperial knowledge that manages and disciplines alterity. This evolves into an arrogant liberal stance that endorses integrationist policies, which politically segregate populations into 'true' citizens, defined by identity and culture, and those deemed in need of a 'civilizing process' through colonialist 'rituals of humiliation.' This approach perpetuates a rigid dichotomy between high culture and popular culture and fosters political/educational discourses that echo and reshape racial narratives from the nineteenth and early twentieth centuries.

We must also be wary of cultural and multicultural rhetoric that might soften the edges of racism without addressing the root issues. These approaches often promote tolerance of other cultures as a superficial substitute for actual equality.

We are concerned that educational research might inadvertently solidify the very issues it aims to resolve. There is an urgent need for this field to analytically reassess its foundational paradigms and address the socio-political structures that sustain the problems it seeks to solve. We must question whether a more critical examination of our research subjects and a reevaluation of the primary categories provided by our contexts could lead to more effective policies. These new approaches might better address the challenges faced by populations whose only fault is their alterity.

Yet, our critique must dig deeper to expose the true challenges within educational activities aimed at peace and coexistence. This critique confronts traditional educational structures, particularly Western schooling, which have been globalized through colonial processes. This examination is vital because formal educational structures are intricately linked to the historical developments that brought about the conceptual dominance of the nation-state, thus reinforcing our critique as one that cannot be easily dismissed.

The rise of mass education through schooling is closely tied to the industrial revolution and the nation-state's development. Both required large populations with basic cognitive and behavioral skills to meet the demands of the nation-state and its economic framework. Therefore, schools are not neutral spaces where knowledge is impartially transmitted from experts to passive learners. In the contemporary era, schools have primarily functioned as tools for sovereigns to unify various local groups under one flag, one language, and one narrative. It's surprising then that peace-oriented groups often choose traditional educational structures to promote their coexistence goals, although it could be argued that while adopting these structures, peace-focused educators adapt them to serve broader purposes than just state mandates.

The fundamental structure and functionality of formal schooling, which are built upon and express a specific paradigmatic perspective, are doubtful in their efficacy for fostering peace. Schools have traditionally served as the main channels for transmitting two interconnected beliefs of the modern Western world: the belief in the individual self and the notion that knowledge exists externally and can be absorbed by this self if properly instructed.

These elements have been integral to the functioning of schools for centuries. Over 5000 years ago, the first schools were established to create a cadre of scribes to meet the bureaucratic demands of large, centralized urban economies. These schools developed three enduring characteristics: students were taught by strangers, separated from family and kin; knowledge was divided into specialized fields; and learning occurred outside the practical contexts where it was meant to be applied.

If the goals of liberal peace-seeking elements are to foster recognition and coexistence, and to understand peacemaking as a dynamic tradition that can respond to contemporary socio-political challenges, then traditional educational structures and their foundational practices may not be the appropriate settings to achieve these aims.

We must reconsider whether frameworks that distance individuals from their families and communities can truly foster peace perspectives that challenge societal norms. Can an educational system that delivers knowledge in fragmented segments (like history, physics, civics) cultivate a holistic understanding of peace and coexistence? Is it realistic to expect that learners, conditioned by conventional schooling, will find relevance in their education if it occurs in settings where knowledge is detached from its functional application? These are significant challenges shared by formal schooling and peace educational initiatives, and they are perhaps even more problematic in the latter, given their starkly out-of-context nature.

I've outlined the results of my engagement with an educational initiative often categorized under peace education. It's been eight years since I last researched these topics actively. My publications from that era are occasionally cited, which seems to satisfy the traditional academic metric of advancing the researcher's career rather than the world. This success has somewhat secured my status at the university, where I am now retired but remain active.

As for any significant influence on policy, be it substantial or minimal, I can confidently say my research has had no relevance at all. At best, it has resonated with a few stakeholders - teachers and parents who remember my involvement with the school fondly, appreciating some insights but largely acknowledging that implementation was unfeasible.

My hope is that from the above text it becomes evident that, in my view, there is a fundamental necessity to analytically examine the prevailing assumptions within peace education that may inadvertently perpetuate the very conflicts they aim to resolve. This includes challenging methodological nationalism and the compartmentalization of education into rigid categories that align with state agendas and Western epistemological frameworks.

The need for interdisciplinary approaches is clear, integrating insights from various fields to provide a more comprehensive understanding of the socio-political contexts of education. Such approaches can reveal the constructed nature of identities and the complex dynamics of conflicts, fostering more effective educational strategies. Moreover, the critique extends deeply into the structural aspects of educational systems, particularly the way schools function within and reinforce the needs of nation-states. This structural critique calls for a reevaluation of how educational institutions serve to assimilate diverse groups under a unified national narrative, often at the expense of suppressing local cultures and histories.

Furthermore, there is a pressing call to rethink the role of education in driving social change. This involves moving beyond the mere transmission of knowledge to passive learners, towards facilitating active engagement and critical attention among students about their cultural and social environments. The text suggests that educational policies should do more than integrate diverse groups into existing frameworks. Instead, there should be a transformative approach that questions and reshapes these frameworks to be more inclusive, egalitarian and reflective of multiple histories and identities.

Practically, the text implies that peace education should not just address conflicts at a superficial or symptomatic level but should engage deeply with the underlying causes, such as inequality, historical grievances, and the ideological uses of education. This deeper engagement requires a fearless (and risky) pedagogy that exposes students and teachers to question and reshape and enrich their understandings and realities.

Lastly, the conclusions drawn from the text call for a commitment to empirical rigor and ethical responsibility in educational research. Researchers should be wary of reproducing power dynamics or colonial legacies in their methodologies and should strive to collaborate with communities to ensure that research outcomes are relevant, respectful, and potentially transformative.

These insights suggest a paradigm shift in how educational research and practice are conceptualized and implemented, urging a move towards more attentive, contextually aware, and structurally embodied approaches to peace education. This narrative underscores the importance of viewing peace education as a dynamic and evolving field that must continuously adapt to the realities of the societies it seeks to serve.

At this juncture (and in short), we face a choice: either succumb to despair or pivot our educational strategies from focusing solely on cognitive categories to actively changing power dynamics through engagement with the world. This shift can be tailored to various interpretations of the prevailing issues and adjusted according to the risk levels acceptable within different sociopolitical contexts where peace education programs are enacted. Each context demands specific practical actions that should be informed by educators who are deeply knowledgeable about local conditions.

In Israel, for example, changes in educational activities could involve altering verbal behaviors to avoid using all-encompassing labels for "the other," engaging in political demonstrations, or initiating regional forums to discuss and negotiate land redistribution locally. These steps, though modest, can represent significant progress compared to the usual outcomes of peace educational initiatives. We would benefit from heeding Buber's appeal: "Only through working on the kingdom of man [is it possible to work] on the kingdom of God ... That which is merely an idea and nothing more cannot become holy." (Buber 1957, p.137) This reminds us that transformative action, not just theoretical ideals, is essential for creating meaningful change.

Lastly, returning to the concept of hope, it is worth considering a modern reinterpretation of Marx's maxim on religion as the 'opium of the masses': 'Hope is the opium of the masses.' We should reject educational hope, optimism, and goodwill to the extent that these sentiments keep us tethered to illusions about the conditions under which education operates. Instead, hope should be re-envisioned as a catalyst for devising strategies to change the educational landscape, eliminating the need for illusions and enabling a more realistic engagement with the challenges we face.

References

Buber, M. (1957). *Pointing the way. Collected essays*, trans. M. Friedman. Routledge and Kegan Paul.

Gatens, M., Steinberg, J., Armstrong, A., James, S. & Saar, M. (2020). Spinoza: thoughts on hope in our political present. *Contemporary Political Theory. 20*(1), 200-231.

Hacking, I. (2011) *2011 Hagey Lecture: How did mathematics become possible?* [Video]. YouTube. https://www.youtube.com/watch?v=PbKUsAR_8DY

Hacking, I. (2004). The complacent disciplinarian. Interdisciplines.org.

Holte, S. (2020). Nietzsche's eternal return and the Question of hope. *Studia Theologica-Nordic Journal of Theology. 74*(2), 139-158.

Jessel, L. (1978). Whorf: The Differentiation of Language. *International Journal of the Sociology of Language,* 1978(18), 83-110. https://doi.org/10.1515/ijsl.1978.18.83.

Maturana, H.R. & Valera, F.J. (1987). *The tree of knowledge: The biological roots of human understanding.* New Science Library.

Maturana, H.R. & Varela, F.J. (1991). *Autopoiesis and cognition: The realization of the living.* Springer Dordrecht.

Sapir, E. (2023). *Selected writings of Edward Sapir in language, culture and personality.* University of California Press. (ed. David Mandelbaum)

Chapter 8
Peace Education: Past, Present and Future

Yumiko Kaneko

The world is not peaceful, and even the path to peace is not clear.

The world is in chaos. The outbreak of Covid 19 in 2020 forced the world to halt its action for almost three years. In the middle of it, Russia, one of the five UN Security Council member states, invaded Ukraine and shocked the world. While this war was still ongoing, another war began in the Middle East.

On another front, countries around the world recorded significantly higher temperatures this year due to global warming.

In Japan, we sensed the rapid progression of global warming in the sheer heat that enveloped us, with a sense of crisis that it would be even more severe next year. Although already an earthquake-prone country with many volcanoes, we have had a higher frequency of stronger earthquakes of intensity 5 around the country since the Noto Peninsula earthquake on 1 January 2024. Typhoons that hit Japan from summer to autumn every year exhibited extraordinary power and new paths this year. Even supercomputers, the pinnacle of human science so far, were said to have been unable to predict the abnormal paths these typhoons took.

Human intelligence has created a variety of wonderful and useful tools, beyond the wildest imagination of times past. While they have been used to make the world better and more peaceful, such tools are increasingly used for destruction, fighting and satisfying human desires, to the extent that it seems they are driving the world to take more critical directions.

One of the conditions that led to our founder's motivation to start Nomura Lifelong Integrated Education work was the insight she drew from her first visit abroad in 1969, through the comparison between Japan and the western nations.

> The history of the rise and fall of the European nations as they waxed and waned across their shifting borders is also a history of blood spilled in the name of revolution or resistance to it, or out of religious fervour or that of war, of blood spilled to win happiness or freedom or dignity. (Nomura, 1996, p. 67 / 1998, p. 37)

These are the soils in which Western thought and religion were born and nurtured.

The Western view of nature is said to be anthropocentric because of the influence of the Christian teaching that nature is to be subdued by man.

In contrast, Japan, being an island nation, certainly had internal conflicts, but has rarely had to fear the threats of foreign invasion in its history. Most of the country has a humid subtropical climate with four distinct seasons, which was conducive to rice cultivation and permanent settlement as well as to the development of national characteristics of mild temper and a keen sensitivity to nature. However, this favourable nature also brings great harm in the form of typhoons and earthquakes that are beyond human control. For this reason, the Japanese have loved and feared and respected nature. The basic idea is not to dominate nature, but to offer prayers to calm nature's anger. In other words, for the Japanese, nature encompasses and coexists with humans, and this view is said to have developed into the Japanese religion of Shintoism.

Extraordinary movements of typhoons and frequent earthquakes leave the Japanese vulnerable in the face of powerful nature that seems to exceed human power and control. The phenomena that are emerging are completely different from previously. And when confronted with these realities, Japan and other societies struggle to find solutions. It makes one wonder, in spite of historical differences, their problems are nothing but homogeneous.

This happens despite the culture and ideas of the people living in different soils giving rise to different ways of viewing and thinking about the world. There is now one global phenomenological world that arose in the 21st century, in which each country, ethnic group and human being is struggling to cope amidst the development of a huge scientific technological civilization.

The Japanese people today seem to have been engulfed by the scientific civilization developed in the West and have become detached from their roots. Could the same be said about all parts of the world? Think of what is happening between Russia and Ukraine, in Gaza, Myanmar and Sudan. Could it be that the whole of humanity has lost its inherent human dignity?

The founder, the late Yoshiko Nomura, stated from the very beginning of this educational work: "At no other time in history have we seen such a grievous loss of the dignity of human life as today." (Nomura, 2001, p. 223 / 2002, p. 36) This is evident since the beginning of the 20th century, in the two world wars that resulted in massive carnage, the disregard for human life such as bullying, suicide, murder and violence that has occurred in every age, and a lack of humanity enslaved by material goods, money and machinery. She continued to highlight that the restoration of human dignity is the first priority.

"Human dignity" refers to the inherent worth possessed equally by all human beings. It is precisely because these are the most dangerous times, in which humanity, the planet and everything else may perish, that a restoration of human dignity is required for all.

This is the significance of our long-standing commitment to human education.

Nomura Center for Lifelong Integrated Education has been active as an educational volunteer organisation since 1962. Distressed by the juvenile issues that began to proliferate in the 1960s, the founder focused on examining the root cause of the youth problems and began exploring the purpose of education, whose role ought to be nurturing human beings. She gained the insight that "the society is a reflection of its education." The conclusions found in dealing with many cases were that there were "fundamental deficiencies in education" and that "a child's world is a reflection of adult society."

Fundamental Deficiencies in Education

Education is meant to be "the work of making human beings more human." The objective of education, then, must be to produce human beings themselves. However, at the time, Japan had just started to recover from their defeat over 10 years after the end of the war, and then entered a period of rapid economic growth. Education no longer nurtured human beings, but had degenerated into a tool for achieving good scores, grades, schools, employment and knowledge, with an emphasis on producing Human Resources useful in the reconstruction efforts. The founder began to realise that the purpose and the means had become mixed up and education no longer served its original purpose, as it turned human beings into a means to an end.

A Child's Society is a Reflection of Adult Society

Through closely dealing with a number of youth problems, it became clear that in each case it was not just the problem of the child concerned, but that its root cause lay in the adult society around the child. The background factors that created this adult society and the characteristics of the period were both found to be deeply connected. When it became clear that the misfortunes of young people had deep roots in the adult population, as well as in the social and historical background, it was concluded that there could be no fundamental solution to problems of youths without taking a comprehensive view of all the factors behind them.

It was from this point that the founder began her endeavour on two fronts: drastic revision of education and reform of the adult society.

Drastic Revision of Education

This was a question of what education is and to whom education belongs, and it meant a return to the origins of education. And if education is the work that enables people to be human, then standing at the origins of education is the same as standing at the origins of humanity. In other words, asking "what education is" is no different from asking "what humanity is", "what it means to live", and "what human values are". What is more important is that this "human being" is not simply an abstract concept, but is an exploration of "Who am I?" and a self-awareness of who I am.

From here, Mrs. Nomura began her activities to reform education, with the aim of returning to the origins of education and to recover education for the benefit of living people by returning to the origins of humanity.

Reform of the Adult Society

The approach to reforming adult society came about through working with many cases among young people, realising that a child's world is a reflection of the adult society, and that each and every problem faced by young people is the result of the composite pollution of a society that is undergoing unprecedented social and historical change. This led her in turn to the conclusion that the first priority is for those adults who are the main players in the social structure - and who should be models for younger generations in families, schools and society - to undertake earnestly to examine their own attitudes, values and lifestyle.

From there, Mrs. Nomura and her fellow members called on all the different strata that make up society, including, not just the world of education, but also the political world, the government, businesses, the media, ordinary families, etc., and while advocating cooperation between home, school and society, they promoted educational activities across the country with a focus on self-learning for adults themselves.

The national conference, which had been held every year since 1970 with over 2,000 participants, continued until the 30th in 1998. Regular seminar courses at a regional level, prefectural conferences and exchange groups were also organized, while requests for lectures were responded to.

In the course of these activities, the organisation was granted approval as a foundation by the Ministry of Education in 1981 and certified as a public interest incorporated foundation by the Cabinet Office in 2013, further stimulating the promotion of its activities.

The founder was motivated to carry out these activities due to the conditions she encountered in Japan, but she also had international motives that arose from her first round-the-world trip in 1969. The experience of seeing Japan in a global context made her aware of both the good and the bad things about Japan, as well as what needs to be done and what should be done. The trip was the first time when she became aware of what being Japanese was.

The final destination of the trip was Hawaii, where Mrs. Nomura encountered the extraordinary feat of the Apollo 11 mission. For the first time since the emergence of primitive life, humanity had set foot on another celestial body and viewed the Earth from an objective perspective. This made her keenly aware of humanity living together on the same small planet, sharing the same fate. However, questions also arose: Why is it that, even though we are now able to travel to celestial bodies 400,000 km away thanks to advances in science, we seem to be incapable of managing the relationship between people on the same planet? Relationships that are supposed to be the closest, between parents and children, between couples, between neighbours and between people at work are becoming increasingly broken and disconnected. Why the paradox?

In 1974 Mrs. Nomura attended her first international conference, the peace conference held in Leuven, Belgium. There she encountered two major questions. One was that the conference was based entirely on Western logic and values and conducted in Western methods based on scientific rationalism, quantification and domination of nature. The other was that the conference was dominated by male theories and ideas.

She thought; "If oriental philosophy and values could have been represented, different perspectives would have been available on the important issues discussed, and the fusion of western rationalism and eastern spirituality could have contributed to the formation of a new way of thinking." (Nomura, 1996, p.70 / 1998, p.40).

This thought informed her activities from then on. She began her work of building bridges of complementarity and integration, from the East to the West, and from women to men.

The first International Forum on Lifelong Integrated Education was held in Tokyo in 1977, and the second was held at UNESCO Headquarters in Paris in 1978. After that, the forum was held every four years, up to the 10th, at UNESCO Headquarters and other locations.

At the 10th Forum, requests were received from participants to "know how Nomura's theory is being put into practice and turned into education in real life." In response, the 11th and 12th Forums were held in Japan, changing the format from that used until then.

Some of the participants were strongly motivated to restore their individual and collective identity through this human education of Mrs. Nomura, and this led to the development of independent branch activities. Currently there are branches in Germany, India, Palestine and Bulgaria, conducting activities in a way that best suits their local needs.

Why Did I Come to Join this Volunteer Organisation that Started with Such Motives?

I first heard about the Nomura Center in the late 1970s, when I was suffering from an illness that I had developed in my student days. Back then, medical science was not as advanced as it is today, and even now there is no treatment that could bring about complete recovery from this illness. I was told by several hospitals that my condition was incurable. The prospect of being saddled with this illness for the rest of my life and the pain I was in made me despair of life.

In the section on a concept of life in Part 3 "Nomura Lifelong Integrated Education: Views on a Human Being" of the Nomura Principles, Mrs. Nomura says, "Humans have resilient restorative power that has continued since the beginning of life." When I heard that, I felt as if a ray of light had shone into my life. I thought, "I am human, so I may also have immense power of recovery" and I found hope in life. Holding onto this hope alone, Mrs. Nomura's deep insight into human nature motivated me to continue to study the Principles.

One of our mottos is the conditions that touch our lives are the teaching materials we use to develop ourselves, and I thought that the illness that touched my life would be such a condition. From there, I began to see the problem was with my sense of values. It was the way of thinking and sense of values that I had acquired through my education in Japan during the period of rapid economic growth after WWII - a way of thinking that did not make the human being an end in itself, but rather a means to an end.

However, after learning about 'human dignity' and realising that "human beings are valuable, not because of what they can do, but because of their very existence", I felt a deep sense of relief; my own existence was precious, and I was able to accept my existence. Through the process of interacting with others, I have come to where I am today. In this way, after a youth that was neither peaceful nor happy, I studied, changed my way of thinking, and put into practice the educational theory that placed flesh-and-blood human beings at the centre of its aims.

This was my personal experience, but as I deepened my learning, I began to see that there was a universal issue at play behind this experience. I was a modern person, who had been at the mercy of a society in which people have become enslaved to objects, machines, technology and knowledge under scientism. But the change I went through signifies myself as a dignified being.

> Human identity, individual as well as collective, can be proved by the simple expedient of allotting us our proper place on a graph representing the structure of the natural world. We all exist at the nexus of time and space and our provenances can be traced back on the eternal chain of time and across the infinite realm of space to the distant moment when life began. (Nomura, 2001, p. 223/2002, p. 36)

My experience led me to the restoration of identity. As students of the Nomura Principles, we, including those who learn at overseas branches, are going through a process of such restoration through practice.

> The challenge for me was to start with something which was unique and from that develop a system of educational principles which would have universal appeal, with the power to convince rational minds and contribute to the reform of education worldwide. I had thus taken on the formidable task of finding a recognised place for oriental philosophy in the pantheon of world thought, while at the same time using it as the basis for the creation of a new universal concept of education for the future. (Nomura 1996, p. 164 / 1998, p. 104)

Nomura identified the fundamental deficiencies in education and constructed this theory with a motive to drastically review education:

> I set out to trace its original purposes, asking myself questions such as
> 'What is it to be a human being?', 'What is it to live life?' and 'What
> is man put on earth for?' The result was that I concluded no amount
> of theorising based on human knowledge and reason would provide
> the answers I needed in my quest to discover and revive the original
> pure functions of education. I needed to look beyond human answers. I
> turned, therefore, to the system that enables humans to live life, and so
> began by observing nature and the universe as they really are." (Nomura
> 1996, p.169 / 1998, p. 108)

She sought a non-judgmental answer to such questions as:

> "What is the structure of the natural world(universe)?
> How is it regulated?
> What laws function in it?
> What is the relationship between the natural world and man?" (Nomu-
> ra 1996, p. 70 / 1998, p. 109)

Nomura suggests:

> The universe as perceived in the oriental view of nature is characterised
> by the symbiotic interrelationship of all things and matters.

> The oriental view teaches that man as well as all living things, matter and
> energy are interdependent and mutually related and that there can be no
> existence outside this....

> Furthermore the whole of existence within this absolute state of equilibri-
> um is in a constant ferment of change, of emergence and decay. Nothing
> rests or stays the same.

> Thus the universe reveals its true feature with the great harmony where-
> by everything changes while everything is related to each other with-
> out being fixed or isolated. It is nature's law of maintaining order in the
> seething world. (Nomura 1996, pp. 172-173 /1998, p. 110)

Thus "Observation of the structure and laws of the natural world cannot but make us realise that we humans are part of nature, incorporated in it as living bodies and sustained by its system and rules." (Nomura 1996, p. 179 / 1998, p. 114)

If we attempt to position humans in this natural world from the perspective of time, humans continue to live in sequential dependence in time. "In the vertical sequence of time human beings exist as a continuous stream of life in a state of interdependence with all other phenomena in nature." (Nomura 1996, p. 180 / 1998, p. 115)

An individual life is part of an eternal chain handed down from its parents and passed on to its children and from them to theirs from generation to generation, repeating the process of continuous discontinuity but never disrupted.

Likewise, humans live collectively in the continuity of time through past, present and future.

In this way we have identified personal existence as well as that of humankind.

Thus, by plotting our lives on the 'vertical dependence in time' sequence, we have visualized human existence. (Nomura, 1996, pp. 182-183 / 1998, p. 116)

Nomura said:

The next exercise is to identify human existence in the spatial domain...I prefer to classify [the environment that surrounds humans] in three [ways]: the human environment, the material environment and the natural environment. The human environment includes inter-personal relations, family, society and humankind. The material environment includes mother earth and the human habitat, and the natural environment includes air, light and heat, humidity and temperature.

An individual human, since he has a body, is a tangible, living, material thing – and at the same time he is a spiritual creature with intangible qualities (i.e. mind, feelings and consciousness).

While his spirit and body are given different labels and assigned different tasks, together they are part of an inseparable entity.

> In the light of the oriental principle of oneness with nature, an individual person and nature represent an inseparable entity. (Nomura 1996, pp. 186-188 / 1998, pp. 119-121)

She continues:

> When we place man in the natural world, we are immediately made conscious of the fact that we humans are at the same time living subjects as well as living objects whose existence is sustained by nature.
>
> If we accept that we are surrounded by an environment that has human, material and other natural components, we must accept too that we would not be able to sustain human life if any one of those was missing. It is evident therefore that we cannot live in isolation or in alienation from others.
>
> If we destroy our habitat, and there is nothing left with which to feed and clothe ourselves, if we strip our mother earth of all that lives and grows upon it, we cannot survive.
>
> If we pollute the air and the rivers and forfeit the light and warmth of the sun, all life on earth including ours will be lost." (Nomura 1996, p. 196 / 1998, pp. 125-126)

Just as we can see in the issue of global warming in the natural environment, it is endangering the survival of not only humans but all living things on earth. As for the human environment, in the most familiar households, family relationships are collapsing, presenting a pathological phenomenon both mentally and physically.

The founder, who astutely grasped the fact that "there is no limit to our folly, which even threatens the survival of our own kind", has continued to loudly appeal that "it is imperative that we bring to the attention of all thinking people the inalienable unity of man and nature" (Nomura 1996, p. 197 / 1998, p. 126).

This is why Nomura Lifelong Integrated Education defines peace as "a state of harmony between the mind, body, and environment".

If the present is the result of an accumulation of the past, the future is created by an accumulation of the present. If we could rectify errors in our way of seeing and thinking, then we would see a bright future.

Throughout human history, humans have sought everything in the external and material world, and clinging to seek things in a finite world inevitably leads to competition over things, and ultimately to killing and destroying each other. We are witnessing humanity at this very limit right now.

We have seen it over and over again throughout history, but unlike the era before the 18th century, which ended with local wars, the 20th century with progress in science and technology has developed into a world war. The 21st century is amid further accelerated and tremendous evolution, with the emergence of AI and other technologies that continue to advance before humans can fully utilize them, and there is a risk of humans who have lost their independence being used by machines.

We need to stop and think again about what the purpose of education should be. This is an age of nuclear weapons, an age that can be extremely dangerous depending on the personality of the people in power. I wonder if the reason we have created such an era is because we humans have not been able to determine what it means to be human beings. Is it not because education has only been seen as tools for acquiring knowledge and skills, and the focus has been placed on our ability to do things. The founder figured out that it is due to a lack of perspective on human education and the humanity of people who use that knowledge and ability.

Having proposed external and objective answers to the question of "what is a human being" from the structure of nature, she attempted to explore the most difficult question, that is to define the qualitative nature of a human being, and she emphasised that "the infinite complexity of our internal world is a lifelong challenge posed to each one of us." (Nomura, 2001, p. 17/ 2002, p. 2)

She elaborated that:

> As a sentient being and the product of his long evolution, there is unfathomable depth to man's nature.
>
> A searching examination of the enigmatic duality of human nature, with

on the one hand its potential for absolute virtue, and on the other a limitless capacity for evil that can stifle a person's intrinsic goodness, can lead us ultimately to answer the question 'What is a human being?'

A human being is ultimately the existence of the wisdom, the perfect reason of the universe.

When love and wisdom take root and grow in a human being who carries the seed of these universal qualities, his inherent dignity is revealed, that is regarded mightier even than the earth. This wisdom could open up a bright prospect for future centuries and realise a long-held hope of humankind.

On the other hand, we can see in the accumulated deeds buried underneath our life over the ages, some would call it karma, the source of the evil that leads to ethnic conflict and war between nations, springing from the individual human's propensity for confrontation, an investigation is called for into these woeful depths of human nature. (Nomura, 2001, p. 17 /., 2002, pp. 2-3)

I believe that without elucidating the depth of humanity, we may not find the next path forward for our challenge of inhuman acts seen today in violence in Gaza.

Such an enquiry deep into human nature, divided between its essential and glorious goodness and the dark secrets of the inscrutable subconscious, can be the first step towards removing all the misfortunes we bring upon ourselves and building the long-awaited ideal society.

Conventionally the field has been treated within the confines of academic disciplines such as psychology and psychoanalysis. Much as the subject of death was long taboo, the unexplored levels of the human subconscious were not acknowledged as a proper field of education, or had escaped its attention.

Only by illuminating them can humankind be rescued from the self-destructive savagery into which it has descended. (Nomura, 2001, pp. 17-18/2002, p. 3)

As in the UNESCO Constitution, "Since wars begin in the minds of men, it is in the minds of men that the defences of peace must be constructed," I feel keenly the desperate need for this human-centred education in today's world, no matter how difficult it may be.

In the 21st century, humans created devices equipped with the most advanced functions in the history of humankind. However, we must know that we humans have unfathomable potential for good and, at the same time, have unfathomable potential for evil hidden deep within ourselves.

Under certain conditions, infinite good and evil can be drawn out from the subconsciousness of anyone. That is why war must never be started. We know from reality that once it is started, it is not the easiest thing to stop. Everyone desires the ideal of "peace," but cannot achieve it because we do not stand on the premise that the origin of both war and peace is within the microscopic human.

Humans inherently have both good and evil, and the gap between ideals and reality may be the gap between good and evil within us. Both ideals and reality are created by humans. As long as we try to overcome our desires, egoism, contradictions and duality, our ideals come a step closer to reality. Nomura Principles for Lifelong Integrated Education demonstrate that overcoming the evilness in our inner world should bring about peace in the outer world.

The Earth is the only planet in the solar system we know of inhabited by living things. It is said that the first life on Earth was born 3.5 to 4 billion years ago, and since then, living things have long transmitted their information to their descendants, and continue to do so.

During this evolutionary process, sea algae, bacteria, and molluscs were created, and it is said that amphibians, reptiles, and mammals like humans were born 230 million years ago.

It is said that the birth of today's evolved, intelligent human, Homo sapiens, after a lengthy period of existence as the biological human beings was only relatively recently, about 300,000 to 200,000 years ago. In terms of the long history of life from a phylogenetic perspective, the history of modern humans is a truly short history that has just begun.

This long process of phylogeny has a profound relationship with the birth of each individual. The whole experience of life on earth is part of the make up of each of us.

The experience of the long past is retained as a superficial memory in part while others are part of our knowledge, habit, talent and ability, making up our personality.

The accumulation of our collective experience of the past has left marks on our mind and body.

The past resides partly in our consciousness and partly sunk in our subconscious. (Nomura, 2001, p. 59 / 2002, p. 30)

"In other words we must be aware that our every action is controlled remotely by our motives in a state of unconsciousness derived from latent consciousness." (Nomura, 2001, p. 63 / 2002, p. 33)

I think that human education now needs to be based on the premise that humans are such profound, complex, and mysterious beings.

The world is now seeing a growing inequality. This is one result of the existing view of education that has placed emphasis on acquiring knowledge and skills. Scientific civilization has truly brought convenience to humans. We must deal with the other side of this benefit.

IT has created a world in which an individual can convey their thoughts anywhere.

Therefore, in today's world, it is not a handful of elites at the top of society, but the consciousness of the vast majority of ordinary people that defines the era. In such a world, if this layer loses its independence and sends messages to share with society in a blind manner, and also influences the next generation, I fear that our irresponsibility, even if we are unaware of it, will lead to mistakes even greater than those of the past.

As an individual, as a society, each and every one of us need to awaken to education aimed at reviving humanity in each individual, in myself, for the peace of the world.

Through mutual education based on the principle of self-education, I would like to continue to promote education encompassing home, society and international community in coordination with family, school and society.

I hope that the future will be brighter for children so as to create a society where they can have dreams.

References

Nomura, Y. (1996, 2001) *Lifelong integrated education as a creator of the future – The principles of Nomura Lifelong Integrated Education I, II.* Tokyo: Mitsumura Educational Co., Ltd.

Nomura, Y. (1998, 2002) *Lifelong integrated education as a creator of the future – The principles of Nomura Lifelong Integrated Education I, II.* Stoke-on-Trent: Trentham Books Ltd.

Chapter 9

Beyond Liberation to Emancipation: Mapping Pathways to Peace Education in the 21ˢᵗ Century

Catherine A. Odora Hoppers

My Understandings of Peace Thought

Peace is a revolutionary idea: peace by peaceful means defines that revolution as **non-violent**. That revolution is taking place all the time. Our job is to expand its scope and domain. The tasks are endless; the question is whether we are up to them…. To work for peace is to work against violence; by analysing its forms and structures, predicting in order to prevent, and then acting preventively and curatively since peace relates to violence much as health relates to illness. The excluded are included not by force… To work for peace is to build liberation, wellness in a world with peace with nature, between genders, generations and races. (Galtung, 2002, p. xi)

This chapter is a collage drawing on my life and work, organized in sections highlighting the key cases, articulations and the interventions that I took from a peace perspective to expand the concept of liberation and pitch higher at the **hard work of emancipation**, in order to map out the pathways to peace in the different contexts where I have worked both nationally and globally.

To begin with, 'Violence' can be described initially as the *movement of carrying extreme force against* X in such a way that it is damaging and destructive or physically injurious to X. By making a person or persons the cause of such a movement, and by giving content to X in terms of objects, animals and persons, the concept of violence can be defined secondly as the *intentional application of extreme force against* X in such a way that it is destructive of objects and physically injurious to animals and persons. This introduces a third level of definition of violence to be the *force which is intentionally brought to bear against* X, which desecrates and disturbs the integrity of X. This definition draws attention to the factor of **intentionality** and **agency**. It also presents violence as action that both hurts and desecrates a person as a person (one individual), as well as his/her integrity as a human being (Degenaar, 1990).

Galtung deepens this definition by outlining the three axes of violence: direct, structural and cultural. **Direct Violence** kills quickly, for instance in a war, killing plus maiming together constitute what is commonly called `casualties' - used in assessing the magnitude of the war. Violence is **structural** when force is not exerted wilfully by a person but by a structure created and perpetuated by a custom or law. The violence which is inbuilt into the structures does not give the citizens equal power and life chances. Even peaceful laws and practices which help to maintain this order can be seen as `instruments', `masks' or `guises of violence'. By `**cultural violence'** is meant those aspects of culture, or the symbolic sphere of our existence that can be used to justify or legitimize direct or structural violence. It is epistemic in the sense that it violates the cognitive space while providing a knowledge base for legitimizing the other violences. Cultural violence, here used interchangeably with epistemic violence, makes direct and structural violence **look, and even feel right,** or at least, **not wrong**. The study of cultural violence highlights the way in which the act of direct violence and the fact of structural violence are **legitimized** and thus rendered **acceptable** in society. According to Galtung, one way in which cultural violence works is by changing the **moral colour of an act from wrong** to **right** or to some other intermediate meaning **palatable to the status quo**. Another way it works is by **making reality opaque,** so that we do not see the violent act or fact, or that when we see it, we see it not as violent (Galtung, 1996).

Direct and structural violence are easy to diagnose. Cultural or epistemic violence is more difficult to diagnose and even more, to develop an active prognosis out of the traumas they bring. In the following sections, I will outline cases from my life which challenged me from a peace perspective that required the recognition of the traumas and conflict that comes with each case and through emancipation as a methodology, I called for institutional, national and global resolutions that involved empathy and healing.

The following sections will show my biographical context, and outline how I have worked to understand the nature of violence; by analysing its forms and structures in education before reaching the stage where I could predict in order to prevent, and then acting preventively and curatively in institutions, at national level and globally. All of the analyses are rooted in my background. I come from a political family that was almost wiped out by the regime of Idi Amin in Uganda. As a witness to the horrors in the 1970s (Direct violence), and the Structural violence that followed plus the misrepresentations (Cultural violence) that underpinned it, I had to tell myself that enough is enough. That I would seek, far and wide, 'kinsmen and women' who were conscientious enough to walk with me as I tried to map out the education for peace in my time.

Case 1: My Biography – Entering the Western Type of Schooling

I was born in Gulu, Northern Uganda. I started school education in a 'school' my mother had initiated in protest against the distance of nearly eight kilometres that children had to walk to the nearest mission station. The school was located under a huge fruit tree straddling a footpath the women of the village used on their way to collect water from the well. Our classroom was situated on one side of this path; and for well over two terms, our paper was the beaten path, and our pens were pieces of twigs we broke from nearby bushes every day on the way to 'school'.

My family was large, non-nuclear, but very organized as a strong Acholi family with a strong sense of kinship. My mother, not literate beyond reading the bible, was a dynamic leader to the only women's group which rejected the national policy of integrating women into development. At that time (the 1960s), 'integration into development' was conducted by well-dressed, sometimes high-heeled Community Development Assistants (CDAs) who carried with them sophisticated baking equipment to show the rural women how to bake cakes, grow carrots and incorporate onions into their cooking. My mother constantly challenged these young ladies to illustrate their dedication to the cause they preached by showing her what they did to bring about 'development' in their real lives beyond the salaries they received from government. The CDAs never grasped the fact that the reason for her insistence derived basically from the proverb "charity begins at home", and from the biblical "remove not the speck in thy neighbour's eyes before you have removed the plank in thy own".

Disgusted with this approach to introducing 'progress', she led her women, by then numbering around 400, into a grower's cooperative society which, for nearly fifteen years, was the only one of its kind in the whole country that was run, managed and controlled only by women. She advised the women to grow cotton as that was the only crop from which they could earn and be assured a more meaningful income annually, but on condition that the same field once cleared of cotton, would be used to grow food crops. Those women prospered. Most of them were illiterate but they were determined to control their destinies.

They used rotational labour to weed each other's fields, negotiated for loans and crop finance from banks and from government and even UN affiliated agencies such as the International Fund for Agricultural Development (IFAD). They protested up to the ministry level if they felt shunned or slighted by the local bureaucracy and demonstrated to the numerous donor agencies and NGOs who visited them in search of models of women's organizations to borrow and transfer, about how they perceived their roles. These women saw themselves as **mothers** fulfilling their role in the nourishment of mankind - their children, their families, their kin - as well as their husbands whom they respected but never allowed to interfere with their group work. This was my introduction, as a child, to feminist action for development.

As I studied and ascended those ladders that all good and successful school children should climb, I looked back and realized that of the group that completed grade seven at primary school with me, I was one of the few who had made it through the gorges and proceeded to the university. I also recalled the rigorous choir practices at that school and how the teachers spent weeks getting us to sing "Auld Lang Syne", "I Sowed Barley in the Meadow", "London's Burning" and "Land of the Silver Birch, Home of the Beavers". None of the teachers had ever seen barley, let alone meadows, birches or even London. I further recalled a few memorable events, especially an award I received from the headmaster on one Parents Day, for reciting by heart a whole chapter from *Rip van Winkle*. The parents had clapped and cheered, but none of them had ever heard of Rip van Winkle, and most of them could neither speak nor understand English, the language of the text.

I also remember clearly the primary leaving examinations and one question that has never left my mind. It was in General Paper, and the question asked who discovered the Murchison Falls (a waterfall not far from my father's ancestral home). The objective options **a**, **b**, **c** and **d** had several European names and **e** had 'none of these'. I had chosen the last one (**e**), but the teacher had insisted that it was one of the Europeans who had discovered it. This waterfall on the River Nile, is part of the boundary between two major ethnic groups in Uganda, with the Acholi - my tribe - to the north of it, and Bunyoro to the south. It was a respected site for ancestral worship by the people who lived close to it. My great grandfather died while on the Bunyoro side of the river early in the nineteenth century, and was brought and buried on the Acholi side as he had wished. A memorial tree had been planted on the grave (way before any of those explorers saw that waterfall), which our family visited regularly. But in the school, we were to say it was some European who had 'discovered' it (Odora, 1993).

Case 2: Beginning Research: First Contact with Research Paradigms

As I commenced my research process, these apparently nonsensical issues began to adopt new significance. Questions like "What kind of education?", "For whom?" and "Why?" were not only matters of personal agony to me, but also questions that seemed to occupy the minds of many other thinkers in education. Was the task of education social mobility, the transmission of the normative heritage of a people, or is it the training of people to work in factories far away from homes that nourished them? Who produces food when all children go to school 6-8 hours every day, and what does compulsory schooling have to say about women's increasing workload and the overall deteriorating food self-sufficiency in Africa?

By then, I had also started to have my own reservations about such proclama-
tions as "Education brings about development", "Literacy means progress",
or even that women's future is best safeguarded in modern development. I
have wondered why the teachers felt so comfortable with educating us about
Rip van Winkle on the Catskills mountains, while ignoring the fantastic narratives of the kind my father told us regularly of famous events that had occurred to the Acholi people on different 'mountains' long ago. I asked myself
why an examination could be set that gave credits for fraudulent responses.
I was disturbed, restless, and felt that I needed to find the tools that would
enable me to critically question an educational system that harboured and
condoned such practices (Odora, 1993).

But once I started from such a position, I discovered that mainstream scientific research has no language with which to accommodate a researcher who is
both a subject and an object. Possession of personal values and such things
as pain, anger and subjective experience I was soon to realize, are equivalent
to high treason in mainstream positivistic thinking and research. It also occurred to me rather late, that the objective in positivistic research is, indeed,
to mould individuals for a life as 'given' and knowledge is posited as something located 'out there' for inquisitive researchers to figure out (e.g. Keeves
1990). Similarly, when I turned to the historical hermeneutics paradigm, I
realized that its objective is the attainment of communication and 'understanding' between the subject and object, in other words, to reach some sort
of consensus. It stresses the growth metaphor particularly that the aim of education is to enhance self-actualization of individuals in a meritocratic form
of social life (Makrakis, 1988).

These paradigms were of little immediate use to me. The first was rather
frightening, and in the beginning gave me an intellectual paralysis because
it would seemingly tell me that it is perfectly natural for all children to learn
by heart Rip van Winkle. Or that the 'distance' that I seemed to be disturbed
about that existed between the school learning and the world outside it was
as God has deemed. It would strongly suggest that I forget about facts of
history, cut out feelings and embark on some neutral value-free investigation
on these questions. It would ignore that I am already part of 'the field', part

of the knowledge 'out there', in other words, I am part of the very history I seek to analyze and the future I'd like to create. It ignores that I am unhappy about the situation and that in that condition, no sane person can talk about 'value-free', 'objective' or even universalistic knowledge.

The second paradigm would encourage me to think about and discuss my concerns, but is pre-occupied with making sure that it is understanding and not change and transformation that I should attain. It does not help me to question the logic of an education that pegs my fate on the extent to which I have imbibed the normative heritage of an alien culture. Neither does it assist me to challenge the apparent innocence surrounding this alien culture whose preoccupation has been with degrading my own.

Case 3: The Search for an Emancipatory Frame of Reference

Then gradually, in solidarity, friends and colleagues began to draw my attention to other ways to perceive and confront reality. They helped me to discover the critical sciences paradigm that focuses on critical values and has an emancipatory interest in eliminating the social and political constraints that distort rational self-understanding. This paradigm I realized, sees knowledge and interest, value and fact, object and subject as closely interconnected. With empowerment as its metaphor, this paradigm sees education as preparing individuals capable of producing and transforming a given form of social life. It stimulates human agents to take an active stand towards social development and urges self-reflection as a primal path by which one can recognize the interconnectedness referred to above.

Then from tools developed by feminist scholars, I realised that the essence of the feminist dialectic also has at its core, an aspiration to emancipation. Embedded in the feminist dialectic is a sociology of knowledge, a conception that the world is known from the varied vantage points of actors differently situated in the social structure. Their view is that knowledge is anchored in, and patterned by the knower's structurally situated vantage point thus making knowledge itself a key problematic.

Truth in any given situation according to this dialectic, is to be discovered in the point of intersection that exists among the competing viewpoints and knowledge systems of the unequally empowered groups involved in that situation. The authenticity of a situation can only be determined when a system of discourse can be achieved that allows for an egalitarian exchange of views in which all parties openly acknowledge both the partialness, and the interest-based character of their views. (Lengermann & Niebrugge-Brantley, 1988).

From indigenization discourse in sociology, I discovered the connection between the application of universalistic sociology, the occlusion of social knowledge, and the social construction of reality. Particularly pertinent were debates among sociologists to the effect that Universalism theory itself has not been examined, criticized or assessed either from the empiricist and pragmatic points of view, or from different paradigmatic views of society (Akinowo, 1988; Park, 1988; Sanda, 1988). They argued that positivistic sociology admits human beings into the arena of inquiry as possessors of measurable primary qualities deprived of such subjective attributes as will, goodness, and destiny. As this way of thinking is elevated to the level of the only valid social knowledge worthy of a science, it means that sociology has got itself trapped in the very limitations of this brand of thinking.

The world is then presented as peopled by object-like beings standing in abstracted relationships to each other and completely devoid of intentions. The subjects of action are ignored as actors, and 'solutions' to various social problems are then imposed onto these 'object-like beings' who are, in reality, the actual living population that make the society. Conscious action does not exist in this framework and populations are 'target groups' without any self-knowledge, tradition, culture. Yet, even as they are taken as if they were bundles of drives and learned reflexes, they are to be beneficiaries of such 'knowledge' (Fay, 1975; Park, 1988).

Some sociologists argued further that what is often assumed as universalistic theories are actually always local views projected large. The social world is constituted by the people who inhabit it, who have integrity of their own, and whose integrity can be denied only at the expense of destroying the foundation of a particular way of life (Park, 1988; Sanda, 1988; Berger & Luckman, 1966).

From the humanistic paradigm and radical philosophy, I gained insight into the commitment to changing relations of subjugation thereby enhancing human freedom, creativity, and thus human justice and a concern to develop a sociology of radical change from a subjectivist standpoint. The radical humanist frame of reference recognizes that human consciousness is dominated by the ideological superstructures with which he/she interacts, and these drive a wedge of alienation or false consciousness between himself and his consciousness which inhibits or prevents his human fulfilment. They place emphasis upon emancipation from deprivation as a way to reconstitute potential.

While the functionalist paradigm stresses the status quo, social order, and integration; and radical structuralist paradigm have key words in concepts like conflict and contradiction, radical humanists see these conflicts and contradictions as symptomatic of subjective conflicts and contradictions. The continuities of the structural problems can thus be confronted by deep recognition that in so many ways we all are part of the system. Secondly, we cannot purport to change something if we are not prepared to begin that process from the self through self-reflection. The underlying edict would therefore be "social transformation through personal transformation" (Burrell & Morgan, 1979).

From philosophy, genealogy as used by Michel Foucault also came in as a useful methodology. Genealogy is an attempt to emancipate historical knowledges from subjection and render them capable of opposition and of a struggle against the coercion of a theoretical, unitary, formal scientific discourse. By that token "archaeology could be the appropriate methodology, and genealogy would be the tactic through which the subjugated knowledges thus released would be brought into play" (Foucault, 1980, pp. 85-86).

Genealogy, Foucault clarifies, is not histography. It focuses among other things, on identifying spaces in which possibilities are created to present new relationships, and provide a new 'landscape'. The objective would then be to write a history of the present, particularly of the conditions that makes us think now, that we are people of a certain kind. Foucault argues that history is incapable of offering us liberation from forms of domination. In genealogy, the search for descent is not a search for firm foundations; on the contrary, it:

...discovers moving sands, fragmented and incoherent events with faults, errors, omissions, faulty appraisals and pious claims and aspirations. The move is, in general, to show that "historical truths" rest upon complex, contingent and fragile ground. (Marshall, 1990, p. 19)

He considers discourses are not only about what can be said and thought, but also about who can speak, when, and with what authority. Discourses embody meaning and social relationships, and they also constitute both subjectivity and power relations. 'Subject' to him carries the twin meaning of an active knowing subject, and of an object being acted upon, a product of discourse. In epistemological terms, the subject both speaks, and is spoken of.

Likewise, 'peace' as commonly understood, to imply the absence of war, of direct, impersonal and/or collective violence is just not adequate. A broad conception of peace encompasses far more than the absence of direct confrontation between states. It includes such factors as the distribution of wealth within states (Brock-Utne, 1989). Cultural violence she states, has socialized society into routinizing this violence to the extent that this embeddedness in structures, institutions and thinking is so hard to challenge, let alone identify:

> ...No oppression is more effective than the one in which the oppressed have internalized the norms of the oppressor. When this is NOT done, the oppressor easily resorts to threats and violence. (Brock-Utne, 1989, p. 3)

Advocates for peace contend that it is a form of violence when structures are put in place that ensure that some get richer while others starve slowly to death, when society is structured so that a few people make big profits from the work and exploitation of many. A definition of peace would therefore extend Brock-Utne's definition of the `distribution of wealth within states', to the `distribution of wealth across regions of the world', and an absence of further intentions to engender and sustain such unjust structures and processes of legitimation of such violence.

One example is Shiva's Third World feminist ecological perspective on structural violence that sees the struggle for femininity as a struggle for certain basic principles of perceiving life; a philosophy of being. The sanctity of science and development alongside it, are exposed, not as universal categories of progress, but as special projects of western patriarchy. Informed by the suffering of those who struggle to sustain and conserve life, the desecration of nature and of natural resources of the Third World in the name of scientific progress and development represents the worst violation of human integrity. This for Shiva is the latest and most brutal expression of a patriarchal ideology which is threatening to annihilate the entire human species:

> ...The violence to nature, which seems intrinsic to the dominant model of development, is also associated with violence to women who depend on nature for drawing sustenance for themselves, their families, their societies. This violence against nature and women is built into the very mode of perceiving both (nature and women), and forms the basis of the current development paradigm. (Shiva, 1994, xvi)

This perspective pins the origins of this violence to the scientific revolution in Europe which transformed nature from terra mater into a machine and a source of raw materials; which transformation removed all ethical and cognitive constraints against its violation and exploitation. Capra captures this particularly sharply in *The Turning Point* (1982). He discusses how modern science devalues the ideas, experience and accumulated wisdom of the majority of humankind. Scientism, he argues, has also subjected to relentless onslaught, indigenous systems of health care, medicine, education, agriculture as well as cosmology.

> ...Nature, in his [Bacon's] view, had to be 'hounded in her wanderings', 'bound into service' and made a 'slave'. She was to be 'put in constraint', and the aim of the scientist was to 'torture nature's secrets from her'. (Capra, 1982, pp. 40-41)

It becomes increasingly clear that scientific neutrality has been a reflection of an ideology, not history, and the spread of this masculinist paradigm of science through development has been at the root of the exclusion of both womens' knowledge and expertise, and of the indigenous knowledges and cultures of the non-west, from discourse and practice.

This is academic speak. When you want to enter policy, and change something, you need to advance your theorization and make it contextually as present as possible.

Case 4: Major Caveats in Placing Peace Studies in Policy and Institutional Practice

As the world settles in to the reality of globalization and the violence and the potentials of peace it brings, it becomes clear that many incongruous facets of human existence have been forced together into a giant tumbler - economy, information systems, finance and people - giving rise to contradictory but also generative responses. Questions around emancipation, co-existence and co-determination, knowledge and citizenship, culture and science, and cognitive justice are being asked at the most penetrating levels.

This chapter posits the **integrative paradigm shift** as a method in this dynamic episode in which knowledge paradigms of those excluded and epistemologically disenfranchised move centre stage, acquire agency and demand a new synthesis, signalling an era in which modernization now proceeds but without the sinister dimensions of Western values. New theories of freedom, understandings of context, diversity, difference and cooperative contemporary change are hallmarks of this generational moment (Odora Hoppers, 2009).

With this new stream, there is a growing maturity of dialogue that is not the result of a paradigm shift, **but is the shift itself**. Thus, from the ignorance and depreciating ideology along with social theories that claimed 'terra nullius' as a convenient rationalization for colonization and ill treatment, **there is a need for honest recognition of the existence of indigenous knowledge systems.** Further, there is **a need for those knowledge systems themselves, not just the recognition that they exist** (Knudtson & Suzuki, 1992). The knowledge paradigms of the future are beginning by reaching out **to those excluded, epistemologically disenfranchised, to move together towards a new synthesis.**

In this synthesis, 'empowerment', which is usually more about resuming power (because power is never voluntarily relinquished), it is recognized that shifting of power without **a clear shift of paradigms of understanding that makes new propositions about the use of that power in a new dispensation, leads to vicarious abuse of power by whoever is holding it – old or new** (Venter, 1997). **Co-optation without a shift in authority, power and**

control is empty.

In this new stream, modernization is about equal access as citizens of a nation and of the world, with an emphasis on **equality**. It is about indigenous peoples reclaiming the custodianship over their knowledge in **public spaces along with the right to speak and be determining agents of cooperative contemporary change and creative knowledge sharing of these knowledge systems** (Odora Hoppers, 2009). It is a rapprochement of modern and older cultures, including modern culture's older roots where each complementing the other opens up the possibility of a viable future for humankind (Huntington, 1998; Fatnowna & Pickett, 2002).

Subaltern agency thus emerges as a process of **reversing, displacing and seizing** the apparatus of value coding which had been monopolized by the colonial default drive. According to Bhaba, it is the contestation of the 'given' symbols of authority that shifts the terrain of antagonism. This he states is the moment of renegotiation of agency. It is the voice of an interrogative, calculative agency, the moment when we lose resemblance with the colonizer, the moment of (in Toni Morrison's words), 'rememoration' that turns the narrative of enunciation into a haunting memorial of what has been excluded, excised, evicted (Odora Hoppers, 2009; Bhaba, 1995).

Case 5: Cognitive Justice in Action in the Academy: the Case of the South African Research Chairs Initiative (SARCHI Chair in Pretoria)

In 2007, South Africa launched the independent "South African Research Chairs Initiative" (SARCHI) as a strategically focused knowledge and human resource intervention that has inter-related objectives of stimulation of strategic research across the knowledge spectrum. Out of the first batch of the Chair Holders was the Chair in Development Education that was hosted by the University of South Africa headed by the present author. The Chair was given 10 years to complete its work as an intervention in the higher education sector. The Chair took the practices in the academy and exposed them from a peace perspective.

It convened an Indigenous Knowledge Advisory Faculty (Knowledge Sages), in the grassroots and brought them into the Academy as experts in dialogues around the development, recognition, protection, of Indigenous Knowledge Systems (IKS), and to ensure that the indigenous voices were heard directly from them. It brought diverse thinkers, Emeritus Professors from quantum physics, law, economics, education, peace and philosophy from all over the world to enter into a serious dialogue on what the world needs to restore humanity and what the academy needs to humanize itself. Masters and PhD students, and Vice Chancellors, leading thinkers, and the IKS faculty were combined at the SARCHI Retreats.

The Chair held Interfaces after the Retreats sponsored directly by the South African Department of Science and Technology. The Interface was an inter-active space where the National Research Foundation and the Department of Science and Technology mandated the university to link with other stake-holders, particularly those at the margins who are the holders of other episte-mologies and producers of knowledge in other systems, and together, work out protocols, terms and conditions for the integration of the different tradi-tions of knowledge.

Together it was a site for the nourishment of emerging leaders with transdis-ciplinary competence in understanding constitutive (underlying) codes that program societal institutions and systems (including disciplines); developing a transnational outlook that is grounded in the African perspective; construct-ing arguments and critical reflection on identified knowledge questions; and establishing a safe and public space as a core social and national strategy.

By integrating citizenship education with academic explorations, research outcomes, and innovations, the Chair brought society face to face with the work of, and insights generated through the academy, previously known as 'experts'. The moral and pragmatic task was to develop new cognitive tools and propositions capable of deciphering the erasure cryptogram that hier-archized and excised the majority of African people from the global collec-tive memory as a positive and substantive contributor to world civilization -- hence denying them active citizenship in key areas of contemporary global currency including knowledge and science. The Chair generated powerful heuristics in terms of theory building, methodological perspectives, and practical interventions in a new ethical dispensation.

The Chair was implicitly future oriented in that the students were encouraged to extend the boundaries of inquiry beyond the immediate specificities of national history. The future oriented methodology was chosen specifically taking into account the potential dangers of the 'vortex' syndrome inherent in societies emerging out of trauma in which the power of that trauma can work adversely to continually suck all analyses and visions back only to the traumatic episode, thereby blocking the possibility for generating comparative and diachronic analyses so essential to making new or fresh propositions.

By turning a title and a status (the SARCHI Chair) into a space, and ethical space, the SARCHI Chair expressed a commitment to actively take up the challenge of fostering a community of thinkers within the higher education in South Africa, as well as strategic players in local communities, including holders of indigenous knowledge. The SARCHI Chair's work in the academy resulted in a metaphysical shift. The Law curriculum in the University of South Africa underwent a transformation. The University of Cape Town's Executive MBA in the Graduate School of Business took the codes produced by the Chair and it has produced remarkable reversals in the way MBA curriculum is taught.

The sector ministries in South Africa who had IKS units were brought into the picture. It enables the development of a weave of ethics, a set of attitudes, and an ethics of the margins capable of producing perspectives on subsistence and survival which are not stymied by the western obsession with hierarchization and alienation of the 'other', but which are civilizational in their own way. It mobilized a cohort of community of thinkers and organic intellectuals (academics, artists, and citizens) around the human condition – i.e. plurality, epistemologies, intercultural dialogue, peace and violence, science and society, knowledge and democracy. The Chair was a yeasting point, a generative hub for leadership building, a facilitative space for intellectual change management, and played the role of an Intellectual interlocutor between the constitution of South Africa, the university's mission/goals, and the implementation arenas.

The space created by the Chair enabled the participants to understand the contexts that have shaped the conceptual history of Indigenous Knowledge Systems (IKS) from **generation to degeneration** and **regeneration**. Issues and values of indigeneity such as autonomy, self-determination, decolonization, restoration, healing, and justice formed the bedrock of the proceedings. IKS as a life force generating renewable energies for cultural, economic, ecological, intellectual as well as other forms of collective wellbeing and survival **was the nexus in the formulation of the proposals for the Interface run by the Chair**. Building bridges to cross from **IKS as a science** to **western scientific paradigms** and back, was at the core of this endeavour in knowledge development in which IKS as a science was included (Odora Hoppers, 2008-2018 Reports to the National Research Foundation, South Africa). This example shows a national and institutional case of building capacity for a transformed thought and practice process in bringing to bear dialogue among knowledge systems. The Chair came to an end in 2018.

Conclusion

In this chapter, I outlined how peace education liberated me by introducing me to a deeper understanding of peace and how I could understand what happened to me. It was an eye-opener. But to take my experiences and make sense of it in public nationally and internationally, I had to adopt an emancipatory frame of reference as Ashis Nandy has stated that the meek do not inherit the earth by their meekness alone. They need defences of the mind and conceptual categories around which they can organise their thoughts and actions (Nandy, 1983). This brought the 'liberated' part of me to work intimately with the 'enemy', people on 'the other side' in insitutions, in policy, with the UN agencies. In other words, the guerrilla and the peacemaker combined into one force, with amazing results!

Six years later after finishing the SARCHI Chair, in November 2024, the Canadian Federal Government awarded the author a **Canadian Research Chair Tier 1 in Pluralistic Societies - Transdisciplinarity, Cognitive Justice and Education** in the University of Calgary, Canada, to introduce elements of what she did in the SARCHI Chair in South Africa to the academy in Canada.

References

Akinowo, A. (1988). Universalism and Indigenization in Sociological Theory: Introduction. *International Sociology* 3(2): 155-160.

Berger, P. L. & Luckman, T. (1966). *The Social Construction of Reality*. Penguin Books.

Bhaba, H. (1995). In the spirit of calm violence. In: G. Prakash, (Ed.), *After colonialism. Imperial histories and post-colonial displacements* (pp. 326-344). Princeton University Press.

Brock-Utne, B. (1989). *Feminist perspectives on peace and peace education*. Pergamon Press.

Burrell, G. & G. Morgan (1979). *Sociological paradigms and organizational analysis*. Heinemann.

Capra, F. (1982). *The turning point: Science, society and the rising culture*. Flamingo.

Degenaar, J. (1990). The concept of violence. In *The influence of violence on children*. Occasional paper No.13. Centre for Intergroup Studies, University of Cape Town.

Fatnowna, S. & Pickett, H. (2002). The place of indigenous knowledge systems in the postpostmodern integrative paradigm shift. In Odora Hoppers, C. (Ed.), *Indigenous knowledge and the integration of knowledge systems: Towards a philosophy of articulation*. New Africa Books.

Fay, B. (1975). *Social theory and political practice*. George Allen & Unwin.

Foucault, M. (1980). *Power/Knowledge. Selected interviews and other writings 1972–1977*. Pantheon Books.

Galtung, J. (1996). *Peace by peaceful means: Peace and conflict, development and civilization*. Sage Publications.

Huntington, S.P. (1996). *The clash of civilizations and the remaking of world order*. Simon & Schuster.

Keeves, J.P. (1990). Social theory and educational research. In: H. Walberg & G. Haertel, (Eds.), *International Encyclopedia of Education Evaluation*. Pergamon.

Knudtson, P., & Suzuki, D. (1992). *Wisdom of the elders*. Allen & Unwin.

Lengermann, P.M. & Niebrugge-Brantley, J. (1988). Contemporary feminist theory. In G. Ritzer (Ed.), *Sociological theory*. Alfred A. Knopf.

Nandy, Ashish (1983). *The intimate enemy loss and recovery of self under colonialism*. Oxford University Press.

Marshall, J. D. (1990). Foucault and educational research. In S.J. Ball (Ed.), *Foucault and education*. Routledge.

Makrakis, V. (1988). *Computers in school education: The cases of Sweden and Greece*. Stockholm University: The Institute of International Education.

Park, P. (1988). Toward an emancipatory sociology: Abandoning universalism for true indigenization. *International Sociology*. 3(2): 161-170.

Odora, C.A. (1993). *Educating African girls in a context of patriarchy and transformation. A theoretical and conceptual analysis*. Stockholm University: The Institute of International Education.

Odora Hoppers, C.A. (2002). Indigenous knowledge and the integration of knowledge systems: Towards a conceptual and methodological framework. In Odora Hoppers. C. (Ed), *Indigenous knowledge and the integration of knowledge systems: Towards a philosophy of articulation* pp. 2-22). New Africa Books:.

Odora Hoppers, C.A. (2009). Education, culture and society in a globalizing world: Implications for comparative and international education. *Compare*. 39(5): 601–614.

Sanda, A.M. (1988). In defence of indigenisation in sociological theories. *International Sociology*. 3(2): 189-199.

Shiva, V. (1994). *Staying alive: Women, ecology and development*. Zed Books.

Venter, L. (1997). *When Mandela goes. The coming of South Africa's second revolution*. Transworld.

Chapter 10
Developing a Planetary Peace Education Agenda

Crain Soudien

Introduction

I am happy to be counted as a peace educator using Robin Burns (personal communication) and Magnus Haavelsrud's explanation of what 'peace education' includes, namely, "social pedagogy, comparative education, critical pedagogy, conscientization, politicization, and more". Pushed, I would describe myself as a cognitive sociologist. I do so with some caution. Cognitive sociology is not yet firmly established in the academy. Working with this reality, I will make the argument that however the academy comes to reckon with cognitive sociology, it is vital for peace education. It offers tools. There are, obviously, others, with which to think through and deal with the issues of mutuality, reciprocity and engagement in the process of managing conflict. Standard definitions of cognitive sociology refer to the ways in which human thinking is shaped and influenced by sociocultural factors. My own approach works in a wider arc. In that wider arc I seek, firstly, to expand the idea of the social to include the multiplicity of means through which human subjectivity comes to be constituted. I do so to deliberately retrieve and hold in sight dimensions of the experience of *being* which fundamentally determine how human beings come to a sense of themselves and their relationships with each other. Amongst these in the many known and unknown factors which steer us in our lives are the economic and the biological. With respect to the first, the economic, our survival as individuals and collectives is based on our management of the basic necessities for life. We build cultures through how we produce and maintain the conditions necessary for our sustenance. In relation to the second, the biological, our bodies, and particularly our brains, are in complex relationships with the social. Their very functioning, the basic metabolic process, affect, temperament and wellbeing as a whole, is influenced, tempered, shaped and even determined by the world in which they are placed. Working with this I seek to find ways, in conscious opposition to standard Kantian discourse which has so effectively embedded in philosophy the formulation of entirely self-standing brains – apart from everything around them - to bring the important new field of epigenetics into our discussions about how our brains work and particularly how biology - our personal biologies, not least of all – relates to the social and vice-versa.

This brief explanation, of course, does not describe the limits of who we are as human beings. How we talk about that which we all have and hold in common as human beings, that which we talk about as our 'universals', is unavoidably always going to be up for debate. This caveat acknowledged, in all the work I do, I proceed from this basic orientation as a framework for understanding our human similarities and differences and particularly how these arise in our sense-making strategies, our approaches to explaining how we differ from and are similar to each other, and, most pertinently for this exercise, how we work with what we understand about difference and sameness. I will, in closing this contribution, set this approach, my attempt at constituting a personal theoretical apparatus, in a *values* frame to argue why it is important for peace education work.

The contribution unfolds in two parts. It begins with a description of my broad field of work as it has taken both intellectual and practical form and then comes to focus on the key ideas and concepts that hold this work together.

What I do

I work primarily in the academy as a researcher and teacher, and, secondarily, as a practitioner in the cultural and socio-political world. This interest, almost inevitably, has my own personal life-space, South Africa, as its immediate focus. From it has come the whole range of human wonder – of beauty and horror, of virtue and venality. These qualities are evident and animative in all the spaces in which I find myself.

As a researcher and teacher, I am located in the university and research arena and as a practitioner in a range of educational, cultural, political and sports organisations. I work in schools, universities, educational agencies, museums, scholarly, educational and cultural associations and sports organisations. In the course of this work, the former, I have written and published widely. In the latter, I have been involved in the establishment, formation and leadership of key cultural and educational organisations and have undertaken consultancies for government, educational and cultural agencies.

The influences that have brought me to this work are my immediate context: South Africa; my parents and my upbringing; my formal education, school and university; and the informal environment of political and ideological elders, mentors, inspirational peers and the many talented young people that have filtered through my life. South Africa, as the scholar Grant Farred (2024) suggests in his contemplation of the effects of apartheid on his life, makes you think. South Africa is for me, as I infer above, a *global ontological hotspot*. It is not the centre of the world – there is no such thing – but it contains, as a few other places in the world do, almost all of the social ingredients which arise in modernity in intense intersectional entanglement – 'race', class, gender, sexuality, culture, language, age, ability, space, well- and ill-being, time and many more. It is a place from which to speak to the world. There is a perversity to living in conditions of utter oppression, Farred (2024) says. This perversity arises out of the insistent *othering* that the policy of apartheid produced. It placed one, in some senses, in a constant state of conflict, conflict with others, conflict with oneself, conflict with the world. Called on to explain one's condition in relation to apartheid, one is either thrust into submissive and deferential bewilderment - it is what destiny has ordained. Or one begins to think. To think about how the situation in which one finds oneself has arisen, to think about oneself and oneself in relation to other people, to think about the nature of life and, powerfully, how one becomes something other than the *other* that is foretold in one's destiny. It is the latter path, I would like to think, I have taken.

The path I took was influenced decisively by the kinds of experiences my parents deliberately crafted for my sister and me. They were deeply conscious of the racializing order into which their children were born and went out of their way to make a better life for us. This meant thinking about where we lived, where we went to school, the stimulation that would help to build our sense of ourselves as human beings. This was modelled in the way they took responsibility themselves in their places of work, recreation and worship. Our home, as a result, was disruptive, social and always stimulating. I met all kinds of people. Most importantly, I learnt to read voraciously. A lot of the world became open to me – not all of it, I now know, but certainly much which sparked a sense of wonder and curiosity. Our parents sent us, their children, to excellent schools. These schools were extraordinary sites of resistance to subjugation. They consciously subverted the educational script of apartheid which had as its objective the socialisation of people not regarded as white into submissive, docile and inferior – in their self-perceptions – human beings. Our schools, both my primary and high schools, invoked the idea of education as a process of open human becoming. They were, looking back on them, and, of course, they would not have used these words, examples of what an anti-racial education looked like. Again, thinking about them critically, as I now think about my literary exposure, they were not unproblematic. They had blind spots. A big blind spot was their Anglo-centric bias. The universe was English. English and all its entailed constructions of worth, of self, and, most relevantly, of *otherness*. I now see how easily *otherness* was subtly inscribed. This difficulty was partially challenged when I went to school in England and then, decidedly, when I came to university in Cape Town. There my education was radically overhauled. I learnt quickly there, largely outside of the university, it must be said, the totally disruptive idea of non-racialism, the idea that 'race' was a social construction. I will return to this in talking of my *values* frame.

These influences from home, school and university came to shape my trajectory, I would like to think, as a scholar-activist. It led me into a study of the country's early trade union movement, and then, more substantially, signalling my entry into what would be my lifelong research focus, into a doctoral study into the making of youth Identity in contemporary South Africa. This was a study based on interviews with over a hundred young people in

Cape Town. It sought to understand how their consciousness as human subjects was formed and particularly their sense of 'race'. This work opened up several veins of research including comparative work on racial and identity formation in the cognate social contexts of the United States of America, the United Kingdom and India.

This early intervention into the discussion of 'race' opened up, significantly, a public career in what is described in the social sciences as 'race relations'. In the last twenty years I have been intensely involved at multiple levels of engagement with processes which can be thought of as 'peace-making', 'reconciliation', 'social-justice', 'healing', and 'public dialogue'.

Formally, and I must emphasize how honoured I have been, I have been fortunate to work in a number of high-level initiatives to deal with the fall-out of our country's apartheid legacy. I have led a number of official government inquiries into conflicts in the education sector. The first was an investigation into a racial conflict at a Cape Town school. The second was a large-scale, nation-wide inquiry into the state of discrimination at South African universities. It was prompted by a demeaning racial incident at a prominent South African university. The incident provoked protest and conflict at the university and at other institutions between white and black members of staff and students. The incident had involved privileged young white men video-recording for the amusement of their peers the subjection of older black support staff in their university residence to a series of humiliating indignities. The report written for the inquiry became the empirical basis for looking at transformation on university campuses. A third inquiry I led arose after complaints were made in the country about biases in school textbooks. The investigation involved scrutiny of the education system's major textbooks and the production of a report which recommended how textbook publishers and writers should be dealing with the questions of social difference.

A by-product of this formal work has been my involvement in important social dialogue initiatives. I have worked and continue to work in interventions which seek to bring stakeholders together around important social issues of the day. Their essential methodological approach has been that of taking the critical stakeholders in a social challenge away from their immediate contexts and to engender the dialogical conditions for them to think about, in dialogue, the causes, issues in the problems and to begin to imagine alternatives.

The work I have done into the making of identity has also given rise to five important developments in my research interest. The first is into the question of violence. In the course of working on racialisation I became aware of the ubiquity of violence as a feature of youth identity. How did young people, however they were racialised, learn violence? I did this work largely to challenge a commonly held trope that violence was a natural attribute of people perceived to be black and that black people were inherently savage, wild and dangerous and, in apartheid terms', therefore, needing to be subjugated and tamed. I worked then with a young man who had been found guilty of murder and been sentenced to a lengthy term of imprisonment. It was one of the privileges of my intellectual life to be able to do so. After he came out of prison I conducted over 60 hours of interviews with this young man and, as a result, wrote a series of articles on becoming, violence and education. The project also stimulated the young man to write his biography. I am in possession of the manuscript and am looking at ways of getting it published.

Related to this work on violence, the second offshoot of my work on identity, I also began thinking about how the affective phenomenon of 'hate' arose in the consciousness formation of people. This led me into the life of another young man, this time a young white man who, as South Africa was transitioning into a democracy led by black people, had deliberately embarked on a killing spree of black people. In one instance, not the only one, he drove into a crowded square in the centre of Pretoria, the administrative capital of South Africa, and armed with an automatic rifle cold-bloodedly mowed down seven people. I used the event to begin a line of thinking, which I have not yet completed, into the phenomenon of hate. Hate, importantly for a text such as this, has a poor scholarly literature. In the most accessible texts at our disposal, it is largely accounted for as the opposite of love, which, not unexpectedly, does have an extensive scholarship. In this piece I begin an exploratory foray – it is brief – into how the phenomenon of hate is produced. This foray draws on the extensive court records of the Pretoria killer's trial, particularly the reports of the psychologists. These reports draw attention to the state of psychology in relation to questions such as hate and help us to understand why cognitive sociology as a field is so important for understanding the questions of conflict, violence and peace.

Related to this work on violence I have also begun to draw on Gandhian ideas of self-sacrifice. Important about this work was Gandhi's thinking on what he called *ahimsa*. Through this idea, which he sometimes described as 'love', he began to articulate the idea of the *other* as being, simply, a different form of ourselves (Gandhi, 1968, p. 180). I have sought to retrieve from this idea the possibility of developing a consciousness which has as its objective the complete and deliberate renunciation of hate.

The fourth area of work stemming from my interest in racialisation is about intellectual formation. This has led me into working extensively in the area of the formation of discourse and particularly the discourse of racism and non-racialism. The way I am doing this is to track the development of the thinking of the key intellectuals of South Africa. With respect to the discourse of 'race' and racism, I have begun, and again not completed, work on the largely unknown but determinative influence of a white Afrikaner intellectual, Geoff Cronjé, on the making of apartheid. Cronjé was a product of Afrikaner nationalism which was unapologetically white supremacist, but, more importantly, of the formative European existentialist intellectual movement of the first half of the 20th century. Important about this movement, epitomised in the work of Martin Heidegger, was its intellectual sublimation of human possibility of people deemed to be 'non-white'. It was, extraordinarily, unable to see, much less work with, its authorisation of the idea of 'race', leading, effectively, to the legitimation of the racial barbarism of the Second World War. South Africa, after the contradiction of racial barbarism was exposed in 1950 in the important United Nations' Statement on Race (UNESCO, 1950) was white supremacy's last, residual workshop. I work with Cronjé's intellectual formation to show how the idea of 'race' is gestated and given substance in the policy of apartheid. As a contrast to Cronjé, I work with the formation of two key counter-thinkers, Ben Kies and Neville Alexander who are responsible for the development of the idea of non-racialism. I have written extensively, and continue to do so, on their contributions to the making of the idea of non-racialism. The new work which is emerging out of this interest is a study of the idea of 'race' over the last 5000 years of the development of what we call 'civilisation'. This is a study which attempts to explain how the ideas of difference have crystallised over this period and to put into perspective how the idea of 'race' emerges in the last 500 years as a recent and modern phenomenon.

The fifth area of my work is in the new area of the social-biological interface. This is exploratory work but has as its objective understanding how the relationship between the body and consciousness works. The way I am doing this is to take an event which happens every year in the lives of non-English or Afrikaans-speaking South African children. This event is the enforced language switch children go through. They are compelled, they have no choice, to move from their mother-tongues, which could be any one of South Africa's indigenous languages, to learn in English or Afrikaans. The argument I am seeking to make is that this switch is traumatic for the children. The switch involves intense body-mind effects. For most, not all, a kind of violence is experienced. This violence comes through the stimulation of serotonin which constricts their neural pathways and the possibility of productive thinking and, critically, for executive functioning. We are now beginning to understand how important executive functioning is for self-control and particularly, for the disciplining of the will to learn to learn. This is a body effect which begins in a social action, the decision to have the children learn through the medium of a foreign language. It is not racial. My interest here is to look at ways of mitigating this trauma. In play here, I argue, is effectively a moment which produces the conditions for peace or conflict in South Africa. It is a moment in which positive cognitive sociology asserts its simple, but as yet not understood, significance for the making of a dignified life for the country's citizens. This will be a critical new development in cognition and sociology and psychology with respect to how consciousness formation works.

This work I have been doing on how people come to consciousness, effectively that of ideation, has led me to working in the cultural and particularly museum field. Most significantly, I have become involved in the establishment of memory projects in Cape Town. The most important is the District Six Museum which I founded with two other colleagues in 1991. This initiative is now a globally recognised intervention in memory and social healing. District Six is a suburb in Cape Town which became, after its proclamation in 1865, the place of refuge for people from all kinds of backgrounds – slaves freed after 1838, migrant workers from the far corners of the earth looking to make a better life for themselves, and political, religious and cultural exiles from all over the world fleeing the pogroms of the early 20th century. The

District Six which they made constituted a reply to apartheid South Africa. It was, with all of its unavoidable problems, a vibrant multicultural refuge for its diverse peoples. Hospitality, referred to as *kanala* by the people of District Six, was its emblematic quality. It took in everybody and became, like the great port melting-pots of the world, Marseille, New Orleans, New York, a great cultural exchange. It offended people such as Cronjé. Cronjé's political acolytes destroyed it through an act of parliament called the Group Areas Act which carved up the physical landscape of South Africa into separate racialised enclaves. 'Race'-mixing was an abomination. It polluted the gift of 'whiteness'. Over 65,000 people were physically carted off the slopes of Table Mountain and dumped into suburbs and townships far from their places of work without the basic amenities to make a decent life. The District Six Museum was established to help the displaced people come back into the city through telling their stories. Its major contribution to healing in Cape Town is the opportunity the displaced have had, and continue to have, of being able to speak of their pain. Following this work, I continue to work extensively in museum and heritage education. This work has taken me into the foremost memory sites in South Africa and an engagement with what I have begun to describe as processes of enfigurement – how people are represented as people - in museums as strategies and pedagogies for building inclusive identities for ourselves. I have tried, in this work, to emphasize how the grand museums of apartheid have, effectively, sacralised white identity. The newer museums, the District Six Museum which I have had a direct hand in shaping as a counterpoint, uses enfigurement in deliberately inclusive ways. It avoids the stigmatising strategies of racialisation. Representation - visual, oral, sonic, tactile, symbolic, is worked with for its conscious pedagogical value.

My Conceptual Framework

In closing, it is important to return to the conceptual frameworks on which I draw. The approach I have taken to thinking about building understanding between and amongst ourselves as human beings – not just making peace but *keeping* it - is that we have to prioritise the critical procedure of sense-making. This, however, is easier said than done. What sense-making procedures do we have at our disposal?

We use multiple forms of sense-making in our everyday lives. Central to most is the process of classification. Classification involves the placement of that which we sense, including seeing, touching and hearing, into categories. As sentient and conscious beings we will always classify. We do so to distinguish different experiences and phenomena in our lives. It produces intelligibility in our communications with each other. When we speak with one another it makes it possible for us to understand – even roughly – what we are talking about. Classification and categorisation, however, are always based on *interpretations* of things. They are never the actual things themselves. The term 'sad', for example, is a classificatory description of a mood. It helps to surface elements of what a mood is all about. It can never, however, capture the complexity of the mood. The description of someone as 'white', to give another example, works at some levels. It describes the colour of a person's skin. Of that there may be little question. But it says almost nothing about the person. And yet, in the way of our common-sense thinking, that which we use in conversation, we assume that it does. Saying someone is 'white' calls up all kinds of fixed explanations of that person.

Because the terms we use are always open for discussion, it is important for a peace-seeking project, to be conscious of how categorisation and classification work in our lives. We need, in terms of this, to always be conscious of the logics, the forms of reasoning on which we draw in our everyday lives. We should, each of us, and this is an act of classification, be able to give a name to the forms of reasoning we use. For myself, I draw on Deleuze (1994) in his comments on how dominant forms of reason work constitutively. He is at pains in his work to break down the ways in which we are *constituted* or shaped as human beings. I am, influenced by Deleuze, what might be called a deconstructionist.

Deleuze's comments are important for coming to an appreciation of how sense-making works in the everyday. The starting point for constitutive reason is, as he says, the idea of a concept (Deleuze, 1994, p. 11). A concept is "a concept of a particular existing thing". Using the principle of what he calls indiscernibles, he explains that there is one and only one thing per concept. In so far, however, as it "serves as a determination, a predicate must remain fixed in the concept while becoming something else in the thing (animal becomes something other in man and horse)" (Deleuze, 1994, p. 12). What he is doing here is to denaturalise how concepts or ideas work. As soon as a concept or an idea is placed in the domain of the social it can become whatever people want it to become. This is how dominance works. "This is why" he continues, "the comprehension of the concept is infinite: having become other in the thing.... (t)his is why each determination remains general or defines a resemblance, to the extent that it remains fixed in the concept and applicable by right to an infinity of things... no existing individual *can* (in the original) correspond to it (the concept) *hic et nunc* (the here and now)" (Deluzue, 1994, p. 12). This is the point, to get to the contribution Deleuze makes to our understanding of difference, where reason struggles with its limits. He explains that "a concept can always be blocked at the level of each of its determinations.... (it may be) forcibly assigned a place in space and time" (Deluzue, 1994, p. 12).

The elements of 'blocking' and 'force' in Deleuze's discussion are relevant for our discussion. I invoke them here to think about how an educational process unfolds. To the deliberate gesture or act of 'blocking' which dominant thinking activates, education seeks to unblock, to 'open'. To the imposition of 'force' it offers instead, openness, an invitational gesture of freedom. How might a reasoning process work with concepts in ways which permit the possibilities of endless difference and to be comfortable with them? Towards making our way into such a space I have sought in the analytic approaches I use to insist that the explanations we make of our social differences are not explanations of social reality in themselves. They are, in Deleuzian terms, open concepts. They involve, each time they are invoked, intellectual work. They demand explanation. 'White' or 'black', or, indeed, any other descriptive concept we might use, are not fixed explanations. A person thought to be 'white' or 'black' is not, *hic et nunc*, the concept 'white' or 'black' itself. They are always, other things. The concepts in their generality explain little. It is here that 'peace' work starts. Our work, each time we are in the presence of difference, which, when one gets to the hard reality of our relationships with each other, is almost all of the time, even with others familiar to ourselves, is to confront the necessity of conscious and deliberative thought. Difference has to be explained and not presumed. An 'educated' person – one who is habituated to the work of thinking – has to proceed from the basic conceptual premise that difference as it is encountered and presents itself has a history. It is the act of learning how to be in engagement with *otherness* however it presents itself – the unspoken and spoken elements of its history - that I am seeking to emphasize.

Learning how to be in engagement with otherness takes Deleuze's (1994, pp. 11-12) insight into 'artificial' blockages seriously. It has to come to terms with the explanation that social difference is learnt. While the fields of sociology and psychology acknowledge this explanation, they have difficulty in working with it to 'unblock' its fixedness in explanations of the difference brought to the social encounter. The point to emphasize here is that if 'race' is not something we are born with, but something which we have learnt and so acquired, we need to be a great deal more helpful in explaining how this – being 'raced', 'gendered', or whatever, comes about. To be more helpful, disciplines and fields such as sociology and psychology have to make the great task of deconstructing how individuals and groups present themselves and interact with each other as necessary features of the life-skills each of us brings into our encounters with each other. We have to be curious about each other. This means, always, respectfully, seeking to understand the other's difference. What this means is not working with the concepts of things in their static ways and 'blocked' forms. I have sought to institute this approach in my work – to insist on the necessity of generating and not simply imputing an explanation about the other on the basis of fixed assumptions. I acknowledge how often this process will lead one into making a mistake. We will make mistakes. We will make mistakes because we will always have unconscious blind spots. We will not know what we don't know. But we want to always be aware of how easily the process of meaning-making in the lives of individual human subjects leads us to simply reduce subjects to their classification or the categories in which social analysis puts them. I have absolutely no doubt about the difficulty of this work but would like to think that it is through difficulty rather than feigned familiarity or presumptive 'knowing' that we begin to manage our differences. Reason is, in this sense, intellectual labour. It is intense. It dislikes shortcuts. It does not permit presumption.

How I work with difference and sameness, to bring this contribution to a close, is underpinned by a three-fold set of concerns. Firstly, in all the different kinds of intellectual and practical activities that I am involved with, which I have described above, I am interested in the modes of reason which have come to characterize our sense-making strategies for working with difference, the fixed categorization analytics which underpin these strategies, and how we constructively develop reasoning cultures which are open and generative. In terms of this I aim to surface the assumptions that are salient, active and constitutive in the making of social difference. Secondly, I seek to understand the inter-relationship between these assumptions and the structural and ideological ecologies in which they appear and how they take practical expression. Finally, I want to be actively involved in the development of learning cultures and practices that offer alternative ways of seeing and being in the world – ways that work productively and generatively with difference in all of its manifestations.

In terms of the concerns I outline above, I have sought to orientate the work I do towards better understandings of how we participate in and nurture as educationists deep learning. By this I mean the kind of learning in which we come to *know* ourselves, to have a conscious sense of ourselves in relation to others, and a sense of what the significance of this knowing is for the wellbeing of all that exists on our wider planet. My aim, in terms of this, is to contribute to the project of a humanism which has a planetary commitment as its first priority. It is the social, economic and cultural context in which knowing takes place which interests me – how it is managed, critically worked with and the uses to which it is put. Contexts, I argue, almost unavoidably, produce for all of us – this is history in constant action – insight and blind spots. Our contexts help us to see some things with utter clarity, others with complete unconscious unseeingness. We have here the great paradox of consciousness.

Flowing from this paradox, my major preoccupation as a cognitive sociologist is how people come to learn in the environments in which they find themselves and how this learning puts them in a position to engage with their worlds critically. This is a particular kind of peace work. In this I have come to be interested in social structures, how social structures work in people's lives and the factors that are present and active in how they make choices. This is about the question of the individual in society and how the individual in his/ her/their life learns their way – in a wide ecological sense - through the time and space of their intersectional entanglements – 'race', class, gender, sexuality, culture, language, age, ability, space, well- and ill-being, time and many, many more. These entanglements come together combustively, producing all of our human triumphs and failings. They are never, however, natural. They are productions. How the human subject – I, we, all of us - comes to formation and consciousness in the world is an important life-skill we should all be making a deliberate effort to become better at. It is a basis through which and from which the process of working with difference is always constituted as an opportunity of generative possibility. It is peace work.

References

Deleuze, G. (1994). *Difference and repetition.* Columbia University Press.

Farred, G. (2024). *The perversity of apartheid.* Temple University Press.

Gandhi, M. (1968). *The selected works of Mahatma Gandhi. Vol. III.* Navajivan Publishing House.

Soudien, C. (2021). A Praetorian sensibility? The making of the humanities and social sciences through the tangled histories of the HSRC and the humanities faculty in Pretoria. In Soudien, C., Swartz, S. & Houston, G. (Eds.), *Society, research and power: A history of the Human Sciences Research Council from 1929 to 2019* (pp. 22-33). HSRC Press.

UNESCO (1950). *Statement on race.* UNESCO.

Chapter 11

The Anthropocene as Challenge to Peace Culture and Peace Education

Christoph Wulf

Introduction

The desire for peace in a violent world led to the founding of UNESCO after the Second World War. Since then, the development of a culture of peace has been a central goal of the international community. Within this framework, the term 'peace' has been expanded. A culture of peace can be defined as "a set of values, attitudes, modes of behavior and ways of life that reject violence and prevent conflicts by tackling their root causes to solve problems through dialogue and negotiation among individuals, groups and nations" (UN Resolutions A/RES/52/13: Culture of Peace). Furthermore, education for peace takes place in many areas of human life without explicitly mentioning peace.

At the heart of peace education is the reduction of violence. The aim is to reduce violence against nature, against other people and against one's own self. Under the influence of peace and conflict research, violence directed toward other people was at the center of peace education in the second half of the 20th century (Galtung, 1975; Senghaas, 1981; Wulf ,1974). At this time, the environmental problems caused by humans were already being recognized and the limits to growth were emphasized (Meadows et al, 1972). However, it was only at the beginning of the 21st century that the violence perpetrated by humans against nature became more of an issue.

In the Anthropocene humans see the world, of which they are a part, as an ensemble of objects that they can use unconditionally for their own interests. It is largely forgotten that humans are part of nature, the world and the planet. The suppression of this insight has led to many negative effects on the living environment of humans, animals and plants. In all cases, it has also made it possible to use violence against nature and against other people. Many problems are the result of this basic human attitude towards nature and the world. Examples include climate change, the destruction of biodiversity, the disruption of biogeochemical cycles, the pollution of the planet and the consumption of non-renewable resources.

The following section explains why the concept of the Anthropocene is suitable for identifying the threatening results of the violence of human activity on the one hand, but also for characterizing the positive efforts of the international community to correct these developments on the other. These aim to reduce violence and its structures in key areas of the planet with the help of sustainable development. Reducing violence against nature is particularly important in this context. Human rights education, education for peace, education for sustainable development and global citizenship education play a central role in these efforts. In conclusion, it will be shown that working on the common heritage of nature and culture offers an important opportunity for the development of sustainability and peace.

The Anthropocene

In the Anthropocene, the aim of peace work is not only to reduce manifest and structural violence against other people, but also to reduce violence against nature. Both forms of violence are intertwined. From the perspective of the social sciences, it is irrelevant whether geologists understand 'Anthropocene' to mean an epoch in Earth's history, a historical period within an epoch or a series of events. What is decisive is that there is hardly any area of the planet in the Anthropocene that is not influenced by the actions and behavior of humans. In many cases, this influence of human action and behavior has consisted in the exercise of violence against nature. Examples include: 1) climate change; 2) the destruction of biodiversity; 3) the destruction of biogeochemical cycles; 4) ocean acidification; 5) pollution; 6) the consumption of non-renewable energy (Wulf, 2020, 2022b). This situation is leading to fundamental changes in our understanding of nature, the world, globality and images of humanity (Wulf, 2010, 2013, 2022b, 2024; Wallenhorst & Wulf, 2022, 2023).

The beginnings of the development of the Anthropocene date back around 12,000 years. At that time, the following occurred: the retreat of the ice, the warming of the earth, the development of agriculture, the development of trade and the spread of humans, Homo sapiens, across the earth. A second phase begins with the spread of the steam engine by James Watt in 1769 and industrialization. It extends into the 20th century, which is the age of the great machines. During this period, the world's population grew from one billion to over six billion people. At the same time, the global economy and energy demand increased by a factor of around fifty. A third phase can be distinguished from this. This covers the period between 1945 and 2015 and is characterized by the explosion of the first atomic bomb, the development of nuclear energy, the tremendous acceleration of life, global economic expansion, the invention and worldwide spread of new media, digitalization, artificial intelligence and robotics. Added to this are far-reaching developments in genetics: the discovery of the double helix structure of DNA, cloning and the manipulation of human genes using CRISPR methods (Wulf, 2020a, 2020b).

A fourth phase is characterized by the adoption of the Sustainable Development Goals by the international community in New York in 2015. In this phase, the aim was to correct the negative effects of human omnipresence and violence on the planet and to improve the planetary situation in many areas. This phase can be understood as an attempt by humans to correct the negative side effects of human action and behavior, some of which were unintentional and some of which were consciously accepted. In connection with the Sustainable Development Goals, there have been increased efforts to reduce violence in many areas of society, particularly with the help of the fourth goal of education for sustainable development, which focuses on education. Although none of these sustainable development goals are entirely new, what is new is their combination into a global system of action and behavior for shaping the future that is accepted by all states.

In order to achieve the goals of sustainable development, the violence of (Western) human planetary dominance must be reduced (Meyer-Abich, 1990; Escobar, 2018). Otherwise, it will not be possible to avert the threat to human, animal and plant life. Can this be achieved within the framework of an 'Anthropocene' concept in which humans are at the center, or does the term unintentionally perpetuate the dominance of humans and the violence they exert? Other terms used to describe the dynamics of the new situation were intended to avoid this. For example, 'Chthulucene' (Haraway, 2016), 'Capitalocene' (Moore, 2016) or 'Plutocene' (Glikson, 2017) present a good case, but only focus on individual aspects of human action and behavior and thus inadmissibly reduce the complexity of the planetary situation. Due to its all-encompassing character and anthropological complexity, it therefore seems sensible to me to continue to use the term 'Anthropocene'. It can be used to characterize many negative developments (Gil & Wulf, 2015; Suzuki & Wulf, 2021) that endanger the foundations of humanity and life on the planet and that urgently need to be corrected. Dealing with these problems has both a universal and a particular aspect. It therefore seems appropriate to speak of a 'pluriversal Anthropocene' in which local, national, regional and planetary elements are intermingled (Wallenhorst & Wulf, 2025 ff.).

Human Rights and Peace Education

With the adoption of the Sustainable Development Goals by the international community in 2015, the efforts of the global community to reduce violence against nature and people have increased. Human rights play an important role in this as a normative basis for action and behavior that reduces violence. For many people, human rights even serve to demand the rights of animals, plants, and landscapes.

To create a sense of belonging to the planetary human community, education and socialization must be based on human rights (United Nations, 1948). "Human rights education and training comprises all educational, training, information, awareness-raising and learning activities aimed at promoting universal respect for and observance of all human rights and fundamental freedoms." (United Nations, 2011) The goal is to reduce human rights violations in all areas of social coexistence. Human rights education is a task for all, from early childhood on, regardless of their nationality and social status. It is a lifelong task that involves the formation of and reflection upon attitudes, actions and behaviors. Such a task involves the communication of relevant information, sensitization to injustice, the development of reflective and critical knowledge about the origins of injustice, as well as helping people to exercise their rights and help others do so. (United Nations 2022) Human rights form the normative basis of education for peace, sustainability and global citizenship.

The Russian war of aggression in Ukraine and the war in Gaza make it clear that people are still threatened by war and violence. Peace is a prerequisite for human life. Not only the lives of individual people, generations or nations, but the existence of humanity as a whole depends on preserving or establishing peace. It is therefore essential to address the preconditions and conditions of war, violence and material hardship in the context of education and to look for ways to help reduce them. Education for peace is an attempt by education to contribute to the reduction of violent conditions. In doing so, it does not fail to recognize that war and violence are often the result of macro-structural system problems, the reduction of which is only partially possible with the help of education. Education for peace is based on the assumption that constructive engagement with the major problems affecting humanity in the Anthropocene must be part of a lifelong learning process that needs to begin in childhood and continue into later life (Wulf, 1973a, 1973b, 1974; Gugel, 1995; Burns & Aspeslagh, 1996; Wintersteiner, 2003; Nipkow, 2007; Calließ & Reinhold, 2013; Obrillant & Wulf et al., 2017; Haavelsrud, 2020).

In Germany, education for peace is part of political education. Since the nineteen seventies it has differed from earlier efforts, which in the sixties understood 'education for international understanding' to be peace education. These efforts were based on the concept that people were fundamentally peaceful and that this was endangered by aggression, whereby peace was considered to be primarily a question of moral behavior. Education for peace also differs from efforts that were concerned with learning peaceful behavior in our awareness of the human aggressive drive structure and which emphasized that an individual desire for peace would lead to political peace. The idea that war begins in people's minds and must be fought there is characteristic of these positions, which hold that the most important thing is to change people's consciousness in order to create social conditions which are more socially just. As important as these efforts to spread a culture of peace are, they are not enough; a more far-reaching examination of the problem of peace is required (Andreopoulos & Claude, 1997; Page, 2008; Trifonas & Wright, 2013;

Bajaj & Hantzopoulos, 2016).

Peace education must also continue to draw on central concepts such as 'organized peacelessness', 'structural violence' and 'social justice', as developed by peace research in the 1960s and 1970s (Galtung, 1975; Galtung, 1981). These ideas make the social character of peace clear and protect against fantasies of omnipotence and naïve oversimplifications of the problem. According to Galtung's distinction, which is still worth considering, peace is not only to be seen as the absence of war and direct violence (negative concept of peace); peace must also be understood as the reduction of structural violence, which is about establishing social justice (positive concept of peace). Based on this understanding of peace, not only war or direct violence between nations and ethnic groups become the subject of education, but also the violent living conditions within society.

Education for peace requires certain forms with which it attempts to promote the development of non-violent learning processes. It will therefore primarily develop forms of learning in which participatory and self-initiated learning takes place (Göhlich, Wulf & Zirfas, 2014). In these learning processes, a large part of the initiative and responsibility should lie with the addressees of education for peace. They are encouraged to develop their peace-relevant imagination. The development of a historical awareness of the emergence and fundamental changeability of conflict formations plays a decisive role here. This awareness contributes to the development and processing of real-utopian designs for changing the world. At the same time, it ensures a future-oriented approach to the problems (Springer, 2013; Senghaas, 1995, 1997).

Education for peace touches on approaches that seek to shape the educational process of the younger generation with related objectives, but under different terms. These include education for international understanding, international education, and Claude development education. A structural problem of peace education and related efforts, however, is that, as education, it is directed at individuals or groups in whose consciousness and attitudes it can bring about lasting change. This needs to go further. For the development of a culture of peace it is essential that it is complemented by practical politics and peace-relevant action.

A great number of educational practices contribute to the reduction of violence and the establishment of peace. Education for peace assumes that the constructive confrontation with the planetary problem of violence is a lifelong learning process that begins in childhood and continues in later life (Wulf et al., 2021). Education for peace makes extensive efforts to reduce violence and to promote the ability of people and societies to develop peace. In a culture of peace, people's actions are guided by the values of peace and contribute to shaping social structures accordingly.

Sustainable Development Goals

The 17 goals for sustainable and peaceful development adopted by the international community in 2015 are aimed at fundamental changes in the following areas (Wallenhorst & Wulf, 2023):

- People: The goals are to reduce hunger and poverty, enable all people to live in dignity and create a healthy environment;

- Planet: The tasks here are the creation of an ecologically healthy environment for humans, animals and plants and the preservation of biodiversity;

- Peace: The reduction of violence and the potential for manifest violence (more than 10,000 nuclear and hydrogen bombs) and the creation of social justice for all people are required;

- Prosperity: The aim here is to improve living conditions through economic and technical developments in such a way that the well-being of all people becomes possible;

- Participation: Since the problems of the Anthropocene are not only local and regional but also global, worldwide cooperation is required to identify and address them.

Education for Sustainable Development

Developments are sustainable if they safeguard the quality of life of current generations and at the same time give future generations the choice to shape their lives (UNESCO, 2017). The goals resulting from this definition are interrelated with a culture of peace and human rights, cultural diversity, democratic participation and the rule of law. A peace-oriented culture of sustainable development is required to transform the economy and society. Its development requires future-oriented models, ideas, norms and forms of knowledge.

Education, training and socialization play an important role in the transformation into a sustainable global society. The fourth goal of sustainable development contains the vision of a globally inclusive, equal, high-quality and lifelong education. It is based on a vision of education and development which is derived from human rights and peace, social justice, security, cultural diversity and shared responsibility (UNESCO, 2001, 2005, 2015a). Education is seen as a common good and a fundamental human right. Realizing these goals is necessary for achieving peace, human self-realization and sustainable development.

Education for sustainability based on the values of peace envisages the development of a twelve-year public school system. Compulsory schooling should last at least nine years worldwide and include free, high-quality education at primary and secondary level. Inclusive here means not only the inclusion of disabled children and young people, but also of marginalized children and young people. Equal access and treatment in the education system will automatically follow. Especially for girls and women, there is still a lot to be done in many regions of the world. In order to promote the knowledge and creativity of children and young people, the quality of education needs to be improved, for example through better teacher training. Finally, the promotion of education and training should not be limited to the school system. Vocational training and lifelong learning needs to be developed and informal and non-formal education promoted. 4-6% of gross domestic product or 15-20% of public spending should be allocated to education (Wulf, 2020a, 2021c).

To meet the challenges of the Anthropocene, education geared towards sustainability and peace must not only be local, national or regional; it must also be global and planetary. After the end of the Soviet Union and the strengthening of the European Union, the emphasis was on efforts to see education in Europe as an international task (Wulf, 1995, 1998). These efforts increased; combined with sustainability, they found their way into the framework guidelines of schools (Wulf & Merkel, 2003; Wulf, 2006; Wulf & Brougère et al., 2018). Dealing constructively with sustainability and alterity became a central task of an education aimed at reducing violence (Wulf, 2016).

Education for sustainable development, global citizenship and peace pursue similar objectives. They cannot always be clearly distinguished from one another; transitions between them are fluid. Depending on the region and culture, these three fields of education have different focuses. They all aim to provide a general education in which differences are of constitutive importance. The aim is a planetary and pluriversal education for all. Its practices have the as yet underutilized potential to reduce violence against nature, other human beings and the violence of people toward their own selves. Education must be developed in such a way that sustainability, peace and global citizenship work together wherever possible (Vare & Scott, 2007; Hallinger & Nguyen, 2020; Wulf, 2022b; Tryggvason, Öhman & Van Poeck, 2023).

Education for sustainability does not aim to impart encyclopedic knowledge, but must select its content carefully (Fischer et al., 2022). It is particularly important to engage with the central values of a pluralistic education that strives to realize human rights and to critically reflect on societal, cultural, social and everyday life processes. Wonder (thaumazein) plays an important role in both aspects. Why is the world like this and not different? Why are people the way they are and why not different? Wonder can become a starting point for the transformation of outdated social structures. Research-oriented learning can contribute to the development of sustainable thinking and acting. Hear questions arise that can become important components of critical educational processes. Wonder, curiosity and questioning lead to educational processes that are of central importance for the development of sustainability, peace and global citizenship (Wulf, 2024).

Education for sustainability and peace is not limited to school education - it is a lifelong task. Children, young people and adults all take part in cultural practices in intergenerational communities. In mimetic processes, they experience how members of the adult generation shape these practices. In doing so, they perform sensual and linguistic, physical and social processes whose educational character cannot be overestimated (Wulf, 2024; Kraus et al., 2024; Kraus & Wulf, 2022; Michaels & Wulf, 2011). Due to the emotional relationships between members of different generations, the experiences in these practices are intense and formative. They create foundations on which other educational processes later build. In the context of realizing education for sustainability, it has become clear that this can only reach its full potential if it is complemented by education for the global community, by global citizenship education, which the UN Secretary-General Ban Ki-moon held to be a necessary complement to sustainability.

Global Citizenship Education

Global citizenship refers to belonging to a planetary community and requires the consideration of corresponding rights and duties (Wulf, 2021b). Thus, all people and all societies have a responsibility for the planet within their own means. This responsibility relates not only to other people, but to animals and plants. The development of a global citizenship that deals productively with differences is at the heart of a new view of humanity and the world that encompasses social participation and cultural participation. It places the individual under an obligation to the global community and the global community under an obligation to the individual. On the one hand, global citizenship is an idealistic aspiration; on the other hand, it has to contend with the limits of different state interests and constraints. The definition of the term refers to people's feelings. Global citizenship "is the feeling of belonging to a large human community. It particularly emphasizes the interdependence of political, economic, social and cultural issues and the interactions between the local, the national and the planetary" (UNESCO, 2015a).

The definition of global citizenship as a sense of belonging takes into account the fact that the term contains the same and different elements in different regions of the world. All people have feelings of belonging to communities. How these are expressed varies. In addition to biological and individual differences, historical and cultural differences play a central role. The simultaneity of disparities between countries and regions, states and their political systems determine the quality and intensity of feelings. The formation of a global community combines desires and imaginations, rational insights and differing feelings and releases energies for action and behavior (Wulf, 2006, 2016, 2021b, 2021d, 2022b).

In the context of efforts to realize education for sustainability, it has become clear that it can only develop its potential if it is complemented by education for the global community, for global citizenship education. The aim of global citizenship education is a political education of the world community that focuses on sustainability and peace. On the one hand, global citizenship education claims to be worldwide, i.e. universally valid, but on the other hand it can only develop through specific content. It must therefore relate local, national, regional, global and planetary thinking and action to each other and thus contribute to a new understanding of transformative education in the 21st century (Andreotti, 2014; Knobloch, 2019; Wulf et al., 2021). Structural and individual perspectives play an important role in this (Resina & Wulf, 2019). In normative terms, they can contain neoliberal or more liberal-critical aspects. The former are based more on the OECD's understanding of education with its international comparative tests. The latter are more inspired by critical theory or pedagogues such as the Frankfurt school of critical thinking or Paulo Freire. They focus on the after-effects of colonialism, imperialism and Eurocentrism. The aim is to teach human rights and democratic behavior and to overcome colonialism and exploitation (Oxley & Morris, 2013; Tarozzi & Torres, 2016). Transformational global learning is required in which knowledge of non-knowledge is a constitutive element. Global citizenship education aims at a planetary education in which pluriversal thinking is constitutive.

In Global citizenship we can distinguish three dimensions (UNESCO, 2015b):

> "Cognitive: To acquire knowledge, understanding and critical thinking about global, regional, national and local issues and the interconnectedness and interdependency of different countries and populations;

> Socio-emotional: To have a sense of belonging to a common humanity, sharing values and responsibilities, empathy, solidarity and respect for differences and diversity;

> Behavioral: To act effectively and responsibly at local, national and global levels for a more peaceful and sustainable world."

How can intangible cultural heritage practices help to engage people in global citizenship? In this process, the cognitive, socio-social and behavioral dimensions must be taken into account and people must be given an understanding of global structures and different cultural identities. To this end, the values and attitudes evident in the practices must be analyzed and critically assessed. At the same time, it is important to develop empathy for others and their diversity and to develop a willingness to take responsibility for global issues and to align one's own actions accordingly (Costa, Alscher & Thums, 2024).

Global citizenship education can be understood as a combination of general education and civic education, incorporating many of the approaches developed over the years within the UNESCO framework, such as 'human rights education', 'peace education' and 'education for sustainable education'. Global citizenship education is not a completely new approach to education, but rather refers to the interaction of many interconnected forms of educational knowledge. A critical attitude towards colonialism, imperialism, racism, post-colonialism and post-humanism also plays an important role. This is clearly understood as constitutive of global citizenship education. It draws attention to the fact that global citizenship education is a pluriversal education that focuses on overcoming Eurocentrism through interweaving the universal and the particular. The aim is to develop a sense of belonging to a planetary community. Global citizenship education encompasses the cooperation of many different communities and an understanding of existing power structures. It requires not only cognitive engagement, but also a social-emotional approach and attitudes of solidarity with them. Global citizenship has two poles: the pole of individual education and the pole of social transformation (UNESCO, 2015b; Knobloch, 2022).

What is achievable and to what extent also depends on the respective social conditions and the historical and cultural context. Although the values themselves do not differ, the forms of peace culture and education differ in the different regions of the world. The implementation of a culture of peace, therefore, requires the consideration of general principles and norms (UNESCO, 2002; United Nations Resolution 2018).

In the Anthropocene, education for peace, sustainability and global citizenship education does not only take place in schools and educational institutions. The extensive heritage of nature and culture offers great potential for education for sustainability and peace.

Nature and World as Object

The spread of human influence across the planet is accompanied by a change in the understanding of nature and the world, which Heidegger had already noted in his essay "Die Zeit des Weltbildes" (1938). According to him a central characteristic of modernity lies in the fact that human beings encounter the world as an object and perceive the world as an image and in images. Human beings no longer see themselves as part of the physical world *(physis)*, as in antiquity, or as part of the *Creatio Dei*, as in the Middle Ages. Instead, human beings encounter nature by perceiving it as an object to be used according to their interests. In the course of the Anthropocene, this attitude towards nature and the world has intensified. Many problems which threaten the survival of humanity are the result of this basic human attitude towards nature and the world. In the Anthropocene humans see the world, of which they are a part, as an ensemble of objects that they can use unconditionally for their own interests. It is largely forgotten that humans are part of nature, the world and the planet. The suppression of this insight has led to many negative effects on the living environment of humans, animals and plants. The reduction of nature and the world to objects and images of human activity reveals a violent attitude. It leads to a very limited perception of the vitality of nature, the world and humans and their 'co-world character'. One consequence of this attitude is an increase in violent behavior. As this attitude is an essential part of the mentality of modern (Western) humanity, it is important to examine its emergence within the framework of an historical anthropology of the present. This requires an examination of human heritage as a prerequisite for present and future action.

Nature and Culture as a Common Heritage

When we speak of nature and culture as the common heritage of humanity, this heritage is seen as an important starting point for shaping the future of societies and cultures that are changing all over the planet. An examination of these conditions offers the opportunity to develop alternatives to the current situation. Young people can develop their own approaches to heritage and engage with it in a critical and productive way. In this process, they come up against 'shifting baselines', which make the preservation and further development of 'heritage' more difficult. Within the framework of UNESCO, five global programs are being developed in which the preservation and further development of the common heritage of nature and culture takes place. This creates opportunities for the appreciation of works and practices from other cultures and the development of planetary identification. With the help of these five global programs, a contribution is made to the reduction of violence, the development of sustainability and global citizenship education. This is done with the help of the World Heritage, the Intangible Cultural Heritage, the Memory of the World Program, the Geoparks and the Biosphere Reserves (Wulf, 2024).

World Heritage

The best known is the World Heritage Program, which began in 1972 and now includes 1154 World Heritage sites in 167 countries around the world. These World Heritage Sites are outstanding testimonies to past cultures and unique natural landscapes. Examples of Sites include the Great Barrier Reef (Australia), the Serengeti National Park (Tanzania), Machu Picchu (Peru) and the Acropolis (Greece).

Intangible Cultural Heritage

Whether dance, theater, music, customs, festivals or arts and crafts - intangible cultural heritage (ICH) is alive and is supported by human knowledge and skills. 730 intangible cultural heritage practices are included in the international UNESCO list. The 2003 Convention is the basis for the selection. Examples include organ building and organ music from Germany, yoga in India and rumba from Cuba (UNESCO, 2003, 2005; Wulf, 2025).

World Documentary Heritage

Since 1992, the World Documentary Heritage has contained important evidence of historical cultural turning points. More than 400 documents from 21 countries are part of the "Memory of the World" program. These testimonies include the Koran manuscript "Mushaf of Othman" from Uzbekistan, the early Korean print Jikji, the Gutenberg Bible and the colonial archives of Benin, Senegal and Tanzania.

Geoparks

Geoparks are regions with important fossil sites, caves, mines or rock formations. They offer the opportunity to better understand planet Earth and the conditions of life by investigating the traces of the past. There are currently 169 designated geoparks in 44 countries. Examples include the Bergstrasse-Odenwald Geopark, the Swabian Alb, the German-Polish Muskau Arch/Łuk Mużakowa, Mount Kunlun (Chile) and Zingong (China).

Biosphere Reserves

With its 727 biosphere reserves worldwide, UNESCO represents model regions and places of learning for sustainable development. In 131 countries, they demonstrate how sustainable development can succeed in a specific landscape and how nature conservation and the economy can be brought together. More than 275 million people worldwide live in these biosphere reserves. They include Paraná Delta (Argentina), Central Amazonia (Brazil), Lake Fana (Ethiopia) and the Rhön (Germany).

Summary and Outlook

With the help of these programs, UNESCO is trying to make clear how important a planetary awareness of the importance of a common natural and cultural heritage is for people's self-image and for the development of a global citizenship oriented towards sustainability and peace. Such an awareness is of great importance for the comprehensive transformations that lie ahead in the Anthropocene. Many of these goals have a planetary dimension and can only be addressed within a planetary framework. The aim is to continuously reduce violent actions and behavior against nature and other people and people's violence toward their own selves. People must be persuaded to participate in these transformations. Whether they will have the desired success is still an open question that constantly invites us work constructively to find answers.

References

Andreotti, V. (2014). Critical and transnational literacies in international development and global citizenship education. *Sisyphus – Journal of Education,*

2 (3), 32-50.

Andreopoulos, G. J., Claude, R. P. (Eds.). (1997). *Human rights education for the twenty-first century.* University of Pennsylvania Press.

Bajaj, M. & Hantzopoulos, M. (Eds.). (2016). *Peace education. International perspectives.* Bloomsbury.

Burns, R.J. & Aspeslagh, R. (Eds.). (1996). *Three decades of peace education around the world. An anthology.* Garland.

Calließ, J. & Lob, R. E. (Eds.). (2013). *Praxis der umwelt- und friedenserziehung.* Vol. 1-3. Schwann.

Costa, J., Alscher, P. & Thums, K. (2024). Global competences and education for sustainable development. A bibliometric analysis to situate the OECD global competences in the scientific discourse. *Journal of Educational Science.* Available at: https://doi.org/10.1007/s11618-024-01220-z.

Escobar, A. (2018). *Designs for the pluriverse. Radical interdependence, autonomy, and the making of worlds.* Duke University Press.

Fischer, D., King, J., Rieckmann, M., Barth, M., Bussing, A., Hemmer, I., & Lindau-Bank, D. (1992). Teacher education for sustainable development: A review of an emerging research field. *Journal of Teacher Education* 73(5), 509-524.

Galtung, J. (1975). *Peace: Research - education – action.* Eljers.

Galtung, J. (1981) Social cosmology and the concept of peace. *Journal of Peace Research* 18(2), 183-199.

Gil, I.C., & Wulf, C. (Eds.). (2015). *Hazardous future. Disaster, representation and the assessment of risk.* De Gruyter.

Glikson, A.Y. (2017). *The plutocene: Blueprints for a post-anthropocene greenhouse Earth (Modern Approaches in Solid Earth Sciences, 13).* Springer.

Göhlich, M., Wulf, C., & Zirfas, J. (Eds.). (2014). *Pädagogische rheorien des learnen.* Beltz.

Haavelsrud, M. (2020). *Education in developments*. Arena Publishing.

Hallinger, P. & Nguyen, V. (2020). Mapping the landscape and structure of research on education for sustainable development: A bibliometric review. *Sustainability*, 12, 1947, 1-16. Available at: doi:10.3390/su12051947.

Haraway, D. (2016). *Staying with the trouble. Making the chthuluscene. Experimental futures*. Duke University Press.

Knobloch, P. (2019). Global citizenship education und die herausforderung epistemischer dekolonialisierung. *Zeitschrift für internationale Bildungsforschung und Entwicklungspädagogik* 42(4), 12-18.

Kraus, A. & Wulf, C. (Eds.). (2022). *Palgrave handbook of embodiment and learning*. Palgrave Macmillan.

Kraus, A., Budde, J., Hietzge, M., & Wulf, C. (Eds.). (2024) *Handbuch schweigendes wissen. Erziehung, bildung, sozialisation und lernen*. 13th ed. Beltz Juventa.

Meadows, D.H. & D.L., Randers, J., & Behrens III, W. (1972). *The limits to growth*. Universe Books.

Meyer-Abich, K. (1990). *Aufstand für die natur. Von der umwelt zur mitwelt*. Hanser.

Michaels, A., & Wulf, C. (Eds.). (2011). *Images of the body in India. South Asian and European perspectives on rituals and performativity*. Routledge.

Moore, J. W., (Ed.). (2016). *Anthropocene or capitalocene? Nature, history, and the crisis of capitalism*. PM Press.

National Platform on Education for Sustainable Development (2019). Federal Ministry of Education and Research – Division "Learning Regions; Education for Sustainable Development", National Actionplan on Education for Sustainable Development. The German Contribution to the UNESCO Global Action Plan. Berlin.

Nipkow, K. E. (2007). *Der schwere weg zum frieden*. Gütersloher Verlag.

Obrillant, D., Wulf, C., Saint-Fleur, J.P., & Jeffrey, D. (Eds.). (2017). *Pour une éducation à la paix dans un monde violent.* L'Harmattan.

Oxley, L. & Morris, P. (2013). Global citizenship: A typology for distinguishing its multiple conceptions. *British Journal of Educational Studies.* 61(3), 301-325.

Page, J.S. (2008). *Peace education: Exploring ethical and philosophical foundations.* Information Age Publishing,

Resina, J.R., & Wulf, C. (Eds.). (2019). *Repetition, recurrence, returns. How cultural renewal works.* Lexington Books, The Roman & Littlefield Publishing Company.

Senghaas, D. (Ed.). (1981). *Kritische friedensforschung.* Suhrkamp.

Senghaas, D. (Ed.). (1995). *Den frieden denken. Si vis pacem, para pacem.* Suhrkamp.

Senghaas, D. (1997). *How to cope with pluralization: Studies on modern cultural conflicts. (InIIS-Arbeitspapiere, 6).* Bremen: Universität Bremen, FB 08 Sozialwissenschaften, Institut für Interkulturelle und Internationale Studien (InIIS). Available at: https://nbn-resolving.org/urn:nbn:de:0168-ssoar-67148-2.

Springer Briefs on pioneers in science and practice (2013). *Dieter Senghaas: Pioneer of Peace and Development Research.* Springer.

Suzuki, S. & Wulf, C. (Eds.). (2021). Pandemien im Anthropozän/Pandemics in the Anthropocene. *Paragrana: Internationale Zeitschrift für Historische Anthropologie.* 30/2020 1/2.

Tarozzi, M. & Torres, C. A. (2016). *Global citizenship education and the crisis of multiculturalism. Comparative perspectives.* Bloomsbury.

Trifonas, P. & Wright, B. (2013). *Critical peace education. Difficult dialogues.* Springer.

Tryggvason, Á., Öhman, J. & van Poeck, K. (2023). Pluralistic environmental and sustainability education – a scholarly review. *Environmental Education Research.* 29 (10), 1460-1485. Available at: https://doi.org/10.1080/13504622.2023.2229076

UNESCO (2000). *International Decade for a Culture of Peace and Nonviolence for the Children of the World*. UNESCO.

UNESCO (2001). *Universal Declaration on Cultural Diversity*. UNESCO.

UNESCO (2002). *Medium-Term Strategy 2002-2007 Contributing to peace and human development in an era of globalization through education, the sciences, culture and communication*. UNESCO

UNESCO (2003). *Convention for the Safeguarding of Intangible Cultural Heritage*. UNESCO.

UNESCO (2005). *Convention on the Protection and Promotion of the diversity of Cultural Expressions*. UNESCO.

UNESCO (2015a). *Rethinking Education*. UNESCO.

UNESCO (2015b). *Global Citizenship Education*. UNESCO.

UNESCO (2017). *Education for Sustainable Development Goals. Learning Objectives*. UNESCO.

United Nations (1948). *Universal Declaration of Human Rights*. United Nations.

United Nations (2011). *Declaration on Human Rights Education and Training*. United Nations.

United Nations (2015). *Sustainable Development*. United Nations.

United Nations (2018). *Resolutions adopted by the Security Council*. United Nations.

United Nations (2022). *World program for human rights education. Fourth Phase. Plan of Action*. United Nations, OSGRY & UNESCO.

Vare, P. & Scott, W. (2007). Learning for a change: Exploring the relationship between education and sustainable development. *Journal of Education for Sustainable Development*. 1(2), 191-198.

Wallenhorst, N., & Wulf, C. (Eds.). (2022). *Dictionnaire d'anthropologie prospective*. Vrin.

Wallenhorst, N. & Wulf, C. (Eds.). (2023). *Handbook of the Anthropocene*.

Springer Nature.

Wintersteiner, W. (2003). *Pädagogik des Anderen. Bausteine für eine friedenspäda-gogik in der postmoderne.* Agenda-Verlag.

Wulf, C. (1973a). *Friedenserziehung in der diskussion.* München.

Wulf, C. (1973b). *Kritische friedenserziehung.* Frankfurt.

Wulf, C. (1974). *Handbook on peace education.* International Peace Research As-sociation.

Wulf, C. (Ed.) (1995). *Education in Europe. An intercultural rask.* Münster / New York.

Wulf, C. (2006). *Anthropologie kultureller Vielfalt.* Bielefeld: transcript.

Wulf, C. (Ed.). (2010). *Der mensch und seine kultur. Hundert beiträge zur ges-chichte, gegenwart und zukunft des menschlichen lebens.* Anaconda.

Wulf, C. (2013). *Anthropology. A continental perspective.* The University of Chi-cago Press.

Wulf, C. (Ed.). (2016). *Exploring alterity in a globalized world.* Routledge.

Wulf, C. (2020). Den Menschen neu denken im Anthropozän. In Wulf, C. & Zirfas, J. (Eds.). *Den menschen neu denken. Paragrana. Internationale zeitschrift für historische anthropologie,* 29(1), 13-35.

Wulf, C. (2021a) .Digitale Transformation und künstliche intelligenz im an-thropozän. *Bildung und Erziehung,* 74, 231-248.

Wulf, C. (2021b). Global citizenship education. Bildung zu einer planetar-ischen weltgemeinschaft im anthropozän. *Vierteljahreszeitschrift für Wissen-schaftliche Pädagogik* 97, 463-480.

Wulf, C. (2021c). Anthropologie und nachhaltigkeit. Zwei visionen und ihre auswirkungen auf erziehung und bildung. In von Carlsburg, G. & Stroß, A. (Eds.). *(Un-)pädagogische visionen für das 21. Jahrhundert* (518-529). Peter Lang.

Wulf, C. (2021d). Emotion and imagination: Perspectives in educational an-thropology. *International Journal of African Studies* 1(1), 45-53.

Wulf, C. (2022a). *Human beings and their images. Imagination. Mimesis, performativity.* Bloomsbury.

Wulf, C. (2022b). *Education as human knowledge in the Anthropocene. An anthropological perspective.* Routledge.

Wulf, C. (Ed.). (2024). *Handbook on intangible cultural practices as global strategies for the future. Twenty years of the UNESCO Convention on Safeguarding Intangible Cultural Heritage.* Springer Nature.

Wulf, C. (Ed.). (2025). *Handbook on intangible cultural practices as global strategies for the future. Twenty years of the UNESCO Convention on Safeguarding Intangible Cultural Heritage.* Springer Nature. OPEN ACCESS.

Wulf, C., Althans, B., Audehm, K., & Engel, J. (2021). Learning as a performative social process: Mimesis, ritual, materiality and subjectivation. In. Kress, G., Selander, S., Saljö, R. & Wulf, C. (Eds.), *Learning as social practice. Beyond education as an individual enterprise* (pp. 103-145). Routledge.

Wulf, C. & Merkel, C. (Eds.). (2003). *Globalisierung als herausforderung der erziehung. Theorien, grundlagen, fallstudien.* Waxmann.

Wulf, C. & Brian. N. (Eds.). (2006). *Desarrollo sostenible.* Waxmann.

Part III: Peace Education in Formal Education

Chapter 12
Peace Education in the United Kingdom

Robin Richardson

Peace Education as World Studies

It is 4.45 in the afternoon of Friday 19 November 1948. The occasion is a meeting of the General Assembly of the United Nations at the Palais de Chaillot, Paris.

The voice heard at 4.45 pm on 19.10.48 is not that of a delegate but of someone claiming to represent 'we the people' of the whole world. A young American, Garry Davis, has risen to his feet in the public gallery and has started to read aloud a declaration he has prepared in advance.

He has barely uttered a single word, however, before he is pounced on by security guards and arrested, and unceremoniously dragged to the nearest exit, and roughly evicted. His speech is read instead by a friend and ally, one Robert Sarrazac, but he too is arrested and evicted. The speech composed by Davis, delivered shortly afterwards in a local restaurant, contains the following declaratory words:

> Mr President, gentlemen. I interrupt you in the name of the peoples of the world who are not represented here … We ordinary people want the peace which only a world government can give. The sovereign nation-states which you represent here are divisive, and are leading us to the very brink of war. I appeal to you to convene immediately a world

assembly which will raise a flag around which all people everywhere may gather, the flag of a single government for a single world ... (Davis, 1948)

Friends and supporters of Davis and Sarrazac who are present include the Nobel Prize winning philosopher and author Albert Camus, and the leading surrealist artist Andre Breton, and also many other French writers, thinkers and creative artists. In the UK supporters of Davis's vision, though not of his brazen interventionist methods, include members of parliament who have recently founded a body known as the All-Party Parliamentary Group for World Government. A year or two later, they will found a charity in London known as the One World Trust (One World Trust, 2014).

The One World Trust, for its part, raises sufficient funds in due course for it to be able to set up a project whose formal purpose is to:

> encourage modification of syllabuses at secondary school level to reflect a world perspective rather than a national perspective, so that an opportunity is given in the curriculum for balancing national loyalty with a measure of conscious loyalty to the human race as a whole in all its diversity. (One World Trust 2014)

The project becomes known as the World Studies Project and its full-time work starts on 1 January 1973. This recollection of an episode in Paris in 1948 evokes the climate of opinion and controversy within which the project was conceived and founded, and within which it had to make its way, or ways. It has to steer a course between, on the one hand, the views and voices of nations and national governments and, on the other, the demands, dramas and desires of 'we the people'.

Other voices whose work influenced the World Studies Project as it took shape in the 1970s included those of Johan Galtung and his fundamental concept of structural violence as a feature not only of relationships between and within countries but also within the life and cultures of education systems (Galtung, 1971, 1974; Curle, 1981); Paulo Freire and his emphasis on liberation and consciousness-raising as distinct from what he called domestication in schools and universities (Freire, 1970); the work of David Wolsk, an educational psychologist based in Canada, on the development of what he called an 'experience-centred' curriculum (Wolsk, 1975); and two bodies of work in the United States associated respectively with the Institute for World Order (Mendlovitz ,1976), whose educational programme was led by Betty Reardon, and *Man A Course of Study* led by Jerome Bruner (Bruner, 1966). The foundational aims of the latter were to impart a sense of respect for the capacities and humanity of humankind as a species, and to leave the learner with a sense of the unfinished business of human evolution.

The principal publication of the World Studies Project's was a practical handbook for classroom teachers (World Studies Project, 1976). This contained much use of collaborative activities and exercises in small groups; games and simulations; fiction and drama; photographs, cartoons and posters; stories, legends and fables; and engagement with local political issues. The title — *Learning for Change in World Society* — gently signalled that its essential concern was conceptualised as 'learning' rather than 'education'.

The principles underlying such pedagogy were later summarised with regard to peace education by Patrick Whitaker, who at the time was the headteacher of a primary school:

- In schools the emphasis should be on learning how to learn, not simply the accumulation of facts.

- Learning is a process, not a destination.

- Pupils and teachers should relate to each other as people and not behave towards each other only in roles.

- The inner intuitive, emotional and spiritual experiences of pupils should be regarded as vital contexts for their learning.

- Encouragement should be given to divergent thinking and guesswork as part of the natural process of creative learning.

- Greater attention should be given to the design of the learning environment with more attention to colour, comfort, personal space and privacy.

- Teachers should be regarded as learners too, learning alongside and from the pupils they teach (Whitaker 1988, slightly adapted).

In short, peace was not only the content of peace education but also an essential part of the pedagogy and practical methodology, namely part of the process. In individual schools and individual classrooms there had to be peace in the relations between teachers and learners, and between learners and each other — and peace not only in the sense of the absence of physical violence and disorder but also in the sense of dismantling structural and cultural violence, and the building and maintenance of a culture in which all people are co-learners.

With regard to curriculum content as distinct from matters of pedagogy, process and context, the World Studies Project focused on (a) war and peace (b) sustainable development (c) human rights and social justice, and (d) ecological balance; and on six overarching sets of concepts or 'big ideas', named as shared humanity; identity, belonging and difference; globalisation and the global village; learning from other places and times; conflict resolution and justice; and open and closed minds.

The first phase of the World Studies Project ended in 1979. Its ideas and ideals were continued and developed, however, in a project entitled World Studies 8-13, which was jointly sponsored by the One World Trust and the Centre for Peace Studies based at St Martin's College, Lancaster (Fisher & Hicks, 1985).

Peace Education as Development Education

Also, and even more significantly and effectively, world studies was developed and expanded in the field known as development education. The close connections between peace and development had been dramatically stated at a peace education conference held at the University of Keele in September 1974, organised under the auspices of the World Council for Curriculum and Instruction (WCCI), based in the United States (Haavelsrud, 1975).

One of the sessions at this conference had featured a meeting and discussion between Johan Galtung, one of the world's leading theorists about peace, and Paulo Freire, one of the world's leading theorists about the concept of development. The two of them met each other for the first time on the conference platform itself, and spontaneously embraced each other. In the course of their conversation Galtung declared "Peace is another name for development, development is another name for peace" (as cited in Haavlesrud, 1976).[1]

In the UK development education was energetically and inspirationally led by a network of, as they were known, DECs — development education centres. These were in the first instance funded by charities and NGOs concerned with overseas aid and development, but in due course they were in receipt of significant funds from central government. A professorial chair was set up at the London Institute of Education, as was an academic journal. For practitioners an association entitled TIDE ('Teachers in Development Education') was set up based in the West Midlands, and a lively magazine was started, *Elephant Times*.

The title of this magazine was derived from a session at a peace education conference that had taken place at Atlantic College in 1981 (Reid, 1984). The speaker had suggested that conversations and disputes about terminology were reminiscent of that ancient and famous Indian fable about six blind people trying and failing to understand the nature of an elephant, based solely on the extremely fragmentary knowledge which each of them had. To know the whole elephant you needed political education *and* development education *and* multicultural education *and* peace education *and* antisexist education *and* personal education. (Richardson 1984, pp. 115-116).

In due course the TIDE network adopted the term global learning to summarise its concerns and it issued a formal statement which began as follows:

> We have come to understand that global learning is as much about *how* people teach and learn as about *what* they teach and learn.
>
> Global learning is not about new subjects or new timetabled content. Instead we have worked collaboratively with teachers, and through their students, to develop projects about all aspects of the life of a school: the so-called hidden curriculum, and the subjects taught and extracurricular activities, since all these offer opportunities to develop children's and young people's skills, dispositions, knowledge and understanding for effective participation in today's interconnected and complex world. (Elephant Education Association, 2025)

Education for Racial Justice

There have been people of Caribbean and South Asian heritage in the UK for many centuries. The symbolic birthday of the present communities, however, was 22 June 1948. On that day the steamship *Empire Windrush* arrived in

London from the Caribbean with about 490 young men on it who had come in response to the UK's need for labour after the Second World War. Most saw themselves as temporary migrants, not as settlers, but in due course they were followed by wives and families, and decided to settle. There was a similar pattern a few years later with migrants from South Asia. They met widespread prejudice and discrimination from the white population, however, and it was not until the 1960s that discrimination against them began to be made unlawful.

In the course of the 1960s there was growing concern amongst parents and educators about the low levels of academic achievement of Caribbean and South Asian children. An official report published in 1969, for example, found that children of Caribbean parents were:

> ...a source of bafflement, embarrassment and despair in the education system, and they often presented problems which the average teacher was not equipped to understand, let alone to overcome. (Rose et al., 1969, p. 281)

Towards the end of the 1970s the then secretary of state for education in England set up an official committee of inquiry into the education of "children from ethnic minority groups". This was chaired by Anthony Rampton, a businessman and philanthropist, and its interim report was entitled *West Indian Children in our Schools* (Rampton, 1981). This was widely welcomed by parents and community activists, not least since it attributed principal blame for underachievement on teachers' expectations, and on routine conventions, customs and procedures in schools, not on the children themselves.

In coming to this conclusion, the committee referred in particular to racism. A racist, it said, is someone who believes that 'people of a particular race, colour or national origin are inherently inferior, so that their identity, culture, self-esteem, views and feelings are of less value than his or her own and can be disregarded or treated as less important (Rampton, 1981, p. 12).

The committee said further that very few people can be said to be entirely without prejudice of one kind or another and that in Britain, due in part at least to the influence of history, prejudices are particularly likely to be directed against non-white ethnic minority groups. A well-intentioned and apparently sympathetic person, it added, "may as a result of their education, experiences or environment, have negative, patronising or stereotyped views about ethnic minority groups which may subconsciously affect their attitudes and behaviour". Consequently African-Caribbean and South Asian heritage may be seen as 'them' or 'these people' and there is a tendency to describe even those born in the UK as 'immigrants'.

By 1981 there had been a change of national government and there was a new secretary of state for education. One of its first actions in response to Rampton's interim report was to dismiss him as chairperson and replace him with someone considered to be more reliable. The report was criticised and disregarded not only by the government but also, at official levels, by the teacher unions. There followed several years during which there was no official acknowledgement nationally that raising the achievement of minoritised students required organisational, attitudinal and cultural change in schools.

There was, however, such recognition in certain local areas, notably in parts of Greater London and the West Midlands. Also, parents and community activists continued to hold the perceptions which they had held since the 1950s. They therefore continued to set up and manage supplementary schools for their children. These continued to be an invaluable base not only for direct teaching and instruction but also for campaigning and advocacy.

A turning point came with the publication of a major document known The Stephen Lawrence Inquiry (Macpherson, 1999). Stephen Lawrence was an African-Caribbean school student who was murdered in a racist attack on the streets of south London in 1993. Sir William Macpherson was a retired judge who presided over an official government inquiry into how the murder had been investigated by the Metropolitan Police Service.

The police's failure to investigate the murder efficiently, accompanied by its failure to treat Stephen's parents and family with decency and respect, was judged by Macpherson to be due to institutional racism, which he defined in terms which subsequently became extremely well-known:

> the collective failure of an organisation to provide an appropriate and professional service to people because of their colour, culture or ethnic origin. (Macpherson, 1999, para 6.34)

The report added that institutional racism can be "seen or detected in processes, attitudes and behaviour which amount to discrimination through unwitting prejudice, ignorance, thoughtlessness and racial stereotyping." The report was about policing, not about education. It had clear implications for educational institutions, however, as for all other public bodies. It influenced the thinking behind the Race Relations Amendment Act 2000.

The Macpherson report was broadly accepted by the government and led to a range of well-funded and well-planned educational projects, both nationally and locally. One of the most high-profile of these projects was the Black Children's Achievement Programme (BCAP), which ran for several years in various forms, and with a range of nomenclature, between 2004 and 2011. It was developed from a series of national projects and programmes in the previous five years which had had the generic title *Aiming High*. The distinctive features of the programme included the following:

1. There was an explicit focus on Black children and young people, together with financial and staffing resources targeted and dedicated specifically towards them.
2. Whole-school approaches and policies were developed with the substantial involvement of senior staff — work in schools was not marginalised by being run by relatively junior staff with little or no support from senior management.
3. An external consultant was attached to each participating school to act as a professional friend, providing support, ideas and advice but also, if considered necessary, criticism and challenge.
4. There was considerable flexibility, such that each school was encouraged and able to devise plans and activities tailored to its particular situation, and to its stage of development and understanding.
5. Parents and members of the local community were consulted and involved.
6. Rigorous attention was paid to monitoring and to the analysis of data.
7. There was a focus on issues of self-esteem and self-image, and on attitudes towards learning and education.
8. Attention was paid to the nature of a culturally relevant curriculum, and to the core concepts which such a curriculum should contain.
9. School-based and school-focused professional development and train-

ing programmes were provided for all staff involved in the project. (Derived from Maylor et al., 2009, pp. 1-6)

In addition to these nine features in each individual participating school, there were regional advisers who had responsibility for providing an additional layer of support, both for schools and for local authorities. Towards the end of the programme, in the period of 2009–2011, it was increasingly integrated with national initiatives concerned with, in particular, tackling socio-economic disadvantage more generally.

It was increasingly recognised after the Stepen Lawrence report and the Race Relations Amendment Act 2000 that racism has two separable but interacting forms, concerned respectively with colour and appearance on the one hand and culture and religion on the other (Commission on the Future of Multi-Britain, 2000, pp. 57-75). Historically, the principal form of racism built around culture and religion targeted Jewish people, or else linguistic minorities, or had been built around supposed differences between Protestants and Catholics. In more recent years, however, this type of racism has particularly targeted Muslims.

The French word *islamophobie* began to be used in West Africa before the first world war. The first uses of its English equivalent in print appear in the 1970s. It began to be widely known from 1997 onwards with the publication of a landmark report by an NGO (Runnymede Trust, 1997) and it was subsequently explained as having four separate but interacting components:

Text and talk in the climate of opinion: All Muslims are perceived to be the same, regardless of nationality, social class, gender, age, political ideology and religious observance, and all as essentially and intrinsically different from non-Muslims, with no values, needs or interests in common.

Violence and abuse: Muslims are at the receiving end not only of hate crime against persons and property but also of micro-aggressions such as taunts in school playgrounds, and 'the unkindness of strangers', as the term might be, in public places.

Direct and indirect discrimination. Muslims are treated unequally in employment and the provision of services and resources, including the criminal justice system and (latterly) counter-terrorism measures, specifically the Prevent programme.

Exclusion and absence ('missing Muslims'). Muslims have very little say in political decision-making and mainstream cultural life. (Richardson, 2017)

Each of these four features can be both a cause and a consequence of each of the others. Clearly Islamophobia, as thus conceptualised, is an example of what the Stephen Lawrence report called institutional racism, and what Johan Galtung called structural violence (1969) and cultural violence (1990). It is relevant and important to note that Galtung saw cultural violence as essentially an example of *post hoc* justification or legitimation of certain behaviours, not necessarily their primary or sole cause. His explanation of the concept was:

... By 'cultural violence' we mean those aspects of culture, the symbolic sphere of our existence — exemplified by religion and ideology, language and art, empirical science and formal science (logic, mathematics) — that can be used to justify or legitimise direct or structural violence. Stars, crosses and crescents; flags, anthems and military parades; the ubiquitous portrait of the Leader; inflammatory speeches and posters, all these come to mind. (Galtung 1990, p. 291)

Inclusion, Diversity, Equalities

It was increasingly recognised in the decade following the year 2000 that procedures and policies for tackling racisms are similar to (but not precisely the same as) those which are needed to tackle sexism and misogyny; exclusion of disabled people; ageism; religious bigotry; homophobia; and transphobia. Accordingly, central government in the UK resolved to merge the three national commissions that had already been set up concerned with race, gender and disability into a single commission, and to add responsibilities to tackle discrimination and prejudice around age, religious heritage and sexual orientation, and to promote human rights.

Most NGOs concerned with equalities were unhappy with central government's decision to set up a new commission with little or no consultation about its detailed terms of reference or about its internal structure and ways of working. The government simply said the new commission should have 'due regard' for three main aims. In a debate in the House of Lords in 2010, a few weeks before the text of the Equality Act 2010 was finalised, a speaker maintained that the due-regard approach in existing race, gender and disability duties "has got us to where we are now, but the proposed duty … takes us no further." He continued:

> What we have now are volumes of equality strategies, schemes and policies, but not a great many desired and required outcomes that add up to recorded equality results. Yes, there are statements of intent, declarations, aspirations, commitments, warm words, policy reviews and mountains of reports, all in order to satisfy the requirement to have 'due regard' … but that standard of due regard is, in my view, woefully inadequate. (Ouseley, 2010)

Responding to this worry that the concept of due regard was woefully inadequate, the government spokesperson promised that the general duty of due regard would be underpinned, clarified and focused by specific duties designed to assist better performance of it, for example to develop and publish measurable objectives, to report progress, and to focus on equality outcomes when progress was evaluated. In the light of this reassurance, the proposal to amend the Bill under consideration was withdrawn. A few weeks later, the Bill received royal assent as the Equality Act 2010.

A few days after that (6 May 2010) there was a general election in the UK, followed by a new administration, a coalition of Conservatives and Liberal Democrats. Barely five weeks later (9 June 2010) the new Home Secretary and Minister for Women and Equalities wrote formally to cabinet colleagues to remind them of their legal duty to have due regard for equality in relation to disability, ethnicity and gender (Dodd, 2010).

Cabinet colleagues were also reminded that duties in relation to age, religion or belief, sexual orientation and transgender were shortly to be introduced, and warned that "there are real risks that women, ethnic minorities, disabled people and older people will be disproportionately affected" by new austerity measures under consideration.

In summer 2010, in short, the outlook seemed promising. There appeared to be a real commitment by the new government to promote a wide range of equalities and in this way to reduce structural and cultural violence in the UK's education systems. Optimism would be further enhanced when details emerged of the government's detailed proposal for ensuring that the duty of due regard was to be focused and supported by duties to collect, analyse and publish relevant data; to formulate and publish specific short-term objectives; and to report regularly on success or otherwise in progress to achieve the objectives. Further, excellent holistic guidance for schools was to be provided to school inspectors about what the concept of due regard entailed in the curriculum and organisation of schools (Ofsted, 2012) and by NGOs concerned with the inclusion of pupils with disabilities in the mainstream life of schools, not in separate 'special' schools (Booth, 2011).

In the event that optimism was premature. The claim in the House of Lords in early 2010 that "the standard of due regard is ... woefully inadequate" proved to be, alas, terribly justified. Ministers and senior civil servants concerned with education simply ignored the new legal requirements in relation to their own internal affairs, and did not make serious efforts to inform schools what they now needed to do, let alone offer helpful guidance and advice.

On the contrary, government ministers led a programme intended to develop what they called a hostile environment in relation to undocumented migrants. Further, it was announced without due deliberation and consultation that the new government did not intend to activate and commence Clause One of the Equality Act 2010, which was concerned with due regard for reducing socio-economic inequality.

Many mass-circulation newspapers and social media platforms enthusiastically supported the scrapping of the socio-economic duty, as also the construction of a hostile environment towards people considered to be outsiders. Further, they ridiculed peace education and its variations and close relatives as outlined in this paper (world studies, development education, racial justice, regard for diversity, inclusion and equalities). It was as if right-wing warnings in the 1980s about peace education (Cox & Scruton,1984) had been vindicated, and could now be safely dismissed as so much political correctness and wokery, despite objections from, amongst many other others (Gillborn, 2015; Bourne, 2021; Meynell, 2024).

From 2018 onwards the four groups to which the Home Secretary had drawn special attention in 2010 — 'women, ethnic minorities, disabled people, older people' — found themselves disproportionately confronted by a very hostile environment indeed, namely the COVID-19 pandemic. As it were, the due-regard approach to equality was shown to have indeed been, as predicted in the House of Lords debate in 2010 mentioned above, 'woefully inadequate'.

Concluding Note

At a meeting in Paris in 1948, recalled at the start of this paper, there was an intervention "for a world assembly which will raise a flag around which all people everywhere may gather, the flag of a single government for a single world". One of the people supporting this ideal, it was further recalled, was the Nobel Prize winning author and thinker Albert Camus.

In his novel *La Peste*, Camus (1947) imagined an outbreak of bubonic plague in a North African city, and implicitly suggested that the pestilence was clearly similar in its deadly effects and outcomes of, as later scholars and activists would put it, to a perfect storm of structural and cultural violence. For people struggling against the plague, and to help or heal those who were infected by it, their lives entailed *"une interminable defaite"*, an unending defeat. But, said one of them, *"ce n'est pas une raison de cesser de lutter:* — that's no reason to stop struggling.

Endnotes

1) The author´s personal note from a panel discussion among Adam Curle, Paulo Freire and Johan Galtung on the topic "What can education contribute towards peace and social justice?" Conference proceedings subsequently published in Haavelsrud (1976).

References

Booth, T. (2011). *Index for Inclusion: developing learning and participation in schools*. Centre for Studies on Inclusive Education.

Bourne, J. (2021, April 20). *Sewell: a report for neoliberal times*. Institute of Race Relations. https://irr.org.uk/article/sewell-a-report-for-neoliberal-times/.

Bruner, J. (1966). Man a course of study. In Bruner, J., *Toward a theory of instruction* (pp. 73-112). Harvard University Press.

Camus, A. (1947). *La peste*. Gallimard.

Commission on the Future of Multi-Ethnic Britain (2000). *The Future of multi-ethnic Britain*. Profile Books.

Cox, C. & Scruton, R. (1984). *Peace Studies: a critical survey*. Institute for European Defence and Strategic Studies.

Curle, A. (1981). The nature of peace. In Reid, C. (Ed.). *Issues in peace education* (pp. 8-11). United World College of the Atlantic.

Davis, G. (1948). *The Oran Declaration*. World Service Authority. https://worldservice.org/issues/febmar97/general.html#oran

Dodd, V. (2010, August 3). Budget cuts could break equality laws, Theresa May warned chancellor. The Guardian. https://www.theguardian.com/politics/2010/aug/03/budget-cuts-equality-theresa-may.

Elephant Times Association (2025). *Global learning and thinking about the curriculum*. https://indd.adobe.com/view/cd947f80-0041-4bfa-b6ab-d4c5f-444f4a6.

Fisher, S. & Hicks, D. (1985). *World Studies 8-13: A teachers handbook*. Oliver and Boyd.

Galtung, J. (1969). A structural theory of imperialism. *Journal of*

Peace Research 8(2), June 1971. At: https://journals.sagepub.com/doi/10.1177/002234337100800201

Galtung, J. (1975). Peace Education: problems and conflicts. In Haavelsrud M. (Ed.), *Education for peace: reflection and action* (pp. 80-87). IPC Science and Technology Press.

Galtung, J. (1990). Cultural violence. *Journal of Peace Research* 27(3), 291-305.

Gillborn, D. (2015). Intersectionality, critical race theory, and the primacy of racism: Race, class, gender and disability in education. *Qualitative Inquiry* 21(3).

Haavelsrud, M. (Ed.). (1976). *Education for peace: reflection and action. Proceedings of the First World Conference of the World Council for Curriculum and Instruction, University of Keele, U.K., September 1974.* IPC Science and Technology Press.

Macpherson, W. et al (1999). *The Stephen Lawrence inquiry.* The Stationery Office.

Maylor, U., Smart, S., Kuyk, K., & Ross, A. (2009). *Black children's achievement programme evaluation.* Institute for Policy Studies in Education, London Metropolitan University.

Mendlovitz, S. (1977). The program of the Institute for World Order. *Journal of International Affairs.* 31(2) 259–65.

Mcynell, L. (2024, January 4). Here's what 'woke' means and how to respond to it. *Dal News.* https://www.dal.ca/news/2024/01/04/woke-politics.html.

Ofsted (2012). *Inspecting Equalities: briefing for section 5 inspection.* Office for Standards in Education, reference 090197.

One World Trust (2014). *Our early history: The first five decades of the One World Trust.* https://www.oneworldtrust.org/early-history.

Ouseley, H. (2010). Amendment 46 to Clause 148 of The Equality Bill, page 95, line 39, House of Lords, 2 March. https://publications.parliament.uk/pa/ld200910/ldhansrd/text/100302-0012.htm.

Rampton, A. (1981). *West Indian children in our schools*. Her Majesty's Stationery Office.

Reid, C. (Ed.). (1984). *Issues in peace education*. United World College of the Atlantic.

Richardson, R. (1984). Culture, race and peace — tasks and tensions in the classroom. In Reid, C. (Ed.), *Issues in peace education* (pp. 115-123). United World College of the Atlantic.

Rose, E.J.B. et al (1969). *Colour and citizenship: a report on British race relations*. Oxford University Press.

Whitaker, P. (1988). Curriculum considerations. In D. Hicks (Ed.). *Education for peace: issues, principles and practice in the classroom* (pp. 20-35). Routledge.

World Studies Project (1976, revised and expanded 1979). *Learning for change in world society: reflections, activities, resources*. One World Trust.

Wolsk, D. (1975). *Experience-centred curriculum: exercises in perception, communication and action*. UNESCO.

Chapter 13
Islam and Peace Education: The Case of Turkey

Mustafa Kölyü

Introduction

Today, a significant portion of the world's population lives in a serious economic, security and social crisis. Although there are various reasons for this situation, it can be said that two main factors are important here. The first is conflict, wars and endless defense expenditures; the second is socio-economic injustice, which is partly related to this (Smith, 1937; Bourne, 2024; Greenburg, 2024). These two negative situations also affect many Islamic countries.

When we look at the issue from the perspective of Islamic countries, the most important breaking point between the western and the Islamic world was the 'Clash of Civilizations' thesis put forward by S. Huntington (1993) and the events of September 11, 2001. Unfortunately, since then, wars, conflicts and many humanitarian problems continue in many Islamic countries (Afghanistan, Iran-Iraq, Syria, Gaza/Palestine). In the face of all these unfavorable situations, some Muslim radical groups believe that social change can be achieved through violence, not peace, and they use Islam as a political tool to gain state sovereignty (Qutb, 1990; Mawdudi, 1980). However, the main purpose of Islam is to establish peace, not violence, in the world and in the universe. Islamic culture is rich in resources on peace, nonviolence, conflict resolution and education.

Today, more than ever, all humanity, regardless of religion, faith, nationality or socio-economic status, needs peace education. Peace education has no religion, race, nationality or country. If we live on the same globe, an event occurring anywhere in the world concerns us all. Therefore, we have to look at events not locally but on a global scale. When understood and practiced correctly, it is possible to find a lot of objective data that will lead us to believe that Islam will make a significant contribution to world peace. The way to achieve this lies in making a culture of peace rather than a culture of conflict prevail.

While many countries (USA, some European Countries, Japan) include peace education from primary school to university level (Harris, 2008; Aktaş & Safran, 2013), unfortunately, as Pakistani scholar Riffat Hassan states, it is not yet possible to talk about peace education at the academic level in Islamic countries. In a book chapter written in 1987, Hassan argues that the concept of peace education is a new concept in the world, that many Muslims today have neither heard of it nor think that peace education can or should be given to humankind, and that there is no such program in any contemporary Muslim society, neither in the academic nor in the social sphere (Hassan, 1987).

Even if Hassan's assessment is partially correct, it is impossible to completely agree with her views. For it is unacceptable that no Muslim has ever heard of peace or thought that peace education could be given to humankind. Because first of all, Islam literally means "peace and well-being". In Islamic societies, the first thing a person says when meeting another person is *"Salaam Alaikum"*, which means "peace and prosperity be upon you". On the other hand, Muslims cannot be ignorant of the many verses in the Qur'an about social and universal peace. However, Hassan is right that there is no serious academic or social work on peace education in Islamic countries in its current meaning and scope.

It is a fact that there have been some studies on peace education in the Islamic world recently (Jafri, 2022; Yılmaz, 2003; Köylü, 2003; Huda, 2010; Sevim & Diler, 2017). Two countries should be mentioned here; Pakistan and Turkey. Especially in Turkey, peace education has been supported in recent years thanks to the "Global Peace Vision" included in government programs and peace education application and research centers have been established within various universities. In symposiums and seminars organized with the support of various state institutions and these centers, course materials, concepts and educational activities on the subject are explained (Çorbacı, 2018). In addition, there are different courses in Turkey that can serve peace education, even if they are not called 'peace education'. These include Human Rights and Democracy and Citizenship courses. However, it should be noted that there is not, yet, an official course called "Peace Education" at any level of education.

This chapter will basically consist of three parts: The first part will focus on the theological foundations of peace education in Islam. In the second part, the characteristics of the Religious Culture and Moral Knowledge course (RCMK) and its program will be addressed. In the third part, peace issues in the RCMK textbooks taught in private and public schools from the fourth grade of primary school to the last grade of high school will be examined. As a method, data collection techniques (document analysis) from qualitative research methods will be used to review the theological foundations of Islam's approach to peace and the RCMK textbooks.

Theological Foundations of Peace Education in Islam

When we look at the Qur'an as a whole, we see that many issues such as the creation of man, the purpose of his creation, his function on earth, his biological and psychological characteristics, and his different structure/characteristics that distinguish him from others in terms of faith are discussed in various chapters (*suras)* in different ways. However, the most striking point among all these is the great value the Qur'an places on human beings. The Qur'an expresses the value it places on human beings in various ways. First of all, the fact that the Qur'an presents man as the caliph of the earth without any discrimination (al-Baqarah, 2:30; al-Naml, 62; al-Fatir, 39) shows that he has an important place among all living and non-living beings. According to the Qur'an, man was created in the most perfect way both physically and spiritually (Sad, 75; Mu'min, 64; Taghābun, 3). Perhaps the reason why he was created in the most beautiful form is that Allah Himself "breathed into him from His spirit". (Sajda, 9; Sad, 72) The Qur'an did not leave this superiority and beauty of the human being only on a theoretical level, but also commanded the angels to prostrate to Adam in order to show that he was superior even to the angels who worshipped him continuously (al-Baqarah, 34; al-A'raf, 11, 179; Sad, 73). Furthermore, the Qur'an declares that the entire universe, the heavens and the earth and all the living and non-living things between them, in short, everything was created for the benefit of human being (Casiye, 12-13; Mulk, 15; Abasa, 24-32; Tin, 5). Indeed, this is a source of great honor for man. In return, man has assumed the burden of 'trust'/responsibility that no living or non-living being can accept (Ahzab, 72).

Another indication of the value the Qur'an places on human beings is the strict prohibition of killing a person unjustly and the threat of eternal punishment in Hell for those who commit this act (Nisa, 92-93; Saff, 27; Isra, 33; Furqan, 68). In this context, the Qur'an considers the unjust killing of a single soul to be the killing of all human beings, and in contrast, the Qur'an states that saving a single human being is equivalent to saving all of humanity (Maide, 32).

In the light of all these verses, the following question can be asked: How can Allah, who places so much importance and value on human beings, allow warfare that may ultimately lead to the deaths of many people? This issue has been debated throughout the history of mankind, with some arguing that peace cannot be established on earth, while others claiming that this seemingly impossible situation can be possible, seeing war as a social anemia or a social disease (Ibn Khaldun, 1981; Huddleston, 1992; Freire, 1979; Köylü, 2003). However, it is a historical fact that humanity continues to wage war and defense for different reasons at full speed (Wright, 1965) and in a much more destructive manner, as in past periods. It is our wish that one day humanity will be completely free from this social and societal disease.

When it comes to peace education in Islam, many people, especially in western societies, have the idea that Islam is a religion of war and violence. Some see Islam as a 'religion of the sword', while others see it as a religion of peace (Kanakri & Shihab, 2024; Khadduri, 1955; Rahman, 1982). Unfortunately, this is one of the most abused issues in both Islamic and western societies (Qutb, 1964, 1977). But what is the real situation? Is Islam really a religion of war or a religion of peace?

In Islam, there two main sources for Muslims. These are the Qur'an and the

Sunnah (the words and actions of the Prophet Muhammad). The period of the Prophet Muhammad can be divided into two time periods. The first is the years in Mecca from his prophethood until his migration (610-622 AD), and the second period is his life in Medina from his migration to Medina until his death (622-632 AD). When we look at the Qur'anic verses chronologically, we see that in the early period of Islam (610-622 AD), the Qur'an did not allow Muslims to fight in any way. They were to refrain from war and bear the harassment and persecution of the polytheists with patience (Hijr, 94; Baqara, 109, 256; Maide, 13), but when Prophet Muhammad migrated from Mecca to Medina, war was permitted (Hajj, 39).

Classical and contemporary commentators interpret the Qur'anic verses on war in different ways. In general, the majority of classical commentators believe that Muslims should fight polytheists and the People of the Book (Christians and Jews) to the extent of their means, and if they are from the People of the Book, they are asked to either accept Islam, pay *jizya* or fight (Abu Yusuf, 1969). If they are polytheists, there is no *jizya* option for them, they will either accept Islam or they will be fought (Kaşıkırık, 2023).

However, when we look at contemporary commentators, we see that they generally argue that the Islamic understanding of war is not offensive but defensive (Shaltut, 1977; Rahman, 1982). In the modern exegetes who advocate this view, the process begins and ends with the verses in Surat al-Hajj, 39 ("Permission is granted to those against whom war is fought unjustly") and al-Baqarah, 190 ("Fight those who fight you in the way of Allah, and do not exceed the limit,") where war is permitted. In fact, these verses clearly command Muslims not to start a war unless the other side fights them. The clearest proof of this is that Allah commanded Prophet Muhammad to invite Muslims to Islam with wisdom and good counsel, and advised him to struggle with the People of the Book in the best way (Nahl, 125). Again, "There is no compulsion in religion. Right and wrong are separated" (Al-Baqarah, 256); "Allah does not forbid you to do good to those who do not fight you in religion and drive you out of their homes, and to treat them justly. For Allah loves those who are just" (Mumtehine, 8).

When we look at the above verses, we see that there are some conditions for the Qur'an to allow Muslims to wage war. These are 1) Muslims are persecuted and wronged; 2) their religious freedom is restricted; and 3) they are expelled from their homeland. In such cases, the Qur'an permits war for Muslims to protect themselves. Although there are a few verses in the Qur'an that command such war (Tawbah, 5), when we look at the Qur'an as a whole, we see that the Qur'an basically prioritizes and commands peace (Eyüpoğlu, 2022).

We understand from the above verses and the practices of the Prophet Muhammad's life that the war permitted in Islam is a war of defense; in a more universal approach, it is a war for the establishment of human rights. This is because Islam is based on peace, and the general principle of Islam is that no living creature should be harmed, let alone killed. Therefore, the purpose of the war permitted in Islam is not to force people to accept Islam, nor is it to expand the borders of a country, to obtain booty, to seize the economic values and sources of income of its leaders, or to gain superiority over others. The main purpose of war is to remove obstacles to defense and religious freedom.

What all commentators, whether classical or contemporary, agree on is that war, if it is unavoidable, must be conducted with a measure of morality and justice. Islam has always upheld the just war theory (the principle of *jus in bello*), even if it permits a limited number of wars. The doctrine of just war in Islam is based on the principles of proportionality and distinction. Accordingly, the principle of proportionality prohibits the use of inhumane weapons on the battlefield. The principle of discrimination, on the other hand, enjoins discrimination between those who actively participate in war and those who do not (Johson, 1997). In fact, this is a universal moral injunction of the Qur'an. In this regard, the Qur'an states: "Fight in the way of Allah against those who fight you. But do not go to extremes. For Allah does not love the excessive" (Al-Baqarah, 190).

As a result of both the Qur'anic injunctions on the theory of just war and the practice of the Prophet Muhammad, the first caliph, Abu Bakr (632-634 AD), laid down the following important rules on the law of war: "Do not betray. Do not commit injustice. Do not plunder property. Do not touch the parts of a dead body. Do not kill children, old people and women. Do not cut down and burn date palms. Nor cut down a fruit-bearing tree. Do not kill cattle, camels, except for food. Along the way you may come across people retreating to shrines, do not touch them, do not interfere with their worship" (Hashmi, 1996, p. 161).

As can be seen, from the earliest years of Islam, Muslims have put forward a law of war, stating that civilians, women and children who do not participate in the war should not be killed and the environment should not be harmed in any way (Kelsay, 2009; Turcan, 2016).

Another important issue in the Islamic peace tradition is tolerance and cultural diversity. While Islam emphasizes similarity, order and solidarity among Muslims, it also advocates cultural diversity and tolerance. In this context, the Qur'an attaches great importance to freedom of belief (Talbi, 1992). In one *surah*, the Qur'an states that people will choose faith of their own free will: "Your religion is for you and my religion is for me" (Kafirun, 6). In fact, the Qur'an itself states that Muslims are under no obligation to convert all people to Islam: "If your Lord had willed, all those on the earth would certainly have believed. Will you then force people to become believers?" (Yunus, 99). In another verse, "There is no compulsion in religion; the truth and falsehood are now well separated" (Al-Baqarah, 286).

After briefly discussing Islam's approach to the issues of war and peace, we can now move on to the issues related to peace education in the RCMK textbooks that are taught in private and public schools in Turkey. For this purpose, we can first look at the RCMK course and its program, and then include information on the subject in the textbooks.

Characteristics of RCMK Course and its Program

The Republic of Turkey is a secular, democratic and social state of law founded on the legacy of the Ottoman Empire. Since its foundation (October 29, 1923), one of the most debated issues in Turkey has been the question of whether or not religion courses can be included in public schools. The reason for this is that the state has adopted secularism as its ideological system, even though the vast majority of the population (98 %) is Muslim. In addition, the principle of secularism in Turkey, unlike in some Western countries, has been strictly enforced (Kuru, 2011; Başgil, 2022). Since the early years of the Republic, religious education has been practiced differently in public schools. In the early years of the Republic, religion courses were not included in the curriculum at all; after the 1950s, they were included in the curriculum as 'elective' courses, and finally, in 1982, they were included in the group of compulsory courses in the Constitution. Since then, religion courses have been taught two hours a week in all public and private schools from the fourth grade of primary school to the last grade of high school (12th grade) under the title "Religious Culture and Moral Knowledge" (RCMK).

Since the 2000s, RCMK courses have undergone significant changes both in terms of curriculum and methodology. As of the 2018-2019 academic year, the programs of all grades have changed, and the textbooks of each grade consist of five units. The topics follow a sequence from simple to difficult. Although the course content is largely Islamic, one unit each of the 11th and 12th grade textbooks is devoted to world religions.

In terms of methodology, based on a pluralistic understanding of religious education, a constructivist method is adopted with an approach that is based on the Qur'an and Sunnah, supra-sectarian and interfaith. The aim here is to present religious subjects to students without pressuring them, considering their personal knowledge and experience. Students of different religions, if present in the classroom, are treated more tolerantly and are not asked to memorize any Qur'anic verses or practice any religious commands but are encouraged to learn about religious and moral issues in a theoretical sense. If a student brings a document stating that he/she is a Christian or a Jew, he/she can be completely exempt from this course. (Tebliğler Dergisi, 1990, p. 553).

Although there is no direct peace education course in the Turkish education system, there are some elective courses such as "Human Rights and Democracy" and "Human Rights and Citizenship". However, the course that can make the most important contribution to peace education is the RCMK course. This is because it is one of the most suitable courses for peace education since it includes moral education as well as religious knowledge. RCMK courses are important in terms of including the main themes of peace education such as freedom of belief, tolerance, cooperation and sharing, universal moral values, respect for others and justice in their curriculum content.

In the following part of the chapter, information will be given briefly about the RCMK curriculum, and then an analysis will be made of the topics in the RCMK textbooks that are thought to be related to peace education.

The Basic Philosophy and Objectives of the RCMK Curriculum (Curricula 2018)

The RCMK Course (Grades 4-8) Curriculum aims to teach Islam and other religions with a descriptive approach. The religion of Islam is discussed within the framework of the basic principles set forth by the Qur'an and Sunnah. The interpretations that emerged in Islamic thought were evaluated with a scientific method and a supra-sectarian approach. Other world religions, on the other hand, have been taught with a scientific method, a religious perspective and a factual approach (p. 17). The same statements are also made in the curriculum of high school (grades 9-12).

In addition, the 9-12th grade curriculum includes the following statements in line with the basic philosophy and objectives of the program:

"(8) Recognize different forms of understanding and interpretation of Islamic thought,

(9) Recognize living world religions,

(10) Respect for different religions, beliefs and interpretations,

(11) Realize that religion is an important element in the relations between people, societies and nations" (p .8).

Vision of the RCMK Course Primary School (Grades 4-8) Curriculum

The vision of the RCMK course is expressed as follows: "To raise individuals who recognize the role of religion in making sense of life; who embrace national, spiritual and moral values; and who have gained the ability to live together with differences" (p. 18). In terms of spiritual and moral values, 10 core values are identified in the current curriculum. These are called 'root values' and include the following values: Justice, friendship, honesty, self-control, patience, respect, love, responsibility, patriotism and helpfulness. According to the curriculum, these values will come to life in the learning and teaching process by being handled both on their own, together with the sub-values they are related to, and together with other root values (p. 12). In the curricula, these values are not seen as a separate program or learning area, unit, subject, etc.; on the contrary, they are included in each of the curricula and in each of their sub-units as the ultimate goal and spirit of the whole educational process (p. 12). In the curriculum for grades 9-12, the vision for the RCMK course is expressed as the same way (p. 66).

Topics related to Peace Education in the Religious Education Textbooks

As we have already mentioned, there are no learning areas directly related to peace education in the current RCMK curriculum. However, there are some topics that indirectly contribute to peace education. Let us briefly touch on them now.

Rights, Freedoms and Religion

Rights and freedoms are one of the most important topics in the RCMK program. Although such topics are included in almost every unit, they are dealt with extensively, especially in the Farewell Sermon (the last sermon of the Prophet Muhammad in 632 AD before his death), which is included in the 4th unit of the 6th grade textbook, "The Life of the Prophet Muhammad". This sermon is not only addressed to Muslims but also to all humanity. The sermon includes the fundamental rights and freedoms expressed in the Universal Declaration of Human Rights. Today, this sermon is frequently read in Friday prayer in mosques and presented to the attention of Muslims. Here, we will only include the parts that are relevant to our subject. Prophet Muhammad said:

> "O people! Your Lord is one and your ancestor is one. You are all descendants of Adam and Adam was created from the clay. The most honorable and valuable of you in the sight of Allah is the one who knows his responsibility towards Him best and has piety. The Arab has no superiority over the non-Arab. The non-Arab has no superiority over the Arab. A white-skinned person has no superiority over a black person, and a black person has no superiority over a white-skinned person. Superiority is only through piety." (Grade 6, 100; Grade 7, 97).

The subject of "Rights, Freedoms and Religion" is also mentioned in textbooks for other grades. For example, in the 3rd unit of the 8th grade "Religion and Life"; in the 5th unit of 9th grade "Geography of Our Heart", and again in the 3rd unit of 10th grade "Religion and Life", the sanctity of human life, universal human rights and freedom of thought and expression are talked about in more detail in the light of the Qur'anic verses and hadiths.

In the activity section, students were asked to interpret the following verse, "If your Lord had willed, all those on the earth would certainly have believed. Then will you force them to believe" (Yunus, 99) in terms of freedom of belief (Grade 10, 82). The subject of *jihad* is covered most comprehensively in the 11th grade textbook. In Unit 3, "Some Concepts in the Qur'an", the following explanation is given regarding the concept of *jihad*: "*Jihad*, which means 'to exert strength and effort, to strive, to tire, to use all the means at one's disposal to accomplish a task', means 'to use all material and spiritual means to strive for the establishment of goodness and the elimination of evil'". (Grade 11, 81)

Islam and Jihad

The author states that *jihad* in Islam has a broad framework of meaning and mentions three stages of *jihad* in the Qur'an. In the first stage, *jihad* is used in the sense of fighting one's own self. According to this explanation, the *jihad* mentioned in the Qur'an is the training and enrichment of one's inner world. It is the effort to get away from the excessive desires of the soul and to approach Allah with good attitudes and behaviors. Therefore, *jihad* is primarily concerned with disciplining one's soul. To reinforce this idea, the author cites the following verse from the Qur'an: "He who wages *jihad* only for himself..." (Ankebut, 6). With regard to the first form of *jihad*, that of one's own self, examples are also given from the Prophet Muhammad. According to a hadith, the Prophet Muhammad greeted soldiers returning from a war and said, "Welcome! You have come from the small *jihad* to the great *jihad*." The Companions asked what the great *jihad* was, to which the Prophet Muhammad replied, "The great *jihad* is the *jihad* against the desires and whims of the soul." (Muslim, Imarah, 150). In another hadith, the Prophet Muhammad said, "The true *mujahid* is the one who wages *jihad* against his own ego and passions in the way of obeying Allah..." (Ahmad b. Hanbal, Müsned, 6(22),

Grade 11, 81-82).

According to the author, the second dimension of *jihad* is the explanation and defense of Islam through words and ideas. This form of *jihad* refers to explaining all the principles and fundamentals of Islam to the members of different religions with the most beautiful style, method and convincing evidence. The author cites the following verse from the Qur'an to support this view. "(My Messenger!) Call to the way of your Lord with wisdom and good counsel and strive with them in the best way ..." (Nahl, 125).

According to the author, the third form of *jihad* is material *jihad*. This is the struggle in the event of an attack on Muslims or to eliminate injustice and oppression. This form of *jihad* is not the main purpose of the religion, but a secondary form of defense that the believers are obliged to undertake in times of necessity. The author claims that all warfare in Islam is a form of defense. It is a defense against actual attacks or preparations for attacks by the other side, or against the destruction of the free environment in which people can make a judgment about Islam. In this regard, he cites the following verse: "Fight in the way of Allah those who wage war against you. And do not go to extremes. For Allah does not love the excessive." (Al-Baqarah, 190; Grade 11, 83).

In the activity section on the subject, students are asked the following question in the context of developing suggestions: "In your opinion, what can be done to emphasize the peace message of Islam? Evaluate by developing suggestions with your friends" (Grade 11, 84).

Teaching Other Religions

In Turkey, the first information about other religions in the RCMK textbooks is found in the 6th grade textbook. Unit 1 of the 6th grade textbook is titled "Belief in Prophet and Divine Book". In this unit, after explaining the belief in God and the prophet from an Islamic perspective, the subject of divine books is included. Here, after giving factual information about the holy books of Torah, Psalms and the Bible, the following statement is made: "There are four Gospels accepted by the majority of the Christian world today. These are the Gospels of Matthew, Mark, Luke and John. These Gospels contain the life of Jesus Christ, His miracles and moral issues such as love, honesty and humility. The originals of other divine books other than the Qur'an have been tampered with and these books have not survived to the present day in their original form" (Grade 6, p. 22).

More extensive information about other religions is included in the 11th and 12th grade textbooks in parallel with students' intellectual and social development. Regarding the teaching of other religions (Judaism, Christianity, Hinduism, Buddhism, Confucianism and Taoism), the following statements are made in the unit program description: "Throughout the unit, the topics are outlined in accordance with the level of the students; an objective and descriptive method is adopted in the narration; care is taken to introduce religions with their own concepts and epistemological assumptions." (Grade 9-12, p. 92).

One of the five units of the eleventh-grade textbook (Unit 5) is devoted entirely to Judaism and Christianity, while Unit 5 of the 12th grade textbook is devoted to Indian and Chinese religions. Considering that all the textbooks are five units each, it can be said that the teaching of other religions is quite extensive.

In the section on Judaism, one of the oldest religions, the history, belief principles, rituals, symbols and holy places of Judaism; the concepts of Hebrew, Israel, Jew and Jewish; the Jewish understanding of the book and prophet; and contemporary Jewish sects are covered. The topic of 'Zionism' is also addressed. Similarly, on the subject of Christianity, the history, belief principles, rituals, symbols and holy places of Christianity; the role of Paul in the institutionalization of Christianity and the formation of belief principles; the Christian understanding of revelation and prophets; and Christian groups (Catholicism, Orthodoxy and Protestantism) are covered. 'Evangelical movements' are also briefly mentioned (Grade 11, 121-150).

In Unit 5 of the 12th grade textbook, Indian and Chinese religions (Hinduism, Buddhism, Confucianism and Taoism) are covered. In relation to these religions, topics such as their history, principles of belief, rituals, symbols and sacred places are presented with visuals.

In the teaching of all religions, information is given in a descriptive and factual manner without making any comparison with Islam, without insulting or discriminating against other religions and their followers, and by referring to their own sources as much as possible. The main aim here is for students to have knowledge not only about Islam but also about other world religions. As we have already mentioned at the beginning, the teaching of the RCMK program is handled with a constructivist approach with a supra-sectarian and interreligious perspective. Thus, it is aimed to prevent students from harboring any prejudices against members of other religions.

Conclusion

War and conflict are an ongoing phenomenon throughout human history. Even though people have lived in peace from time to time, this state of peace has not been sustained and nations have fought each other for different reasons. However, today's modern world has reached a very different point in this regard. Today's wars and conflicts are incomparably more destructive than the wars and conflicts of the past. All countries, whether developed or undeveloped, allocate a significant portion of their national revenues to military expenditures for defense purposes, even if they are not actively fighting each other. These endless military expenditures cause societies to regress economically and socially in many areas.

This is where peace education plays a very important role. Although some scholars argue that world peace cannot be achieved, it is possible to build a more peaceful world with a total world-wide education. Slavery was once like this, but there is no longer the institution of actual/physical slavery in the world as there was in the Middle Ages. Through peace education, people can at least be made aware of what is going on in the world, what wars and conflicts cost, and that the money spent in this field could be spent on meeting much more basic human needs. The way to do this is through education.

Many disciplines can contribute to peace education, but religions can make the most important contribution. Although there is a worldwide decline in interest in religion and a trend towards deism, atheism and new religious movements, it is still possible to believe that religious beliefs have an important role to play in this regard. Monika K. Hellwig writes on the subject:

> No academic discipline offers a better or more fitting context for social justice and peace education than religious studies. Almost all imagin-

able courses in this field must include some observation of and reflection on lifestyle, values, social choices and decisions, relationships among groups, attitudes to wealth and power, and responses to suffering and violence, because all of these are dependent upon faith and beliefs. (Hellwig, 1986, p. 15)

Similarly, R. S. Johnson states:

Religion offers no short-term solution, no palliative or panacea for the world's ills likely to find an immediate application. But unquestionably religion offers to men the only final solution of the world's problems, but it is a long-term solution. (Johnson, 1970, p. 349)

Of course, not only religious beliefs but also their teaching is of utmost importance here. If we, as citizens of the global village, are passengers on the same ship, we should all try to contribute to world peace as much as we can.

References

Abu Yusuf, Y.I.A. (1969). *Kitab al-kharaj*, vol. 3. Leiden E.J. Brill. trans A. Vben Shemesh.

Hanbel, A.B. (1989). *Müsned*. Cilt: 1-6, Beyrut: Daru'l Fikr.Aktaş, Ö, Safran, M. (2013). "Evrensel bir değer olarak barış eğitiminin tarihçesi," *TSA*, s. 2, 131-150.

Başgil, F. (2022). *Din ve laiklik*. Kubbealtı yayınları.

Bourne, R. (2024). *The war on prices*. Cato Institute.

Buhari, (1991). *El-camiu's-sahih*. Çağrı Yayınları.

Çamyar, S, & Yaldız, H. (2023). *Din kültürü ve ahlak bilgisi 7. Sınıf*. Ankara, Gün yayıncılık.

Çorbacı, O. K. (2018). Din kültürü ve ahlak bilgisi müfredatında barış eğitiminin yeri. *2. Uluslararası Din Eğitimi Kongresi*, 244-251.

Doğan, R. (2023). *Din kültürü ve ahlak bilgisi 11. Sınıf*. Ankara, Gezegen yayıncılık.

Dönmez, K., Özyurt, S. & Taş , U.(2023). *Din kültürü ve ahlak bilgisi 6. Sınıf ders kitabı*. Ankara, Devlet kitapları.

Dâvûd, E. (1992). *Es-sünen*. İstanbul: Çağrı Yayınları.

Eyüpoğlu, O. (2022), *Kur'an'da itaat kavramının sosyal psikolojik tahlili*, 2. Baskı, İstanbul: Üniversite Yayınları.

Freire, P. (1970). *Pedagogy of the oppressed*. Herder and Herder.

Greenburg, J. & Healy, M. (2024). The U. S. Military's sexual assault crisis as a cost of war. *Boston Institute, Brown University*, 1-42.

Harris, I. (2008). *Encyclopedia of peace education*. Teachers College, Columbia University. http://www.tc.edu/centers/epe/

Hashmi, S.H. (1998). Islamic ethics in international society. In Mapel, D. & Nardin, T. (Eds.), *International society: diverse ethical perspectives* (pp. 215-217). Princeton University Press.

Hellwig, M. (1986). Religious studies. In Johnson, D. (Ed,), *Justice and peace education: models for college and university faculty* (pp. 15-26). Edwin Mellen Press.

Huda, Q. (2010). Peace education in Muslim societies and Islamic institutions. *Die Friedens-Warte*, *85*(3), 69–84. https://www.jstor.org/stable/26524858

Huddleston, J. (1992). *Achieving peace by the year 2000: a twelve point proposal*. Oneworld.

Huntington, S. (1993). The clash of civilizations. *Foreing Affairs*, Summer 72, 22-49.

Khaldun, I. (1981). *The mukaddimah: an introduction to history*. Princeton University Press.

Jafri, Q. A. (2022). Islam and peace education in Pakistan. In Hermansen, M., Aslan, E., & Erşan Akkılıç, E. (Eds.), *Peace education and religion: perspective, pedagogy, policies* (pp. 489-503). Springer VS.

Johnson, R. C. (1970). The Influence of religious teaching as a factor in maintaning peace. In: Wallace, V. (Ed.), *Paths to peace: a study of war its causes and prevention* (pp. 336-349). Melbourne University Press.

Johnson, T. J. (1997). *The holy war idea in western and Islamic tradition*. The Pennsylvania University Press.

Kanakri, M. & Shihab, M. (2024). Is Islam religion of peace or violence and terror? A socio-cultural study. *International journal for arabic linguistics and literature studies*, 6/5, 82-91. DOI: https://doi.org/10.31559/JALLS2024.6.2.3

Kelsay, J. (2009). *Arguing the just war in Islam*. Harvard University.

Khadduri, M. (1955). *War and peace in the law of Islam*. Johns Hopkins University Press.

Konaklı, N., Çınar, H. & Emiroğlu, S. (2023). *Din kültürü ve ahlak bilgisi 10. Sınıf*. Ankara, Devlet kitapları.

Köylü, M. (2003). *Islam and its quest for peace: jihad, justice and education*. The Council for Research in Values and Philosophy.

Kuru, A.T. (2011). *Pasif ve dışlayıcı laiklik: ABD, Fransa ve Türkiye*. İstanbul Bilgi Üniversitesi Yayınları.

Mawdudi, A. (1980). *Jihad in Islam*. International Islamic Federation of Students Organizations.

MEB (1990). Tebliğler Dergisi.

MEB (2018). *Din kültürü ve ahlak bilgisi dersi öğretim programı (ilkokul 4 ve ortaokul 5, 6, 7 ve 8. Sınıflar*. Ankara.

MEB (2018). *Din kültürü ve ahlak bilgisi dersi öğretim programı (ilkokul 9, 10, 11 ve 12 sınıflar*. Ankara.

Milli Eğitim Bakanlığı (2018). *Din kültürü ve ahlak bilgisi dersi (9-12. Sınıflar) Öğretim Programı*. Ankara.

Müslim (1992). *El-camiu's-sahih*. Çağrı Yayınları.

Nesai (1992). *Es-sünen*. Çağrı Yayınları.

Özdemir, F, & Çamyar, S. (2023). *Din kültürü ve ahlak bilgisi 8. Sınıf*. Ankara, Anka yayınları.

Qutb, S. (1964). *Islam: the misunderstood religion*. Al-Assriyya Printing Press.

Qutb, S. (1977). *Islam and universal peace*. American Trust.

Rahman, F. (1982). *Islam and modernity: transformation of an intellectual tradition*. University of Chicago Press.

Riffat, H. (1987). Peace education: a Muslim perspective. In Gordon, H. & Grob, L. (Eds.), *Education for peace: testimonies from world religions* (pp. 90-108). Orbis Books.

Sevim, F, Z & Diler, R. (2017). Din kültürü ve ahlak bilgisi (DKAB) derslerinde barış eğitiminin yeri. *Uluslararası sosyal araştırmalar dergisi*, C, 10, S. 51, 833-846.

Shaltut, M. (1977). Koran and fighting. *Jihad in medieval and modern times* (pp. 26-86). transl. and annotated by Rudolph Peters. Leiden: E. J. Brill.

Smith, A. (1937). *The wealth of nations*. Modern Library.

Talbi, M. (1992). Religious liberty: a Muslim perspective. In Swidler, L. (Ed.), *Muslims in dialogue: the evolution of dialogue* (pp. 465-482). Edwin Mellen Press.

Taşın, Z. (2023). *Din kültürü ve ahlak bilgisi 12. Sınıf*. Ankara, Özgün matbaacılık.

Taşkıran, A. et al (2023). *Din kültürü ve ahlak bilgisi 9. Sınıf*. Ankara, Korza yayınları.

Turcan, T. (2016). İslâm hukukunun klasik ve çağdaş doktrinlerinde cihad. İslâm kaynaklarında, geleneğinde ve günümüzde *cihat*, İstanbul: Kuramer yayınları, 281-308.

Wright, Q. (1965). *A study of war*. 2nd ed. University of Chicago Press.

Yılmaz, H. (2003), *Din eğitimi ve sosyal barış*. İnsan yayınları.

Chapter 14
Towards Peace Education Beyond Division on the Shared Korean Peninsula

Soon-Won Kang and Soonjung Kwon

Introduction

The Korean peninsula was divided in 1945, the year when Japan's colonial rule over the region came to an end with the conclusion of World War II. Ever since, the two Koreas—one representing communism (North/Democratic People's Republic of Korea/DPRK) and the other capitalism (South/Republic of Korea/ROK)—have been in a state of antagonistic confrontation. The catastrophic results of Korea's national division are revealed clearly in the stories of divided Korean families. We begin this chapter with Soon-Won Kang's family story:

My father in-law was born in 1919 in Kaesong, North Korea. When Japan's colonial rule ended, he feared for his life, thinking that—as the second son of a rich landowner—he might be killed by his family's tenants in the name of 'liberation for the people of communist North Korea'. His family decided he should leave home for a while and find safety in the South. He left before the Korean War began, and up to the time of his death in 2003, never returned to his homeland, despite the fact that he had left behind a wife and two children in North Korea. Living in South Korea, he initially tried to return home, but due to the breakdown of inter-Korean mutual exchanges, he could not do so. Ten years later, in 1957, he decided to marry my mother-in-law, and went on to have four children with her.

After marrying my husband in 1982, I watched my father-in-law weep every New Year's Day and on his father's and mother's birthdays, because he blamed himself for being a bad son, an unfaithful husband, and a bad father to his children in North Korea. However, he never told us the names of his family members in North Korea. In 2000, President Kim Dae-jung opened the door to North Korea and initiated the Sunshine Policy. Due to the June 15 Joint Statement, a limited number of separated family members in both Koreas were able to contact their remaining families in order to plan a reunion. My husband and I asked my father-in-law to apply to meet his family in North Korea. It was then that I saw my mother-in-law's face turn pale.

The miserable situation of divided families has been a critical issue worrying the people of the Korean peninsula, in light of the future possibility of reunification. Notwithstanding the complicated family disturbances within the humanitarian dimension, however, it is urgent that the matter be solved, to allow reunions for elderly Koreans of separated families before their death (Kim, 2013).

Regarding the division of the Korean peninsula, both politics and culture in South Korea are dominated by the notion that peace between North and South must be conditioned on national prosperity and military power. The South Korean Constitution nominally guarantees freedom of speech, press, petition and assembly for its nationals, but behavior or speech in favor of the North Korean regime can be punished by the National Security Law. That law was applied specifically under the military dictatorships of the 1960s-1980s, when those who took a critical stance against the regime were imprisoned, and some political prisoners were put to death without trial. This law has led to a dominant perspective in South Korea that exacerbates the culture of violence in schools (Kwon et al, 2018) and hampers unification education as well (Chung & Kim, 2007).

Thus, the basic orientation of unification education (UE) in South Korea is anti-communist and aims at implementing peacebuilding on the Korean peninsula by force so as to eventually defeat North Korean communism. (Han, 2016) 'Unification' does not mean 'peaceful coexistence on the Korean peninsula'. As a coordinator of the Peace Education Committee of Christian Academy in 1995-1997, Soon-Won Kang initiated an examination of the polemical side of unification and peaceful coexistence in the Korean peninsula, and—

together with schoolteachers, social activists and peace education academics—proposed redirecting UE towards the concept of universal peace education. They developed the project "Coexistence in the Classroom," which was the beginning of the peace education movement in schools in South Korea. (Kang, 2000) In the 1990s several peace education NGOs set up and developed peace education from below, different from the UE-style peace education from above (Kang & Oh, 2020).

Cho et al. (2019) classified the developing trends of peace education in the ROK into three stages: 1980s-early 1990s, introduction of peace education from abroad by mostly Christian groups; late 1990s-early 2000s, exploration and contextualizing of peace education by peace educators and NGO activists; and since the late 2000s, differentiation of peace education into various peace-related themes according to local and global contexts. According to this classification, Soon-Won Kang is one of the peace educators who led critical peace education theory and practice from the 1990s, with her background of engagement in the student movement and night school movement as a college student in the late 1970s-1980s. Soonjung Kwon, one of the 3rd stage scholars, endeavored—while studying at Hanshin University—to apply Minjung theology (a grassroots theology that resisted the dictatorships in South Korea) to peace and human rights concepts developed at University for Peace in the 2000s. Since then, Kang and Kwon have participated in the interconnecting of peace education with human rights education, multicultural education, democratic (global) citizenship education, ESD, etc. According to their framework, UE that advocates building peace by force should be transformed into peace education promoting peaceful means for the sake of peaceful coexistence on the Korean peninsula.

Such a transformative perspective holds that peace education is a reasonable alternative to UE, for peacebuilding beyond division in the Korean peninsula, and for building consensus in civil society (Lee et al., 2018; Moon & Lee, 2019). In cultivating competency toward a comprehensive peace, peace education analyzes the social, political and economic drivers of the national division, advocates a balance of power as opposed to the 'dominance' emphasis of UE, and supports the resilience of Korean identity in a shared peninsula. (Reardon, 1988; Kang, 2019; Carter, 2015)

The Social Impact of Division on South Korea

In the Korean peninsula, the term 'unification' was first used on a national level by the Unified Silla dynasty (AD.676-935). From then, through the Goryeo and Joseon periods, a unified dynasty persisted in the Korean peninsula up until the colonial period in the 20th century. Korea, the sole unified nation of the Korean peninsula, was then relegated to the condition of a Japanese colony. Koreans' independence movement against the Japanese colonial rule was politically rooted in anti-Japanese nationalism, so the potential division of the peninsula into South and North after liberation in 1945 was deemed unacceptable. Under the divided condition, 'national unification' was the common political slogan of those on both the left and the right. Nevertheless, the division of the peninsula became unavoidable as a result of agreements made in discussions at Yalta, Potsdam, and Moscow trilateral meetings, as it was deemed necessary to stop the Cold War order that was spreading. (Hong, 2012)

Shortly after the division, the ROK proclaimed itself the sole legitimate government of the Korean peninsula and began referring to the North as an unlawful occupant of the northern part of the land. Armed with the nationalist view that "one nation, two countries" was untenable, the DPRK instigated the Korean War in 1950, resulting in three years of unrelenting destruction. In July 1953, without ROK participation, the United States, China and the DPRK signed an armistice agreement, and that ceasefire still remains in effect. Galtung (1985) characterized the division of the Korean peninsula as a convenience for the superpowers, not a deliberate choice made by the people of Korea, arguing that it was a clear expression of occidental racism, as the Koreans' sentiments, philosophies, and history were ignored.

After liberation, the dominant political forces in the ROK promoted a national unification ideology centered on the notion that "Korea was, and must remain, one nation." This played on the chauvinistic nationalism of the people within the domestic political realm, rather than developing a clear understanding of the matter within a global context (Lee, 2024). In particular, since the responsibility for the devastating Korean War was shifted unilaterally onto 'the other side', South and North Korea perceived each other as enemies and banned all exchanges. The authoritarian governments that took power after the Korean War, in the South and the North respectively, maintained a state of hostility, using the division as a rationale for sustaining their regimes (Im, 2015).

The ROK and the DPRK joined the United Nations concurrently as individual sovereign nation-states in 1991. However, Article 3 of the Constitution of the ROK states that "the territory of the Republic of Korea shall be the entire peninsula and its annexed islands," covering the area north of the military demarcation line, which is not currently under the jurisdiction of the ROK. Moreover, Article 4 states, "The Republic of Korea aims for a peaceful unification and implements policies for peaceful unification based on a free democratic order." On the other hand, the Constitution of the DPRK proposes a socialist unification, for which Article 9 states, "The DPRK will achieve a complete socialist victory by strengthening the people's regime in the northern part of the peninsula and by achieving the goals of the three revolutions of ideology, technology, and culture, and will struggle for the realization of national reunification on the principles of independence, peaceful unification and national unity." The divergent directions of unification sought by the two Koreas are based largely on political calculations and associated ideological considerations.

We may compare Korea and Vietnam, both of which were divided after colonization in the wake of the Cold War order that emerged after the Second World War. Both countries suffered tragic destruction and damage on the scale of a world war. On the Korean peninsula, the two Koreas are technically still at war, as testified by the stationing of North Korean soldiers in the Demilitarized Zone, standing against the United Nations forces. In Vietnam, however, the intense fifteen-year long Vietnam War, which devastated the Vietnamese people and land, concluded in a socialist victory and defeat for the US. Contrary to fact, Koreans have been taught in school that Vietnam collapsed and that South Korea must strengthen its military build-up and grow its economy in order to overwhelm the North in every respect, in preparation for potential attack (Yoon, 2015).

In 1989, a contrasting perspective emerged when ROK society became fascinated with the German model of economic unification by absorption, despite the fact that the East/West division of Germany had stemmed from different reasons (Lee & Song, 2014). With this perspective, there began to develop the belief that the Korean peninsula would be peacefully reunified through the economic incorporation of the collapsed DPRK and its subsequent absorption by the ROK. However, the anticipated economic reunification by absorption has not materialized over the last three decades, and instead of collapsing, the DPRK has armed itself with nuclear weapons, threatening peace and security on the Korean peninsula and beyond (Moon, 2015). This raises the question of "why" the Korean peninsula was divided and has remained shrouded in uncertainty and instability in both local and global contexts.

Critics of Unification Education: Can Non-violent Peacebuilding through Education be Taught in Schools Without Questioning 'Why?'

Kang (2018) has classified the development stages of UE as shown in Table 1. Considering the historical context of inter-Korean relations and UE development, peace and unification beyond division is complex and multi-layered. UE has swung from ideological indoctrination based on anti-communism and national security under the conservative regimes, to history and values education based on peaceful coexistence and regional solidarity under progressive governments.

Table 1 - Stages of unification education (Kang, 2018)

Stage and period		Focal points of UE	Key political matters
1	1945 - 1971	Aggressive, warlike, anti-communist UE	Korean War (1950-53) "Declaration on August 15 peaceful unification agenda" (1970)
2	1972 - 1987	UE for national security, maintaining the regime	July 4 Inter-Korean Declaration (1972) October Revitalizing Reforms (1972)

3	1988 - 2007	UE as a process for peacebuilding in the Korean peninsula	Global shift from Cold War to neoliberalism Inter-Korean Basic Agreement and Denuclearization (1991) June 15 Joint Summit Declaration (2000) Inter-Korean Summit (2000, 2007)
4	2008 - 2017	Weakening period of UE/ national security focus	Denuclearization & Open 3000 May 24 measures (2010)
5	2017 -	Peace-oriented UE	Inter-Korean Summit (2018) US-DPRK Summits (2019)

Since liberation, the ROK has had a series of regimes with diverse ideological deviations, from right-wing conservative governments to so-called left-wing progressive governments. As shown in Table 1, under the conservative regimes, "unification" was emphasized as the unifying ideology, while the term "peace" rather than unification was preferred during the periods of progressive governments. UE has been continuously administered through the framework of the national curriculum. In the third national curriculum of the ROK, adopted in 1963, UE was established as an independent subject referred to as "Anti-communism Education":

> Whatever the fight, in order to win the fight, you have to be superior to your opponent. That is more so in the fight against the Communist Party. We must cultivate superior ability to compete with the North Korean puppets in all aspects: politics, economy, military, culture, and social life…If we develop political, economic, and military capabilities that can overwhelm the Communist Party, with national unity, we will be able to do what we want, either by means of a general election, or by the uprising of the North Korean compatriots, or by whatever other means, and

we will defeat the Communist Party and achieve the democratic unification we desire. (Ministry of Education, 1970)

Since 1980, however, UE has often been covered as a subject area in ethics and
moral education or social studies curricula. During the 3rd stage, in particular,
UE seemed to take a peace-oriented approach based on universal principles,
following the practical dialogue and exchange programs that characterized
inter-Korean communications (Park, 2017). Today, however, after the failure
of the inter-Korean summit and the DPRK-US summit in 2019, and now with
global war in Ukraine and Israel, neither inter-Korean communication nor
positive UE is officially allowed. A new Cold War is settling over the Korean
peninsula, and so new policy adjustments are required (Hwang, 2024). It is a
critical turning point of UE for peaceful coexistence in the shared peninsula.

From 1999 to the present, the formal definition of UE has been the description
given in Article 2 of the "Unification Education Support Act." "Unification
education" refers to education designed to cultivate the values and attitudes
necessary for achieving unification based on belief in a free democracy, a
sense of national community and a firm view of national security. According
to this definition, UE presupposes political neutrality, and prohibits misuse
for personal or partisan purposes. Moreover, according to Article 11 of the
Act (Accusation), "When a person has provided unification education, the
content of which constitutes infringement of the basic order of free democracy, the Minister of Unification shall request the correction thereof or lodge an
accusation against him or her with an investigation agency, etc." Therefore,
it is dangerous for an educator to deal with controversial matters, even for
a culture of peace in the Korean peninsula. Consequently, critical questions
are excluded from discussions in classrooms, and teachers customarily avoid
generating controversial debate on such topics (Kang, 2013). This is opposite
from the UNESCO direction of peace education (Kwon & Kang, 2013; Kang,
2021).

In this context, UE without critical awareness is not peace education in the
universal sense but rather moral education for indoctrination. Therefore, with
respect to the reconceptualization of UE as peace education aimed at resolving conflicts which originate from division, it should be focused on overcoming the antagonistic image of the North Korean regime and increasing con-

tact with the DPRK to build mutually beneficial relationships as neighboring sovereign nation-states (Kim et al., 2013). It should also be geared towards helping South Koreans build the mindset needed to overcome the division and pursue co-existence with the North in the 'shared peninsula' (Kwon et al., 2014). This further requires the establishment of strong reciprocal relations with neighboring countries in order to build a peaceful North East Asian community, extending beyond peacebuilding on the Korean peninsula (Kim, 1997; Kang et al., 2021). Thus, as a Korean representative, Soon-Won Kang initiated Korea-Japan peace education dialogue for Asian solidarity in 1998-2005 (Kang, 2005).

According to the Asian Human Rights Charter (1998), the people of Asia have suffered great hardships and tragedies due to wars and civil conflicts which have caused many deaths, mutilation of bodies, external or internal displacement of persons, break up of families, and in general the denial of any prospects of a civilized or peaceful existence. Thus, most Asian countries are still divided by ethnic and social barriers. In this Asian context, unity and solidarity should be reviewed beyond the narrow spectrum of nationalistic unification, demolishing all kinds of dividing barriers. Peace education in this region should be preceded by critical reflections through a postcolonial lens on whether the division and South-North imparity in the Asian context, which appear to be set in stone in the realm of international politics, were indeed inevitable. In relation to the division of Korea, this should be a crucial theme for education toward peace and active citizenship in Northeast Asia, which is one of the world's leading zones of economic activity, but is also a powder keg of political flashpoints (Kang & Kwon, 2011; Moon, 2018).

From Unification Education to Peace Education Beyond Division in the Shared Peninsula

UE was inaugurated in the idiosyncratic situation of the Korean peninsula. Since 1999, UE in schools has been administered at the discretion of teachers at each school, in accordance with the "Unification Education Support Act". It is worth noting that the Moon Jae-in government undertook measures in 2018 to modify the "Unification Education Guidelines," transforming the UE curriculum to focus on what is needed to build peace and prosperity in the

Korean peninsula. The new "UE guidelines" include 15 key future directions with perspectives and directions that can emerge from understanding the matters of unification, North Korea, inter-Korean relations and the future image of a unified Korea. The guidelines also clarify that the roots of division and matters of unification must be understood from a global perspective as well as from the vantage point of national identity; it is only through international cooperation that peace can be achieved globally, going beyond the unification of Korea and the North East Asian region. Despite limitations on the practice of education for a culture of peace within the current legal boundaries, it seems quite similar to our format of our peace-oriented approach to UE. Unfortunately, such initiatives were not very successful, even under the previous Moon government (Lee, 2024).

The peace education framework of transferable action posits a move from a culture of violent division into one of nonviolent coexistence—for instance, with the Korean peninsula transforming from operation as two imaginary enemies, into neighboring countries coexisting in the shared peninsula. UNESCO APCEIU has carried out two kinds of sub-regional projects: one on peace education in Korea in view of UNESCO peace education (Kang & Oh, 2020), and the other on peace education in Northeast Asia (Kang et al., 2021). Soon-Won Kang coordinated both research projects, and proposed a comprehensive peace education model based on mutual respect for all North East Asian countries. This was a peace education model for coexistence based on the UNESCO values for peace: how to resolve the negative images formed out of stereotypes, prejudice, hostility and discrimination, which result from segregation and separation in a divided society, through programs for authentic mutual understanding. When inter-Korean exchanges and cooperation evolve qualitatively, based on mutual trust, the two 'UN member country' Koreas can develop common peace education within the UNESCO universal framework of peace education on the shared peninsula.

Firstly, peace education on the Korean peninsula should employ a universal framework. As described by Kofi Annan (former UN Secretary-General), humanity's pursuit of future peace must shift from a perspective of military-based national security to one of comprehensive human security (United Nations Development Program, 1994). The new model should recognize that the peace process is a continuous one, and that it needs to be monitored by every citizen with a checklist developed from the perspective of human security in both North and South on the Korean peninsula, and shared by both Korean states. It should help eliminate divisive social barriers, thereby contributing to a proactive peacebuilding process from military security to human security demands of both South and North. Here, we should promote a more multidisciplinary approach in considering how to change the current UE model—that is, in a way that incorporates both the specificity of the Korean peninsula division and the universality of peace education for conflict resolution on a shared peninsula.

Secondly, from the de(post)-colonial perspective, a creative peace education curriculum is needed to form a social consensus on how to dismantle and reconstruct dividing barriers such as the Korean demilitarized zone (DMZ), the peace walls in Northern Ireland, and the green line in Cyprus. This can be sublimated into division aesthetics (Kang, 2017). Since the division is related to international and global contexts, peace education should include education for international understanding, done in cooperation with neighboring countries, and transcending chauvinism based on national homogeneity. Thus, we endeavor to develop a peace education network among people from divided societies, with the goal of building solidarity for peace and security from below, viewing reality through 'de-colonized lenses' and utilizing comparative analysis (McGlyne et al, 2013). Consequently, the peace education curriculum should include interpretation of the Korean division from a postcolonial perspective: one that allows students to critically review the ideologies of colonialism and imperialism, and to understand that they function as two sides of the same coin (Abdi et al., 2015; Kang, 2019).

Finally, UE based on this peace education format should adopt a framework for intergenerational, lifelong learning in the twenty-first century, a framework which will nurture the communal capacity to live together. Unification is at the heart of intergenerational debate related to the divided families, whose suffering is the core historical trauma of divided society (Zembylas, 2015). From the viewpoint of humanitarianism, we strive to restore justice for the mutual healing of victims and perpetrators of violence, in the divided society as well as in people's daily lives. Supporting humanitarian exchanges and cooperation for the victims of division and linking them to the school curriculum is an important key to achieving peace-sensitive education

(Kwon, 2015; Kwon & Kang, 2021). In this light, UE should help all generations create transferable actions to overcome warfare and encourage peaceful co-existence.

Conclusion

Peace education is transcendent, which offers it a place in all educational sectors—homes, childcare centers, schools, community centers, NGOs and service-providing centers—taking the learner from birth to grave through all forms of learning. When gathering diverse voices in peacebuilding processes to overcome division, it is imperative to set clear guidelines, so as not to isolate any of the victims of division or political circumstances. There is an acute need to listen to the victims of the violent division system in peace education.

Accordingly, more than importing westernized pedagogy into the local situation, we are developing our own peace pedagogy derived from our own political, social and cultural context. Peace pedagogy that encompasses a peaceful understanding of oneself at the global level focuses on questioning why in some regions wars have not taken place, internally or internationally; where wars are most concentrated and who is most affected; what efforts should be made to prevent wars; and how to resolve cultural conflicts and create a new culture of peace. Such pedagogy not only fosters peaceful values and attitudes, but also builds critical awareness about the structure of peace, which can be used to help nurture resilient, active citizens who can deal with controversial issues.

A divided society is a violent society in which two different systems are hostile to each other for reasons that may be political, ideological, economic, social, cultural or religious. Whatever the cause of division, the violent society resulting from division creates more hatred and conflicting belief systems. Because the Korean peninsula continues to be one of the world's most notorious, potentially explosive places, with two hostile ideologies remaining in conflict, we are endeavoring to collaborate in the development of more comprehensive peace education. In order to create a sustainable, co-existent community in the Korean peninsula, UE should be re-conceptualized into peace education with transferable action from the culture of violent division to the culture of peaceful symbiosis on the shared peninsula.

References

Abdi, A. A., Shultz, L. & Pillay, T., (Eds.). (2015). *Decolonizing global citizenship education*. Sense Publishers.

Asian Human Rights Commission (1998). *Asian Human Rights Charter: A Peoples' Charter*. https://www.google.com/search?source=hp&ei=irw-%20 XrL0BMuiwAPyrZN4&q=asia+human+rights+charters&oq=Asia+hu-man+rights+chater&gs.

Carter, C. C. (2015). *Social education for peace. foundations, curriculum, and instruction for visionary learning*. Palgrave Macmillan.

Cho, J., Kim, E., Moon, A. & Yoon, B. (2019). *Reality and issues in peace education*. KINU research book. Institute of Unification.

Chung, H. & Kim, J. (2007). *Understanding unification education towards peace*. Unification Education Center of the Ministry of Unification. (in Korean).

Galtung, J. (1985). The Cold War, peace and development: A comparison between the Atlantic and Pacific theatres. *Current Research on Peace and Violence*. 8(3/4), 101-111.

Han, M. (Ed.). (2016). *Education for making unification*. Education and Science Company. (in Korean)

Hong, S. (2012). *Hysteria of division*. Changbi. (in Korean)

Hwang, J. (2024). The new security challenges on the Korean Peninsula. *Global Asia*. 19(1), 90-94.

Im, D. (2015). *Peace maker: The 25 years of Inter-Korean affairs in North Korean nuclear weapons*. Changbi. (in Korean)

Kang, S. (2000). *Education for peace and human rights*. Hanwool. (in Korean)

Kang, S. (Ed.). (2005). *Peace Education from below in Korea and Japan*. Community. (in Korean)

Kang, S. (2013). How peace education has tried to overcome the division of Korea into two nations: Practicing peace-reunification education in schools.

In Harris, I. (Ed.), *Peace education from the grassroots* (pp. 151-171). Information Age Press.

Kang, S. (2017). *A journey to the Integrated School Movement in Northern Ireland: Beyond division.* Hanwool Academy. (in Korean)

Kang, S. (2018). The limit and possibilities of unification education as peace education beyond division in South Korea. *Asia Journal of Peacebuilding, 6*(1), 133-156.

Kang, S. (2019). Tuning of unification education toward peace beyond division in the Korean Peninsula and education for international understanding. *Journal of Education for International Understanding, 14*(1), 1-33. (in Korean)

Kang, S. (2021). Localization of the UNESCO peace education into the Korean Peninsula. *Korean Journal of Sociology of Education, 31*(4), 1-32. (in Korean)

Kang, S., & Kwon, S. (2011). Reunification education viewed from peace education of Northeast Asia. *Korean Journal of Comparative Education, 21*(3), 95-126.

Kang, S., Liu, C., Matsui, K., Monkhooroi, Park, B., Huang, M., & Dugarsuren, O. (2021). *Peace education in Northeast Asia: A situational analysis.* RR-RND-2021-040. APCEIU.

Kang, S. & Oh, D. (2020). *A critical review of peace education in Korea: In view of UNESCO peace education.* APCEIU Research Report. Seoul: APCEIU. (in Korean)

Kim, D. (1997). *Kim Dae-jung's three-stage approach to Korean reunification: South-North confederal stage.* The Center for Multiethnic and Transnational Studies, University of Southern California.

Kim, B., Kim, M., Park, H., Lee, S. & Cho, E. (2013). *Division and life without peace on Korean Peninsula.* Acanet. (in Korean)

Kim, J. (2013). *Modern novels and trauma of division.* Somyung. (in Korean)

Kwon, S. (2015). *Violence in South Korean schools and its relevance to peace education.* Unpublished doctoral thesis. UK: University of Birmingham.

Kwon, J., Choi, K., Cho, M. & Park, S. (2014). *A Study of peace-unification education strategy for peace and co-prosperity.* SNU Policy Research Paper of the Committee for Unification Preparation. (in Korean)

Kwon, S. & Kang, H. (2021). Exploring the educational possibility of preventing school violence by cultural transition: Reflecting upon school violence through the objectification phenomenon and revisiting the value of peace, human right, and relationship. *Journal of Korean Education, 48*(4), 63-84.

Kwon, S. & Kang, S. (2013). A study on the UNESCO guideline of education for peace and international understanding. *Journal of Education for International Understanding, 8* (2), 51-82.

Kwon, S. & Kang, S. (2015). A study of complementarity on peace education and human rights education. *Journal of Education for International Understanding, 10*(1), 31-62. (in Korean)

Kwon, S., Walke, D. & Kristjansson, K. (2018). Shining light into dark shadows of violence and learned helplessness: Peace education in South Korean schools. *Journal of Peace Education, 15*(1), 24-47.

Lee, D. & Song, Y. (2014). *A study of action plan for peace-unification education.* UNESCO Policy Research. KNCU. (in Korean)

Lee, K., Lee, S., Chung, Y., Chung, J., & Choi, K. (2018). *How to do peace education on Korean Peninsula: Stories of peace education with friends.* Salimter (in Korean)

Lee, W. (2024). *Social stories in the South and the North.* Seonin. (in Korean)

McGlynn, C., Zembylas, M. & Bekerman, Z. (Eds.). (2013). *Integrated education in conflicted societies.* Palgrave Macmillan.

Ministry of Education. (1970). *The Road to unification by defeating communism. For Middle Schools.* National Textbook Publisher. (in Korean)

Moon, A. & Lee, D. (2019). *Peace Education for enduring, transversing and undoing division system.* Peacemomo. (in Korean)

Moon, C. (2015). *The 70 years of division: Asking a road to 15 June (Sunshine pol-*

icy) again. Yonsei University Press.

Moon, C. (2018). Barriers to community-building in Northeast Asia: Geopolitics, nationalism and domestic politics. In Hayes, P. & Moon, C. (Eds.), *The future of East Asia* (pp. 267-307). Springer Singapore.

Park, C. (2017). The Status and challenges of unification education in Republic of Korea after 2016. *Moral and Ethics Education, 54*, 265-288. (in Korean)

Reardon, B. (1988). *Comprehensive peace education: Educating for global responsibility.* Teachers College Press. Translated into Korean by S. Kang (2021).

United Nations Development Program. (1994). *Human development report.* Oxford University Press.

Yoon, C. (2015). *Vietnam War and the social history of Korea.* Blue History. (in Korean)

Zembylas, M. (2015). *Emotion and traumatic conflict.* Oxford University Press.

Part IV: Informal and Non-formal Education, Communication and Cognitive Justice Initiatives

Chapter 15
Durable Peace Education towards Sustainable Communities

Mazin B. Qumsiyeh, Kamal Jarrar and Mona Sader

Introduction

In conflict situations especially those involving colonialism and anti-colonial struggle, there is invariably a different perception of what 'peace' means. In fact, many wars are fought in the name of bringing peace. To colonial settlers, peace is essentially pacification and quiet (Ishida, 1969). To oppressed people, peace means restitution of justice, removal of oppressive regimes, and living on our lands (Kerr & Mobekk, 2007). Yet, concepts like peace and justice are themselves contentious and lend to different interpretations (Fogarty, 1992; Smith, 1993). People generally accept the notion that some sort of social justice is a prerequisite to calmness and peace. What substantiates this is that wars and civil strife is inexorably linked to some grievance. In many cases, we noted end of conflict or its relative stabilization when some grievances are addressed and resolved, what we might call a compromise as in the case of Aceh (Aspinall, 2008) and Northern Ireland (Hancock, 2008). Peace studies are now in vogue globally to digest information and produce road maps that could end conflicts 'peacefully'.

In the case of the protracted conflict in Palestine that pitted the Zionist movement plans to create a Jewish state in Palestine against the indigenous people of Palestine, the 'peace' negotiations failed for many researched reasons

(Qumsiyeh, 2004; Salinas & Rabia, 2009; Moughrabi et al., 1991). Both sides in this conflict credit 'education' or lack of 'peace education' with a lack of progress towards peace (Peled-Elhanan, 2013; Bar-Tal, 2011; Aweiss, 2011). The concept of peace education though is contentious in defying clear definitions as the concept of peace is becoming prevalent at least in the global north and mainstreamed in international interventions in conflict zones (Stetter, 2021; Harris, 2009; Bajaj & Hantzopoulos, 2016).

Some authors seem to focus on peace education as a form of acceptance of different narratives in conflict situations or even ideas of normalizations under occupation (Bekerman & Zembylas, 2011). The Berghof Foundation uses an expansive definition of peace education which we like: "the process of acquiring the values and knowledge and developing the attitudes, skills and behavior to live in harmony with oneself, with others, and with the natural environment." (Jäger, 2015) Taking this definition we would like to address the tools and mechanisms that bring this kind of education to achieve that kind of sustainability. The goal of this study is to offer a reflective analysis of peace education's role in fostering sustainable communities using Palestine as a model.

Relationship of Peace Education to Sustainability

There are many limitations to the traditional 'peace education' models but after the second world war and now it is proliferating at university campuses with departments and courses that focus on 'conflict resolution'. Limitations include emphases on 'nation states' as actors, ignorance of cultural and societal differences, lack of understanding of socio-political forces that shape people's lives and 'orientalism' (Zembylas, Charalambous & Charalambous, 2016; Said, 1978; Han & Moquino, 2018). Peace education aimed at ensuring safety and quiet for only one side of a conflict cannot achieve sustainable long-term results. In examining the voluminous literature on peace education, one finds some literature referring to sustainability. This belongs in two categories: 1) Sustainability of peace education, and 2) sustainability of societies (including harmony with the environment) and their actual ability to live in peace based on justice (the positive peace not merely lack of conflict). We believe peace education cannot be separated from sustainability of communities (especially indigenous communities). In fact, it is worth having an integrative and holistic approach to peace building that takes all issues into consideration (Yanniris, 2021; Brantmeier, 2013). Peace education that is holistic helps fulfil conditions of harmony between people (based on justice) and harmony with nature (see also the UN Sustainable Development Goals for guidelines). The latter goals can be advanced via systematic education which leads to harmony and 'sustainability' (Goi, 2024; Jershey & Kopnina, 2020). We may define a wider scope of peace education as education that leads to reducing and eliminating all violence (to fellow human beings and to nature) and results in a way of life of sustainability where humans and nature both prosper without fear.

Education for Peace: Decolonization Versus Normalization

Colonizers seek to control not only the land and military but also aim to reshape the mindset of the oppressed people (Qumsiyeh & Amro, 2019). There are a myriad of programs that purport to teach peace but are essentially normalization programs that delay peace. Examples of these are "Seeds of Peace" (Biton & Salomon, 2006) and environmental peacebuilding efforts that actually harm the environment (Ide & Tubi, 2020). As both colonizers and oppressed people in Palestine can be considered mentally colonized, (Khalifah & Qumsiyeh, 2021) peace education can focus on either 1) normalization where the narrative accepts the colonizers or 2) liberating minds leading to justice and sustainability. The former 'normalization' can lead to authoritarian tendencies and entrenching colonization (El Kurd, 2023). The impact of peace education in this context is nuanced. While many use language of peace, the outcome over eight decades of these programs in Palestine is the illusion of a 'peace process' that actually gives time to the colonizers to further expand their colonization activities (Qumsiyeh, 2009). Such normalizations without addressing root causes of conflict are also by nature short lived and ready to 'burst' at any crisis such as the era that started on 7 October 2023 (Mens, 2024). Peaceful education is seen in this process as getting together, altering curricula towards acceptance of the other. However, applying peace while injustice persists is impossible, especially in ongoing, long-standing conflicts that socially, psychologically, and politically affect people. Teachers and learners are often directly impacted by the colonizers' actions, such as land confiscation, home demolitions, assassinations, killings, or, at best, being restricted from moving freely in their own land.

A second challenge to peace education done without the context of space and time is the idea that you can educate oppressed people about peace while the boot of the occupier is on their neck. Many schools in Palestine are subjected to attacks by Israelis or settlers. How can children be taught to live in peace while their lived experience is anything but peaceful and their basic rights (even to education) are being violated? Younger generations instinctively understand that justice is the foundation of peace, and this can be achieved by advancing justice-oriented education.

Peace education that is lasting and important for human well-being needs to be reinforced and developed over long periods of time (Salomon 2013). In fact peace education is part and parcel of struggling for justice and hence is a form of resistance (Qumsiyeh, 2010; Qumsiyeh, 2015).

There is a tendency to foster peace education that connects people globally to become "better global citizens" (Reardon, 1988). However, the latter may have different interpretations which may differ from the interpretation of Reardon and say Fanon and is better reshaped as a decolonized global citizenship (Fanon & Sartre, 2003). Peace education disconnected from de-colonization only prolongs colonization (Andreotti, 2011; Hajir & Kester, 2020). In Palestine, we may adapt the Gandhian method of education that leads to self-reliance away from Western models of subservience (Dey, 2021).

Implementing Peace Education for Sustainability in Context of Palestine

Everyone claims they want peace. As noted above though the form of peace and goals of peace education can be dramatically different depending on the position of the person within the conflict (from a privileged colonizer or from the oppressed community). In examining aspects of promotion of peace in Israeli schools for example, we notice emphases on peace as a form of 'getting along' between the remaining Palestinians (having become a minority in the Israeli system after the ethnic cleansing) and the majority colonizers. Hence, even the lofty goals of 'coexistence' are not met in practice (Vered,

2015). Implementing peace education in Palestine involves navigating a myriad of challenges, from political sensitivities to cultural differences. Programs must be tailored to respect and incorporate local values and traditions while promoting the key prerequisite to peace which is decolonization. These programs can be conducted across various educational settings. Schools can incorporate liberating peace education into their curricula through subjects like civic education, history, and social studies. Teachers are trained to use interactive pedagogies that encourage critical thinking and dialogue among students (Tandon, 2014). It can focus on giving hope for examples based on the only positive possible outcome of colonial/anti-colonial struggle: the one democratic state for all its citizens. Using example of actions that led to dismantling apartheid while accepting whites in South Africa can be a model (though this is still a work in progress).

Non-governmental organizations and community groups play a crucial role in delivering peace education through workshops, art programs, and sports activities. These settings provide flexible and responsive environments where participants can explore peace concepts in a more personal and impactful manner. Initiatives such as peace camps and leadership training sessions help bridge the gap between formal and informal education, providing structured yet adaptable learning opportunities that are crucial in volatile environments.

How We Became Involved in Peace Education *Sensu Lato*

Beyond the concept of education for 'conflict transformation' (Ozerdem, Thiessen & Qassoum, 2016), we believe peace education that focuses solely on human to human interactions is not sustainable (Esteves, 2020). Peace should focus also on human-nature interactions. That is a sustainable peace important for sustainable human and natural communities. It is indeed a major part of the reason a group of volunteers founded the Palestine Institute for Biodiversity and Sustainability at Bethlehem University (PIBS-BU, http:// palestinenature.org). Our vision was to help foster sustainable human and natural communities. This is an imperative thing for us Palestinians as for all human beings but our situation of colonization and oppression that is one of the longest that lasted in the 20th and 21st century, made this work more urgent. The first author taught courses and published research in conflict resolution, peace, justice, and sustainability. All our team is motivated by these lofty principles of justice and sustainability. The institute evolved with four main lines of work: research, education, conservation, and community service. But in all these our motto and guiding principle remains RESPECT (for ourselves, for other human beings, for nature) and we consider this critical for peace making at all these levels (Qumsiyeh, 2023). To achieve education for children for example, we structured programs that ensure children learn to enjoy each other's company, to relate to adults and other children with mutual respect, and through practice respect animals and plants and soil and all elements of earth around them. This generates first an inner peace (we have thus become an oasis of peace and hope) but it also generates outer peace in components of our earth (Brantmeier, 2007). Peace education structured along these principles can help in decolonization in a colonial context, equality in case of discriminatory societies (like civil rights), and environmental justice where there is injustice. Not only does this kind of peace education lead to sustainability of the communities and harmony with nature but also can itself become sustainable and integrated education within a flourishing society.

References

Andreotti, V. (2011). (Towards) decoloniality and diversality in global citizenship education. *Globalisation, Societies and Education.* 9(3-4), 381-297.

Aspinall, E. & Centre for Humanitarian Dialogue (2008). *Peace without justice? The Helsinki Peace Process in Aceh.* Geneva: HD Centre for Humanitarian Dialogue.

Aweiss, S. (2011). Culture of peace and education in Palestine: the Palestinian context. In: E. Mathews, (Ed.), *The Israel-Palestine conflict: parallel discourses* (pp. 224-246). Routledge.

Bajaj, M. & Hantzopoulos, M. (2016) Introduction: Theory, research, and praxis of peace education. In: Bajaj, M. & Hantzopoulos, M. (Eds.), *Peace education: International perspectives* (pp 1-16). Bloomsbury Publishing.

Bar-Tal, D. (2011). Challenges for constructing peace culture and peace education. In Mathews, E. (Ed.), *The Israel-Palestine conflict: parallel discourses* (pp. 209-223). Routledge.

Bekerman, Z. & Zymbylas, M. (2011). Teaching contextual narratives: Identity, memory and reconciliation in peace education and beyond. Cambridge University Press.

Biton, Y. & Salomon, G. (2006). Peace in the eyes of Israeli and Palestinian youths: Effects of collective narratives and peace education program. *Journal of Peace Research.* 43(2), 167-180.

Brantmeier, E. (2007). Connecting inner and outer peace: Buddhist meditation integrated with peace education. *In Factis Pax: Journal of Peace Education and Social Justice.* 1(2), 120-157.

Brantmeier, E. (2013). Toward a critical peace education for sustainability. *Journal of Peace Education.* 10(3), 242-258.

Dey, S. (2021). The relevance of Gandhi's correlating principles of education in peace education. *Journal of Peace Education.* 18(3), 326-341.

El Kurd, D. (2023). The paradox of peace: The impact of normalization with Israel on the Arab World. *Global Studies Quarterly* .3(3), 1-11.

Esteves, A.M. (2020). Peace education for the Anthropocene? The contribution of regenerative ecology and the ecovillages movement. *Journal of Peace Education.* 17(1), 26-47.

Fanon, F. & Sartre, J.P. (2003). *The wretched of the Earth, 1961.* UK, Grove Press.

Fogarty, B.E. (1992). Peace and justice: Towards a culture-neutral view. *Peace & Change.* 17(3), 267-285.

Goi, C.L. (2024). *Teaching and learning for a sustainable future: Innovative strategies and best practices.* IGI Global.

Hajir, B. & Kester, K. (2020). Towards a decolonial praxis in critical peace education: Postcolonial insights and pedagogic possibilities. *Studies in Philosophy and Education.* 39(5), 515-532.

Han, D. & Moquino, T. (2018). Moving beyond peace education to social justice education. *AMI/USA Journal*. 8-10.

Hancock, L.E. (2008). The Northern Irish peace process: from top to bottom. *International Studies Review*. 10(2), 203-238.

Harris, I. (2009). Peace education: Definitions, approaches, and future directions" *Peace Literature and Art* I. 77-96.

Ide, T. & Tubi, A. (2020). Education and environmental peacebuilding: Insights from three projects in Israel and Palestine. *Annals of the American Association of Geographers*. 111(1), 1-17.

Ishida, T. (1969). Beyond the traditional concepts of peace in different cultures. *Journal of Peace Research*. 6(2), 133-145.

Jäger, U. (2015). *Peace education and conflict transformation*. Berghof Foundation Operations GmbH: https://berghof-foundation.org/.

Kerr, R. & Mobekk, E. (2007). *Peace and justice*. Polity Press.

Khalifah, C. & Qumsiyeh, M.B. (2024). How the colonizers are also mentally colonized: An Israeli-Palestinian example. *Palestine-Israel journal* (in press).

Mens, J. (2024). The 'Age of Normalizations' – An Overdue Post-Mortem. *Israel Journal of Foreign Affairs*. 18(1), 23-34.

Moughrabai, F., Zureik, E., Hassassian, M. & Haidar, A. (1991). Palestinians on the peace process. *Journal of Palestine Studies*. 21(1), 36-53.

Ozerdem, A., Thiessen, Ch., & Qassoum, M. (Eds.). (2016). *Conflict transformation and the Palestinians: The dynamic of peace and justice under occupation*. Routledge.

Peled-Elhanan, N. (2013). *Palestine in Israeli school books: Ideology and propaganda in education*. Bloomsbury Publishing.

Qumsiyeh, M. B. (2004). *Sharing the Land of Canaan: Human Rights and the Israeli Palestinian conflict*. Pluto Press.

Qumsiyeh, M.B. (2009). True peace based on human rights versus the endless 'peace process' based on lies. In Salinas, M. & Abu Rabia, H. (Eds.) *In resolving the Israeli-Palestinian conflict: Perspectives on the peace process* (pp. 131-138). Cambria Press.

Qumsiyeh, M.B. (2010). *Popular resistance in Palestine: A history of hope and empowerment*. Pluto Press.

Qumsiyeh, M.B. (2015). Evolution of armed to unarmed resistance in Palestine. In: Dudouet, V. (Ed.), *Nonviolent resistance and conflict transformation* (pp. 77-99). Routledge.

Qumsiyeh, M.B. (2023). Developing institutions that serve national goals: Case study of the Palestine Institute for Biodiversity and Sustainability. *Al-Quds Journal for Natural Sciences, 1*(3), 6-10.

Qumsiyeh, M.B. & Amro, A. (2019). Liberation from mental colonization: A case study of the indigenous people of Palestine. In Kleibl, T., Lutz, R., Noyoo, N. & Bunk, B. (Eds.), *The Routledge handbook of postcolonial social work* (pp. 185-196).

Reardon, B. (1988). *Comprehensive peace education for global responsibility*. Teachers College Press.

Said, E. (1978). *Orientalism*. Pantheon Books.

Salinas, M.F. & Rabia, H.A. (Eds.). (2009). *Resolving the Israeli-Palestinian conflict: Perspectives on the peace process*. Cambria Press.

Salomon, G. (2013). Lessons from research on peace education in Israel/Palestine. *Asian Journal of Peacebuilding, 1*(1), 1-15.

Smith, R.C. (1993). Concepts of peace. *Political Science, 45*(2), 198-208.

Stetter, S. (2021). *What fosters and what hampers sustainable peace education*. Report for the Project "Mapping Sources of Mutual Distrust in Palestinian-Israeli Relations." Ramallah: The Palestinian Center for Policy and Survey Research.

Yannis, C. (2021). Education for sustainability, peace and global citizenship: An integrative approach. *Education Sciences, 11*(8), 430.

Zembylas, M. & Charalambous, C. & P. (2016). *Peace education in a conflict-affected society*. Cambridge University Press.

Chapter 16
CEPPA Foundation's Journey: Towards the practice of Peace Education in Costa Rica

Celina Garcia and Jose Daniel Romero

Introduction

How do we stop the circle of violence in a country of entrenched customs that does not allow children to move in the classroom? How do we transform the cognitive dissonance of education if the teaching staff has been educated under that same system? How do we form communities of peace, as Martin Luther King dreamed, if we still teach the glories of wars and overlook the world's efforts for peace? How do we teach a whole country that there are also cooperative games in which everyone can have fun?

In the last 35 years, we have learned experiences in Peace Education in Costa Rica, thanks to the Creative Response to Conflict (CRC) program and the Alternative to Violence Program.

Above all, can we inspire, in traditional education, the joy and enthusiasm of teaching and learning? Can we achieve the joy that inspires Waldorf, Montessori and other educational philosophies that encourage the child's freedom to move and sing? As Ken Robinson pleaded for this for years and now that joy is practiced in many schools in England.

It has been 35 years and, thanks to the training CEPPA (Center for Peace

Studies) Foundation received in the Creative Response to Conflict (CRC) program, we have made progress because we never imagined that the opposition from the Ministry of Education could be so strong. In the first few years of CRC's acceptance, our teacher training was very well received, but then, it became practically impossible. Even so, we have continued in a few schools and the results are proven through positive evaluations of children, educators and parents.

Through practice, we have learned that it is essential not only to train the teachers, but also the student population and the parental figures.

New trends in education in many countries point to the advantages of full student participation in the classroom and extracurricular work. Throughout our experience, with the principles of the Creative Response to Conflict Program, i.e., self-esteem, cooperation, and communication, we have learned that these ideals are the basis for combating bullying, teasing, fights, and other forms of violence in education.

CRC takes us even further because it has values that should precede the teaching of human rights. It includes internalizing the feelings of children and adolescents, creative conflict management, and games in which everyone wins because everyone has fun at the same time.

What interest can a child have in reciting human rights if her teacher puts tape over her mouth or sticks tacks in her skirt to keep her from getting out of her chair? What confidence can a child have in peace education if we exercise power in an aggressive, abusive, and unjust manner, using traditional authoritarian structures?

Peace education is the presence of peace in the classroom, under 'my' responsibility, practicing it every day until it becomes 'my' way of being, inside and outside the classroom. Only when we reconcile with ourselves and develop our own self-love, can we project peace to others. This is why educators who have participated in our training feel that the philosophy and practice of peace is "the gateway that opens the good and positive in a person," helping to cultivate and mature the spirit of self within the students.

We have made our way in peace education and, through the following document, we intend to share the context, values and pedagogical practices that have been fundamental in our work.

1. Beginnings of the CEPPA Foundation

The Alternative to Violence Program (AVP) was developed by a group of Quaker educators for educational purposes in the United States in 1985. The name they used, Creative Response to Conflict, CRC, is aimed specifically toward schools and colleges. Thanks to a grant, its director, Priscilla Prutzman, was invited to come to Costa Rica for two consecutive years to train the first group of educators. This is how peace education was introduced in Costa Rica for the first time. Celina and Priscilla also took the program to other Latin American countries. It is indisputable that the themes of self-esteem, self-worth, cooperation, and creative conflict management, are basic principles of the CRC. We believe that children, educators, and parents should be included in the process of transforming a culture of violence into a culture of peace.

At the same time, the CEPPA Foundation introduced the PAV, an alternative to violence program, aimed particularly at prisoners. Martha Moss, a Quaker friend of CEPPA who had been a facilitator of the program in the United States, trained the CEPPA team in 1990.

The first training took place at La Reforma Penitentiary Center, with officials from different departments, who said, "We were able to see, with our own eyes, that the PAV really works because it can transform violence into cooperation, companionship and solidarity".

Celina Garcia, Director of CEPPA Foundation, has focused her efforts on the care of people deprived of liberty, children and adolescents in schools and professionals whose work is focused on the transformation of violence, which has led her to find her purpose in life.

From March 1990 to July 2024, the lives of more than 25,000 people have been changed through the training provided by CEPPA Foundation, with participants from Costa Rica, El Salvador, Peru, Brazil, Colombia, Mexico, Nicaragua, the United States, Germany, Switzerland, Egypt, Myanmar, Thailand, and the Middle East.

All of the people who have received the programs have experienced positive changes in their lives, giving them the strength and skills to turn their violence into peace.

Celina García, through the CEPPA Foundation, has produced 53 publications. Among them are: The translation and adaptation of the *Manual of the Alternative to Violence Program* (1994), which adapted the original English version to Spanish from several perspectives. It acknowledges the Latin American socio-cultural reality to whom the translation is addressed, in addition to including cooperative games, songs, and exercises of our culture, taken from the different countries CEPPA has visited. The translation of the *Creative Response to Conflict Manual* (1992) which offers a true methodology of peace practice in schools; *The Arias Peace Plan* (1988); *Education for Peace* (1989); *A Constitution for the Federation of the Earth* (1991); *Workplace Communication and Stress Management* (1997); *Building a United Family* (2000); *Stop the Abuse!* (2007); *Disarming the Mind of Man* (2007); *Self-improvement and Intelligent Management* (2008); *Comprehensive Program for Social Reinsertion* (2014); *Human Rights for Those Sentenced for Violence* (2016); *Tenga Paz* (2019); *Peace Studies as an Academic Discipline; Thematic Guide on Commercial Sexual Exploitation; Workshops for the Prevention of Commercial Sexual Exploitation of Children; Strategic and Project Planning; Work Motivation and Stress Management; Youth Leadership; How to Build Synergy for Children and Adolescents; Restitution as an Option to Prison; Education for Peace in Times of Crisis; The Daily Practice of Ethics in Public Administration in a Culture of Peace.*

2. Methodology and Pedagogical Practices used at CEPPA Foundation

People are not born hostile, aggressive or violent, nor are they born apathetic. They learn to respond to the inevitable problems and conflicts of life through their experiences within their environment.

Children have the right to grow up in schools that help them develop, not only intellectually, but also socially and morally. The educator must reaffirm the child's many and varied abilities, and the attitudes and skills that can help them live and work cooperatively with others, first in the classroom and at home, and later as citizens.

It is urgent for educators to provide concrete answers to society's concerns about violence and destructive attitudes that are the source of so many traumas in society.

It is for this reason that the CEPPA Foundation in recent years has developed projects based on the values of CRC, to help educators and students manage conflict in a positive way, transforming their environment into a community that is based on mutual respect. All of CEPPA's programs and projects, though they target different populations and have different forms and perspectives, have the following values and pedagogical practices.

2.1. Participatory and Experiential Methodology

Unlike lectures that are unidirectional, the success of our programs depends on the active and constant participation of the group, including their valuable contributions. Our methodology is participatory and experiential. Under this methodology, the process and practice of life without violence begins, and guarantees significant short-term changes.

Let us remember that peace is subject to human experience, which means that war and violence are not considered to be 'genetically integrated' into human nature, but are seen as aspects of a culture that can be varied. As the famous UNESCO motto says, "War and violence are in the minds of men" (Reardon, 1984), which emphasizes that the peace educator should not teach what to think, but how to think, since the former implies an opinion or a policy which cannot be defined as a responsible and ethical way of teaching, while how to think includes the needs, problems and ways to achieve peace.

The most important and valuable thing is practice, as a famous Chinese proverb says, "I hear and forget, I see and remember, I practice and understand". This proverb expresses what many treatises cannot do. It lets us know that warnings or calls for attention are easily forgotten. This methodology is based on a continuous cycle.

- Experience, by means of an exercise or practice.

- Expression of feelings. What does this exercise mean to me, my students and my children?

- Reflection. What is happening in my social environment, what does our society say about this environment?

- Life application. How can I use it in my personal, work and family life?

- Regarding participation, it should be clarified that it should be voluntary. If the sessions are positive and fun, it is very likely that everyone will want to participate. However, some may not want to do so. This calls us to remain flexible and welcome the participant in case he/she changes his/her mind and wants to participate with the group.

Regarding this practice, K.M.G. (inmate of the Jorge Arturo Montero Institutional Care Center), mentions in his evaluation, "I like that they ask everyone to give their opinion, it fosters fellowship and we learn from each other" (Personal communication, January 11, 2024).

2.2. The Game as a Learning Strategy

Play is one of the most effective therapies in the psycho-pedagogical conception that allows children and adults to overcome different difficulties and learn at the same time.

Cooperative ('joyful') games are an integral part of the learning processes at the CEPPA Foundation. Apart from the displacement in the physical space, it energizes the participants and allows for pauses between long exercises. As mentioned by Parraga, Vera, Mendoza, et al (2021), "The teaching-learning process is of quality when people develop by playing in a comfortable environment, when playing there is a feeling of confidence and freedom, one learns unconsciously dispersing traumas and developing skills".

From this practice, the group can have very deep discussions after simple activities such as the elephant/palm tree and squirrels. After a 'joyful' one, facilitators ask why that was included in a conflict resolution workshop and sometimes, the answers lead to a deep discussion that can be directed to the session's theme.

In the PAV manuals, where it says "respect or trust the process," the group expands on the text and comments on what is learned in different ways. This includes, of course, that play is also "to have fun and manage everyday stress."

Undoubtedly the merrymakers are a hallmark of CEPPA Foundation's programs. As Ana Aguirre mentioned in her evaluation of the transformative mediation module, "What I enjoyed most were the dynamics of the merrymakers, especially the squirrels and the cooperative machine, as they help a lot to take away stress" (Personal communication, October 24, 2013).

For his part, J.D.D. (deprived of liberty at the Jorge Arturo Montero Institutional Care Center), reflects on the practice of joyful people. "I firmly believe that one cannot deal with the most serious things in this world unless one understands the most amusing ones. Laughter is the sunbeam of the soul and without sun nothing can grow or live" (Personal communication, July 2010).

2.3. Practice of Working in a Circle

Another important practice in our workshop is to work in a circle as a symbol of equality. The circle is the physical expression of equal participation, while revealing a balance of power.

Sitting in a circle replaces the idea that the educator is the sole possessor of knowledge and truth.

2.4. Flexibility of Agendas

Plans and agendas are a means to an end, not an end in themselves. The changes that are made must fulfill a need of the group, much more than the original plan.

When you change a plan, you meet the needs of the group and show them that the session was designed especially for its members, and that it is not a model to which the group must conform. When students participate in the decisions, you develop much more of a sense of group and, therefore, a more supportive environment. Changes can be made at the beginning, or as the session develops.

A very real concern of some educators interested in Peace Education is the belief that they must choose between complying with curricular programs or doing peace education practices. However, through the practices of the Creative Response to Conflict Program, we have demonstrated that the two are interestingly and effectively intertwined.

The only limitation to combining the peace education techniques practiced from the CRC with the curriculum is imagination, because there are many and varied ways to do it and, with practice, the students themselves come up with very original ideas.

Many of the self-affirmation or self-esteem exercises we practice in our workshops (Interview with a Friend, My Own Album, etc.) are directly related to the development of literacy skills.

With each of these practices, we intend to create an atmosphere of cooperation and self-esteem in education, stimulating academic interest in a very significant way. This is revealed, almost immediately, in a very active participation in the learning process.

With these practices we consider that it is time to recognize that intellectual formation without moral and ethical values is destroying the social fiber and the environment in an almost irreversible way. The recognition that the future of education must be education for peace, with the certainty that these practices work and change lives, as mentioned by the majority of people who have participated in our training.

A.P.C. (inmate of the Luis Paulino Mora Institutional Care Center), commented, "It was a unique experience, because something that I have struggled to learn throughout my life, I came to understand in three days and it taught me how to leave many violent things behind. An interesting and important experience, I think and I am sure that if we had had the opportunity in our childhood, adolescence and youth about these techniques many of us would not be in these places, because they are very important to minimize violence" (Personal communication, May 21, 2016).

Another comment to highlight is that of K.A.R. (Inmate of the Jorge Debravo Institutional Care Center), who states, "More than grateful to the program facilitators, their teachings changed our lives and helped us to generate greater value for ourselves" (Personal communication, June 7, 2023).

Finally, we highlight what Carlos Flores Chávez (University Community Work Student) said, "I thank the CEPPA Foundation team for all the help provided, for their human quality, their knowledge and wisdom; I learned a lot from them. May God bless you for such a noble cause" (Personal communication, January 20, 2024).

Conclusion

Undoubtedly, the long experience and practices of the CEPPA Foundation have shown that peace education is one of the best means to form subjects that can respond to violence with responsibility and morality. The practice of peace begins and ends in ourselves as facilitators or educators, which means that we must first form an atmosphere of trust and respect with the participants. This way peace is not taught, but practiced. It emerges from the experience itself.

The philosophy, exercises, and techniques of the practices develop self-esteem, cooperation and communication, offering a true methodology of practice for peace. It is not a discourse without roots in reality, it is a way of shaping it for those who practise it.

Note by Daniel Romero

As for CEPPA's journey, everything that can be quoted and mentioned about Celina Garcia would fall short. She is one of the most outstanding women and pioneers in peace studies in the Central American region, since her main interest, trajectory and true impact have been marked by her social actions. An educator for peace in schools, prisons and communities at high social risk, who does so with the purpose of responding to the deepest and most urgent needs of society, especially in the prevention of violence, the cradle of traumas in people, which often lead to criminal behavior.

At the same time, we give thanks to dreams, especially Martha's, who had a dream, which we at the CEPPA Foundation have tried to turn into reality. Thanks to all the university students who do their communal work in CEPPA, facilitators, whose dedication and commitment have made CEPPA's adventure possible.

In recognition of CEPPA Foundation's journey, we can only act, taking up the many proposals for peace education and crime prevention through effective non-violent alternatives. We hope from CEPPA Foundation, to continue working in the legacy of eradicating violence from our society and to fulfill Celina's dream of life: That we do not need prisons to sentence human beings who were also victims of violence, to prevent to not regret, because "The Culture of Peace is in our hands".

References

García, C. (1989). *Peace education as an academic discipline*. Monograph, San José, Centro de Estudios para la Paz.

Párraga, N., Vera, F., Mendoza, A. et al. (2021). The game as a psycho-peda-gogical strategy and its impact on the educational quality of middle school students. *Revista Científica Dominio de las Ciencias (7)*, 903-919. DOI: http://dx.doi.org/10.23857/dc.v7i1.1747.

Reardon, B. (1984). Principles and standards for curriculum development and teacher preparation. In Haavelsrud, M. (Ed.) Unpublished manuscript for the *UNESCO teacher´s handbook on Disarmament education*, Archive A-0303 on Peace Education in www.arkivportalen.no, Norwegian University of Science and Technology Library and UNESCO archives.

Chapter 17
Education for Conflict Transformation

Diana Francis

My First Experience of Peace Education

My parents were conscientious objectors in World War 2 and I took my Christian pacifism from them. They were members of the Fellowship of Reconciliation (FoR), a Christian pacifist organisation, which started in the UK and soon became an international network called IFoR. At the age of fifteen I took part in an FoR youth conference, where I was involved in discussions about war, peace and my beliefs. Then, the following summer, I joined its young people's camp, where we worked in the mornings, refurbishing an old building. In the afternoon we held discussions and made presentations to each other and, in the evenings, we visited local youth clubs to make our presentations about pacifism to the young people there, answering their questions and responding to their challenges.

Since that first, powerful experience of being educated and educating others, I have been a constant 'peace activist' and communicator, involved in demonstrations, civil resistance, public speaking and holding conversations with people of all shades of opinion.

Later Learning in an International Context

When I was in my thirties, I was asked to represent our national FoR branch at an international gathering of IFoR on an ashram in Kerala, in Southern India. There, I was elected to IFoR's Steering Committee and, three years later, I was made its president, in which role I served for eight years.

At that time the IFoR focus was more on nonviolent struggle against oppression than on conflict resolution or reconciliation (which cannot be reached until the violence of extreme injustice has ended). During my years with IFoR, I met with nonviolent activists from different countries, learning about the challenges they faced and how they were responding to them. I was inspired by their courage and determination: resisting apartheid in South Africa, confronting President Marcos's regime in the Philippines, finding the power of solidarity in the face of oppression in several Latin American dictatorships.

Two travelling peacemakers and educators from IFoR, Jean and Hildegard Goss-Mayr, were travelling constantly, inspiring, educating and supporting these activists. They emphasised the need for absolute respect for all people, in whatever circumstance, and for dialogue, first and last, at every stage of conflict. Those two things have remained at the core of what I have tried to practise and convey to others.

Jean and Hildegard worked in the spirit of Paulo Freire's *Pedagogy of the Oppressed* (1972), with its concept of education as empowerment enabled by eliciting from people the knowledge they already have. These two great educators began by asking activists to define and name the violence or injustice that needed to be addressed, depicting it diagrammatically as an inverted pyramid, and then to give names to the pillars holding it up on either side: the different elements of their society supporting the oppressive system and needing to be removed or transformed. The next diagram consisted of a succession of concentric circles, with the activist group itself at the centre and the expanding circles around it representing the different categories of people to be won over to the cause. The final diagram depicted the steps of progress they wanted to see: steps up from oppression to liberation. These diagrams enabled cogent and creative thinking as the basis for effective action (see diagram "Stages and Approaches to Conflict Transformation", next page).

Then, in the 1980s, IFoR's focus on nonviolent means of addressing violent injustice, as the prerequisite for reconciliation, was proved to have been justified by the successes of nonviolence that began to be achieved in countries

Stages and Processes in Conflict Transformation

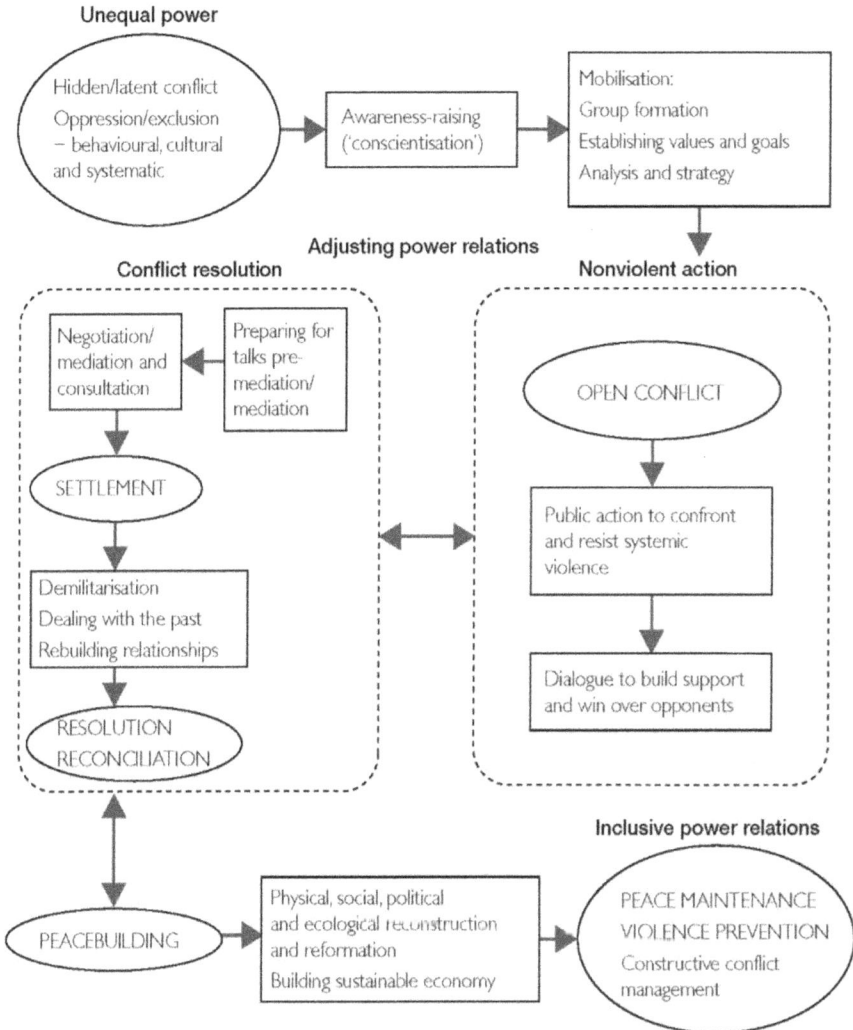

Diagram 1: Stages and Approaches to Conflict Transformation
(Diana Francis, 2015)

where it had worked. In Latin America, there was a shift from military to civilian rule and, in 1986, the dictator in the Philippines, President Marcos, was nonviolently overthrown by the Christian base groups that Jean and Hildegard had long supported. A few years later, in South Africa, where, among thousands of others, two IFoR workers had been jailed, apartheid was being dismantled.

These examples of successful nonviolent struggle were followed by massive changes in Europe, brought about by nonviolent 'people power' in what had been the Warsaw Pact countries and the Soviet Union. Beginning in 1988, with civil resistance in Czechoslovakia, in the form of student-led street protests, and in Poland with the mass strikes called by the trade union, Solidarity, the nonviolent revolution spread. By the end of 1989 the Berlin Wall had come down and the Eastern bloc was rapidly disintegrating. The following year saw Lithuania's declaration of independence from the Soviet Union and the reunification of East and West Germany. Soon the Warsaw Pact was gone and the Soviet Union was at an end.

This process and its outcomes were, of course, hugely uplifting for those who had longed for freedom, and those of us who were promoting nonviolent action for needed change were elated. However, as time went on, new problems began to arise in Europe. People found themselves living in a new and unfamiliar world.

In particular, those in the former Soviet territories were now no longer citizens of the Soviet Union, so who were they? Who were to be their new leaders, in what entities? Many turned to their old family histories and identities. If they were living in places where a particular ethnicity had predominated, they often resented the number of ethnic Russians living there and wanted their own former language back, with a government that represented their history, not their recent past.

This all came as a shock to those of us who had, till then, been used to thinking of nonviolent action as a means for addressing the violence of oppression. Now in the former Soviet region the problem was the conflict of clashing aspirations and fears that could lead to physical violence. To address this situation in Europe, new thought-frames, strategies and skills were needed, with a focus on conciliation. At home in England, neighbourhood mediation centres were beginning to be established and, as I neared the end of my second term as IFoR president, I trained, began to practise as a neighbourhood mediator, and then to train others.

Training and Learning in PhD Research

The Development of My Own Learning and Practice

My resolve to focus on peacemaking at home came to an abrupt end when, in 1991, I was asked to respond to training requests from activists in Serbia, when the wars that were to break up Yugoslavia began. I was to work – and learn – in different entities within that region for the next decade. In that time I also worked in many places elsewhere and in 1994 I learned that a radical new research programme was being offered by the School of Management Studies at the University of Bath, where I live. Entitled 'Action Research in Professional Practice', it offered researchers the chance to scrutinise the practice not of others but of themselves, writing their thesis in the first person. For their findings to have any convincing validity, they needed to bring in the voices of others involved – as participants or co-facilitators – as well as providing 'thick description' (detailed, first person, contemporaneous accounts) of the events and interactions in question, allowing the readers (in the first place their examiners) to make their own judgements about any conclusions reached, on the basis of the detailed material provided.

I felt this research experience would give me a chance to think hard, with both support and challenge, and to reflect on the highly responsible work in which I was now involved; an opportunity also to educate myself further on theory and strategic tools that could be useful to me and to those whom I was helping to educate. I hoped it would enable me to become more self-aware and observant of my effect on others, and so to hone my skills as a facilitator of learning.

The title I chose for my research, "Respect in Cross-cultural Conflict Resolution Training", was wordy but accurate (except that, as will become clear, I should have replaced 'Resolution' with 'Transformation'). I chose 'respect' as my focus, first as the underlying value for nonviolence and for the thinking and behaviour of all players in peace-related work. It was also essential to the practice of a trainer/educator/facilitator and important for all participants in any process. And theory must be respectful, in being realistic and helpful to participants in understanding how best to act for change in respectful and powerful ways.

Summaries of Three Sample Case Studies

In what follows, I have drawn on three sample accounts in my PhD thesis, to illustrate some of what I learned in the process.

Early Work in a Post-Soviet Context

The 'cross-cultural' part of my working title was deeply relevant at that time, as I was beginning to work in the North Caucasus region of the former Soviet Union. The first was held in the Mountains of the North Caucasus. The workshop culture in which I had done my learning, thus far, was non-hierarchical and informal, facilitating or enabling learning rather than being didactic. (Back then at least, there was no Russian word for 'facilitate'.) However, the informality of our interactions with our participants – and those encouraged between them (especially since many of those with whom my colleagues and I were working were 'important' in their own societies) – came as something of a culture shock to them. Gradually though, their resistance dissolved and they engaged with the process with great energy, accepting and learning from what we came to recognise as a methodology based on what could be seen as our ideology as trainers. The wonder was that they accepted it and learned from it.

We held evaluation sessions with the participants at the end of each afternoon, giving them the opportunity to tell us what they had found helpful and what not, with a column on the flipchart sheet for suggestions for future sessions.

My co-facilitator and I also debriefed together, assessing the participants' evaluations and their implications for the following day. If, after consideration, we decided not to change our plans, we explained why the next morning. We also discussed with each other our 'performance' as facilitators, through open self-assessment and giving each other supportive feedback, along with any suggestions for adjustment.

During sessions, if energy seemed to be dropping, we would introduce a (non-compulsory) game to revive us all. Some participants at first objected, feeling games to be undignified and irrelevant, but soon they became a source of shared fun which brought the group together.

Note 1, re language: My co-facilitator and I were not competent Russian speakers, so we relied on translators for the workshop sessions. Mostly we used consecutive translation, which could have been difficult for all of us. Somehow, though, the rhythm of speaking and pausing is less problematic than one might expect, the slower pace enabling greater succinctness. The one disadvantage was not to be able to eat and chat with participants outside of sessions.

Note 2, re gender: Most of the participants were male and both they and the few women present clearly saw their dominance as proper. We did not then challenge this directly, as we might have done, but later I was to plan and co-facilitate a good number of extended workshops for women alone, which had an easier flow, were really vibrant and allowed the women to talk about gender issues as such.

Note 3, re mediation: When we discussed mediation it became clear that the mediator's role, in the minds of most participants, was one of an external authority whose task was to arbitrate. There was an initial objection, from the men in particular, to the proposition that the mediator's function is to facilitate or guide a dialogue, with the aim of finding agreement between the conflicting parties on a constructive way forward.

Note 4, re theory gap: The term 'conflict resolution', which was then prevalent in the theory of peace and conflict, was not helpful when we were thinking about conflict situations in some parts of the region where power relations were so unequal and oppressive that any challenge from below was impossible and the conflict remained 'latent' – waiting to happen. (Here we were back in Goss-Mayr territory.)

In conversation with a colleague, I devised a diagram that depicted a succession of stages or processes, beginning with severe oppression or injustice, then moves to a process of awakening and mobilisation for nonviolent action, which builds the power of the oppressed to the point where the oppressors accept the need for dialogue. At that point negotiation and resolution become possible and can allow real peace to be built and maintained. This diagram was referred to by the participants as 'the snake', on account of its shape. (Not long after, the term 'conflict transformation' was added to the conflict vocabulary and I renamed the diagram as 'Stages and Processes in Conflict

Transformation'. First published in my post-PhD book (Francis 2002, 49), it has gone through a variety of developments, in response to input from workshop participants down the years.

Note 5, re co-facilitation: 'Co-facilitator' or 'colleague' are frequently recurring words in this and other accounts. Not working alone, especially in extended workshops, has always been important to me – for mutual support and exchange and to demonstrate the advantages of cooperation and complementarity. Below is an example of where, in the most unfortunate context, that was not possible.

Pan African Workshop for Women

This workshop was a painful example of the considerable difficulties (in those days at least) in achieving any sense of justice or equality in the relationship between Africans and 'white' Europeans, given the unaddressed impact of slavery, colonialism and neo-colonialism. I always tried to avoid invitations to work in Africa because, at that time, it seemed that European trainers were in demand because they were respected, whereas more local ones were not. I saw that as internalised and continued oppression.

Then, one day, the London NGO for which I had worked in the Caucasus asked me to lead a Pan-African workshop for women activists. I first refused but, under pressure, agreed to do it on condition that an African co-facilitator could be found. One was: a highly experienced and able woman to whom I was introduced. We got on well and worked together easily on the preparation but then, at the last minute, she suffered a bereavement and had to pull out. I asked the African head of programme, who had employed me, if she could be my co-facilitator. However, she said she lacked experience and wanted to be there as an observer, as did another African staff member. The only plan I could think of was to see, on arrival, whether someone in the participant group would be willing to co-facilitate or, failing that, to enlist an advisory group, to give me feedback and guidance.

In the event, when I explained why I was there as a sole, white European facilitator, there were several participants who were angry, noting that I had two African colleagues with me (my employers) and asked why they could not be my co-trainers. They, in turn, insisted that they could or would not step in, having come to learn.

When all avenues had been exhausted, the participants settled down and engaged with the process in a very productive way. I had been warned that there might be tensions between those from the Northern and Southern regions of Africa but perhaps the resentment at perceived neo-colonialism had brought them together, as no tensions of that kind arose and the participants worked harmoniously together. This experience deepened my conviction that it was unhelpful and disrespectful to send, without some special reason, white Europeans to undertake work in Africa that could well be done by Africans. Hopefully things have moved on in the intervening decades.

International Training at the WCC

While my research was still ongoing, I was invited by the World Council of Churches (WCC) to co-facilitate a nine-day training in nonviolent action, finding my own co-facilitator. This event was joined by participants working for peace and justice in different countries across the world. Though they came from different cultures, they shared one religion and had similar goals. The purpose of this workshop was to give them an opportunity to learn from each other's experiences and reflect together, in order to discover new ways of seeing things and to acquire tools and skills which would be of use in their own, different contexts.

I was introduced by South African colleagues to a pastor from King Williamstown, whom they considered to be extremely able. He was a member of his local peace committee and, in the run-up to the post-apartheid elections, had been working for the Ecumenical Monitoring Programme. We had an opportunity to meet beforehand, to get to know each other and to do some advance planning. Since the participants' situations would be so varied, we decided to use the 'Stages and Processes' diagram as the framework for our planning of the event, providing a broad but structured agenda.

The fact that we two facilitators were so comfortable with each other – and represented both North and South, black and white, male and female – was particularly important, as this was to prove an extremely challenging event.

It began with an official welcome from the organiser, self- introductions by the participants – to each other in pairs and then to the rest – and an introduction from me to the purpose of the workshop and its character. Anger was expressed by some in the participant group when it was explained that, although the workshop had been advertised to some as a 'training for trainers', it had been named simply as a 'training' to the rest of us, and some of that anger carried over into subsequent sessions. Ironically, in the event, this challenging, sometimes turbulent workshop must have taught even those who were already trainers more than they could ever have imagined.

During that introductory session we opened with questions about the word 'conflict'. What were the associated words that sprang to mind in response to it? Once the negative ones were exhausted, the participants came up with the positive things that could come out of it, such as fresh understanding or new ideas. Then 'the 'snake' was introduced as the framework for our nine-day timetable, taking us through the different stages and processes in conflict transformation. Some of the participants objected that we were trying to achieve too much and that the days would be too packed. The balancing of time, energy and content is always a challenge in such events, but by the time we reached the end of our nine days, they were in the event, satisfied.

(We felt unable at the time to explain that the content of the sessions would be interspersed with songs and games, fearing that without a thorough explanation there would be objections to the idea of apparently childish things for serious adults. In the event they proved to be a wonderful release, particularly for those traumatised by violence in their home situations. Together with the silence and song with which we began each day, and the daily worship prepared by the base groups, the games did much to bind the group together.)

Finally in this opening session, George introduced his proposal for 'base groups', whose members would meet after the initial plenary evaluation, to review each day, and later report to the facilitators. These groups (sometimes known as 'home groups') not only provided participants with a place of belonging but also gave us facilitators an important means to stay in tune with participants and be responsive to them. We tailored the following day's agenda with all this in mind, summarising all the feedback the following morning, before presenting the new day's agenda.

When George and I debriefed together at the end of that first day, we felt that we had handled things as well as we could and, within the following days, the dynamics grew rapidly more positive.

There was a later row between certain participants, about the request from some of the women to form a women's group – no doubt in response to the vocal role of one or two dominant men. The request was seen by some as divisive and as disrespecting the existing base groups. However, a women's group was eventually formed and accepted by everyone. I think it played an important role in bringing in a gender voice which in those days was often not heard.

All this was another reminder that workshops of this kind have their own counter-cultural culture, which is likely to come as a shock to many. The fact that the group will be focused on nonviolent responses to conflict may be explicit, but in its process it will contain much that is unfamiliar or uncomfortable for some. When that factor is combined with the intensity of working in a residential community, with a wide variety of experiences and expectations, it would be surprising if there were to be no turbulence.

Language was inevitably a factor in the power dynamics of an international workshop run in English, though with interpretation for those who needed it. The advantage always remains with confident English speakers and in this case the Latin-American participants suffered because they had inadequate support from their interpreter.

All that said, helped by the silence and singing with which each day began, and by the shared worship led by participants, a sense of mutual belonging grew in the group; also a strong engagement with the many ideas and tasks which they undertook together. George and I were now seen to have been very flexible and responsive and, as one group pointed out, we had not only learned about the different stages and processes in conflict but lived them, together.

As I noted in my journal afterwards, 'respect' had held good, both as an explicit core value, both for nonviolent approaches to conflict in general and for us in the here-and-now. It can also be seen as the litmus test for what constitutes cross-cultural training.

Gathered Learnings from all My Work

Functions of Facilitation

As will be clear from the different research accounts above, facilitators in this kind of work have many different roles or functions. The first, essential task for them is to create (and if necessary, adjust or recreate) the structure of the workshop itself: its agenda, which must be presented and agreed, even if it is subsequently changed. Then (not mentioned in the examples above) they need to ensure that 'ground rules' – as far as possible elicited from the participants – are listed and agreed by the whole group, providing the framework for all to behave respectfully towards each other. The three rules that stand out for me are to keep to agreed times, to listen to each other attentively and without interruption and to speak one at a time. Participants may come up with several others. However, they will be meaningful only if adhered to and reminders to that effect are ultimately the responsibility of the facilitators. It is their job to ensure that all participants have a voice and are respected and respectful; also that they are encouraged and enabled to empathise with each other.

Some theoretical and process input and guidance is needed in the educational process, and is the basis for eliciting the ideas of participants, drawing from them their existing experience and knowledge as the basis for creative thinking. Time and reflection are also important for sound judgement in decision making. Feedback to and between participants on the way they engage with tasks will help them to develop their skills, particularly in communication. At the same time, facilitators need to be open to feedback from participants, to show them respect and to receive guidance. Daily evaluations will provide one opportunity for that.

Tried and Tested Concepts and Processes for Learning

Important underpinning for Goss-Mayr models' for analysing oppressive situations, building movement and setting goals, and the Stages and Processes diagram (see diagram above) is provided by 'Galtung's triangle'. Defining violence in general as "Avoidable insults to basic human needs", such as "killing, maiming, denial of physical resources, overriding of group identity, and

repression", Galtung represents it as a triangle with three aspects: "direct violence" comes at one of the bottom angles, "structural violence" at the other of
them and "cultural violence" at the top. "Direct violence" is to be understood
as a "direct assault" on any of these needs; 'structural violence' as the systems,
relationships and structures that cause ongoing, widespread harm, and "cultural violence" as "those aspects of culture" which "make[s] direct and structural
violence look, even feel, right - or at least not wrong" (Galtung, 1990, pp. 291-
305). This fundamental thinking points also to the different levers for change.

'Conflict' as such is not violence. Collins Dictionary defines it as "serious
disagreement and argument about something important". However, since
those are often related to the most unimportant things, I prefer to think of the
word's etymology, which means literally a clash or friction. How it is dealt
with it is what matters. Respect and empathy rule out violence.

Role-plays, if they are regarded not as a game but as a way of experiencing
and testing things, are the most powerful tool for learning about empathy,
which can counter strong negative feelings and prevent them from being expressed in their raw form. Learning can be had from playing both 'negative'
and 'positive' roles in them – and from playing the roles of third parties who
have been caught up in the clash. Their 'feedback', along with that of appointed observers, will be important to the learning of all those involved,
especially if it is offered in a non-judgemental way.

Basic listening skills can be practised in pairs, in which each person has a turn
as the speaker and one as the listener, with a good debrief between the two
before roles are swapped. There are many possible permutations of these, for
instance whether the listener remains entirely silent or makes brief interventions for clarification or to express sympathy. Again, having an observer can
be helpful.

An important exercise for analysing and understanding a conflict and bringing empathy into negotiations is 'needs and fears mapping', in which the
conflict is defined and the competing positions of the different parties are
articulated and written down. Those need to be represented and discussed
but are likely to prove incompatible until the needs and fears behind those
positions are identified. Adding those layers of understanding can release
the parties from the boundaries of their positions and lead to a far more cre-

ative process in which new openings appear on both sides (Cornelius & Faire, 1989).

One other exercise that I have found really helpful over the years – this time primarily for individual self-examination, but also for exploring and shifting thinking – is called 'line-ups' or 'continuum lines'. An imaginary line is drawn across the room, with one end designated as representing total positivity about something and the other end total negativity (or two diametrically opposing positions or statements). Participants are invited to take their place, physically, somewhere on that line, according to their self-assessment or opinion. Then the facilitator invites volunteers to speak to the rest, from where they are standing, explaining their chosen positions; then the discussion may be pursued in different ways. This works well for reflection on large issues, such as 'competing goods': for example, the relative importance (or compatibility) of personal freedom and public safety.

These things, along with facilitator input and feedback, and regular group-work and presentations on various tasks, form the basis of most of my workshops.

A Much Later Workshop

Once I had completed my PhD, from which I had learnt much, I continued with a wide variety of training and facilitation work in many different parts of the world. Then, out of the blue, I was asked to undertake a task in which identity remained a vital issue, but this time all the participants shared one very specific identity. It took place in 1998, in Northern Ireland when, after the signing of the Good Friday Agreement, the violent conflict between the (Protestant) Unionist /Loyalist and (Catholic) Republican communities and paramilitaries was coming to an end. The Northern Ireland Assembly would soon be reopened for cross-party politics and paramilitary leaders were required to disband their organisations and, in some cases, would become civilian politicians.

Because of connections made in work elsewhere, I was asked to facilitate a workshop in Belfast for the brigadiers of one of the smaller Unionist paramilitaries, who were tasked with disarming and disbanding it. They were accompanied in this five-day workshop by their right-hand men and together they made a sizeable group.

I had expected to be co-facilitating with a male colleague but, in the end, he was given some other task in what turned out to be a wider gathering. I had no time to consider what it would be like to work with them alone, as a woman, or how, as a pacifist, I would feel to be working with a roomful of men who had 'done time' for murder (that being how their military killings had been classified) and had only recently been released from prison. I should add that my sympathies, as someone 'of the left', had always been more with the Republicans than the Unionists.

In the event, these men treated me with respect and I quickly warmed to them. They talked about their time in prison with deep regret. As they now saw it, they had wasted their years there 'on body-building and metal work', while the 'Shinners' (paramilitaries fighting for Sinn Fein) had studied and 'got themselves degrees'. As a result, as they described it, the Shinners were now being driven around in large cars, having found a place in the new politics, while they themselves were nobodies and felt that they were finished. Their honesty and humanity touched me deeply and I really wanted to help them to find a way forward, in tackling the very difficult task of disarming their group. (They had been given temporary jobs as 'community workers', as a cover, but had no idea how to proceed.) It was clear to me that they really needed support in finding a way to move on.

They participated eagerly in the various processes we went through: reflection and analysis on their current situation, 'brainstorming' and strategising on possible ways forward, then identifying the steps to be taken in the immediate and longer-term future. At the end of one evening, I found myself in a largely empty room, sitting opposite one of the men. Having, I think, had rather too much to drink, he started to unburden himself to me, pouring out his worries about his clearly much-admired father and wondering what he would think of him, his son, now that he was planning this exit from the fight for the Union. He told me proudly how many men his father had killed, how he had been employed as a hit man in France, in exchange for weapons, and how he himself had not lived up to these 'achievements'. Then he suddenly recollected himself and remembered who I was, saying, "But Diana, what can you be thinking of me?"

I said that I thought he was very brave, to be planning to do something so different and difficult: to turn his whole life around. Then, clutching one knee, he said "This leg wants to go forward but this leg (clutching the other one) just doesn't want to come." I was deeply touched. That simple and eloquent statement took me to a place that I could never have imagined I could reach, and I will always be grateful to him. This whole workshop, which ended on a very positive note, with profuse thanks to me, had been a powerful education for me, removing my prejudice, opening my heart and deepening my understanding.

A Final Thought

The work of conflict transformation has had its successes and I will always admire those who have contributed to them. They give me hope. Now what is needed, urgently and radically, is its application in the world of International Relations, to transform the geopolitics of confrontation and ever more violent conflict into the geopolitics of cooperation, which alone can save us all from extinction. Now who will educate the politicians?

References

Cornelius, H. & Faire, S. (1989). *Everyone can win: How to resolve conflict.* Simon and Schuster.

Francis, D. (2002). *People, peace and power: Conflict transformation in action.* Pluto Press.

Freire, P. (1972). *Pedagogy of the Oppressed.* Penguin.

Galtung, J. (1990). Cultural violence. *Journal of Peace Research, 27*(3): 291 – 305.

Chapter 18
Good Living and Feeling-Thinking Approach: Latin American and Indigenous Gift for Global Peace Education[1]

Amada Benavides de Pérez [2]

South narratives have a big place in peace education and peacebuilding. They show different ways to understand the relations between people, communities and nature. As the effect of knowledge illustrates, some narratives from North academic institutions, and NGOs sometimes, have ignored narratives and research from the Global South, and at times even regarded them with contempt. In this presentation we will explore how many spaces exist for teaching and learning from each other.

The first part of my presentation is based on what Boaventura de Sousa Santos refers to as "Southern Epistemologies" (2016). I strongly concur with De Santos about the pre-eminence that academic thought has in academic-Cartesian thought, and the loss in value that has occurred in research - transformation based on other types of knowledge.

After centuries of trusting colonization, capitalism, militarization and patriarchy, results that are produced by this epistemology are exhausted: the environmental crisis and capitalism, the damage caused by the militarist and macho culture, instances where violence is accepted as the only way to resolve conflicts, the competition to achieve goals, the exploitation of nature, among others. It requires a profound change of paradigms, and many of them can be found in what is known as the GLOBAL SUR.

This concept is not given by a geographical definition, but instead it refers to places in the world that share similar settings related to domination, colonization and the silencing of knowledge and matters known that were despised because they were not validated by logic and Cartesian methods. This has been defined as EPISTEMICIDIO.

Bringing this knowledge to light is thanks to a group of people around the world who are part of the postcolonial mindset. This highlights criticism of the excesses to which the extreme confidence in the Cartesian scientific logic and the Eurocentric world view led. It rescues "the immensity of alternatives of life, coexistence and interaction that have been relegated and destroyed by the theories and concepts developed in the Global North and employees throughout the academic world that does not identify other thought options" (de Sousa Santos, 2016, p. 20).

De Santos states that there are other ways of understanding and transforming the world: other conceptions of time, space, productivity, consumption and resistance. However, this does not mean to completely disregard the scientific knowledge that has led to advances in science, technology and research, but it does imply recognizing that this has reached a limit and that alternative solutions must be sought to make the profound changes we need as humanity. de Sousa Santos calls this plural, horizontal and equitable search Intercultural Translation (de Sousa Santos, 2016, p. 22).

Intercultural Translation helps us to broaden our view of multicultural standards, which can contribute to greater knowledge, well-being, and relationships more harmonious with nature, coexistence, justice and power, among others. It consists of looking for specific concerns, threats and assumptions that are common to different cultures, identifying differences and similarities, to develop, when appropriate, new hybrid forms of cultural understanding and intercommunication that can be useful to deepen interactions and strengthen alliances in the search for common benefit.

This method gathers traditional knowledge known of ancestral peoples; strongholds intuition and new forms of expression from art, dance, music, based on the recognition of the body as the first scenario that experiments with emotions: enjoyment or violence; and it asks us to look at active and passive resistance, collective knowledge and puts emphasis on the power of the oral word, more than writing and literature.

Although postcolonial and other studies are very well known in academia, the trickledown effect of knowledge shows how some narratives from more privileged academic institutions and NGOs have ignored narratives and research from native and traditional communities, and, at times, with contempt. We will explore how many spaces exist for teaching and learning from each other. In the 2019 International Institute on Peace Education, we wanted to open up dialogue, and challenge these prevailing perspectives held by some, and contribute to change the existing narrative.

The following ideas represent the intent for such goal. This presentation helps us observe and consider three proposals from Latin America on education for peace, based on the perspective of postcolonial studies:

1. Feeling-thinking (sentipensante) pedagogy
2. Good living
3. Sweeten the word to resolve conflicts

1. On Feeling-Thinking (Sentipensante) Pedagogy

The language that speaks the truth is the sentient language.
The one who can think feeling and feeling thinking
(Orlando Fals Borda, 1981)

Our educational systems, inheritors of paradigms conceived under the interests of science to promote the Industrial Revolution and productivity, base their certainty on knowledge and research. The distance between this method and practice has created enormous barriers that prevent people from applying this method to daily life. The schools have also neglected and eliminated from their curriculum any type of experience that leads to identify, regulate and process the emotions and conflicts that arise from them.

Since 1960, sociologist Orlando Fals Borda proposed to work from the sentipensante language, "the prodigious trance of feeling – thinking" (Fals Borda,

1981). This concept pertains to the riverside communities of the Sinú River, which use it to recognize the subjects and communities that are in touch with their nature and have submerged themselves in the aromas of the river, the movement of the waters; they have resisted domination, miscegenation; they deeply combine the transformation of thinking, feeling. Sentient training is an emancipating pedagogy that recognizes that all subjects are producers of knowledge, works on integrality, promoting multiple learning that takes into account the knowledge and traditions of subjects and communities, that is, not just about acquiring and executing these useful lessons, instead one must make an attempt to apply and appropriate such knowledge, and by collecting these methods one can redefine the original intent, bringing forward as a base the struggles and challenges many people have endured in time of conflict (Fals Borda, 1981, pp. 149-174).

Sentipensante pedagogy goes beyond research. It is a lifestyle that is based on recognizing the knowledge of communities, exercising empathy with others, respect and appreciating differences.

Sentipensante pedagogy is the basis of popular education, which has two foundational axes: an epistemological vision to generate knowledge from a critical perspective, and the proposal of research - action - participation that does not create distance between the subject and object of research, but instead generates a horizontal relationship where everyone learns from everyone; these improved actions are possible thanks to the systematization of experiences for the production of knowledge that can be transferred to other communities and improve the quality of life of the communities that generate them.

Based on this paradigm, the Schools of Peace Foundation is actively working on a proposal to conduct Experiential Pedagogical Workshops. Experiential Pedagogical Workshops contribute to the construction of knowledge that combines theoretical, conceptual and practical components, which are in themselves, the presentation of didactic and pedagogical strategies. These workshops open spaces intended for the participants to socialize their experiences and strengthen the group's knowledge and communication. They are based on recreational, artistic, experiences, and exemplification through cases, which provide tools for participants to develop skills as multipliers, with techniques that are easy to use and understand for a very heterogeneous and plural audience. This methodology arranges the teaching of knowledge, the training of skills and aptitudes and the renewal of attitudes for coexistence and peace. More specifically, it is sought that each participant can have relevant information that gives them access to better and higher levels of training with which they can become an agent of transformation for their communities. They are dynamic, interactive, participative workshops, in which the movement is privileged, the recognition of oneself and the other, and various strategies are used such as: music therapy, dance for peace, biodanza, elaboration of individual and collective mandalas, lines of life, theater of the oppressed, painting and graffiti, among others.

2. Good Living (Buen Vivir)

> The concept of Good Living or Living Well comes from the indigenous words Sumak Kawsay (in Quechua) - Suma Qamaña (in Aymara), which really speak of the Full Life, in fullness, in harmony and balance with nature and in community, so it is also called the Good Living. The ancestral thought of Good Living is an old-new paradigm, which proposes a life in balance, with harmonious relationships within each human being, between people, community, society and the mother earth to which we belong. (Rodriguez Salazar, n.d.)

In times of multiple global crises, the "Good Living" is proposed as an alternative method to the current system focused on the exploitation of nature and human beings.

El Buen Vivir is both a philosophical proposal, based on the indigenous ancestral wisdom of the Andean and Amazonian peoples, and a political proposal that was put into practice in Ecuador and Bolivia with the governments of Rafael Correa and Evo Morales, respectively (El Portal de la Economía Solidaria, 2010).

As a philosophical proposal, it is based on the paradigm of caring for life and taking care of everything in our ecosystem and beyond. It arises from indigenous claims as a profound criticism and rejection of the collapsing Western civilizing model. The "Good Living" as an alternative, includes proposals to reestablish the balance of life on the planet, from the defense of nature (pachamama / mother earth / gaia) and the ancestral knowledge of peoples and nations, which have other world views or practical philosophies (Rodriguez Salazar, 2013). It is based on four pillars that apply to all fields of life, are expressed in multiple ways and include different dimensions and relationships, from personal to cosmic: (a) principle of relationality, (b) complementary duality, (c) correspondence and (d) reciprocity.

As a political bet, the pachakutec, the cycle change (revolution, transformation), echoes the indigenous resistance that is strengthened in the social upheavals in Ecuador and Bolivia since 2000 and was legally promulgated in the Political Constitution of Ecuador (2008), where "it is a fundamental right of the population to live in a healthy and ecologically balanced environment, which guarantees sustainability and good living, sumak Kawsay" is recognized (In the same way, in the National Plan for Good Living 2009 - 2013 and the Political Constitution of Bolivia of 2009, the Plurinational State is established, which "assumes and promotes as principles the sum qamaña (to live well)".

Living Well gives priority to nature rather than to humans. These are the characteristics that are gradually being implemented in the new Plurinational State of Bolivia (El Portal de la Economía Solidaria, 2010).

Good Living allows us to find solutions to many of the current global issues, in times of multiple crises and an urgent search for answers to resolve worldwide conflict, which calls for new civilizational paradigms in the 21st century.

Table 1: Good Living Principles (Amada Benavides de Perez)

Principles in relation to life	
1) Prioritize life	2) Reach consensus agreements
3) Live in complementarity	4) Living well is not "living better"
Principles regarding respect for others	
5) Defend identity	6) Accept differences

7) Respect differences	
Principles regarding respect for nature	
8) Prioritize cosmic rights	9) Balance with nature
10) Protect seeds	11) Take advantage of water
12) Reincorporate agriculture	13) Recover resources
14) Exercise sovereignty	
Principles of community	
15) Retake Abya Yala. Create community	16) Know how to eat
17) Know how to drink	18) Know how to dance
19) Know how to work	20) Know how to communicate
Essential principles	
21) Simple life and balanced production	22) Social control. Work in reciprocity
23) Do not steal and do not lie (ama sua and ama qhilla inquechua)	24) Respect women
25) Listen to your elders	

3. Sweeten the World to Resolve Conflicts

Everything you do has to be done with a cold heart. It must be done with the sweetheart. And it must be done with that much empathy. That means that between the two worlds there are things known as a hot word and a cold word. Hot words are all negative and cold words are all positive. When that order is altered then we say we must cool the word, we must sweeten the word. But not from the word, but from the concept of knowing the care of the word of life, of the care of the air of life. (Centro Nacional de Memoria Histórica, 2017, p. 23)

Colombia is the home to more than seventy indigenous communities surviving the very different types of colonization suffered by our country since the Spanish colonization. They are located throughout the country's rural regions, and many communities are living with no more than a thousand people who share a common lifestyle, languages and dialects, culture, rites and legends.

Some of them live in La Chorrera, a department of the Amazon to the southwest of the country. It is made up of 22 indigenous councils belonging to four groups: uitotos, boras, okainas and muinanes, with a population of 3,823 inhabitants at present. These peoples are retaking their identity and their traditional indigenous organizations, they have organized collectively making symbiosis of legal structures in Colombia and their ancestral organizational forms. "Every night they meet in the malocas, their house of knowledge, to communicate with their ancestors and keep alive an ancestral culture that was about to become extinct" (Centro Nacional de Memoria Histórica, 2017, p. 83).

One of the main concerns as a whole is to keep alive the historical memory of their communities, and for that they have prepared the new generations to search for their own roots and request help in national think tanks and universities. This is what de Santos calls Intercultural Translation.

Among the many learnings that the academy of these towns has received is the practice of ENDULZAR LA PALABRA [English: Sweeten the Word]. They consider that "tobacco, coca and sweet cassava are a trinity. Tobacco is the representation of the divine, the coca of the human and the sweet yucca of the woman." Every ritual ceremony begins in the maloca with the use of these three elements under the guidance of the grandparents. Ceremonies that last all night, and that thanks to these elements, allow dialogue to open and "access with a good spirit and without major consequences to a difficult and painful story to prevent the violence that it brought back from being resurrected." This ritual "is sweeten the word of life. It is sweetening the difference. It's the harmony in the difference." "It invites us to cool the word and strip away any connotations of denial, exclusion, invisibility and inequity" (Asociación Indígena de Cabildos y Autoridades Tradicionales De La Chorrera, n.d.). It is a new proposal to resolve conflicts, cooling the word, so that it does not hurt the other.

Epilogue

In the face of the serious problems, we face today as humanity, these proposals from the Global South can provide an answer to today's global crisis.

The need to break with the Cartesian paradigm that privileges reason over feeling, competition over cooperation, consumerism over moderation is challenged by new ways of understanding relationships with ourselves, with others, with nature and with the transcendent. This has a philosophical, metaphysical and anthropological significance which should also take into account indigenous worldviews.[3]

The secrets that reveal these routes from Latin America are a gift for the world that seeks new alternatives in the crisis of the models and paradigms that govern humanity since the 16th century. Our challenge is to learn from them and to put them into pedagogical proposals that make possible the construction of cultures of peace.

Endnotes

1) A first version of this document was presented at the meeting of the International Institute on Peace Education, Cyprus 2019.

2) Member of the United Nations Working Group on the Use of Mercenaries as a Means of Violating Human Rights. Office of the High Commissioner for Human Rights. Geneva, Switzerland, between April 2004 and July 2011. President of the group in April 2004 - February 2006. Member of the Global Campaign for Peace Education, Hague Appeal for Peace, International Institute on Peace Education, International Peace Bureau, Latin American Peace Research Council, Global Alliance for Ministries and Infrastructures for Peace, Colombian and Latin American and Caribbean Networks for Human Rights Education. As a member of these teams, Mrs. Benavides has had the opportunity to provide consulting, training, and research in peace education and human rights education throughout the Americas, Africa, and Europe. *For further biographical information see Biographical notes*

3) "In Philosophy, transcendence is the opposite of immanence. It refers to

that which is beyond consciousness, above its natural limits. Hence, it is associated with the idea of superiority... From the point of view of metaphysics, transcendence refers to that which is not part of tangible reality and which, in this sense, is considered infinitely superior" (Enciclopedia Significados, n.d., para. 4).

References

Asociación Indígena de Cabildos y Autoridades Tradicionales De La Chorrera. (n.d.). *ENDULZAR LA PALABRA* [unpublished PowerPoint slides].

Centro Nacional de Memoria Histórica. (2017). *Endulzar la palabra, memorias indígenas para pervivir*. Centro Nacional de Memoria Histórica.

Constitution of the Republic of Ecuador. October 20, 2008, Republic of Ecuador.

Constitution of the Republic of Ecuador. February 7, 2009, Republic of Ecuador.

de Sousa Santos, B. (2016). Epistemologies of the South and the future. *From the European South, (1),* 17–29.

El Portal de la Economía Solidaria. (2010, February 23). *"Vivir Bien" – propuesta de modelo de gobierno en Bolivia.* https://www.economiasolidaria.org/eu/noticias/vivir-bien-propuesta-de-modelo-de-gobierno-en-bolivia/

Enciclopedia Significados. (n.d.) *Trascendencia.* https://www.significados.com/trascendencia/

Fals Borda, O. (1981). La ciencia y el pueblo: nuevas reflexiones sobre la investigación-acción. *La sociología en Colombia: balance y perspectivas*. Memoria del III Congreso Nacional de Sociología, Bogotá, agosto 20-22 de 1980, pp. 149-174.

Gil Farekatde, Gil (2017). *Gift of Murui grandparents for future generations*. Centro Nacional de Memoria Histórica. Endulzar la Palabra. Memorias Indígenas para Pervivir..

Rodríguez Salazar, A. (n.d.). *Teoría y práctica del buen vivir: Orígenes, debates conceptuales y conflictos sociales. El caso de Ecuador.* [Unpublished doctoral dissertation]. Universidad del País Vasco.

Rodriguez Salazar, A. (2013, June 1). *25 Postulados para entender el Vivir Bien.* https://filosofiadelbuenvivir.com/25-postulados-para-entender-el-vivir-bien/

Secretaría Nacional de Planificación y Desarrollo – SENPLADES (2010).The Republic of Ecuador. National development plan: National plan for good living 2009-2013. Building a plurinational and intercultural state. Summarized version.

Chapter 19
Peace Education:
A Lay Perspective

Ela Gandhi

Generally the majority of people around the world are concerned about the situation both in their own country and worldwide. Some of the most critical problems facing the world in the present time are located in three fundamental issues that we face today; the first is the wild and ruthless scramble to accumulate as much wealth as possible, the second the scramble to gain power so that accumulation of wealth becomes possible and accessible, and three, this scramble has seen the loss of fundamental universal values of compassion, honesty, integrity, courage and concern for the other and the environment. A direct result of these three elements is the proliferation of violence, wars, violent conflicts, unbridled environmental degradation and exploitation of both other people and the earth's resources for profit and power.

If we accept this analysis of the situation then we see that the root cause is unbridled and unscrupulous materialism. How then can we change this mind set?

We see that our education system is geared towards producing a mental attitude that one receives education to be able to secure a good job so that you earn a good wage or to be able to set up a business so that you can make profit and become rich. Wealth is the important and all embracing criterion to want to learn. If a child is inclined towards art then parents and society deters him or her from pursuing it further as there is no wealth in it. This perception of education needs to change so that society also changes, or vice versa.

The present trend in education and in society generally is to encourage a culture of buying and of wanting things. Advertisements, media and our education system promote consumerism. But what we see is the unacceptable inequality and abject poverty on the one hand and the absolute opulence and unharnessed wealth accumulation on the other, with many trapped in between trying to reach the top. The top is wealth. But what we see is that to protect the ownership of the wealth we build walls, fences and armies. We build lethal weapons to arm the soldiers.

We are now voting governments into power because we feel that they will be able to protect our wealth and security. We are not interested in a government that cares for the poor, the down trodden and the marginalised. We use them to gain votes but we do not care where they live, how they are able to access food, care for their children or obtain health care. We support populists who fan the hidden fears and prejudices in the people and breed hatred, divisions and enmity. Experience has also revealed that while there is a transfer of power from one regime to another, the economic conditions of the vast numbers remain unchanged. The tyranny continues in new vestments.

So what needs to be done? A sustainable method needs to be found. That method is through education. Gandhiji began this experiment in South Africa in 1904. The experiment was as he put it after the realisation that the good of the individual is contained in the good of all; that work is important both to establish one's dignity as well as to earn a living and that therefore all work should be respected equally; that work of the tiller of the soil and the handicraftsman is the most important. Following on this realisation in 1904 he bought a piece of land in a rural area and invited those who were prepared to live according to this ideology to join him. A Settlement of some hundred people began this experiment. Everyone took the same wage. Everyone engaged in food growing activities. Everyone worked in the press to bring out a weekly newspaper aimed at education, information dissemination and mobilization of the masses against injustices they faced. Here all faiths were respected and people shared each other's beliefs to develop a better understanding of other's faiths. According to Gandhiji this understanding deepened their knowledge of their own faith.

Here they began to learn about a culture of nonviolence and to apply the principles to their own lives. It was education while working. Children learnt while on a nature walk. Gandhiji saw the link between all disciplines or subjects and children were taught accordingly. Similarly their parents too learned while engaging in the various activities.

They learned to become self-reliant and they learned to develop new skills in sewing, leather work, cooking and cleaning. They also learned how to deal with issues of garbage disposal and toilets that were environmentally friendly. Recycle, reuse and reduce started at the Phoenix Settlement in 1904.

But life was never dull - they played games, they played football and cricket and other games. They went for picnics, walking to beautiful picnic spots. So education was also fun and retentive. It was never stressful but rather learning happened in creative playful ways.

But above all education was geared towards developing a humane personality. Compassion, a sense of justice and respect for all of mother earth's creations were some of the basic values inculcated at the Settlement. Children on their nature walks with Gandhiji not only learned about the different plants, trees, butterflies and other insect life, but also how important they are and why we should nurture them. This kind of training started at a very early age.

Soon after birth until 10 years are the most crucial years when a child learns about its surroundings and what it means to him/her and about how to take care of each object, person and animals. What a child learns at this age remains a part of the person's ideology throughout life.

Gandhiji realised, through these experiments, that if we ask others to change or behave in a certain way we have to first implement the changes in our lives. Practise what you preach was a firmly embedded motto in his educational experiments. The move from an urban lavish life style to a simple rural life style where all chores were performed by all with no distinctions in terms of roles. Imparting of education was about doing things and learning both how to excel at what you do and learn self respect and respect for others,

Gandhi Development Trust began an education programme in the early 2000.

Initially we focused on a peace education programme at high schools. But later we decided to focus on the early learning stage with children 3-10 years of age.

We read about research which indicated that when animals are abused and badly treated in a home, there's a strong chance that people are also being abused in that home. There could be abuse of children, gender based violence or ill treatment of the elderly and those living with disabilities.

A study carried out by the Massachusetts Society for the Prevention of Cruelty to Animals and a North-eastern University survey found this link between animal cruelty and abuse in the home (Arluke & Luke, 1997). Furthermore Phil Arkow, a lecturer at Harcum College where he developed a course in Animal Assisted Therapy and Activities and was coordinator of the National Link Coalition, also affirmed this link between animal abuse and human abuse. More recently a report produced by Animal Defense Fund in 2023 (USA) found that 89% of women in abusive relationships reported that their pets were also under threat from abuse.

We therefore opted to focus on animals in our training modules for children. We also focused on humane education. Children who grow up in abusive environments often become less caring and humane and so end up as abusers themselves. By telling caring stories linked with animals a sense of caring love and compassion is aroused in children. Coupled with this training we also introduced training in developing food gardens. Nurturing plants and seeing them grow and caring for them instilled a sense of caring responsibility and love in children. Similarly relationships with pets also instil love and affection.

This training reduces the possibilities of them becoming bullies, abusers and instead enhances the possibility of them becoming caring loving compassionate human beings and increases the chances of them also becoming responsible citizens.

When adults disrespect, neglect, abuse or harm an animal, it starts a process of loss of feeling in our children – they witness the neglect, hurting, harming or killing of an animal without feeling a response because this becomes a normal sight.

Once children become unfeeling, abuse, neglect and cruelty become a habit or part of a child's life and accepted as normal.

The main objective of humane education is to develop in children the ability to understand and share the feelings of another being – human and animal.

This is the gift a parent/caregiver can give to a child - filling the child up with positive emotions which will stay with the child throughout their life, giving the strength to deal with challenges, the ability to bounce back from setbacks, and the ability to show unconditional affection in relationships.

When young children do not have parental affection - the most valuable birthright - we damage them. Such effects are not always seen in childhood or even adolescence and young adulthood, but they can come back in mid-life.

Perhaps humans can learn something from animals about parental affection: look at the picture of a hen with her chicks. How she cares for them under her wings, showing them love and warmth. The hen may be frightened off by dogs and snakes, but if their fright is for their children, they fight it out beyond their strength to protect their children.

Parents/Caregivers have a responsibility to develop and support good values in their children – showing love and kindness to animals will teach them to do the same and this extends to the way they will treat humans, as well.

This seems like an ideal situation in our violence torn world, but one has to start somewhere. Gandhiji said, "The basic premise of Nayi Talim (New Pedagogy) was that education had to be rooted in the culture, life and needs of the people" (M.K. Gandhi, 1962). It was defined as "education for life, education through life and education throughout life." As opposed to rote learning, it emphasised developing one's holistic personality through doing, thinking, caring and serving. The objectives of Nayi Talim were three- pronged. Firstly, it was people centric. A child belonging even to the lowest stratum of society must receive basic education. Education has to be free and compulsory up to the age of 14 years. Women must have equal rights to education as men.

To achieve this, Gandhiji said: Firstly "the Vidyapeeth (University) must go to the village" (M.K. Gandhi, 1962, p. 76).

Secondly, the new education system had to be character centric. It must build the child's moral character right from the time of the kindergarten. He emphasised that literary training itself added not an inch to one's moral height or character- building. Essentials of all religions should be taught to pupils for moral upbringing and also to promote communal harmony and universal brotherhood.

Thirdly, basic education had to be craft centric. Learning would now be reconnected to doing. Education and work should not be separated. "I hold that true education of the intellect can only come through a proper exercise and training of the bodily organs – hands, feet, eyes, ears, nose, etc. I would begin children's education by teaching them a useful handicraft and enabling them to produce from the moment they begin their training. I hold that the highest development of the mind and soul is possible only under such a system of education. However every handicraft has to be taught not merely mechanically as is done today, but scientifically-that is, the child should know the why and wherefore of every process. I am not writing this without some confidence, because it has the backing of experience. I have myself taught sandal making and even spinning on these lines with good results" (M.K. Gandhi, 1962, p. 74).

These then are some of my experiences in peace education. It is somewhat different from the usual courses in conflict resolution, negotiations and peace pacts. This is a preventive approach, an approach if widespread can bring about personality transformation that would eliminate exploitation, greed, scramble for power and hatred. It will help human beings become independent, self reliant, confident, compassionate men and women for whom war and violence would naturally be remote.

References

Arluke, A. & Carter, L. (1997). Physical cruelty towards animals in Massachusetts 1978-1996. *Society and Animals*, 5(3): 1955-204.

Gandhi, M.K. (1962). *Village Swaraj*. Compiled by H.M. Vyas Navjivan Publishing House.

Chapter 20
Joint Israeli-Palestinian Media to Promote Conflict Resolution

Hillel Schenker

My decision to become active in peace education via the media to promote a resolution to the Israeli-Palestinian conflict was a direct result of the 1973-74 Yom Kippur War and its aftermath. I served seven months in the Combat Engineering Corps on the Golan Heights. War is clearly hell, and that experience convinced me that I had to find a way to prevent future wars by being involved in seeking a resolution to the Israeli-Arab and Israeli-Palestinian conflict. My primary tool for doing this was peace journalism, which I later learned was a discipline developed by Prof. Johan Galtung. I already had skills and experience in journalism, as I had served from 1966 to 1969 as the editor of the English-language *Mishmar* (The Guardian), the quarterly publication of one of the three major kibbutz movements, the left-socialist Hashomer Hatzair Kibbutz Artzi movement.

Starting Out: New Outlook

The first vehicle I joined was the Tel Aviv-based English-language *New Outlook* magazine, the unofficial organ of the Israeli peace movement. *New Outlook* had been founded in 1957 after the 2nd Arab-Israeli war by a group of center-left independent Israeli Jewish and Arab journalists. Its Statement of Purpose declared that "it is the desire of the sponsors and editors of *New Outlook* that this publication serve as a medium for the clarification of problems concerning peace and cooperation among all the peoples of the Middle

East...."

The editors' approach was based upon Martin Buber's philosophy of dialogue, expressed in his famous 1923 essay "I and Thou." Then a professor at the Hebrew University of Jerusalem, Buber wrote a greeting to readers in the first issue, published in July 1957, which provided the publication with its title:

> Dear Friends,
>
> The future of the Near East depends on a comprehensive cooperation of Jews and Arabs. The hour is come for the Peoples to get a new outlook, in order to see where their great common interest lies and to act accordingly in common. (Buber, 1957)

Founding editor Simha Flapan was also a graduate of the left-socialist Hashomer Hatzair movement and a longtime kibbutz member. He and a colleague journalist, Dr. Ze'ev Katz, a member of the editorial board of *Haaretz*, brought each of the early issues to Prof. Buber at his home in Jerusalem for discussion before publication. Flapan, although not a formal academic, is considered the father of the "New Historians" — Benny Morris, Ilan Pape, Avi Shlaim, Tom Segev and others who challenged the official Israeli narrative of the history of the conflict. He did this with his two books, *Zionism and the Palestinians* (1979) and *The Birth of Israel: Myths and Realities* (1987).

Sadat Sends a Greeting

New Outlook demonstrated that it succeeded in its aim of holding a dialogue with the Arab world. In 1977, on the eve of his historic visit to Jerusalem, the Egyptian President Anwar Sadat sent a greeting to the opening of the journal's 20th anniversary symposium in Tel Aviv. This was the first ever communication by an Arab leader to an Israeli body:

> In the name of peace I take this opportunity to send a message of justice to the 5th international symposium of New Outlook. You have come from the four corners of the earth, of many persuasions and philosophies. You have come in the spirit of seriousness and amity. The Palestinian dimension of the tragic conflict which has haunted the Middle East for so long. Allow me distinguished delegates to express the hope that your deliber-

ations will prompt you to see the living reality of the Palestinian people and their inalienable right to statehood. For this is the only way to bring about fruitful dialogue between Arabs and Israelis. It is only within the bounds of the truly new outlook on the world of human affairs that men of goodwill may find their ways towards building peace together and beating their swords into ploughshares. Only then will they be able to lift the nightmare of renewed military confrontation from the suffering anguish of our peoples.

Mohamed Anwar El Sadat (New Outlook, Dec.1977-Jan.1978)

I became managing editor of *New Outlook* in December 1977, and the first issue that I edited, dated December 1977/January 1978, featured the title "Dramatic Days in November." It contained the greeting and the major presentations at the symposium. On the cover appeared a photo of President Sadat and Israeli Prime Minister Menachem Begin with representatives of a delegation from the conference, including Dr. Nahum Goldmann, head of the World Zionist Organization and the World Jewish Congress. Goldmann had been denied the opportunity to meet with Egyptian Presidents Sadat and Gamal Abdel Nasser by Prime Minister Golda Meir, which might have prevented the bloody Yom Kippur War. Also in the picture were former French Prime Minister Pierre Mendès-France, leading Israeli academics, some prominent Jewish Americans and the *New Outlook* editors.

President Sadat's visit to Israel and speech to the Knesset was the first step that led to the 1978 Camp David Accords and the Israeli-Egyptian peace treaty in 1979.

A senior member of the Egyptian delegation to the Knesset told us that it was reading *New Outlook*, which reached them via Europe, that convinced them that there was a possibility of peace with Israel. This was, of course, in the days before the Internet, when print journalism was the only option.

So peace journalism was able to have an impact on developments.

When Enemies Dare to Talk

The next *New Outlook* initiative took place in November 1978. While President Carter was hosting Prime Minister Begin and President Sadat at Camp

David, an unprecedented two-day Israeli-Palestinian dialogue was carried out at the fabled American Colony Hotel in East Jerusalem. The Israeli participants included leading Israeli writers Amos Oz, A.B. Yehoshua and Amos Elon, along with leading center-left politicians. The Palestinian delegation included Dr. Haider Abdel Shafi from Gaza who would become their spokesperson at the 1991 Madrid conference and West Bank mayors associated with PLO. What made this two-day dialogue particularly important was the fact that all the participants committed in advance to the publication of the exchange in book form. It was published as *When Enemies Dare to Talk: An Israeli-Palestinian Debate* (Flapan, 1979). Among the primary lessons that evolved from the discussions was, for Palestinians, the realization that the powerful Israelis have genuine fears for their survival. For the Israelis, one of the primary lessons was that the Palestinians considered the PLO, the Palestinian Liberation Organization, to be the authentic representative of their people's struggle for liberation.

Meeting with Palestinians in East Jerusalem

During this period a Palestinian Arabic-language newspaper, *Al Fajr* (The Dawn), was published in East Jerusalem as the unofficial voice of the PLO in the occupied territories beginning in 1974. In 1980 they decided to publish a weekly English-language edition. In the first issue they concluded the opening editorial with a call for dialogue with peace-loving Israelis. In response, a meeting of the *New Outlook* and *Al Fajr* editorial boards was arranged at the Philadelphia Restaurant in East Jerusalem. I was one of the Israeli participants in that meeting.

Over the course of 13 years, from 1977 to 1990, I continued working at *New Outlook* in various capacities, as managing editor, senior editor, special projects Director and, from 1987 to 1990, North American representative.

My assignment as North American representative was to coordinate the realization of an idea that evolved out of the initial encounter between the *New Outlook* and *Al Fajr* editorial boards. The idea was to organize a joint Israeli-Palestinian conference in the United States, whose government and public opinion were considered a key to promoting a resolution of the conflict.

In the mid-80s, dialogue between Israelis and PLO members began to proliferate. The Palestinians realized that if they wanted to achieve national liberation, it was important to speak with mainstream Israelis who defined themselves as Zionists. Peace-seeking Israelis realized it was important to speak with Palestinian members of the PLO, the official representatives of the Palestinian people. This led the right-wing Israeli government — led by Likud Prime Minister Yitzhak Shamir, who replaced Begin — to issue a ban on Israeli-PLO meetings. However, there was one legal loophole. Meetings between Israelis and PLO members were okay if they took place within an academic framework.

The "Road to Peace" Conference at Columbia University

The venue we found was Columbia University. In March 1989, it served as the location for the two-day 'New Outlook-Al Fajar Israeli-Palestinian Road to Peace Conference'. One of the American participants in the organizing committee, Prof. Nubar Hovsepian, represented Prof. Edward Said's American Council for Palestinian Affairs. Prof. Said, the noted author of *Orientalism* (1978) was a professor of literature at Columbia.

About 25 center-left Israelis and 25 Palestinians from the occupied territories and the PLO participated in the conference. Among the Israelis were Members of Knesset Shulamit Aloni, Yossi Sarid and Yair Tzaban, who would later become members of Prime Minister Yitzhak Rabin's government that would sign the 1993 Declaration of Principles, the 'Oslo Accords', which declared mutual recognition between the Israeli government and the PLO. The Palestinian delegation included senior PLO representative Dr. Nabil Sha'ath and the West Bank Palestinian leader Faisal Husseini. Dr. Sha'ath would later tell me that after the conference he flew to the PLO's Tunisian headquarters to tell Yasser Arafat that the Palestinians had partners for peace. One of the international speakers at the conference was Prof. Galtung, who believed that such civil society initiatives were a key to peace-building.

Unfortunately, in 2023-24 during the Israeli-Hamas War, Columbia University would become the scene of clashes between 'pro-Palestinian' and 'pro-Israeli' students, rather than a setting for peace education and conflict resolution.

The Oslo Accords were supposed to produce a resolution to the Israeli-Palestinian conflict within five years, by 1999. However, they did not provide a clear endgame based upon an end to the occupation and the establishment of a Palestinian state in the West Bank and Gaza, with East Jerusalem as its capital, alongside the State of Israel. The 2000 Camp David Summit conference between Israeli Prime Minister Ehud Barak and Arafat, hosted by President Bill Clinton, did not produce an agreement, and the Oslo Process collapsed with the outbreak of the Second Intifada in 2000.

New Outlook had closed at the end of 1991 and *Al Fajr* closed soon afterwards — both essentially due to lack of funding.

Palestine-Israel Journal - the First Joint Publication

In January 1994 the first issue of the East Jerusalem-based *Palestine-Israel Journal* (www.pij.org) was published, founded by veteran Palestinian journalist Ziad AbuZayyad and veteran Israeli journalist Victor Cygielman. Abu-Zayyad had been the editor of the Arabic edition of *Al Fajr*, while Cygielman had been a longtime member of the *New Outlook* editorial board. Its original goal was to accompany the Oslo Process with analysis and recommendations for how to complete the process. When the Oslo Process collapsed with the outbreak of the Second Intifada, the journal continued to publish, with the goal of providing analysis and recommendations for resolution of the conflict. With Israeli and Palestinian co-editors and managing editors, and with an equal number of about 15 Israeli and 15 Palestinian members on the editorial board — mainly academics, civil society activists and media practitioners — it continued to provide a platform for analysis and recommendations towards a resolution of the conflict.

I joined the staff in 2002 and since 2005 have served as the Israeli co-editor alongside Palestinian founding co-editor Ziad AbuZayyad.

Every issue has a central theme, with an approximately equal number of articles written by Palestinians and Israelis, along with a few international contributors. Issues have dealt with such topics as education, refugees, settlements, the environment, youth, women and the role of the international community. One issue was devoted to the "Israeli-Palestinian-German Relationship," with the support of the German Foreign Ministry. Another issue,

"Lessons from the Northern Ireland Peace Process" for Israelis and Palestinians was supported by the Irish government.

Continuing to Work Together Despite the Tragic War

Today the *Palestine-Israel Journal* is one of a small number of joint Israeli-Palestinian organizations continuing to work on peace education and peace-building, despite the tragic war. They include the joint Bereaved Family Forum, composed of Israelis and Palestinians who have lost a family member to the conflict, and Combatants for Peace, composed of Israelis who fought in the Israel Defense Force and Palestinians who participated in armed resistance who now believe that non-violence is the only answer.

Together with my colleague Ziad AbuZayyad, we have guided the preparation and publication of many of the over 70 issues of the journal. We also have provided a joint editorial for each issue we worked on.

The vicious Hamas attack on October 7, 2023, which killed 1,200 Israelis, the overwhelming majority of them civilians, along with the taking of more than 250 hostages, created a major crisis in Israeli-Palestinian relations. This was followed by the disproportionate Israeli response leading to the death of over 41,000 Palestinians in Gaza [this was the number when this article was prepared: Ed.], the displacement of the overwhelming majority of Palestinians from their homes and the destruction of much of the physical infrastructure. For the Israelis, October 7 was the worst blow in the country's history, shaking their sense of security and arousing memories of the Holocaust. For the Palestinians, the war has evoked a sense of a Second Nakba (catastrophe). The first Nakba took place in 1948 when, during the course of the First Arab-Israeli War, over 700,000 Palestinians were driven out of or fled from their homes and became refugees.

Both Israelis and Palestinians are guilty of war crimes during the current war. Israel has been charged by South Africa before the International Court of Justice with the crime of genocide, a case still waiting for a final verdict, though interim measures have been ordered. Meanwhile, Israeli Prime Minister Benjamin Netanyahu and former Defense Minister Yoav Gallant, along with Hamas leaders, have been issued warrants for their arrest by the chief prosecutor of the International Criminal Court.

WhatsApp and Joint Appeals for Peace

This crisis created a major challenge for the *Palestine-Israel Journal*. There were natural tensions at the beginning of the war, but Palestinian Co-Editor Ziad AbuZayyad suggested that we open a WhatsApp group for all 15 Israeli and 15 Palestinian members of the editorial board. Throughout the war, we have maintained a rare ongoing dialogue between us.

The issue that was about to be published in October 2023 was devoted to "Democracy", the major topic on the internal Israeli agenda before the war, due to the attempt to undermine the independence of the courts. This was also a major issue on the Palestinian agenda, given that elections for the Palestinian Authority Legislative Council and president have not been held since 2005-06. We managed to add a joint editorial, "Amidst the Horror Lies an Opportunity for Peace" (Schenker & AbuZayyad, 2023a).

And in November 2023 we issued a "Joint Israeli-Palestinian Call for Peace" (Schenker & AbuZayyad, 2023b).

It was only in September 2024 that we were able to complete and publish our first post-October 7, 2023 issue, devoted to "A Joint Search for a Way Forward: From Conflict to Conciliation" (Schenker & AbuZayyad, 2024).

Prof. Johan Galtung's Principles for the Middle East

As Prof. Galtung wrote in an article on "Peace Journalism and Reporting in the United States" (2015): "To say something about peace journalism, something has to be said about peace, to say something about peace, something has to be said about conflict and its resolution." In discussing how to deal with Israel and the Arab world, he wrote about the need for:

> Work on (a) Palestine recognized; (b) a two-state solution; (c) a Middle East Community (MEC) of Israel and five Arab neighbors; (d) 1967 borders adjusted; (e) Create an Organization for Security Cooperation in the Middle East simultaneously. (Galtung, 2015)

That brings us to where we are today. Prof. Galtung's proposals are at the heart of what is necessary to move forward. Both Israeli and Palestinian society are experiencing an extreme sense of trauma, and, consequently, an inability to feel a sense of empathy towards the other. Yet the very concept of **peace** must be returned to the Israeli-Palestinian and international discourse alongside the need for a resolution of the conflict.

One of the results of the current tragic war is the fact that the international community can no longer ignore the Israeli-Palestinian conflict. Prof. Galtung's first element, (a) "Palestine recognized" is clearly a factor, as Spain, Norway, Ireland, and later Slovenia, have joined Sweden as European countries that have recognized a Palestinian state. In the latest issue of the *Palestine-Israel Journal*, Alon Liel, a veteran Israeli ambassador and former director-general of its foreign ministry, wrote an article titled "The Recent Palestinian Recognition Momentum," promoting the importance of this process (Liel, 2024).

Element (b), the two-state solution, has clearly returned to the fore of the international community's response to the crisis. That includes [former, Ed.] US President Joe Biden's plan for a post-war two-state solution with the aid of a "revitalized Palestinian Authority," which he unfortunately only gave lip service to, and the statement by Saudi Arabia that post-war normalization with Israel depends on the creation of a clear path towards a Palestinian state alongside the State of Israel.

As for (c), a Middle East Community of Israel and its Arab neighbors, that is the essence of the Arab Peace Initiative adopted at the 2002 Arab League Summit Conference in Beirut. The API offers Israel recognition and normal relations with all 22 Arab states, backed by the 57 Organization of Islamic Cooperation members, based on an end to the occupation, the establishment of a Palestinian state in the West Bank and Gaza with East Jerusalem as its capital and an agreed-upon solution with the Israeli government to the refugee problem. That was at the heart of the statement by Jordanian Foreign Minister Ayman Safadi during the UN General Assembly meeting in September 2024, when he declared that "while Netanyahu says Israel is surrounded by enemies who want to destroy it, we're here, members of the Muslim-Arab Committee mandated by 57 Arab and Muslim countries... All of us are willing to guarantee the security of Israel, in the context of ending the occupation and allowing the emergence of Palestinian state" (Al Jazeera, 2024).

Issue (d), the 1967 borders adjusted, is the principle of mutually agreed-upon land swaps that was included during the 2013-14 negotiations led by US Secretary of State John Kerry as an element in the Arab Peace Initiative. According to Dr. Shaul Arieli, an Israeli expert on the settlement project, an exchange of 4% to 5% of land adjacent to the internationally recognized Green Line would mean that 80% of the settlers would be included within the sovereign state of Israel, neutralizing the settlement problem.

As for (e) Create an Organization for Security and Cooperation in the Middle East, we, the co-editors of *Palestine-Israel Journal*, Ziad AbuZayyad and I actually participated in such an initiative. In 2011, German-Iranian Prof. Mohssen Massarat convened a Conference on Security and Cooperation in the Middle East at the Evangelical Academy, Bad Boll, Germany, with participants from Egypt, Jordan, Iran, Lebanon, Israel and Palestine, modeled on the 1973 Conference on Security and Cooperation in Europe. A second session was held a year later at the School of Oriental and African Studies in London. Though there was no continuation, the seeds of the idea were sown.

Trump and Netanyahu

It is hard to predict the impact of Donald J. Trump's victory in the 2024 US elections. On the one hand, as an isolationist who is opposed to getting involved in wars, he will probably try to end the Israel-Gaza war. On the other hand, he has demonstrated no sympathy for the Palestinians and it is hard to believe that he will continue to promote President Biden's post-war two-state solution with the aid of a "revitalized Palestinian Authority." It can only be hoped and encouraged that Saudi Arabia, which has declared that it will only be ready for normalized relations with Israel if there is a clear path to a Palestinian state, will be able to influence Trump's approach to the region given his transactional approach to international affairs.

As for the Israeli scene, Prime Minister Netanyahu has apparently guaranteed the survival of his government for a full term until the 2026 elections. The addition of the four Knesset members from the small right-wing New Hope Party gives him a 68-member majority out of 120 Knesset members. Yet the polls still say that the opposition would defeat him in the next elections.

One of the challenges is that the opposition leaders haven't articulated a clear alternative policy to the current extreme government's approach, which would place the need for peace back on the country's agenda and address the need to resolve the Israeli-Palestinian conflict. This is also something that has to be encouraged both by internal Israeli factors like *Palestine-Israel Journal* and also the international community.

Threats to Freedom of the Press in Israel

Today, freedom of expression and independent journalism in Israel are under threat from the extreme right-wing government. Following comments made at a conference in London by *Haaretz* publisher Amos Schocken defending the Palestinians' right to resist the occupation, the government has mandated that any government-funded body refrain from communicating with *Haaretz* or placing advertisements in the paper. This would be a major economic blow. The Knesset also passed an initial reading of a bill that would close the relatively independent public TV station Kan and replace it with private media vehicles.

Meanwhile, the *Palestine-Israel Journal*, as a not-for-profit publication, is faced with a severe challenge to its existence because of the constant and urgent need for emergency funding. The government has also tried to place obstacles to international fundraising for all civil society not-for profit organizations. Prime Minister Netanyahu clearly aspires to Hungarian Prime Minister Viktor Orbán's and Trump's approach to independent media and civil society.

Despair is Not an Option

Although the current reality is bleak, peace journalism, as practiced by *Palestine-Israel Journal* continues to serve as a platform for "A Joint Search for a Way Forward." Despair should not be an option, for either Palestinians or Israelis. We need new, farsighted leadership, on both sides. And we need the international community ready to play a proactive role in promoting a resolution to the conflict.

References

Al Jazeera English [@AJEnglish]. (2024, September 29). *Video: Jordan's FM pushes back against Netanyahu's "enemy" claim.* X. https://x.com/AJEnglish/status/1840421226696654901

Buber, M. (1923). Incorporated in a greeting in *Outlook* (1957), 43.

Flapan, S. (1979). *Zionism and the Palestinians.* Croom Helm.

Flapan, S. (1987). *The birth of Israel: Myths and realities.* Pantheon Books.

Flapan, S. (Ed.). (1979). *When enemies dare to talk: An Israeli-Palestinian debate (5/6 September 1978).* Croom Helm.

Galtung, J. (2015). Peace Journalism and Reporting in the United States. *Brown Journal of World Affairs. 22(1), 1-13.*

Liel, A. (2024). *The recent Palestine recognition momentum.* Palestine-Israel Journal. https://www.pij.org/articles/2293/the-recent-palestine-recognition-momentum

Said, E. (1978). *Orientalism.* Pantheon Books.

Schenker, H. & AbuZayyad, Z. (2023a). Amidst the horror lies an opportunity for peace. *Palestine-Israel Journal.* https://www.pij.org/articles/2258/amidst-the-horror-lies-an-opportunity-for-peace

Schenker, H. & AbuZayyad, Z. (2023b). A joint Israeli-Palestinian call for peace! *Palestine-Israel Journal.* https://www.pij.org/event/86

Schenker, H. & AbuZayyad, Z. (Eds.). (2024). A joint search for a way forward FROM CONFLICT TO CONCILIATION. *Palestine-Israel Journal* (Vol. 29 No. 1 & 2). https://www.pij.org/journal/112

Chapter 21
Peace Activism
Is Peace Education

S. P. Udayakumar

Inquisitive young minds do have a quest to know more about the world they live in, its ills and their cures. As a young man, I could not understand why human beings should ever fight with each other and kill brutally to achieve their goals; nor could I comprehend why all the science and technology and the modern developmental paraphernalia let the poor and vulnerable people down and they should suffer from poverty and misery. Although I was not well-informed, I always had an inkling that everything was not all right around me in my world. It bothered me vaguely, made me think in unclear terms, and I was driven to seek quick and easy solutions.

The predicament continued and got worse when I took up teaching English in a senior secondary school in a remote village of Tigrai province, a mountainous and windy region of northern Ethiopia. I used to flee to the national capital, Addis Ababa, at every possible opportunity to escape from the war-torn and famine-stricken Tigrai and get a gasp of fresh air. There I came across a UNESCO publication in a library that carried a chapter on the International Peace Research Association (IPRA). Hurray, that was what I was looking for! I wasted no time in writing to its Secretary General and to Robert Aspeslagh, the executive secretary of the Peace Education Commission of IPRA about my interest in joining them.

On returning to Tigrai, I founded UNESCO Clubs in the schools at Maichew and Makale. The Stalinist and militarist government of Mengistu Haile Mariam did not like it but had to put up with it because of the UNESCO tag attached to the effort. Eventually, I began to write and speak about peace education in Ethiopia in newsletters and international conferences on peace research. Robert Aspeslagh acted as my mentor and when Robin Burns took over the reign of PEC from him, she nominated me for the International Scholars Program at the University of Notre Dame, Indiana. That formal initiation into the academic discipline of peace studies coupled with a previous brief stint at the University of Oslo took me all the way to the University of Hawai'i at Manoa where I worked as a research assistant to Professor Johan Galtung for more than three years and pursued my doctoral studies.

I founded the South Asian Community Centre for Education and Research (SACCER) and prepared to come back to India in order to undertake some educational and research ventures in the region. Professor Johan Galtung, my boss, teacher, guide, thesis committee member, co-author and friend, added 'Action' to my dream project: SACCER Action. I had absolutely no idea that the suffix Johan Galtung added was going to be my vocation for the rest of my life. He did not want to stop with education and research but insisted on following up with suitable action. He had the ingenuity to think about both peace research and peace work.

I ended up as an anti-nuclear activist conscientizing the Indian public about the perils of Uranium mining, nuclear reactors, radioactive waste, and atomic bombs. In this day and age of the twin-evil of Nuclearism-cum-Fascism, that tends to threaten the contemporary nation-state system and endanger all our survival, wellbeing, identity and freedom (as Galtung would list), we ought to educate the global civil society about all this. After all, Fascism is the ideology behind Nuclearism and Nuclearism is the penultimate expression of Fascism. Education or conscientization in this larger social context implies political socialization, to be more precise, protest socialization.

Protest Socialization

Human socialization is predominantly political, and this political socialization begins with one's birth and ends only with death. However, the term 'political socialization', which came into existence in 1960 and gained prominence in the 1970s, has been mainly used to refer to youthful learning processes (Jaros 1973, p. 8). Political socialization is generally defined as "the developmental process through which persons acquire political orientations and patterns of behavior" (Dennis, 1973, p. 5). Much of the research in this subject concerns itself with the enquiry about the etiology of the system or the aggregate of the individual's political behavior (Dennis, 1973, pp. 5-6). The traditional concern of researchers has been the political development of the young to see how youngsters gain their political orientations.

There have been two major categories of concern in political socialization research: system-level effects which demonstrate the relevance of socialization for the operations of political systems, and individual-level concerns which illustrate the processes by which individuals are politically socialized (Jaros, 1973). The latter concentration is the best developed area which concerns itself with Greenstein's questions "who learns what from whom under what circumstances with what effects?" (Jaros, 1973, p. 139). Several different theories such as the 'systems persistence theory' of Easton and Dennis, psychoanalytic theory, learning theory, and cognitive development theory have provided the guidance in political socialization research (Jaros, 1973, pp. 136-147).

Among these, the psychocultural approach regards political socialization as a simple process and assumes that significant socialization experiences take place early in life, that these experiences are neither intended to have political effects nor are the political effects recognized, and that the socialization process is a unidirectional one in which the 'basic' family experiences have a significant impact upon the secondary structures of politics. If we expand this early and latent political socialization, according to Almond and Verba, we may find the sources of political attitudes include early socialization experiences, late socialization experiences during adolescence, and postsocialization experiences as an adult that are both political and nonpolitical, and intended and unintended to have an effect on political attitudes (Almond & Verba, 1965, pp. 266-271).

A closer scrutiny of the larger society with its multifarious socialization agents and processes for history constructions, identity formations, future envisionings has to be focused on 'social education'. Such an approach becomes even more crucial when the role of the formal school system in influencing the people's concept of history, identity and futures is quite limited, and the majority of the people do not undergo the 'schooling' process in many South countries anyway.

Like teachers and traditional story-tellers, the role of politicians in influencing the masses' concepts of identity, history and futures through their public speeches is rather important. The 'state-politician-public policy' trio plays the 'school-teacher-textbook' mix with almost the same functional roles. Street-protestor-government policies/projects combine have come to play such a vital political socialization function in today's 'globalized' world that keeps fighting against monetization, mechanization and marketization of everything in life. The recent fight against the Russian-sponsored nuclear power plant at a village called Koodankulam near the southernmost tip of India can be an illustrative case study.

The Koodankulam Case

The Rajiv Gandhi government in New Delhi signed the Koodankulam nuclear power project (KKNPP) deal with the Mikhail Gorbachev government of the Soviet Union on November 20, 1988, barely two years after the nightmarish Chernobyl accident that had taken place on April 26, 1986. Although many local farmers in and around Koodankulam felt enthused about potential high land value, job prospects for their youth, overall growth and a better life, the nuclear fears did run quite high, especially among the coastal fishing communities. They were afraid of plant interference in fishing, disposal of the hot and radioactive coolant water into the sea, overall impacts on fish and marketing, and even eventual evacuation from their native villages.

Thanks largely to a handful of social activist groups, public opinion was mobilized against the nuclear power plant and Rajiv Gandhi was forced to put off the foundation laying ceremony that had been planned for December 19, 1988. Between 1989 and 1991, the situation changed rapidly as the Soviet Union collapsed, Mikhail Gorbachev lost power and Rajiv Gandhi (who had been out of power) got killed, and consequently, the Koodankulam project was shelved.

However, the project was restarted in March 1997 when the Indian prime

minister Deve Gowda and the Russian president Boris Yeltsin signed a supplementary deal to the 1988 agreement. The anti-Koodankulam campaign
was also revived slowly with talks and seminars on the issue organized by
several groups and the nuclear weapons issue was also included ever since
the May 1998 nuclear tests (Pokhran II) of the Vajpayee government. What
started off with the NIMBY (Not In My Backyard) factor, became more comprehensive and principle-oriented.

Koodankulam continued to be the rallying point as it provided immediacy,
a sense of urgency and focus. The *Anumin Nilaya Ethirpu Iyakkam* (Nuclear
Power Project Opposition Movement) was created on November 14, 1999, at
Nagercoil and sporadic small-scale mobilization went on. When prime minister A. B. Vajpayee signed the final agreement on the Koodankulam Nuclear
Power Project on November 6, 2001, a broad umbrella organization called
People's Movement Against Nuclear Power (PMANP) was founded at Mad-
urai on November 10, 2001. It was later broadened and re-christened as People's Movement Against Nuclear Energy (PMANE) in order to include the
nuclear bomb and related issues also.

The facts that this kind of 'development' project could damage the ecological
balance of this sub-region, give rise to environmental hazards, and undermine the rights to life and to livelihood of the farmers and the fisherfolks
alike. Such concerns have never been important for the state elites. For them,
development means economic growth reflected in enhanced statistical aggre-
gates and not the cumulative pursuit of happiness of individual citizens or
communities. In their scheme of providing larger economic good for a large
number, sociological and environmental consequences matter little.

In the globalizing pro-development, economistic environment, a nuclear
power station built in their midst looks appealing for the poverty-stricken
farmers as (many of them wrongly assume that) it could increase their land
value; offer them lucrative jobs; generate more economic opportunities; bring
more visibility, attention and resources to their communities and enhance the
overall development of the area. The mostly illiterate and semi-literate rural
people of this area are largely unaware of the consequences of power plant
accidents or a nuclear war and of the fact that the Earth can be blown up sev-
en times over by the nuclear powers around the world.

When the patriarchal State thrusts developmental projects down their throats in a high-handed manner with little public participation or democratic dialogue, the relatively-privileged top layer of the rural societies plays along (and seeks to make the best out of the situation), and others passively accept due largely to the 'we-cannot-fight-the-government' or 'why-should-I-stick-my-neck-out' or 'who-cares' or 'if-someone-organizes-against-something-s/he-must-have-some-selfish-agenda-in-it' and other such apolitical attitudes that are prevalent in the contemporary Indian political culture (or lack thereof).

However credible it may be, the State looks down upon any opposition to a 'development' project as anti-national and even unpatriotic. The State ignores, insults, or intimidates the unorganized and self-motivated dissenters and violates their democratic rights. If and when they or the situation gets out of control, the State and/or its agents would not even mind incinerating them. This 4-I strategy (ignore, insult, intimidate, incinerate) of the modern State is rather universal.

Although anti-nuclear activities and sentiments were not hitherto totally unknown in the southernmost tip of India, and the area woke up to the nuclear reality as far back as in 1988 when the Koodankulam project was first proposed, the Koodankulam conflict has been rather dormant. There have been intermittent encounters between the State and the oppositional movement/s with mixed results.

The Manmohan Singh government (2004-2014) tried to thrust a pro-nuclear energy policy down the throats of Indians despite their stiff resistance all over the country. In a highly and densely populated country like India, nuclear energy with deadly wastes would pose serious dangers and threats to the common people. The current and intensified phase of the struggle against the KKNPP erupted in 2011 and went on continuously for almost three years. The Tamil Nadu police registered more than 353 cases with serious charges such as 'sedition,' 'waging war on the Indian State,' 'attempt to murder (state officials)', and so forth against 5296 named accused and 221483 unnamed accused at the Koodankulam police station alone. This is a history of sorts in independent India.

Although the protestors were invited to meet with the chief minister of Tamil

Nadu and the prime minister of India, there was hardly any dialogue between the government and the people. Johan Galtung establishes that "dialogue is based on questioning." He adds: "The conflict party opens with '!'. The breakthrough comes when he changes to '?'. At that point real dialogue, mutual search and discovery start." According to Johan Galtung, "conflicts must be transformed so that the parties can live creatively and non-violently and the violence avoided. The parties have to break down the polarisation within themselves and between them because it makes empathy, dialogue and creativity as impossible as deep understanding and dialogue with ebola, HIV, cholera or bubonic plague, with scorpions" (Galtung 2004, p. 170-179).

Nonviolent Protests

Instead of engaging in a meaningful dialogue, the Indian authorities unleashed all kinds of atrocities on the protestors such as imprisonment, curfew and prohibitory orders, intimidation campaigns, home searches, physical attacks on our persons and properties, police atrocities, and other such high-handed behaviour. The protestors were forced to seek justice from the people of India through multifarious peaceful and nonviolent protests. They undertook a whole array of actions to push their anti-nuclear agenda.

Over 100 actions have taken place. There is only space here to name types of action: for a full list see Appendix 4.

Types of Action: Hunger strikes; meeting with officials; organizing seminars, conferences, teach-ins and other 'educational' activities; reaching out with information to people from the villages to district, state and national levels; using diverse media from the printed to the digital; special activities with and by women, youth; rallies, ritual events for different religious groups; boycotting nuclear plants and their workers; special actions for and by specific groups of people including women, children and youth, and promotion of alternative energy.

All these democratic, peaceful and nonviolent protests were actually undertaken with the 4-P principles proposed by Swami Vivekananda: Purity, Patience, Perseverance and Prema (Love) (Vivekananda, 1894).

References

Almond, G. & Verba, S. (1965*). The civic culture: Political attitudes and democracy in five nations*. Little Brown and Company.

Dennis, J. (1973). *Political socialization research: A bibliography*. Sage.

Galtung, J. (2004). *Transcend & transform: An Introduction to conflict work*. Pluto Press.

Jaros, D. (1973). *Socialization to politics*. Praeger.

Vivekananda, S. (November 30, 1894). [Letter to Dr. Nanjunda Rao]. Retrieved from https://vivekavani.com/li-dear-beloved-letters-swami-vivekananda/

Chapter 22

Africa Peace and Development Network: The Past, Present and Future of Peacebuilding

George Mutalemwa

Introduction

This paper seeks to contribute to knowledge regarding a newly established network, namely the Africa Peace and Development Network. Four issues constitute the kernel of this chapter on the network popularly known by its Swahili acronym MAMA, derived from *Mtandao wa Amani na Maendeleo Afrika*. First, the paper attempts to summarize the historical development of the Africa Peace and Development Network; second, explain the reasons for which MAMA was established; third, assess its strengths and weaknesses; and fourth, discuss its vision for global peace and development. All is done with a special focus on Africa. The reason for this summary is to take stock of the major developments, keep the readership informed and preserve and promote the values for which the network was founded. The chapter employs literature sources in print and digital forms, testimonials and the author's personal experience while striving to avoid any conflict of interest, as the author is also the co-founder and leader of the network. The name MAMA was first introduced on 4 November 2022 during a conference of the Africa Peace Research and Education Association (AFPREA) in Juba, South Sudan. AFPREA is a regional member of the International Peace Research Association (IPRA). On the same day, a WhatsApp Group also known in Swahili as *Amani na Maendeleo (MAMA)*, meaning Peace and Development, was set up. However, it should be noted that finding the right name required a great deal of searching. As Anna Tibaijuka would later rightly put it, MAMA is a network with a beautiful name (Tibaijuka, 2024). In my view, it is beautiful because of its varied dimensions. First, it represents a network that is determined to promote peace and development in Africa. Second, it is in Swahili, which represents the African identity and origins of the network. Third, it recognizes the role of women in peacebuilding around the world and across Africa.

Indeed, the establishment of MAMA is a tip of an iceberg of preparatory activities that started in 2018, when three pioneers of the network held their first meeting in Vechta, Germany, sponsored by the University of Vechta through its International Office. Prof. Dr. Prof. h.c. Egon Spiegel from the University of Vechta in Germany, Prof. Dr. Liu Cheng from Nanjing University in China as well as UNESCO Chair and Dr. George Mutalemwa from St. Augustine University of Tanzania in Tanzania discussed and agreed upon four activities:

- co-editing a special issue on peace studies and sustainable development to be published by St. Augustine University of Tanzania;
- organizing an international peace conference in Tanzania;
- organizing a workshop also in Tanzania;
- organizing an exchange program for students and staff.

Shortly after the Vechta meeting Prof. Lester R. Kurtz from George Mason University in Fairfax, Virginia, USA, joined the pioneers of the network which would later be known as MAMA.

However, before the implementation, COVID-19 struck and ushered in a new way of organizing. With travel restrictions in place and safety precautions in mind, the conference and workshop plans were halted. It was not until May 2024 that MAMA teamed up with several peacebuilding associations in Africa to organize a major international conference in Arusha and Mwanza, punctuated by meetings with the Maasai communities affected by challenges in Loliondo and the Serengeti area, and a visit to Julius Nyerere's birthplace in Butiama, all in Tanzania. The conference took place after the pioneers had established weekly webinars on 27 October 2021, first known as "Peace Studies for Sustainable Development in Africa," and later on as "Global Peace

Studies for Sustainable Development in Africa."

The prefix "Global" to the webinar name reflects the nature of the network, which was transcontinental right from the beginning, bringing together pioneers representing Africa, Europe, America and Asia. Speakers and participants came from different parts of the world. The content of the talks given was also international, taking into account the transdisciplinary, interdisciplinary and multidisciplinary nature of both Peace Studies and Development Studies. It was, in fact, our new collaborators from the University of Congress in Argentina, who added "Global" to the name when they offered to create flyers to promote the webinars and to livestream them on their YouTube Channel.

Some Notable Achievements

By the end of the year 2024, MAMA had organized 144 webinars. As webinars were going on, the pioneers were co-editing books. The first book, *Peace Studies for Sustainable Development in Africa: Conflicts and Peace Oriented Conflict Resolution*, was published in 2022 as part of the book series *Advances in African Economic, Social and Political Development* (Spiegel, Mutalemwa, Cheng & Kurtz, 2022). The second book, *Peace as Nonviolence: Topics in African Peace Studies* was also published in 2024 by Springer, in the same book series (Spiegel, Mutalemwa, Cheng & Kurtz, 2024). These publications were not only an opportunity for contributing to knowledge, especially among young African scholars, but also a springboard to network creation.

Two kinds of networks can be deduced from the above, a network of authors and editors, and a network of webinar participants and speakers. The two networks morphed into each other, enriched each other, and one: the MAMA network emerged. While the original idea was to publish one book in lieu of the special Issue in the *Journal of Sociology and Development*, the enthusiasm of the African scholars redounded in the publication of a 700-page book, and encouraged MAMA to consider a second publication, equally well received.

The end of the second book began preparation for the third book, still under review, titled *Networking for Peace and Development in Africa: Legacy, Transformation and Sustainability*. This book is based on webinar presentations and aimed at consolidating the network, recognizing the importance of the webinar topics and appreciating the offers of the speakers to serve the network through their talks. It is set to be published in 2025.

A number of factors may account for this extraordinary productivity. First of all, young African academics need to publish their scholarly works. Second, and related to that, publishing companies often privilege authors from the northern hemisphere over those from the so-called global south (Neba & Bain, 2024). Third, most of the editors are world class authors, including, for example, Prof. Lester R. Kurtz who is the editor of the world famous *Encyclopedia of Violence, Peace and Conflict* (2022). Fourth is the quality of the publisher, Springer International.

Thus the MAMA network is built on the solid foundation laid down in 2018 by the first meeting of the would-be pioneers of the network in Germany, followed by the *Global Peace Studies for Sustainable Development in Africa* webinars, as an academic association of researchers, activists, and all people who care about peace, wellbeing, dignity and the environment. It is not a political organization though it discusses political issues. It is not a religious organization though it discusses spiritual matters. It is definitely not an economic organization seeking profit, though MAMA discusses economic affairs. MAMA is a civil society organization led by academics in search of knowledge, intellectual development and wisdom.

In 2017 the General Assembly of the Association of Catholic Universities and Higher Institutes of Africa and Madagascar passed a resolution for each member institution to have a department of Peace Studies. During the General Assembly, I was elected Executive Secretary of the Association. As soon as I finished reading all the Resolutions, I was inspired to prioritize Peace Studies over and above all else. The establishment of a department of Peace Studies had practical as well as ontological value. Experience shows that in General Assemblies and various other meetings, there is more of talking than doing. I wanted to change that.

However, I had little knowledge of the field, and in fact I still have a lot to learn in Peace Studies. Luckily, I had worked with Prof. Dr. Prof. h.c. Egon Spiegel during my work and PhD studies at the University of Vechta in Germany from 2009-2015. Prof. Spiegel researched, taught and published on Peace Studies. Once during my stay in Germany, he asked me to proofread a book *Peace Studies in a Globalized World: An Illustrated Introduction to Peace Studies* which he co-authored with Prof. Liu Cheng (Cheng & Spiegel, 2015).

It followed that when I was confronted with the implementation of the resolution to mainstream Peace Studies, (Mutalemwa & Trochemowitz, 2022) I went to Prof. Spiegel and found him very enthusiastic about the idea. The advice I got during the 2018 meeting in Vechta gave birth to the webinars, conference, publications and eventually MAMA. The method of implementation became global and more inclusive than narrowing Peace Studies down to Catholic institutions in Africa. In this way, MAMA has a universal outlook and identity, working for the common good.

In relation to the resolution institutionalizing Peace Studies, there was a much more fundamental reason to focus on peace, especially in Africa, in the sheer number of violent conflicts on the continent, which has caused untold suffering and loss of people's lives (Pul, 2014). Can Peace Studies prevent, minimize or stop violent conflicts? We answer in the affirmative. Peace is too precious to lose. It is a skill to be taught and learnt. It is a value to be inculcated and promoted. It is a treasure not to be taken for granted but rather to be nurtured and sustained.

Once a person recognizes a value, gets a useful skill and has knowledge about the value and skill, it would be a contradiction in terms and self-defeating to go against the value, skill and knowledge. Universal values of truth, justice, kindness, love and peace apply to everyone. The kind of education and training promoted by MAMA seeks to build minds and hearts that not only know about peace, but act peacefully. Peace becomes a culture, part of human nature and a method of life. The opposite of peace is thus uncultured, inhuman and lifeless. For this reason we argue that violent conflicts and wars are the very antithesis of peace, and should be strongly opposed, unanimously prevented and completely stopped.

MAMA and Theory of Change

The establishment of the Africa Peace and Development Network (MAMA) is informed by two theories, one building on the other. These theories are the People's Organizations Development Theory (PODT) (Mutalemwa, 2015) and the University Revitalization Theory (URT) (Mutalemwa, 2018). The former was created in 2015 as part of my PhD thesis at the University of Vechta focusing on people's organizations, the latter also by me in 2018 with a focus on higher learning institutions. Both of them have four stages of implementation. They can be summarized as Needs Assessment, Organizing, Networking, and Transformation.

In both theories, actors start as individuals at a micro level who identify a problem, need or issue. Then individuals talk to one another about the problem they face and move to a second level, which is known as a meso level and establish an association to address the problem. After the second level, the association creates a network in the third or macro level. Finally, the individuals (micro), association (meso) and network (macro) experience transformation, which seems to be the last stage, by accomplishing fulfillment of the reason for being. However, it should be noted that unlike linear development, after this final stage, individuals and associations identify new challenges, which call for a repeat of the process. This goes on in a spiral, each time causing a new kind of development.

It can be inferred that the establishment of MAMA followed the same stages explained in the PODT and URT theories above. Starting with stage one (Needs Assessment), identifying the need to mainstream Peace Studies in Africa, I reached out to my friend Egon (Prof. Egon Spiegel). Egon invited Prof. Liu Cheng to discuss the issue at hand. Soon afterwards, Prof. Lester R. Kurtz was invited to participate. In the second stage (Organizing), the four of us came together to identify activities and plan implementation.

A problem remains a problem unless people begin to talk about it and strive to find solutions. Talking is necessary but not sufficient. When people stop at talking, without walking the talk associations, networks and institutions including states fail.

MAMA leaders decided to walk the talk, and create the network organically, inviting other networks, and was in turn invited by other networks to collaborate, becoming a network of networks. The earliest collaborators included:

- Universidad de Congreso (UC), Mendoza, Argentina through Dr. Mariana Covolo;
- Catholic Peacebuilding Network (CPN) through Prof. Gerald Powers

and Fr. William Headley;

- International Federation of Catholic Universities (IFCU/FIUC) through Prof. Francois Mabille;
- International Peace Research Association (IPRA) through Prof. Matt Meyer;
- World Intellectuals' Wisdom Forum (WIWF) and Commonwealth Interfaith Network (CIN) through Dr. Thomas Clough Daffern;
- African Peace Research and Education Association (AFPREA) through Dr. Charles Wasike;
- St. Augustine College of South Africa through Prof. Terry Sacco;
- AttentionAge.org through Mr. Peter Barus, Vermont, USA;
- Human Dignity and Humiliation Studies Network through Dr. Evelin Lindner (Global Citizen);
- International Institute on Peace Education (IIPE) through Prof. Janet Gerson.

--and the list is growing.

Each of these institutions has various partners and therefore they amplify MAMA's activities just as MAMA is keen on spreading the word about the activities of each of these institutions. This list of partner networks certainly builds on institutions earlier mentioned: the University of Vechta, Germany; UNESCO Chair at Nanjing University in China; George Mason University, Fairfax, Virginia, USA and St. Augustine University of Tanzania.

Completion of the Networking stage leads to the fourth stage, Transformation. The PODT and URT theories are silent on when transformation takes place. As far as MAMA is concerned, there are some indicators even at the initial stages of building and consolidating the network. But Transformation is a process.

For example, we can consider the transformation of MAMA against the original objectives. One was to offer a ninety-minute webinar session on a weekly basis. This happened without a miss. Another was to produce scholarly work, and two books have been published. The major objective, to establish a peace and development network, has been accomplished, and the network is growing. More than 240 members are on the WhatsApp Group, and many others engage through email. In 2024, we established a five-member steering committee in Mwanza, Tanzania, to help develop the network. The members have drafted a MAMA Constitution to be discussed and approved by the full membership.

The task of building a strong and sustainable network is enormous. After two years, the to-do list is still long. Creating a network is one thing; maintaining, improving and solidifying it must be sustained. I would like to argue that we are still at the creating stage, and this should be the focus of our evaluation. We need to increase open and inclusive membership. We are not only interested in number, but also in quality. Ideally, a person interested in joining the network is admitted without any fees, application or registration procedure.

Three Pillars of Network Formation

Three pillars are essential in gauging the development of a young network such as MAMA. These include formalization, motivation and promotion. At this initiation stage of the network, we feel that even if members do not have to be registered it is still vitally important to register the network so that it is recognized by regulatory authorities in Tanzania, where its headquarters are. The registration process is already in progress. This constitutes the process of formalization, which is essential at this stage of network formation. With the formalization in place, the legality of the network would be established and as such its existence and operations cannot be questioned because MAMA exists by law.

The formalization process goes hand in hand with the motivation of members to stay interested in the work of the network. This is happening by incentivizing participants through offering them certification. Ideally, we plan to offer certificates to each participant who has attended at least ten webinars. Those who have attended twenty webinars will get a different kind of certification and the same will apply to those who attend thirty or more sessions. We are aware that this is just a token of appreciation. A similar token is planned for our speakers who make these webinars possible much like our esteemed participants.

MAMA considers the award of certifications as one of the steps to motivate participants and speakers. The next step is offering participants academic credentials. Specifically, we plan to offer a master's degree in African Peace

Studies. This will largely be pursued online but with a possibility of in person interactions. One of the major advantages of the online program is to reduce the cost around tuition, accommodation and travel. Conversant with the economic challenges facing Africa, the online program maybe the panacea for higher learning and indeed the future of learning in Africa as we envisage quality education for all. The other advantage is certainly an opportunity to learn from speakers from potentially any reputable university under the sun and at no cost. MAMA can thus revolutionize online education thanks to the digital revolution. This would be another way of motivating people to stay with and in the network while increasing their academic qualifications. Plans for the M.A. program are under way. As we strive to motivate others, we also get motivated by those who collaborate with us and amplify our work such as CIRAD-IFCU (2022) which shares MAMA's work through their website and LinkedIn platform.

So far our medium of communication has been English. However, we are aware of the need of involving non-English speakers as well. To bring these people on board, we need to get ready and include participants and speakers from other languages. So far, we have had requests from French and Spanish speakers. Certainly, we will need volunteers who are conversant with these languages. Another language that would motivate more speakers and participants would be Swahili. For MAMA with its roots in Tanzania, the inclusion of Swahili would be logical and welcome. The issue here is not the choice between this language and the other: It is about giving participants an opportunity to use the language they are most comfortable with. This opportunity would be a practical contribution to decolonial studies by privileging local languages, cultures and knowledges.

The inclusion of participants from different linguistic backgrounds would help diffuse the values of the network in various geographical locations. With time, MAMA branches may spring up and grow in those regions. In the end, MAMA would be present in every region and country. For example, there could be MAMA-French, MAMA-Spanish and MAMA-Swahili. Alternatively, the network may be named after the country in which it exists such as MAMA-DRC Congo and MAMA-Colombia or any other appropriate name. In Tanzania for instance, we are discussing the introduction of JAMAA (Jukwaa la Amani na Maendeleo Afrika Asilia) as an authentic platform of peace and development for the Swahili speaking world.

Having touched upon the question of formalization and motivation as essential pillars of the network creation, we proceed with an equally important pillar, namely promotion. In order to make people know, like and trust the network, MAMA needs to make itself known far and wide. This act of promoting the network has to be done well and consistently. Hence, we need professionals to assist with publicity and advertising. Some of the tools to help with this promotion include: website, social media, magazines and use of partner networks to amplify MAMA's objectives, values, mission and vision. The following section sums up the vision, mission, objectives and values of the network.

Vision, Mission, Objectives and Values

Vision

We envision peaceful, safe, inclusive, sustainable and developed societies around the world and across Africa.

Mission

Promoting education, research and advocacy that support peace, nonviolence and sustainable development in Africa.

Objectives

The following are the four major objectives of the network:

1. Advocating for and maintaining the link between peacebuilding and sustainable development.
2. Promoting training avenues for women, youth, children and special needs groups on human rights, justice and environmental sustainability.
3. Enhancing community engagement for conflict resolution through nonviolence.
4. Promoting coalitions of peacebuilding networks locally and internationally.

Core Values

The core values of the network are universal and they include but are not limited to the following:

Peace, Ubuntu, nonviolence, truth, justice, dignity, equality, human rights, environmental justice, inclusion, unity, well-being, professionalism and freedom.

Moderation Skills and Webinar Organization

Besides the encouraging team spirit, the offers to give talks and the enthusiasm of participants in MAMA activities, especially as regards the weekly webinars; the moderation aspect is worth highlighting. One may attribute moderation skills of the series of weekly webinars, Global Peace Studies for Sustainable Development in Africa or Global Peace on a number of factors. The first one is passion. The moderator is passionate about the webinar. As the co-founder of the series, the moderator has prioritized the series and he sees to it that it is brought to its logical conclusion. The second factor is consistency. The moderator has tried to remain consistent in organizing regular webinars every Wednesday. This consists in sending out two thousand five hundred invitation emails and following a specific format of the webinar by greeting and welcoming all participants, introducing the theme and the speaker through presenting their brief bio.

Every talk is followed by an open discussion. After the discussion, the speaker is invited to wrap up their talk. Then the moderator thanks the speaker and the participants and announces the talk theme for the next week. Another factor for the successful moderation is openness. This openness is multifaceted. First of all, the range of topics is almost infinite. All topics are interesting as long as they address matters of peace and development. There are no taboo topics. At least we have not come across any. Second, everyone has an equal chance of making a presentation, asking a question or making a comment. It is a place where the moderator and co-founders want to make everyone feel at home, respected, valued, loved and trusted. In the world where some people do not see eye to eye for political, economic, ethnic or religious grounds, openness to all is the best medicine. Another factor for the success of the moderation is team spirit.

Although the moderator has organized all the webinars and moderated almost all of them, the moderation has benefitted a great deal from co-moderators and volunteers. In order to build and maintain teamwork, the moderator has asked and guided some participants to help with the moderation. This has been done, as rarely as three or four times out of 144, by invited moderators. The idea is to give an opportunity to other people to moderate the sessions and also to break the monotony where only one man does the moderation always. What I find most interesting is when some participants take on the moderation task impromptu. This has happened especially when the internet connection is interrupted and the regular moderator cannot begin or continue with the service. It is interesting because with this kind of spirit and teamwork, participants own the webinar. Ownership of the process is crucial. This gives me confidence that even in my absence the webinar can go on uninterrupted. This is my hope and strategy.

The other factor in the quality of moderation is communication skills. This entails keeping people informed and interested in the session, articulating ideas, summarizing key talk points, using words and language that participants can easily understand, making complicated ideas simple to understand, listening carefully and paying attention to both the speaker and the participants, including comments and questions in chat and maintaining eye contact. With participants coming literally from all parts of the world, we are aware that there are many people who are struggling with English much as there are many whose English is as good as it can be. Therefore it is imperative to take cognizance of the linguistic differences. The moderator is like a midwife, maintaining the bond between the participants and the speaker and indeed the network.

Rebuilding Africa and the Sudan Case

One of the tasks of the Africa Peace and Development Network (MAMA) is certainly not of recolonizing the Continent but restoring the unity of Africa as before the onset of colonialism. Unfortunately, colonialism set a precedent of fragmentation of Africa rather than its unity as engineered by the likes of Nkrumah and Nyerere in the 1960s. Instead of forging African unity as a means to build a peaceful, robust and prosperous Africa, disunity has underdeveloped some countries. The case in point is The Sudan. This country has been cut into halves due to violent conflicts emanating from a scramble for natural resources, one part of the nation taking a lion's share at the expense of the other. The resultant separation of Sudan and South Sudan as two distinct states seemed to some people to be the best solution.

However, separation has never been a solution to any development program, including peacebuilding. A solution lies in unity and in eradicating the root cause of the problem. For those who support and encourage separation will soon realize that inequalities within South Sudan might lead to a fragmentation of South Sudan. Soon there will be a new country known as North South Sudan and another one known as South South Sudan and who knows how farther the separation can go, *ad infinitum*?

Turning to Sudan, the world is witnessing another serious fight between major rival factions of the military government (OCHA, 2025). For the protagonists of separatism, the establishment of Sudan minus South Sudan meant a stronger Sudan. But now Sudan is being weakened by endless fighting, loss of lives and destruction of the infrastructure as well as derailment of the national economy. If we follow the separatism logic, soon we will witness at least two new states: Sudan North and Sudan South or East Sudan and West Sudan. Separatism is reckless and meaningless. An oasis in the African desert is probably Tanzania, which is a union of Tanganyika and Zanzibar. Its limitations notwithstanding, this kind of unity remains a lodestar for the rest of the continent and indeed of the world.

Talking about unity, it is difficult, for example, to prove that England is stronger today than before 'brexitting' from the European Union. Conversely, it is equally mindboggling to claim that the European Union is stronger today than before brexit. Other examples of separation include the balkanization of the Soviet Union. The attempt to divide regions of Ukraine would definitely weaken the country (Carbone, 2023). Several other cases may be presented. Suffice to say that in MAMA we also believe that united we stand, divided we fall. Therefore Africa should remain intact as states work towards African unity while remaining vigilant against attempts to recolonize the Continent as Mniga (2024) argues.

Critical Questions from Some Participants

The success of the Africa Peace and Development Network (MAMA) has largely come from inspiring comments from webinar participants. These comments have served as a motivation and feedback to spur on the noble peacebuilding service. It is by way of feedback that participants express their feelings and thoughts towards the network and the activities it carries out.

I am including these questions from one participant, which might be useful for the other people and the network. They are especially relevant to me as I try to present a picture of the network and what it stands for in this first self-evaluation attempt. The participant is curious about the larger mission of the webinar, the presence or absence of the local supportive community and the participation of fellow Africans. All these questions were asked before MAMA was established. Nevertheless, they remain relevant and representative because some people might have asked or wish to ask the same or similar questions. In my conclusion, I will try and answer these questions albeit briefly by way of summarizing the chapter.

"Larger Mission? I have appreciated the webinars. You have, as you always do, welcomed me. Egon Spiegel is most friendly. Still, I wonder what this is building toward. Is the webinar simply a spinoff from the pending book publication? Or, is it your personal relationship with the German university? I know you to be a man who thinks big. Is there a larger mission here than simply providing, for whoever is interested in attending, a seminar series on peacebuilding? If there is a larger mission and I can help, I would like to explore it with you."

"ACUHIAM: The Association is a continent-wide cohort of Catholic universities. Its member institutions must have a range of issues that concern them. Yet, all the action 'seems' to be coming from you. And, that energy is directed to peacebuilding. Is there a supportive community for peacebuilding within ACUHIAM other than yourself?"

"Participants: In the first webinars, I saw on the screen largely white faces - German professors? - and few Africans. As we progressed, I saw more Africans. Several weeks ago, when I asked, you acknowledged that many of the African participants were students doing advanced academic work and, perhaps, some teaching. They appeared young, eager and inquisitive.

More recently, you've drawn more experienced presenters, e.g., Sr. Ann (Mozam-bique), the South Africa speaker, Dr. Thadeus and Hippolyt Pul. And, there seems to be a wider mix of participants. One young man last week was from the Ivory Coast. Is there some pool, list or source from which you are inviting?" HB 2023

In conclusion, having looked at the origins of the Africa Peace and Development Network (MAMA) and the achievements through webinars, publications and the creation of a global network of peacebuilders and sustainable development professionals, we sum up the grand mission of the network as the promotion of education, research and advocacy that support peace, non-violence and sustainable development in Africa. In so doing, MAMA strives to groom young scholars to assume leadership through education and training that prioritize values of peacebuilding and Ubuntu. To succeed in this, MAMA needs concerted efforts of all like-minded stakeholders worldwide. Among the key stakeholders are local actors such as local universities, for example, St. Augustine University of Tanzania and, by extension, the Association of Catholic Universities and Higher Institutes of Africa and Madagascar. These and other African institutions need to support members who take innovative initiatives. It should all be done in the spirit of genuine cooperation based on trust rather than unfair competition nurtured by jealousy.

Sometimes, Peace Studies and Development Studies are misunderstood because both seem to be outside of the common academic disciplines such as medicine, business, law, engineering and the likes. We argue that Peace Studies is a unifying academic field and the same applies to Development Studies. That is why many medical doctors, lawyers engage in peace and development studies. Peace becomes a unifying academic discipline. Without peace, nothing goes well. All in all, as a network with roots in Africa, MAMA will thrive by remaining Africa-centered and transdisciplinary both in terms of themes presented and the inclusion of more and more Africans and Africanists in all the network programs. The good news is that there are many well-meaning people around the world who are keen to collaborate with Africa for the good of the Continent, its people's and their environment. MAMA is developing a database of African peace and development scholars to support our common vision. Africa cannot afford to take a back seat.

Acknowledgements

As we thank speakers, participants, authors and well-wishers, we gratefully recognize the generous financial support from the Ministry of Education and Culture of Lower Saxony in Germany towards our publications and webinar series.

References

Carbone, M. (2023). When elephants fight, it is the grass that suffers: The Russo-Ukrainian conflict and the decentring-recentring conundrum in EU-Africa relations. *Journal of European Integration* 45(3), 539-557. https://doi.org/10.1080/07036337.2023.2190108

Cheng, L. & Spiegel, E. (2015). *Peacebuilding in a globalized world: An illustrated introduction to peace studies.* People's Publishing House.

CIRAD-FIUC (2022). *Cycle of webinars on peace studies for sustainable development in Africa.* https://www.cirad-fiuc.org/en/cycle-of-webinars-on-peace-studies-for-sustainable-development-in-africa/

Kurtz, L.R. (2022). *Encyclopedia of Violence, Peace and Conflict,* 3rd ed. Academic Press.

Mniga, M. (2024). *Recolonizing Africa: An ethnography of land acquisition, mining and resource control.* Taylor & Francis.

Mutalemwa, G. (2015). *People's organizations in Tanzania: Strengths, challenges and implications for development.* University of Vechta.

Mutalemwa, G. (2018). African diaspora and the revitalization of African universities. *Journal of Sociology and Development* 2 (1), 150-174.

Mutalemwa, G. & Trochemowitz, S. (2022). Mainstreaming peace studies in African higher learning institutions. In Spiegel, E., Mutalemwa, G., Cheng, L., & Kurtz, L. (2022). *Peace studies for sustainable development in Africa: Conflicts and peace oriented conflict resolution.* Springer.

Neba, A. & Bain, L.E. (2024). The perilous path: reimagining promotion and tenure in African academia. *Pan African Medical Journal.* 49(5). 10.11604/pamj.2024.49.5.44855

OCHA (2025). *Sudan: Humanitarian situation in Wad Medani, Aj Jazirah State - flash update No. 01* (As of 16 January 2025). https://reliefweb.int/report/sudan/sudan-humanitarian-situation-wad-medani-aj-jazirah-state-flash-update-no-01-16-january-2025

Pul, H. (2014). *Proposal for institutionalizing education, training, and research in peace studies.* ACUHIAM.

Spiegel, E., Mutalemwa, G., Cheng, L., & Kurtz, L. (2022). *Peace studies for sustainable development in Africa: Conflicts and peace oriented conflict resolution.* Springer.

Spiegel, E., Mutalemwa, G., Cheng, L., & Kurtz, L. (2024). *Peace as nonviolence: Topics in African peace studies.* Cham: Springer.

Tibaijuka, A. (2024, May 24). *Ujamaa, ubuntu and new Pan Africanism: The future of world peace* [conference keynote address]. Pan African Peace Conference Arusha, Tanzania. [Video]. YouTube. https://youtu.be/X2fmbE6eq-E?si=f-PU5ygFy30PSUCzm

Chapter 23
Peace Education through Museums for Peace in Japan and Abroad

Kazuyo Yamane

I became involved in peace education because my father was a survivor of the atomic bomb dropped on Hiroshima on August 6 in 1945. I grew up seeing the keloids, burn scars from heat rays from the atomic bombing on his arm. On the other hand, my mother was Japanese-American born in the US and grew up there until she was 13. She was a teacher in Japan during World War II and was taken to a police station to check if she could understand English news. Perhaps it was to find out if she was a spy. She could not use English because it was regarded as an 'enemy language' during the war. She sent me to her relatives in the US after the war so that I could study there, because it was what she couldn't do because of the war. I wrote my MA thesis on Japanese American literature which was not known in the 1970s at the University of Puget Sound in Tacoma, Washington. The history of Japanese Americans who were put into concentration camps during World War II made me think of human rights issues.

After I returned to Japan, I became a public high school teacher in Hiroshima and promoted peace education in the late 1970s. Then I began to teach Peace Studies at Kochi University (a national university) in Kochi City. On the other hand, I began to get involved with peace museums in Japan such as Grassroots House in Kochi, Kyoto Museum for World Peace at Ritsumeikan

University and those abroad. Such experiences led me to work for the International Network of Peace Museums (INMP) and the Japanese Citizens' Network of Museums for Peace.

1. Peace Education at Schools and Universities in Japan

It was common that an emphasis was put on atomic bombing on Hiroshima and Nagasaki in peace education in the 1970s. An emphasis was put on the atomic bombing which is Japan's side of World War II as a victim. Japan's dark history of colonization of Korea and invasion of China and other countries were not dealt with at many public schools. There have been serious issues of school textbooks in which historical truth such as the Nanjing Massacre and Korean women who were forced to work as sexual slaves for Japan's military have not been dealt with seriously. A unique peace museum focusing on textbooks was established by Kazuko Yoshikawa in 1997. It was called "the Peace, Human Rights and Children Center/the School textbook Institute" (Yamane, 2009, pp. 119-132).

In 2011 the author found that Japanese students' historical viewpoints are very different from international students. Students of Ritsumeikan University, including students from China, the Republic of Korea and so forth, and those at American University in Washington, D.C. went to Hiroshima and Nagasaki in August for ten days. American students had learned that the atomic bombing was necessary to end World War II without learning the result such as atomic bomb victims' suffering. Chinese and Korean students had learned how much their people suffered from Japan's invasion and colonization without knowing the consequences of the atomic bombing. Japanese students were shocked to learn about Japan's aggression against China, Korea and so forth at the Nagasaki Museum for Human Rights and Peace [1]. It is because they didn't learn about the historical facts at school, and the media haven't reported them much. However, it was possible for Japanese and international students to learn different historical perspectives when they visited peace museums in Kyoto (Kyoto Museum for World Peace), Hiroshima (Hiroshima Peace Memorial Museum, etc.) and Nagasaki (Atomic Bomb Museum, Nagasaki Museum for Human Rights and Peace). Regardless of historical concepts of atomic bombing, students became good friends through such peace education by visiting peace museums (Yamane, 2014, pp. 117-128).

2. Peace Education through Museums for Peace

It should be noted that the term 'museums for peace' is used to include peace museums, peace centers, art museums, and any museum which aims at promoting peace for a better future.

The Peace Museum, Grassroots House (Kusa-no-iye) was established in Kochi City, Kochi Prefecture in November 1989 as "a private facility for peace, education, and environmental issues". Kochi is the birthplace of the movement for freedom and human rights in Japan. In order to convey the reality of war and the preciousness of peace to the next generation, "they collect and organize materials, create peace education materials, and make them available for loan to a wide range of citizens" according to its website.[2] I became a member from its opening because it promised to be a good place for citizens to work for peace.

Peace education has been promoted not only in schools but also in the community. Children visit the peace museum and learn what happened in Kochi during World War II. Exhibited are not only the US air raids on Kochi where over 400 people were killed and injured but also Japan's aggression towards China and Korea. Japan colonized Korea in 1910 until 1945 and Korean people suffered from Japan's colonization. Japan invaded China in 1931 and Chinese people suffered from Japan's aggression until 1945. This exhibition at the Grassroots House is very different from exhibits at public peace museums where only Japan's victimhood tends to be exhibited. Japan's dark history tends to be hidden at school textbooks and public museums, but honest exhibition has been displayed in the private peace museum.

Mr. Shigeo Nishimori, the founder of the peace museum, asked me to attend the first International Conference of Peace Museums held in Bradford, England in 1992. Members of the museum funded my fare. This changed my whole life because I felt a great responsibility to report peace education and peace work at the Grassroots House abroad, and also to report various activities at peace museums in other countries to Japanese citizens. The International Network of Peace Museums (INPM) was founded in 1992. Its newsletter was initially edited by Dr. Peter van den Dungen, then a peace history lecturer in the Department of Peace Studies at Bradford University, commencing in 1993. It became possible to exchange ideas among peace museums.

I started publishing International *Exchange News* after I returned home in 1992. There are links that show the author's activities in introducing international news to the Grassroots House in Kochi, in Japanese, from 1992 to 1998. There are also Grassroots House *International Exchange Newsletters* in English which show various international exchange activities at the Grassroots House in Kochi. [3]

The Japanese Citizens' Network was formed in 1998 when the 3rd International Conference of Peace Museums was held in Osaka and Kyoto. Its newsletter called *Muse* was first published in 1999.

Mr. Yutaka Maruyama, a co-coordinator of the Japanese Citizens' Network of Museums for Peace, stated:

> I read a glimpse of the 'International Exchange News of the Grassroots House' published by Ms. Yamane. I was amazed to see that there were people from Europe, the US, China, Korea, Indonesia, East Timor, India, Kenya, Croatia, the UN, UNESCO, and so on. It shows a history of grassroots democracy from Kochi, which has been transmitted to the world through the English version of Grassroots House Newsletter. This is the origin of the English version of Muse Newsletter.[4]

There is a link to Muse Newsletter from 1999 to today in English and Japanese.[5]

2.1 Peace Work that has Resulted: INMP and the Japanese Citizens' Network of Museums for Peace

There are many war museums in various countries. When abroad I found it was not easy to find museums for peace. War museums tend to glorify war while museums for peace tend to criticize war and aim at creating peace through peace education. This is the type of peace that is positive peace that is based on "the presence of attitudes, institutions, and social structures that are able to sustain peace and reduce harmful conflict."[6]

The world's first 'peace museum' was established by Jan Bloch in Lucerne, Switzerland in 1902. "The museum was meant to warn the world of the dangers of another great war and thereby to contribute to its avoidance, but ironically it became a victim of it, and was dissolved in 1920" (van Dungen, 2006, p. 30). In 2002, "various organizations in Lucerne came together to organize a series of events in order to commemorate and celebrate the 100th anniversary of the inauguration of the world's first peace museum" (van Dungen, 2006, p. 30). Fortunately, I had a chance to attend the symposium and learned about the history of the first peace museum in the world.

2.2 Networks of Museums for Peace

There are several networks of museums for peace in order to support and encourage one another. The International Network of Peace Museums was founded in Bradford, England. Later, the name was changed to the International Network of Museums for Peace (INMP) to include various museums for peace. The international network will be considered first. Then the promotion of peace education by two organizations of peace museums in Japan will be considered: Association of Japanese Museums for Peace, comprising relatively large museums; and Japanese Citizens' Network of Museums for Peace, which attracts more small grassroots museums.

2.2.1 The International Network of Peace Museums & INMP

The first International Conference of Peace Museums was held at the University of Bradford, the UK, in 1992. It was organized by the Give Peace a Chance Trust, a small Quaker charity. At that conference, the International Network of Peace Museums was founded, initiated by Dr. Peter van den Dungen. He became the Network's coordinator and also edited the Network's newsletter. The newsletters are available on the INMP website. [7] The Network held regular international conferences, approximately every three years. Other host venues included: Stadtschlaining, Austria (1995); Osaka and Kyoto (1998); Ostende, Belgium (2003); Gernika, Basque Country, Spain (2005); Kyoto and

Hiroshima (2008); Barcelona (2011); No Gun Ri, the Republic of Korea (2014); Belfast (2017); Kyoto (2020 – online), and Uppsala, Sweden in 2023. The name of the Network was changed in 2005 to the International Network of Museums for Peace to include those which had an objective of peacemaking.

The **mission** of the International Network of Museums for Peace (INMP) is to enable museums for peace (and related organizations) to resource, to collaborate, and to mutually support each other in their work for peace. The mission, vision and goals of INMP are made clear on the Network's website.[8]

2.2.2 The Association of Japanese Museums for Peace

The Association of Japanese Museums for Peace was founded in 1994 with the aim of "developing peace promotion projects by working together to conduct surveys and research to inform people about the horrors of war and to help realize peace" (Kawasaki City, 2021). There are ten member organizations: Peace Museum of Saitama, Kawasaki Peace Museum, Kanagawa Plaza for Global Citizenship, Kyoto Museum for World Peace, Osaka International Peace Center, Hiroshima Peace Memorial Museum, Nagasaki Atomic Bomb Museum, Okinawa Prefectural Peace Memorial Museum, Himeyuri Peace Museum and Tsushima Maru Peace Memorial. *(This is from north to south.)* "Together, these 10 museums receive approximately 4 million visitors annually" (Kawasaki City, 2021).

Through the display of historical artefacts and photographs, and through their interpretation panels, these museums address not only the issues of Japan's war damage and that of other countries, but also poverty, discrimination, environmental problems, and other social violence that prevents people from fulfilling their full potential. The museums are "for peace" because they encourage their visitors to participate in efforts to create peace and social justice.

2.2.3 The Japanese Citizens' Network of Museums for Peace

A third organization of peace museums is the Japanese Citizens' Network of Museums for Peace. This was founded in 1998 when the third International

Conference of Peace Museums was held in Kyoto and Osaka.

Part of the rationale behind having two Japanese networks is that some publicly-funded peace museums in Japan tend to emphasize Japan exclusively as victim in World War II – victim of the atomic bombing and victim of US air raids on different Japanese cities. They do not explain Japan's history as an oppressor and perpetrator of war. Since the 1990s, there has been nationalistic pressure to prevent the depiction of Japan's aggression of other countries at public peace museums. However, private grassroots peace museums do have the freedom to make exhibitions on Japan's dark history; the consequence, however, is that they then face financial difficulties as they are not able to access any subsidies from national/local governments. This tends to affect such peace museums in terms of financial problems, but they have freedom of speech.

The three networks are not distinct and there is overlap between them. In particular, Ikuro Anzai, the Honorary Lifelong Director of the Kyoto Museum for World Peace, has played an important role in all three networks. He organized three INMP conferences in Japan and, from 2017 to 2020, he was the second INMP coordinator. A scientist by background, Anzai has played an important role in the anti-nuclear movement, writing about the dangers not only of nuclear weapons but also of nuclear energy. In 2023, he became the director of the Hiroshima, Nagasaki, Bikini, Fukushima Museum for No Nukes (Dengonkan) in Fukushima.

3. Practice of International Exchanges among Peace Museums

Following are some examples of international exchanges by the Grassroots House where the author was in charge of international exchanges as a volunteer from 1992 to 2010. Kochi City was air raided by US bombers in World War II and over 400 people were killed and injured. Citizens donated war related artifacts to the Grassroots House so that the war will never be forgotten. On the other hand, the members of the Grassroots House investigated what the soldiers from Kochi did in Korea and China during World War II. A group of citizens went there and were shocked to learn about the history of Japan's aggression towards these countries. Such exchanges with people in

Asia were not easy because the Japanese government has not acknowledged the past war. However, activities for peace and reconciliation began at the grassroots level.

3.1 Exchanges with Museums for Peace in Asia

3.1.1 The Exhibition Hall of Evidence of Crime Committed by Unit 731 of the Japanese Imperial Army founded in 1985 in China

First, what is the 731 Unit? It was a unit that existed in the Imperial Japanese Army during World War II, located in Harbin Heibo, Heilongjiang Province, China. The first unit commander was Shiro Ishii (Lieutenant General of the Army Medical Corps), and the unit had a large group of facilities equipped with special prisons and facilities for testing and producing germ and biological weapons in order to complete the development of germ weapons in secret. For human experimentation, people from anti-Japanese organizations captured by the Japanese military police were used as experimental materials; the number is said to have been about 3,000, including women and children.

The 731 Exhibition Hall and the Grassroots House had an agreement called the "Cooperation Agreement between the Exhibition Hall of Evidence of Crime Committed by Unit 731 of the Japanese Imperial Army and the Grassroots House Peace Museum." It is a significant citizen-level movement to build peace in East Asia. Before signing the agreement, there were citizens' efforts to learn about the history of Japan's aggression of China. This is because the dark history was not written in school textbooks and was not taught at school. The media did not report it much and many people didn't know about it. The background is that after Japan's defeat in the war, the Allied Forces arrested the war leaders and charged them with crimes at the International Military Tribunal for the Far East, but the officers of the 731 Unit were exonerated as war criminals by handing over the data of human experimentation to the US and being placed under their protection, and the existence of the unit was hidden for a long time after the war.

The members of the Grassroots House decided to investigate what former soldiers in Kochi did in China, and they visited China six times for research trips. They visited such areas in 1991 on a China Peace Trip and interviewed local residents. The record is in Grassroots House Booklet No. 1 titled "Remember Your Past Experiences and Use them as a Warning for the Future" (Chinese proverb). The author attended the 6th Peace Trip to China and a booklet was published by the Grassroots House: "Germ Warfare had been Carried out: Report of the 6th China Peace Trip to China" in 1999. It was not easy to learn about the reality of Japanese Germ Warfare in China because Chinese people could not trust the Japanese. The situation might have been different if the Japanese government dealt with the history, apologized to the Chinese people sincerely and compensated them for damage. However, the Japanese government still doesn't make efforts to face the facts and this is why it was not easy to communicate with the Chinese people. However, their attitude toward the Japanese people began to change when the members of the Grassroots House listened to their stories and began to organize an exhibition on the 731 Unit in Kochi and support a Chinese lawsuit against the Japanese government for apology and compensation. The members of the Grassroots House believe that the "cooperation agreement" was operated by citizen participation, and it has significance as a citizen-level movement to build peace in East Asia.

3.1.2 The Museum of Colonial History founded in 2018 in the Republic of Korea

The Museum of Colonial History was founded in order to "remember the history of the period of Japanese imperialist occupation as a whole, to properly record the history of the reckoning of the past, which was promoted by citizen power, and to steadily carry out its role as a historical educational institution for the youth and citizens to lead it into the future" (INMP, 2020, p. 252).

There have been three exchange agreements signed with Japanese peace museums: Grassroots House (Kochi); the Women's War and Peace Museum/Women's Active Museum (Tokyo); and the Korea Museum (Tokyo). As for the Grassroots House, the friendship exchange agreement was signed in September 2019 by Masahiro Okamura, director of Grassroots House, and Seungeun Kim, Chief Curator of the Museum of Colonial History in Korea. They agreed to deepen mutual investigation, research, and exchange of the historical facts of the Japanese imperialist war of aggression against the Korean peninsula and colonial rule; and to promote mutual human exchange in order to deepen a friendship suitable for the 21st century, based on respect for individual dignity and basic human rights.

It should be noted that Yeonghwan Kim who is the Chief of the External Relations Team at the Colonial History Museum worked at the secretariat of Grassroots House between 2001 and 2006. He played a very important role to educate people, especially young people and also facilitated a series of friendship visits between Kochi and Korea. For example, he gave a lecture as a guest speaker at Kochi University where I used to teach, and he suggested that students visit the Grassroots House. Some started visiting there and got involved with an event to invite a Korean woman who was forced to work as a sex slave by Japanese military during World War II. The students were shocked to listen to her testimony and one of the students began to study such sexual slavery issues at graduate school. Thus, Yeonghwan Kim educated students and citizens about the past history in Japan and also played a very important role in exchanging ideas, people and exhibits. Such international exchanges helped people in Japan and Korea to understand each other and build trust between them.

3.2 The Exchanges with Museums for Peace in Europe

3.2.1 England: Peace Museum in Bradford

The Peace Museum was founded in 1998 and it tells the stories of peace, peacemakers, and the peace movement, honours the history of 'people of peace' (INMP, 2020, p. 287). In 2024 the peace museum was moved to Salts Mill, a busy culture and retail complex, in the Bradford suburb of Saltaire, a UNESCO World Heritage Site. Information is available on the website.[9]

Dr. Peter van den Dungen, the first INMP coordinator, and Dr. Clive Barrett, the Chair of the Board of the Peace Museum, visited the Kyoto Museum for World Peace. There have been many exchanges such as publishing books and articles. For example, Peter van den Dungen and the author wrote "Peace Education through Peace Museums" in the *Journal of Peace Education* (Dungen & Yamane, 2015, pp. 213-222). *Museums for Peace in Search of History, Memory, and Change* edited by Joyce Apsel, Clive Barrett, and Roy Tamashiro highlights "the inspiring as well as conflicting representations and purposes of diverse museums for peace around the world... the volume demonstrates that some museums reinforce hegemonic narratives, while others resist authoritative tropes to reveal silenced histories, including peace histories."[10] Both Clive Barrett and Kazuyo Yamane contributed a chapter called "Museums for Peace and Reconciliation in East Asia".

3.2.2 Italy: Peace Museum Project

Piera and Giancarlo Caramellino in Milan participated in the International Conference of Peace Museums held in Kyoto in 1998. Piera visited Grassroots House with other participants from England and Austria after the conference. There was an exhibition on US air raids of Kochi during World War II to educate children and citizens about the war. It reminded her of the US air raids on an elementary school in Milan where 184 children (205 children including those who were killed outside school) were killed on October 20 in 1944. Piera started the project of promoting peace education by discovering photographs, documents, and testimonies related to the air raids, and held events to inform people about their air raid experiences. Thus, she educated children about US air raids in Milan after being influenced by Grassroots House. It was moving to attend a peace rally to convey to school children information about the history in Milan when the author was invited there.

3.2.3 Spain: Peace Museum in La Vall d'Uixó

There is another example of the influence of the Grassroots House in peace education at the University of Jaume I in Spain. The author gave lectures on Peace Studies at the graduate school there three times in the early 2000s. The peace education and activities at the Grassroots House were introduced as an example to promote peace education at schools and communities. Then a Spanish graduate student, Nati Fortea, read Grassroots House Newsletters carefully and asked me to meet with one of the candidates for Mayor. I didn't think that it would be easy to establish one, but she initiated the founding of a Peace Museum in La Vall d'Uixó, Castellón in Valencia, Spain in 2000. It was a great joy for me to visit the peace museum where many photographs of children who had visited there were exhibited at my next visit there. Unfortunately, the Peace Museum is closed as of 2024, but it shows one of the effects of peace education at the university which led to founding a peace museum to promote peace education.

There are other peace museums in Europe with which international exchanges have been promoted such as the first Peace Museum in Wolfsegg in Austria, the Anti-War Museum in Berlin, the International Peace Poster Documentation Center in Bologna, Peace Lab Museum in Collegno, Italy, Gernika Peace Museum, Yi Jun Peace Museum in The Hague, and so forth.

3.3 Exchanges with Museums for Peace in the USA

Swords Into Plowshares Peace Center and Gallery in Detroit was founded in 1986. The mission is to convey the message of peace through art, and to document the need to transfer resources spent on war to the social needs of people around the world.[11] The Grassroots House donated the exhibit of "The Atomic Bombs and Humanity" in 1995, and an art work was sent to the Grassroots House from Detroit.

Conclusion

Museums for peace have been promoting peace education not only at schools but also communities. After conducting the study of activities of grassroots museums for peace, it became clear that there are various international exchanges that would build trust among humans and promote peace and reconciliation, which could contribute to preventing war and stopping war. There are restrictions by the central and local government at public museums for peace in terms of the contents of exhibition and programs, but there has been freedom of speech in the case of grassroots museums for peace. Many private museums for peace prefer having freedom to obtain public subsidies.

Issues for grassroots museums for peace have been financial, and their activities for peace have not been widely known not only in Japan but also in other countries. It is necessary to contact the media so that their activities for peace through the INMP and the Japanese Citizens' Network of Museums for Peace would be reported more not only in Japan but also in the world. This would encourage people to prevent war and also deal with war nonviolently.

Endnotes

1) The peace museum used to be called "Oka Masaharu Memorial Nagasaki Peace Museum", but the name was changed in April 2024. It is because testi-

monies from a victim have revealed that the late peace activist Masaharu Oka engaged in sexual violence.

2) What is Peace Museum/Grassroots House? http://www.maroon.dti.ne.jp/kusanoie/shoukai.html

3) INMP Newsletter No. 40, 37 at https://inmp-news.museumsforpeace.org/

4) An article, "Introducing INPM/INMP Newsletters to Japan since 1992 while reporting international exchange abroad in English" was published in the INMP Newsletter #40 in 2024. https://sites.google.com/view/inmp-museums-for-peace/newsletters?authuser=0 All the INMP Newsletters are available at https://sites.google.com/view/inmp-museums-for-peace/newsletters?authuser=0.

5) A link to Muse Newsletter from 1999 to today in English and Japanese: https://jcnmp-web.jimdofree.com/. Muse Newsletter was published with not only news in Japan but also the other countries' news between 2003 to 2010. It was thanks to Dr. Peter van den Dungen and others who kept sending news for Muse Newsletters.

6) What is Peace? Types, Examples, Learning Opportunities by Thomas Brown at https://globalpeacecareers.com/magazine/what-is-peace/

7) INMP website: https://sites.google.com/view/inmp-museums-for-peace

8)   https://sites.google.com/view/inmp-museums-for-peace/home?authuser=0. A short history of the International Network of Museums for Peace (INMP) is summarized in the INMP Newsletter No. 18 in 2017.

9) The Peace Museum in Bradford. https://www.peacemuseum.org.uk/

10) Museums for Peace In Search of History, Memory, and Change at https://www.routledge.com/Museums-for-Peace-In-Search-of-History-Memory-and-Change/Apsel-Barrett-Tamashiro/p/book/9781032270012?srsltid=AfmBOorhAYn-vtaLPHeLW6neALL2ygP_Tbt7vgWzLdm05qC-PK5q-C50a

11) Swords Into Plowshares Peace Center and Gallery: https://www.

swordsintoplowsharesdetroit.org/

References

There are books and articles that were published by the INMP members and the information is available on the INMP website. https://sites.google.com/view/inmp-museums-for-peace

Grassroots House. *What is Grassroots House?* Available at: http://www.maroon.dti.ne.jp/kusanoie/shoukai.html (Accessed: May 15 2024). .In Japanese.

Kawasaki City (2021). *Nihon Heiwa Hakubutukann Kaigi* (the Association of Japanese Museums for Peace). https://www.city.kawasaki.jp/shisetsu/category/21-21-14-0-0-0-0-0-0-0.html

Van den Dungen, P. (2006). Preventing catastrophe: The world's first peace museum, Ritsumeikan. *Journal of Peace Studies* 18(3), p. 30 (full No. 65). https://www.ritsumei.ac.jp/ir/isaru/assets/file/journal/18-3_DUNGEN.pdf.

Van den Dungen, P. & Yamane, K. (2015). Peace education through peace museums. *Journal of Peace Education.* 12(3), 213-222

Yamane, K. (2009). *Grassroots museums for peace in Japan: Unknown efforts for peace and reconciliation.* VDM Verlag.

Yamane, K. (2014). Contemporary peace education in peace museums: Student visits to Hiroshima and Nagasaki. *Kyoto: The International Studies Association of Ritsumeikan University* (pp. 117-128).

Yamane, K. & Anzai, I. (Eds.). (2020). *Museums for peace worldwide.* Kyoto: Organizing Committee of The 10th International Conference of Museums for Peace, Kyoto Museum for World Peace, Ritsumeikan University, Kyoto.

Part V: Personal Journeys in Peace Education

Chapter 24
Educating for peace in Ukraine

Yurii Shelizhenko

Lifelong Journey Towards Peace

Intuitive leaning to a culture of peace from childhood coupled with a challenging environment full of militarist influences forced me to have a lot of conversations with different people during my life trying to persuade them that violence is a problem, not a miraculous solution to all problems as people used to think. No wonder that the spontaneous lifelong war resistance led me to study and teach peace consciously.

I learned about an ugliness of compulsory military service from my father who served only half a year instead of two years in the Soviet army, had conflicts with commanders due to his sharp feeling of injustice, subjected to *dedovschina* [hazing] and was dismissed early on health grounds. My mother likes to tell an episode from kindergarten age when father tried to teach me to fight but I refused, after he failed to reply convincingly to my question how could I beat others if they feel pain.

I was born in 1981 and grew up in the moment of detente in the aftermath of the Helsinki Declaration. I enjoyed and took seriously, perhaps more seriously than others, simple visions of peace embedded in popular culture, fairy tales and science fiction. Warmongers were antagonists in many popular fairy tales for children by Georgiy Pocheptsov and Alexander Volkov; there was a book *Gelsomino in the Land of Liars* by Italian writer Gianni Rodari, and there was the wonderful musical film "Miraculous Voice of Gelsomino".

Science fiction replaced fairy tales in my reading in adolescence, and one of my favorite short novels was *A piece of wood* by Rey Bradbury, the story about an inventor who tried to end wars by making rust destroy all weapons, and I laughed reading how a stupid general makes desperate attempts to continue war armed with a chair leg even after the destruction of weapons. *Bill, the Galactic Hero* by Harry Harrison exposed the absurdity of the whole idea of war. I drew an inspiring vision of a future of scientific progress in a more peaceful and united world from novels like Isaac Asimov's *I, Robot*, Kir Bulychev's *The Last War*, and *The Inhabited Island* by Strugatsky Brothers demonstrated how technologies could be misused for propaganda and perpetuation of war exhausting and polluting the whole planet. There was also a translated collection of antiwar sci-fi novels entitled *Peace to Earth*.

I recall antiwar posters, mostly on nuclear disarmament, found in the first years of independence of Ukraine in the darkest corridor of my school where very few people went. Also I remember, when assigned to deal with scrap papers and books for recycling, how I found behind a closet a pile of books in English, one of which, I believe, was an annual report about conscientious objection to military service in Europe. Perhaps someone took it from abroad. Of course, there were no courses on human rights.

Conscientious objection, as well as pacifism in general, was a taboo in my school and later in university where I studied mathematics. When I started to issue a student newspaper in university and published Sakharov's call for peace and disarmament, unexpectedly I became an enemy of the administration. Near that time, during mandatory military registration, I insisted on attaching an antiwar poem to my file in the local recruitment office.

Since a usual way for young students at that time was to study at a military faculty and prepare to be officers in reserve instead of conscription, I was surveyed for that in 1999 and it ended badly. The psychological test asked, inter alia, am I ready to drop an atomic bomb and kill 100,000 enemies to save 1,000,000 Ukrainians. I rejected this offer to enter officer training writing my conscientious objections on a reverse side of the survey form. The objections reminded officials that Ukraine gave up nuclear weapons, a right decision, and proposed to abolish all nuclear weapons in the world. I responded similarly later to an invitation to work in a defense think tank. It was delivered personally to me as a prospective student.

In 2000, I wrote a letter to President Kuchma calling on him to abolish the Ukrainian army. I proposed to abolish the army in order to prevent the mass killing of people in wars, and later received a mocking reply from the Ministry of Defense.

At that time I refused to celebrate Victory Day and went to the central streets of a celebrating city alone with a banner demanding disarmament. I did this because all my life I preferred to search for truth, refusing to adopt popular traits and superstitions. Even in childhood I preferred to receive my open-air education not in gangs thriving in the 1990s but on street protests of different democratic parties and different religious gatherings, mostly Christian, rarely Krishnaite (group of independent Hindu traditions).

In different moments of my life I joined nonviolent rallies for the dissolution of the Soviet Union and independence of Ukraine, for changing authoritarian regimes of Kuchma and Yanukovych, and for other political causes.

Mostly, we had no genuine antiwar rallies in Ukraine, and I avoided participation in circuses for one or another partisan or bureaucratic reason far from honest pacifism. One exception was my personal protest at the Victory Day, and another is my participation in the protest of the association of humanists against NATO and Ukrainian involvement in the Iraq War. I was invited to the protest in 2003 after winning their 2002 competition for the best humanist essay; in that year I also won an UNHCR competition for the best essay about refugees and exiles in the history of Ukraine.

I was invited several times to a conference of young scientists in Moscow with presentations of my studies in mathematics. Once organizers invited me to submit an abstract for a round table discussion of humanities. I submitted a slightly pacifist, very theoretical abstract, promoting less coercive and more interesting education facilitating harmonious individual and social development. It was accepted. But in Moscow I faced 'anti-terrorist' measures and an atmosphere of fear and suspicion everywhere. The newspapers enthusiastically promoted a war in Chechnya, so I added to my presentation explicit condemnation of all wars and a call to end the war in Chechnya in a peaceful way. When I said that, one attender interrupted me with the words

"I am an officer and will not listen to that". He left and a few other few people followed.

Despite the lack of proper peace rallies, I found ways to express peace values in the thick of the biggest political turmoil in my country.

Witnessing the Revolution on Granite in 1990 I sympathized with demands of students against conscription into the Soviet army, but these young men laughed at the suggestion of a boy runaway from school that it would be better to abolish all armies.

During the Orange Revolution in 2004 I volunteered for a dialogue group seeking common ground between protesters and counter-protesters. Later I was invited to a patriotic youth camp, where I started a little workshop on creativity and social changes to discuss a better world without borders, free and peaceful, with diversity of cultures and languages, to the great disappointment of organizers who expected from activists more Ukraine-centric activities. Despite that, during several years I was regularly invited to creative youth seminars, making presentations, organizing panels, and answering radical questions with peaceful ideas.

During Euromaidan in 2013 I published a brochure, or rather a first short book about this historical event, urging the importance to stick to politics of nonviolence, criticizing violent tendencies and right-wing politics, including linguistic exclusion and delusions regaining nuclear weapons.

Almost all my life I had a hope that publicism, prose and poetry could change minds of people. I published some pieces of my own antiwar fiction and poetry in Ukrainian but realized that many people quickly judge it as naive and unrealistic, being indoctrinated to give up all the best hopes and fight ruthlessly for mere survival. Still, I spread my message, some readers liked it and asked for an autograph or said to me it is a hopeless but right thing to do.

Rarely did the media accept my articles and creativity full of dissent with things that are universally accepted and full of dreams that most people easily give up. The start is a dream about peaceful development of society with free people having a say in public matters, with a public sphere not alienated by manipulators, with individuality not subordinated to the cruel uniformity by demands of self-sacrificing for the peculiar version of 'greater good' that apparently only a few people enjoy and most people suffer.

I started to create media to find a reader; I published a newspaper at my school, my university, my home, my street, sometimes with others, sometimes alone. I was on the editorial board of an unofficial online student newspaper in Kyiv National University, then wrote a lot of freelance articles for different online and offline media, was a reporter, columnist, editor of a division for social problems, author of editorials. For more than a decade I published my own newspaper, until the format of newspapers became too outdated.

Once in 2011 the popular news and opinions portal Ukrainska Pravda published my article on how all presidents of Ukraine including the incumbent of the time, Viktor Yanukovych, deceived voters, promising to abolish conscription and never delivering. In other opinion pieces I opposed notions of the need to ignite popular anger and violent political action, calling for reason and peaceful creativity.

In all this media activity I tried to promote intuitively perceived values of peace beyond the political struggles. This cost me popularity and other perks. I was still constantly engaged in such struggles by friends seeking advice, and many times found it necessary to express moderate opinions on heated political matters, insisting on universal values, legitimacy and reconciliation. It was valued for a long time, but later many people adopted radical views, some moderate friends in the parliament lost their seats, and my contributions were not required any more.

My skills in conversation with authorities and in critical publicism were still needed for local small businesses, since the local authorities violently extorted bribes destroying those unwilling to pay.

Bureaucratic intricacies I faced required professional training, so additional to my first education in mathematics I started to learn law, and after publishing several articles started to think about an academic career.

In 2019 I had a feeling that instead of waiting for the emergence of a genuine peace movement that could be joined I needed to create such a movement myself. I shared this idea with several friends who were critical of mainstream militarism, raising human rights and pacifist concerns rather than partisan rhetoric that radicalised more from day to day both in pro-Russian and pro-Western circles (some of these friends later turned to both sorts of radicalism, unfortunately).

Cruel methods of military mobilization in Kharkiv, along with hopes for new President Zelensky elected on a platform of peace, created a moment when public expression of pacifist views was possible and necessary. So, learning by doing, I prepared documents for registration of the Ukrainian Pacifist Movement and notification of public protests against cruel conscription under Ukrainian parliament and Office of the President in the first day when the parliament gathered after a snap re-election.

I had read more literature on peace and made a leap in my studies of English language more actively discovering resources and events of the international peace movements. The three-days webinar of the International Peace Bureau on the history of peace movements (IPB, 2020) and Devi Prasad's (2005) book on the history of War Resisters' International were particularly helpful. I started to study the history of the culture of peace and peace movements in Ukraine, presented it at an international conference of historians, in 2020 prepared and published a short educational film in Ukrainian and English "Peaceful History of Ukraine" (Sheliazhenko, 2020) and demonstrated it to hundreds of students when lecturing in legal theory and history in university and college.

I organized several educational webinars of the Ukrainian Pacifist Movement on the WRI Declaration, right to peace in the Constitution of Ukraine, and on the right to refuse to kill. Then, invited by Japan nuclear abolitionists, the Japan Council against Atomic and Hydrogen Bombs, to participate in the action Peace Wave, I received by post a set of posters depicting horrors of the atomic bombing of Hiroshima and Nagasaki, and I convinced a local library to exhibit them.

Another interesting international activity of the time was cooperation with the Eastern European Network for Citizenship Education. In this framework I organized two webinars on the current situation and perspectives of peace education in the countries of the Eastern Partnership and Russia (EENCE, 2021, 2022).

Peace Studies in the Formal Education System

I committed to legal education in 2010, which cost me a lot of time and money. My master's thesis defended in 2016 was on a case law of the European Court of Human Rights in cases related to armed conflicts and its relevance to war in Eastern Ukraine.

Moving forward in PhD studies and lecturing, I started to include in my academic activities elements of peace studies, for example, emphasis on the role of human rights as safeguards of peace.

In 2021 I defended my PhD thesis developing, with legal reasoning and case law, the Kantian philosophy that links personal autonomy and eternal peace, since both were and remain fundamental values inspiring me. I suggested a constitutional reform strengthening human rights guarantees necessary to help people make independent and responsible choices, not be manipulated by powerful and rich radicals fighting each other and inflicting on the public costs of their ugly struggle for monopoly. In my dissertation I proposed a concept of informed autonomy as a vision of development of the legal culture based on the knowledge of the legal technologies of dynamic peace and communicative democracy, processes of meditation, mediation, and nonviolent resistance to injustice and aggression (Sheliazhenko, 2021, 2021b). Peace education was a part of this concept. I presented the concept during an online webinar at Warwick University (The Ends of Autonomy, 2020).

In the course of my legal studies I wrote a letter to the ministry of education suggesting that Ukraine needs to replace military patriotic upbringing with civic education for democratic citizenship, focusing on human rights. This proposal was welcomed and "taken into consideration," according to a reply, though the old-style militaristic indoctrination was not abandoned and civic education remained optional depending on local circumstances.

At that time, I was challenged to join a new master's program in mediation and conflict management funded by the European Union and hosted by a business school in my university. This program helped me to sharpen understanding and skills of peacebuilding dialogue facilitation. I defended a master's thesis dedicated to a concept of liberal peace management by nonviolent means, through mediation, and, as a part of master's research,

I experimentally proved that people tend to underestimate expressions of peace and overestimate expressions of violence. I called it a "conflict bias", a cognitive bias that is a tendency to focus on contradictions taken as granted without saying the underlying harmony (Sheliazhenko, 2020a). As one vivid example I pointed out that we usually discuss the 20th century as an epoch of two world wars, although these wars took only one tenth of the century and serious progress was made in development of technologies and skills for nonviolent life and institutions of nonviolent world governance, including the United Nations. I recalled several books dedicated to the history of science, communications, art, literature, negotiation techniques, diplomacy, and suggested that most of our history textbooks, focused mainly on wars, are probably distorted by a conflict bias and need methodological correction because, apart from the history of wars, we need to study more deep and comprehensive history of peace. I implemented this insight in my courses on national and international legal history, trying to show my students how the moral power of human rights in history overcomes the old dangerous delusion of 'might is right.'

In the course 'Jurisprudence', explaining basics of legal and political theory, I added the UN Sustainable Development Goals to a module on functions of the state, focused on a theory of democratic peace discussing political regimes, mentioned peace as a social norm that must be protected by the law and started the final module with basics of international law, including human rights law.

In my course 'Constitutional Rights, Freedoms, and Duties of Human and Citizen' I paid special attention to discussion of a link between human rights and peace and to the constitutional right to alternative service. Apart from Ukrainian students, I lectured to foreign students, and one student from Israel told me that he went to study in Ukraine because there was no other legal way to avoid military service in his country.

In several historical disciplines (World History of Law and State; Intellectual History of Law and State; History of Law and State of Ukraine) I put emphasis on the development of the legal system facilitating peaceful coexistence of different people, stopping "the war of all against all", starting from restriction of blood feud in the early stages of development of a legal system (for example, it was limited and later prohibited by Ruska Pravda medieval code in 'Kyivan Rus'). Among modern tendencies with deep historical roots shaping the future of law I discussed development of nonviolent, non-coercive methods of dispute resolution like principled negotiation techniques and mediation, restorative justice, mitigation of punishments, e.g. replacement of incarceration with probation. I demonstrated evolution of legal systems from attempts to achieve peace in a small community a long time ago to current aspirations for universal and lasting peace on our common planet. This was formulated in my final slide "What is a Future of Law and State?" in one of the historical courses as follows: "Culture of peace and human security; further disarmament (Costa Rica abolished military in 1948, there are 22 such nations)". Teaching intellectual history of law, I emphasized that scientific and philosophical approaches to legal studies are historically linked with an old notion of the moral value of peace, and I loved to quote "The Outline of History" by H. G. Wells (1921): "A sense of history as the common adventure of all mankind is as necessary for peace within as it is for peace between the nations."

In the course "Models and Styles of Mediation" transformative and humanistic methods were explained, including a need for reframing destructive conflicting narratives into constructive narratives of cooperation. This course presented mediation as a practice of peacebuilding on all levels, and the changing character of the justice system from a coercive to a voluntary basis.

Preparing my lectures and slides for the Media Law course, I cited as a warning 30-year prison sentences, issued by the International Criminal Tribunal for Rwanda to journalists who incited genocide. The introductory module of the course urged that propaganda of war and hate speech violate human rights and usually are prohibited by the law with serious sanctions. I suggested that media professionals must learn and practice peace journalism, pay special attention to efforts of conflict resolution, reconciliation and life of non-combatants, because excessive attention to violent conflicts encourages cruelty and escalation. Also I explained that the main reason to practice peace journalism should be not a fear of punishment by the court, but understanding the lack of ethical commitment to peace. Additionally, irresponsible complicity with warmongering brings all the pains of war including restrictions of the freedom of speech, harming the journalists who were not responsible enough to resist warmongers or even knowingly promoted war for reasons of personal gain, thirsty for fame, career, money and power.

I developed these lecture courses on legal theory and history and defended my PhD thesis before the full-scale Russian invasion. Two months before the invasion, I sent to President Zelensky a letter with an article and slides asking to implement proposals of my study of human rights violations, to protect properly by the law of the human right to conscientious objection to military service in Ukraine according to international standards. My letter was redirected from the Office of President to the Ministry of Defence with a formulation that my research must be taken into account in the activities of the ministry, but I received a reply totally denying any Ukrainian human rights obligations.

Educating Civil Society

After the Russian invasion, there were a lot of requests to write or speak about the situation in Ukraine. I included elements of peace education in all such speeches, interviews and other publications. One example is my interview with Werner Wintersteiner (2022) about activities of the Ukrainian Pacifist Movement.

For the purposes of research and education, I prepared a scheme and timeline of escalation of conflict between Russia and Ukraine using the framework of the nine-stages model by Friedrich Glasl. This model was first presented at the round table on fundamental problems of jurisprudence at the National Academy of Legal Sciences of Ukraine, then I presented it many times during public talks. My draft paper on it was published in an academic blog with Glasl's comments (Sheliazhenko, 2023). Unfortunately, sometimes I felt that people were not interested in objective 5, analysis of conflict escalation and were interested only in seeking whom to blame, what side to take, or rather sought arguments in favor of their side already taken.

Another aspect of my struggle for peace education during full-scale Russian aggression was a resistance to militarization of the Ukrainian education system. When the candidacy of a new minister of education and science Oksen Lisovyi was announced and advertised as a soldier taking charge of reforms in a militarist direction, I immediately exposed him as plagiarising, before he was appointed, though the scandal in media didn't stop his appointment (Sheliazhenko, 2023a).

I facilitated modules in online courses "Leaving World War II Behind", "Peace Education and Action for Impact", "Unarmed Civilian Defense Instead of War" by the World BEYOND War, that are usually organized on the Canva platform. Students watch video presentations, some of which I made, read learning materials, and post on forums their answers to proposed questions and exercises; facilitators engage in conversations, making comments and suggesting further reading. These courses were based on a comprehensive concept of a global security system alternative to war (Gittins, 2020) developed and promoted by the World BEYOND War network. Also, the network holds annual #NoWar conferences where I participated in a panel dedicated to nonviolent resistance to war in Ukraine and presented my vision of a de-escalation ladder (World BEYOND War, 2023). On the conference a project of unarmed civilian protection was presented, I was a part of team working on this project and helped other activists to learn historical roots of conflict between Russia and Ukraine (Sheliazhenko, 2023b).

Making my presentation at the course "Neutrality in the 21st Century and Why It Remains Relevant" organized by the International Peace Bureau, I explained that the concept of neutrality needs development on the basis of proactive pacifism and education for structural changes in societies; consistent neutrality, not complicity in warmongering, must include nonviolent resistance to war and militarism (IPB, 2024).

A lot of time I dedicated to comparative studies of cultures of peace, with support of the Peace Institute in Ljubljana, and to field studies of human rights defence. I co-authored several annual reports of the European Bureau for Conscientious Objection on compliance of European states, with their obligations to protect human right to conscientious objection to military service. My initiative was to add in 2024 a new chapter of the report "Conscientious Objection in Time of War and Other National Emergencies" (EBCO, 2024). Working in the Ukrainian Pacifist Movement, I helped War Resisters' International to report violations of the said right in Ukraine; they also kindly added in the report that: "The Security Service of Ukraine accused Yurii Sheliazhenko – legal scholar, human rights defender, and executive secretary of the Ukrainian Pacifist Movement, who provides legal assistance to conscientious objectors to military service – of 'justification of the Russian aggression' on the grounds of the statement 'Peace Agenda for Ukraine and the World' which actually condemns Russian aggression. His house was searched, and his computer and smartphone were seized. Amnesty International reports that such charges are extensively used to disproportionately restrict freedom of expression" (United Nations, 2024a). In a letter to President Zelensky that was a pretext to repressions I called to replace military patriotic upbringing with peace education. Regarding these repressions, I published an article in a German journal on my participatory research into political repression against the peace movement under martial law from the point of view of a victim (Sheliazhenko, 2023c).

From comparative studies, I presented results in a lecture "What Ukraine could learn from Slovenia's culture of peace" in the Research Centre of the Slovenian Academy of Sciences and Arts, video (ZRC SAZU, 2023) and abstract (Sheliazhenko, 2023) were published.

Free Civilians School of Pacifism

In July 2024, I launched a new educational project, Free Civilians School of Pacifism, aimed at the development of peaceful planetary citizenship and worldview. Currently it functions only in the Ukrainian language, but I have an idea to translate and adapt my textbook and other learning materials into English and Russian, revise lists of recommended reading taking into account differences in peace literature accessible in the said languages, and make the course truly global, not just in its content but also in its coverage. It could also help to convey wider the Ukrainian vision of peace developed by the Ukrainian Pacifist movement (2022; 2024).

The Free Civilians School of Pacifism offers a peace education course that consists of five lectures, summarized in chapters of a short open access textbook. Sign-up and studying is free of charge. Every student receives slides of lectures, a list of recommended reading, additional learning materials, and is encouraged to take tests after every lesson. After the end of course, a final test must be passed to obtain a certificate of finishing the course.

Topics of the lectures offered are: Nature of Pacifism; Right to Peace; Right to

Conscientious Objection; Nonviolent Protection of Peace; and Organization of Peaceful Future.

The first lecture (Nature of Pacifism) gives basic definitions: pacifism is a peaceful way of life, readiness to resolve disputes peacefully, and in narrow sense a conviction that war (mass killing) is unacceptable; peace is a dynamic life free from violence, i.e. infliction of harm by any means. Also, the first lecture elaborates a concept of conflict and the need to keep all conflicts in the win-win phase, explains development of different forms of knowledge of peace in spheres of religion, philosophy and science, and introduces practical work for peace, peace movements and international institutions of peace. It mentions that Jacques Novicow, a delegate from the Ukrainian city of Odessa, participated in the 1901 International Peace Congress in Glasgow where the term "pacifism" was coined, and explains his beliefs that development of transport, communications and industry brings world peace closer. Among additional course materials there is a collection of quotes on peace from secular humanist and religious sources from Christian, Islamic, Judaic, Buddhist, Vedic and other traditions. Being a Quaker, I explain the historical role of Friends in the development of popular understandings of peace, and I added to the collection elements of the Quaker peace testimony (Quakers, 2024); some students joined my effort to set up a Quaker meeting in Ukraine (Free Civilians, 2024) that contributes to a lack of peace churches.

The second lecture (Right to Peace) explains that jurisprudence is a system of knowledge and practices of transforming reality from what it is to what it ought to be to achieve justice, to ensure common good and satisfy all reasonable individual needs. Since peace is a need of every human and every healthy community, it is a human right that must be observed voluntarily and, in case of deviations, enforced in peaceful ways. The need of institutional arrangements to implement the right to peace is discussed; historic role of states is mentioned, as well as abuses of power to use force by governments, and new institutions of international peace with the central role of United Nations are introduced. The lecture encourages study of the UN Charter and Universal Declaration of Human Rights. The necessity of world governance based on inclusive democracy, nonviolent dialogue and conflict resolution is underlined, and historical experience of fallen empires that tried to conquer the world is mentioned to show that militarism causes grave mistakes that should not be repeated.

The third lecture (Right to Conscientious Objection) shows that individual conscience restrains persons, communities and governments from cruelty and unnecessary violence, so human right to conscientious objection to participate in violence, and especially in war or preparations to it, must be protected by the law as a vital safeguard against abuses of power. The lecture emphasizes the special role of the right to refuse to kill that the sanctity of all life entails. The human right to conscientious objection to military service is covered by a right to freedom of religion or belief in its internal aspect is mentioned, and that nobody under any circumstances including martial law shall be subject to coercion which would impair his or her freedom to have or to adopt a pacifist religion or belief. Relevant provisions of Article 35 of the Constitution of Ukraine, Article 18 of the International Covenant on Civil and Political Rights, and Article 9 of the European Convention on Human Rights are explained with a case law of the Constitutional Court of Ukraine, European Court of Human Rights, jurisprudence of Human Rights Committee and Working Group on Arbitrary Detention. Materials for the lecture include translations in Ukrainian of the most important international documents on the human right to conscientious objection to military service, including the 2022 UN Human Rights Council resolution "Conscientious objection to military service" co-authored by Ukraine during the Russian aggression.

The fourth lecture (Nonviolent Protection of Peace) explains that a hope for a better world without wars and without violence is preserved and gradually made happen because we can and we learn how to protect ourselves creatively by nonviolent methods. Truth-telling, disobedience, dialogue, solidarity and conscientious objection are introduced as day-by-day routine methods of nonviolent resistance and unarmed protection of civilians. It is emphasized that civil disobedience makes violent governance futile. Also, a duty to protect peace nonviolently and not encourage warmaking and other injustices by inaction is discussed. Advocacy of peace and conscientious objection to military service in the media, human rights defending work is explained along with other instruments of the nonviolent protection of peace.

The fifth lecture (Organization of Peaceful Future) starts with a vision that in the world where people have skills to resist violence in nonviolent ways and everybody refuses to kill there will be no wars. The lecture presents a worldwide ecosystem of peace movements, such as peace-centered religious traditions and international secular networks like the International Peace Bureau, War Resisters' International, European Bureau for Conscientious Objection, World BEYOND War, campaigns for nuclear disarmament. It discusses symbols of peace movements: the dove, the Broken Rifle, the Peace Sign, etc. It mentions that our peace work continues in hostile environments where many people wrongly put their trust in miraculous powers of violence, but crimes are not stopped by punishments, revolutions don't bring justice, and wars don't bring peace. Peace movements are challenged to face these naive beliefs in miracles of bloodshed and show societies that you need to prepare for peace, not war, if you want peace. The lecture calls to contribute to peace movements using all knowledge and skills of civilian life.

Future of Peace Education

My experience in peace education helps to understand better how to apply in the realities of Russian aggression against Ukraine the universally accepted strategies of peace education set up by United Nations in the 1999 Declaration on a Culture of Peace, 2015 Sustainable Development Goals, 2016 Declaration on the Right to Peace, 2023 New Agenda for Peace, and 2024 Pact for the Future, as well as in the Recommendation on education for peace and human rights, international understanding, cooperation, fundamental freedoms, global citizenship and sustainable development, adopted by UNESCO (2024), with its emphasis on promotion of a culture of peace and non-violence and ambitious goal to ensure that all learners acquire the knowledge and skills needed to promote sustainable development by 2030.

The main challenge is that, in contrast to these UN and UNESCO guidelines, currently governmental policies in many countries are aimed at militarist indoctrination. For example, the Law of Ukraine "On the main principles of state policy in the sphere of the establishment of Ukrainian national and citizenship identity" adopted by parliament in 2022 (Ukraine, 2022) and "Strategy of strengthening Ukrainian national and citizenship identity for the period up to 2030" adopted by the Cabinet of Ministers of Ukraine in 2023 focus on military indoctrination of the population from childhood and the formation of 'defensive consciousness' (Ukraine, 2023). This policy, that seemingly expects continuation of Russian aggression for long years ahead, faces no challenges in absence of genuine peace movements and publicly active peace churches in society. External incentives are needed to convince the Ukrainian government to support development of peace education or, at least, to not obstruct civil society efforts.

Peace education in times of worldwide crisis plays the crucial role of nonviolent resistance to harmful ignorance and superstition, belligerent nationalisms, imperialisms, opportunisms and war profiteering, especially any forms of militarism.

In the Soviet Union's system of "military patriotic upbringing" the ideal citizen was seen as a loyal conscript obeying commanders without questions. Russia and Ukraine are both post-soviet nations that inherited this paradigm and still tend to bring up obedient soldiers rather than responsible, free and peaceful citizens. It was deeply embedded into official policies even during détente and after the end of the cold war, when the worldwide moral impulse to educate for peace was so powerful that even standards of patriotic upbringing were unable to prevent some enthusiastic peace educators in the Soviet Union and post-soviet countries to teach the next generation that all people are brothers and sisters and should live in peace (Sheliazhenko, 2021a).

A deep trauma caused to Ukrainian people by Putin's brutal war increases hatred and destructive attitudes in my country to everything related to Russia: to culture, to religion, to language, and even to persecuted opponents of Putin's regime. So, attempts to limit the use of language commonly abused to express hatred to Ukraine are understandable; but at some point the Russian ruling class must abandon its politics of denial of Ukraine independence on the fringe of genocidal intentions, and the Russian church must stop shameless spiritual encouragement of war and nuclear escalation, and then a window of opportunity must be opened for reconciliation. Peace education on both sides could help to heal the trauma, return to language's role as the medium of peaceful communication, and mitigate wartime linguistic taboos.

While the necessity of peace education is obvious to transform the mentality and behaviour of an aggressor state, the importance of peace education for the victim should not be underestimated, because nonviolent resistance means stopping violent behavior of others while not behaving like them, sticking to the light side of human nature (IPB, 2024a). As I said in an interview with Pressenza:

> Without peace initiatives, or with so weak peace initiatives as currently, Putin will continue to attack, and Zelensky will continue to counter-attack, and they will have supporters. To cease it, we must tell the truth not only about wrongness of Russian aggression, but about wrongness of any war and violence in principle and need to consider and implement peaceful solutions. Narrative of inevitability of war must be changed, we need to find nonviolent way to transform the behaviour of aggressor State and ensure restorative justice, compensation or at least mitigation of pains of all wrongs done. This is a big work which needs engagement of lot of people, lot of resources, research and education and dialogue efforts. (Zanella, 2024)

In the light of the European aspirations of Ukraine a culture of peace must be developed at least for a level comparable to the European norm. Peace education could help to fill in this gap. With Western choice of our nation, some elements of a developed culture of peace, such as human rights and citizenship literacy are introduced into formal educational courses and are developing in informal courses. However, there is a lack of systematic approaches to peace education, and the official 'peace through strength' doctrine along with a cultivated absolute trust in armed forces and national security agencies excludes the most important nonviolent approaches and marginalizes 'peace by peaceful means' visions, or rather tries to eradicate them as threats and weaknesses.

The future of peace education in Ukraine depends on whether the government, civil society and academic community will be aware of the need to develop a genuine and consistent culture of peace, able to support and encourage efforts in the field.

Worldwide peace movements and partners in human rights and environmentalist movements need to engage more actively with Ukrainian civil society to initiate and support peace education projects, articulating the necessity of peace education for social development, preserving political neutrality (especially in sensitive matters of analysis of conflict escalation, level of democracy in Ukraine, etc.) but helping to remedy general lack of knowledge. It would be unwise to "let Ukrainians themselves decide whether they choose militarism or peace culture", because the military propaganda forces public opinion to despise peace leaving no space for genuine discussion and choice, and because there could be no democratic choice in favour of militarism. Such a choice fundamentally erodes democracy replacing it with military command-and-control ushering dictatorship. But the topic of erosion of democracy, along with other topics on which Russian propaganda speculates, is too painful to address it bluntly.

In education for peace for victims of aggression, you must be cautious not to insult them by repeating anything, even formally correct or ostensibly 'realist' statements, that were weaponized by an aggressor in psychological warfare. That's why many notions of the international peace movement need reframing to get people in Ukraine to think seriously about anything close to such notions, not just reject them as the enemy's narrative.

For example, contrary to the narrative "Ukraine should not join NATO to avoid nuclear war" popular worldwide among peace movements, any attempts to convince Ukrainian people currently that NATO membership will not bring security to Ukraine will be not only unpopular but will immediately face accusations of repeating narratives of Russian propaganda, and in some sense these accusations will be plausible. Much better to discuss principles of global security, like the principle of common security, and whether NATO membership is possible without escalation to nuclear war, asking Socratic questions and suggesting wise options without direct opposition to questionable options already adopted too deeply, so only with time and a changing environment people might reconsider it. If we ask: "Can Ukraine become a NATO member without escalation to nuclear war between Russia and NATO?", it could be argued that it is possible, and even useful for stopping Russian aggression and reaching global de-escalation, if Ukraine will join the Treaty on the Prohibition of Nuclear Weapons first (Sheliazhenko, 2024b). This way of thinking also helps to educate on dangers of nuclear war, needed since fear of nuclear war in Ukraine according to surveys is one of the lowest in the world.

For the same reasons, it would be counterproductive to attempt to convince Ukrainians, at least those who don't have basic peace education, that they don't need weapons to achieve peace. A much better approach is to show that dialogue, diplomacy and nonviolent communication could empower people and protect from aggression, and that democracy not weakens but strengthens the country. If we allow military dictatorship the war will be lost, and the aggressor will benefit from destruction of Ukrainian democracy.

Enthusiasts currently working on peace education projects in Ukraine despite the hostile environment need to focus on creation of accessible educational materials in all fields of peace culture, cover more people and offer digestible practical pieces of knowledge that suit needs of people and are not causing immediate alienation because of intentional attacks on narratives of war propaganda and militarist ideology. However, the end goal must be to return people to a civil mindset.

Peace education must develop knowledge and skills of nonviolent resistance to Russian aggression, starting with resistance to Russian disinformation and aggressive strategic communication. That's why it is important to use political imagination, to propose alternatives to political views and solutions existing in pro-Russian parts of the international peace movement instead of trying to promote pro-Russian narratives in peace education. That approach is necessary for Ukraine, but it could also develop peace education worldwide.

I hope with time there will be more books, films, podcasts, games, and other different educational materials in Ukrainian; also, that many people start to learn English because of the pro-Western course of Ukraine, and it will bring Ukrainians closer to high-quality peace education in English.

The challenge of peace education in a militarist environment needs smart intellectual responses, and it would be good if more scholars consider their moral duty not to serve war efforts but to join or start genuine peace efforts. Scientists could contribute to ending the war in Ukraine and all wars as citizens, by joining peace movements; as researchers, helping to understand the war, its causes and ways to peace; as educators, teaching peace; as experts, warning about consequences of militarist stupidity and helping to make decisions ceasing violence; as visionaries, imagining and building practical models of the world without wars; as leaders, pioneering in organization of knowledge-based nonviolent society (Sheliazhenko, 2022). Peace movements also need to engage and incentivise scientists and educators not just as speakers with a status, but as intellectual leaders who have expertise to organize more successful peace movements.

Peace education as a comprehensive study of a nonviolent way of life needs a powerful kickstart, and sooner or later the growing need of relevant knowledge and skills will give that impulse.

Among priority tasks of peace education today, in my view, is the urgency to deal with illiteracy in matters of peace, helping people to understand that peace through communication with others is real and peace through killing all perceived enemies is a naïve delusion; to contribute to de-escalations, peace processes and development of institutions of peace; to resist military disinformation, psychological and ideological manipulations and other forms of war propaganda; to give people necessary skills for a nonviolent way of life, including skills of advocacy of peace and conscientious objection to military service, human rights defence, nonviolent resistance to war and militarism, unarmed protection of civilians; facilitate social change, profound transformations in politics, economy, science and culture of daily life, individual and collective, necessary to build a better nonviolent society free of the scourge of war.

References

EBCO. (2024). *Conscientious objection to military service in Europe 2023/24. Annual Report.* Available at https://ebco-beoc.org/sites/ebco-beoc.org/files/2024-05-15-EBCO_Annual_Report_2023-24.pdf

EENCE. (2021, November 21). *Peace education for citizenship in Ukraine and Europe. A record of webinar organized in the Eastern European Network for Citizenship Education (EENCE).* [Video]. YouTube. https://youtu.be/et48uqw0myc

EENCE. (2022, Octobre). *Approaches to building of culture of peace and critical study of armed conflicts in civic education. A record of webinar organized in the Eastern European Network for Citizenship Education (EENCE).* [Video]. YouTube. https://youtu.be/qQcGDYs5hrw

Free Civilians. (2024). *Quakers gathered at the Oasis of Peace.* https://www.

civilni.media/127/

Gittins, P. (2020). *A global security system: An alternative to war (fifth edition).* World BEYOND War.

IPB. (2020). *IPB reflects on 200+ years of peace movements.* International Peace Bureau. https://ipb.org/ipb-reflects-on-200-years-of-peace-movements/

IPB [IPB International Peace Bureau]. (2024, April 12). *Neutrality session 4.* [Video]. YouTube. Available at https://youtu.be/Dg2oQBWH-qg?t=4799

IPB (2024a). *2 years of war in Ukraine – A pacifist comment.* International Peace Bureau. https://ipb.org/2-years-of-war-in-ukraine-a-pacifist-comment/

Prasad, D. (2005). *War is a crime against humanity: The story of War Resisters' International.* War Resisters' International. https://www.vredesmuseum.nl/download/deviprasadbook2005.pdf

Quakers: Friends of Ukraine (2024). *Peace testimony.* https://friends.org.ua/peace-testimony-eng

Sheliazhenko, Y. [Yurii Sheliazhenko]. (2020, September 20). *Peaceful history of Ukraine.* [Video]. YouTube. https://youtu.be/tQTspdu6HXU

Sheliazhenko, Y. (2020a, November). *Conflict bias and vision of liberal peace management through mediation.* [Conference presentation]. The State, Regions, Business: Informational, Social, Legal, and Economic Aspects of Development. Kyiv, Ukraine.

Sheliazhenko, Y. (2021). *Legal foundations of personal autonomy of private persons and organizations: Theoretical aspect.* [Doctoral dissertation, Krok University]. https://library.krok.edu.ua/media/library/category/disertatsiji-avtorefe-rati-vidguki/df-26-130-005/shelyazhenko_2021-disertatsija.pdf

Sheliazhenko Y. (2021a). *Peace education for citizenship: a perspective for Eastern Europe.* Pravdoshukach. https://truth.in.ua/en/public/1162/

Sheliazhenko Y. (2021b). Concept of liberal peace management through mediation. *Legal Bulletin.* 2, 114-119. https://ssrn.com/abstract=3879889

Sheliazhenko, Y. (2022). *What scientists could do to stop the war in Ukraine.* [Online presentation]. Science4Peace Forum. https://science4peace.com/Public-Events/Entries/2023/1/science4peace-forum.html

Sheliazhenko, Y. (2023, August 8). *War and nonviolent intervention: Tracking Russia-Ukraine conflict escalation and finding possible ways to peace.* Wissenschaft und Frieden. https://wissenschaft-und-frieden.de/blog/sheliazhenko-war-nonviolent-intervention/

Sheliazhenko, Y. (2023a). *Militarist and plagiarist Oksen Lisovyi should not be Ukraine's Minister of Education and Science: Report of the Ukrainian Pacifist Movement.* Ukrainian Pacifist Movement. https://ssrn.com/abstract=4408126 or http://dx.doi.org/10.2139/ssrn.4408126

Sheliazhenko, Y. (2023b, January 20). *A graphic history of Ukraine and the current conflict.* World BEYOND War. https://worldbeyondwar.org/a-graphic-history-of-ukraine-and-the-current-conflict/

Sheliazhenko, Y. (2023c). *Dissenting to war in Ukraine.* Forum Wissenschaft, 1/24.

Sheliazhenko, Y. (2024). *What Ukraine could learn from Slovenia's culture of peace.* [Conference presentation]. Unconditional Peace. Politics. Histories. Memories. Futures. Institute for Cultural and Memorial Studies ZRC SAZU.

Sheliazhenko, Y. (2024a). *Ukraine must support the elimination of nuclear weapons.* World BEYOND War. https://worldbeyondwar.org/ukraine-must-support-the-elimination-of-nuclear-weapons/

The Ends of Autonomy [The Ends of Autonomy]. (2020, July 11). *Yurii Sheliazhenko, 'Informed autonomy: conceptualization of freedom in the digital age'.* [Video]. YouTube. https://youtu.be/aLKAnnBqV70

Ukraine. (2022). *Decree of the President of Ukraine on the introduction of martial law in Ukraine.* https://zakon.rada.gov.ua/laws/show/64/2022#Text

Ukraine. (2023). *Draft law on amendments to the Laws of Ukraine "on citizenship of Ukraine" and "on ensuring the functioning of the Ukrainian language as the state language" regarding the conditions for admission to Ukrainian citizenship.* https://itd.rada.gov.ua/billinfo/Bills/Card/40141

Ukrainian Pacifist Movement (2022, September 21). *Peace agenda for Ukraine and the world. Statement of the Ukrainian Pacifist Movement, adopted at the meeting on International Day of Peace 21 September 2022.* World BEYOND War. https://worldbeyondwar.org/peace-agenda-for-ukraine-and-the-world/

Ukrainian Pacifist Movement (2024, September 22). *Ukrainian vision of peace. Statement adopted by general assembly of the Ukrainian Pacifist Movement on the International Day of Peace 21 September 2024.* Free Civilians. https://www.civilni.media/111/

UNESCO. (2024). *Recommendation on education for peace and human rights, international understanding, cooperation, fundamental freedoms, global citizenship and sustainable development.* https://unesdoc.unesco.org/ark:/48223/pf0000391686_eng.locale=en

United Nations. (1999). *Declaration and programme of action on a culture of peace.* https://digitallibrary.un.org/record/285677?v=pdf

United Nations. (2015). *2030 agenda for sustainable development.* https://docs.un.org/en/A/RES/70/1

United Nations. (2016). *Declaration on the right to peace.* https://digitallibrary.un.org/record/858594?v=pdf

United Nations. (2023). *A new agenda for peace.* https://www.un.org/sites/un2.un.org/files/our-common-agenda-policy-brief-new-agenda-for-peace-en.pdf

United Nations. (2024). *Pact for the future.* https://www.un.org/sites/un2.un.org/files/sotf-pact_for_the_future_adopted.pdf

United Nations. (2024a). *Written statement submitted by War Resisters International, a non-governmental organization in special consultative status.* https://un-docs.org/en/A/HRC/57/NGO/308

Wells, H. G. (1921). *The outline of history: Being a plain history of life and mankind.* Macmillan Company.

Wintersteiner, W. (2022). *Ukrainian Pacifists: War is a crime against humanity.* War Resisters' International. https://wri-irg.org/en/story/2022/ukrainian-pacifists-war-crime-against-humanity

World BEYOND War [World Beyond War]. (2023, October 1). *#NoWar2023 panel: Nonviolent resistance to war in Ukraine.* [Video]. YouTube. https://youtu.be/LjrTUzLEDoO

Zanella, M.C. (2024, August 26). *Yurii Sheliazhenko: "We must change the narrative of the inevitability of war."* Pressenza. https://www.pressenza.com/2024/08/yurii-sheliazenkho-we-must-change-the-narrative-of-the-inevitability-of-war/

ZRC SAZU [ZRC SAZU]. (2023, December 26). *Brezpogojni mir. Politika. Zgodovina. Spomini. Prihodnost. - Yurii Sheliazhenko (14/16).* [Video]. YouTube. https://youtu.be/ermvg_QvCrk

Chapter 25

An Exiled Burmese Educator's Journey for Peace and Reconciliation at Home: An Honest Reflection

Maung Zarni

Introduction:
Societal, Political and Biographical

If peace-makers, -builders and -educators are so successful we would certainly not be living in this wretched world where over 100 million people have been rendered war- and conflict-fleeing refugees, and many millions more are trapped inside their own nations as the Internally Displaced Persons (IDPs, another technocratic euphemism from the United Nations for war- and conflict-fleeing persons).

As persons, peace-educators are believers, in final analysis, individuals who refuse to give up on the ideals of harmony among different human communities and peace as the preferred reality to wars and conflicts, which without fail entails death and destruction of increasingly unimaginable scale.

Their intellectual efforts at peace education-activism cannot be divorced from who they are, individual(s), choosing to pursue and contribute to such a thing as 'peace', which is in turn a non-lucrative act, typically thankless, while having little chance of success.

I feel it is relevant here to share a glimpse of my own personal background which has directly guided my efforts at peace making in my strife-torn native country of Burma or Myanmar.

I grew up in the country's cultural heartlands of Mandalay under the violent and repressive military dictatorship in the 1960s and 1970s. Importantly, my extended family of parents, grandparents, aunties and uncles were a socially liberal, but spiritually devout Burmese family, with an inter-generational tie to the country's most militaristic and nationalist organization – the armed forces.

I was born in 1963, one year after General Ne Win's military coup which deposed the representative government of Prime Minister U Nu, an avowedly pro-peace nationalist politician influenced by Buddhist teachings of Metta or universal compassion. While being exposed to Vipassana meditation and Buddhist philosophy of Impermanence, I was at the same time exposed to various strands of contradictory norms and values. Soaked in ethno-majoritarian and rather militaristic version of patriotism, I *grew up* (Zarni, 2012) admiring all the males in military uniform – uncles and great uncles in our family who were in the various branches of the country's armed forces. I learned to dissemble the army-issue 9-mm pistol which an uncle who grew up with me in the same extended family home on the West Moat Road in Mandalay brought home during his brief visit from 'the front lines' where he was engaged in counter-insurgency military operations against the country's 'multi-ethnic and multi-coloured insurgent groups' (such as the armed and outlawed Burmese Communist Party, the Karen National Union, the Shan State Army etc.).

Institutionally, Burma's new military rulers had refashioned radically the post-independence state, from its nascent civilian parliamentary democratic orientation to the neo-totalitarian state that would suit their dictatorial reign. In those mid-decades of the Cold War, both the Western Bloc of liberal democracies and the Communist and Socialist regimes of the Eastern Bloc or the non-aligned bloc had shelved various normative documents and inter-state treaties including, and most importantly, the Universal Declaration of Human Rights and the Convention on the Prevention and Punishment of the Crime of Genocide, adopted in December 1948. As long as General Ne

Win, 'our dictator', stayed clear of the West's fight to contain both China and USSR and claimed to be fighting the Burmese communists, his repressive junta was left alone to do what it did best – repress the multiethnic society, particularly dissidents and insurgents who sought ethnic political autonomy.

The Burmese society I knew in my formative years – I left for California in 1988 at the age of 24 - was only nominally Buddhist in that its Buddhism, the predominant religion of the country, where there exist significant pockets of Christians, Muslims and Hindus, was in its ritual practices and cultural façade. Both the state and the society have become progressively more violent, militant and genocidally racist over the last three decades since my 1988 departure.

The foundational Buddhist principle of *Metta* or non-discriminatory loving kindness has never guided our cultural practices. Just as a truly love-based Christian community, a peace and truth-anchored Jewish community, peace and equality-driven Islamic *Ulma* or Hindu community of One-ness of humans, would never conceivably – and theoretically – harm any other fellow human groups, with different belief systems. But again, Burma's Buddhist society, people and leaders are not different from all other existing 'faith' communities, in terms of our multiple layers of religious and racial bigotry, material/class exploitation and conflicts, gender inequalities, moral and spiritual corruption and political violence.

The result of Burmese Buddhists coming short – far, far short – of their own philosophical and spiritual ideals of Impermanence, universal loving kindness, etc. was a social and political order full of multiple forms of violence. The dominant Burmese national culture has historically condoned – even encouraged! – domestic violence (wife beating), produced and validated popular genocidal psyche through popular sayings and proverbs (e.g., annihilate one's enemy from its root or punish dissenters up to seven successive generations), institutionalized male supremacy and complete domination over females and sings the praise of recognizably marshal or militaristic strains of ethno-nationalism vis-à-vis non-Buddhist communities (such as Muslims and Christians) and non-Burmese ethnic communities, with their own distinct historical memories, political aspirations and rights to self-determination, constitutionally guaranteed, both in spirit and in writing (in the case of

Shan and Kachin people).

While oppressed by the dominant Burmese Buddhists, the cultural and ethnic Others have their own version of moral internal contradictions in the
form of dominant minority vs 'lesser' or weaker minorities. However, my
focus here is on the war-making by the dominant Burmese society and its
state institutions, particularly our national armed forces, in the name of the
people, country and, outrageously, in defence of Buddhism.

Growing up in such a society, one experienced the insidiousness of violence
in multiple ways and sites. In our everyday oral expressions, in culturally
rooted proverbs, in our inter-personal communications, as well as within
the web of institutional practices (for instance, law enforcement and security agencies and their essentially repressive and violence-ridden official behaviours towards civilian populations, including Buddhist monks and nuns).

It is often said that soldiers/generals appreciate peace more than civilians
because they operate in the institutions whose signature nature is to inflict
violence – that is, murder.

I disagree.

In my observations, having spent a significant amount of time with the an-
ti-Burmese junta resistance fighters from the Karen National Liberation Army
(KNLA) 20 years ago, I realize civilians in war-torn and politically repressive
society, as well as 'insurgents', long to stop fighting, violence and war. Karen
National Union, the political umbrella of the KNLA, is the oldest ethnically organized movement struggling for political autonomy since 1947, a year
before the British colonial rulers let go of Burma, their colony in mainland
Southeast Asia. For at least three generations, the Karen people in Eastern
Burma have only known violence, military operations and fierce fighting between their liberation organization and the central state actor, the Burmese
armed forces. Young KNLA resistance fighters – and their civilian peers – in
their post-teen years just want a peaceful normal life where they can go club-
bing, attend trade schools or colleges, watch a good thriller in a city theatre,
or simply tend to their family business or farm. They told me they are tired of
the cycle of armed conflicts. But at the same time, they and their Karen communities of resistance are not prepared to lie down and take violent abuses,

land and resource grab by the Burmese military – notorious for its lawlessness and egregious human rights crimes.

It is in this context I sought to support the Burmese resistance movements, first by Aung San Suu Kyi and her non-violence political platform and subsequently the armed multi-ethnic resistance movements – or 'insurgencies', as the state-centric international policy wonks and scholars would label them.

Peace, not as a Spiritual Pursuit but as a Strategic Option

My entry into 'peace education' is not based on some kind of belief in the presumably inherent virtues of peace. Even that most iconic 'prophet' of non-violence – Mahatma Gandhi – did not begin his activism as an advocate and educator of non-violence as an act of resistance to British rule in India. Gandhi was recruiting his fellow Indians to go and fight on the side of the British imperialists out of his strategic miscalculation that the British would be favourable to Indians' demand for independence, in exchanges for the military contributions by the Indian recruits towards the Raj's war efforts during the First World War. His sole disappointment with Britain's attempts to hold on to its crown colony of the Indian subcontinent eventually led him to consider and adopt non-violent but open confrontation with the British authorities in British India.

As a Burmese student dissident at the University of Wisconsin at Madison, I cut my teeth in international non-violence activism and advocacy in the consumer boycott, divestment and shareholder activism modelled after the successful anti-apartheid divestment campaign against South Africa which ended with the release of Nelson Mandela in 1990. The Free Burma boycott movement was established and expanded as an international support pillar for Aung San Suu Kyi's non-violence resistance against the Burmese military dictatorship a few years after the anti-apartheid divestment benefitted massively from the arrival of the 1st wave of the Internet, widely available among student and faculty populations across elite American universities and colleges, as well as the commercialized availability of the Internet through the AOL as the service provider. Thanks to the ever-expanding reach of the new Information Technology – albeit in its rather primitive 'dial-up' form for online access to the worldwide web of Netscape, the Free Burma campaign I was building and coordinating with other fellow activists across the globe – we had a network of activists spanning 28 countries on several continents – became one of the Internet's first and most successful human rights campaigns dedicated to a single country in the 1990s and early 2000s (Zarni, 2000).[1]

The international success of our worldwide grassroots campaigns culminated in both the corporate divestment from the military-ruled Burma by over 100 multinationals - most famously Pepsi Cola - and the enactment of economic sanctions against Burma by the United States and the European Union. But the Burmese junta found enough wiggle room to keep the Foreign Direct Investment flow into its coffer for two concrete reasons. First, in the global capitalist economy, there were also foreign investors and businesses, outside these regions of liberal democracies, that were not subjected to national laws, or domestic consumer pressure. Companies and state-owned enterprises from Burma's Asian neighbours including China, India, and Southeast Asia were eager to fill the investment and business vacuum created by the divestment and departure of Western corporations. And second and lastly, US and EU sanction laws or policies came with large enough loopholes and exemptions for energy corporations that were heavily invested in Burma's natural gas, oil and other extractive industries such as valuable hardwood.

However, my own initial euphoria, as a Burmese activist, in witnessing our Free Burma efforts were bearing fruit in terms of corporate divestment as evidenced in the headlines we as activists were making and in terms of the number of foreign investors withdrawing their business ties with the Burmese military junta, was short-lived. The Free Burma campaign was not making a dent in terms of its original two-fold mission. Our aim for the grassroots activism globally was to weaken the Burmese junta financially and to strengthen the hand of the Aung San Suu Kyi-led Burmese democratic opposition which adopted non-violence as its principal strategic platform. I wrote the mission statement for our collective activism, and specifically for the Free Burma Coalition which I was leading.

Honest reflection made me realize that what appeared to be successful in the Western public eyes as measured by the significant media coverage wasn't really changing the reality on the ground. The junta's repressive behaviour continued towards our democratic opposition – Suu Kyi remained in captivity, under house arrest – while the public in Burma were no longer inspired to turn the society into a decidedly anti-junta revolutionary society.

Meanwhile, through my face-to-face meetings with US officials in Washington, involved in both formulating and executing Burma sanctions policy, I reached a conclusion that the United States was not really a principled supporter of the Burmese democratic opposition – much less the federalist ethnic armed resistance organizations such as the Karen National Union. In those days, the Western policy circles and the public at large held Aung San Suu Kyi in highest regard. And yet the US was not going to explore any concrete and impactful ways to support various armed and non-violence opposition movements against the junta whose crimes were already well-documented. They used forced labour on large scale joint-venture infrastructure projects, for instance, the building of a natural gas pipeline which was jointly constructed by the California-based US oil company Unocal (later acquired by Chevron Oil). Myanmar junta and the Thai energy corporation known as PTTE committed war crimes and crimes against humanity including the use of sexual violence against ethnic minority women in Shan, Karen and Rohingya regions. A small circle of Burmese dissidents in exile who attempted to push Washington to go beyond what we then called 'sanctions orthodoxy' started to explore any possibilities of re-igniting a deadlocked or non-existent political process. We felt that the sanctions and isolation of Burna were hurting ordinary factory workers, depriving the society of any international exposure, intellectually, culturally and ideologically.

Witness to Burma's Civil War as A Transformative 'Education' for an Educator-Activist

In the spring of 2003, I jumped with excitement when my ethnic Karen dissident colleague invited me to go into the Karen National Liberation Army-controlled civil war region of Eastern Burma and to see first-hand life on Burma's front-line war zone. Although it was a very personal occasion – she was going for a marriage ceremony with her fiancé who was commander of the well-known KNLA Brigade Five - we were both aware of the potential transformative experience I was going to have. Remember, I was raised a Burmese ethno-nationalist in an extended military family, who viewed the non-Burmese and non-Buddhist ethnic people as second-class communities in the country where the majority Buddhist Burmese public perceived themselves as the rightful guardians of the core political state of the Union of Burma, throughout the country's history, both pre- and post-colonial.

My own close relatives in the Burmese national armed forces fought the KNLA and other ethnic armed organizations from when I formed my consciousness as a young boy in a large city, privileged and protected from any realities of the country's wars, which were being fought on the ethnic borderlands.

I stayed in the KNLA Brigade Five with the Karen 'insurgents' for nearly one month in April. I had numerous and frank conversations with Karen fighters, representing 3 different generations. I ate with them. I cracked jokes with them. I took long walks with them.

Learning from them through conversations and my own realization how impoverished and option-less were these ethnic communities really compelled me to un-learn my own ethno-centric prejudices which bordered on internal colonial attitude towards those who were portrayed in our popular and official narratives as, basically, lesser than us, the dominant Burmese Buddhists.

No amount of talks and theoretical studies about the principle of ethnic group equality or the need for peaceful resolution of the political differences and even conflicts over territorial claims and material interests would ever be a substitute for the immersive educational experience – albeit my stay with the Karen 'insurgents' was not designed as such – I was undergoing.

This 'semi-accidental' educational experience had a profound and lasting effect on my old 'Burmese supremacist' or colonial mindset. I felt ashamed seeing everything Burma through the militaristic, Burmese-centric lens, typical of virtually all classes of Burmese, irrespective of their educational attainment, wealth, profession or geographic location.

Beyond Rational Analysis: Empathy as a Part of My Peace Activism

In doing 'peace' some years later, my first-hand witness to the Karen people – 'insurgents' – on the receiving end of the Burmese militaristic nationalism, which the political state and the main controlling organ have come to embody and the (dominant) Burmese Mind is infused with, has proved to be of immense help.

Additionally, facilitating dialogue in a society or culture, where talking to 'the enemy' is considered a sign of weakness or cop-out, requires not just the political courage but the cultivated ability to put oneself in leading perpetrators' shoes. The perpetrators are typically humans – just like everyone else – whose behaviour and policy choices turn inhuman. There is always something human common across these categories – our own human fears, preferences for security, aspirations and interests. But both victims and victimizers need self- awareness.

Empathy ought to be a pillar of peace efforts.

The maxim that "we don't talk to our friends, but our enemies, if peace is the objective" applies in my own peace efforts. My initial phase of staunch anti-junta opposition which ended with the realization there is no state actor, near or far, for the Burmese opposition who was prepared to provide significant support – material, diplomatic or political – to help the Burmese tip the point of conflicts in our favour. Without some serious support from a sympathetic state, preferably in the neighbourhood, or simply a state actor with global reach (for instance, the US), I realized that we, the Burmese opposition, were staring at the permanent stalemate. There is no Zero Sum (winner takes all) scenario, however hard the Burmese dissidents, armed and non-violent, try.

Peace Activism Act I: Talking to the Enemy and Educating the Grassroots

There were two types of peace activism which I had felt compelled to undertake based on the emerging situation on the ground inside Burma, and the un-favourable international factors (specifically, the lack of significant support for the Burmese resistance), over the last 20 years.

First, political dialogue with the leadership of the military junta from 2003 onward, until the junta's efforts to block the emergency aid delivery or offers to millions of the Burmese victims of Cyclone Nargis which devastated Burma's rice delta, the Irrawaddy Delta, and parts of the central Burmese coast, which spans about 1,300 miles in the Bay of Bengal.

Up until this point, I only had rudimentary technical understanding of negotiations in conflict situations. Through the Rockefeller Foundation's Next Generation Leadership program (2001-2003) and the Georgetown Leadership Seminar established by the School of Foreign Service at Georgetown University (2004), I was given opportunities to learn about 'difficult conversations', a closest thing to negotiations to end conflicts.

Living and working as a Free Burma grassroots organizer in Washington, I became well-acquainted with Matthew Daley, a Korean War army vet and former member of the Secret Service who was then serving as deputy assistant secretary of state. Daley was a maverick who pointedly told me that his US government's policy towards Burma may be giving the Burmese opposition a false hope – as a similar false hope was given to the anti-Soviet Hungarian dissidents in the 1950s. (Then the Eisenhower Administration publicly encouraged the Hungarians to rise up against the Moscow-controlled Budapest regime, and then let them be mowed down by the security forces in 1956). He knew that I was disillusioned with the US sanctions orthodoxy and increasingly losing confidence in the leadership of Aung San Suu Kyi, who, from her house arrests, offered the Burmese opposition supporters – among whom I counted myself as one – little more than vague liberal sound bites and a continuing call for more sanctions. What the opposition needed was a serious political program and concrete steps towards forcing her military captors to liberalize their vice-like control over politics, economy and society. That was not forthcoming. And none of the Western state actors was prepared to do the heavy lifting for the Burmese opposition.

While there was a growing dissatisfaction among the circles of her leading supporters in the armed resistance movement, primarily along the Thai Burmese border regions of Karen, Karenni and Mon, as well as in the diaspora, no one was prepared to do anything to deviate from her pro-sanctions stance.

Her vague liberal words were biblical in the Burmese opposition. In the eyes of the adoring Western policy world, Aung San Suu Kyi – then nicknamed The Lady – could do no wrong.

It was against this backdrop that I decided to explore ways to break the political stalemate. In the early 2000s, there was no armed resistance among the majoritarian Burmese opposition, worthy of its name. On the part of our 'enemy', the Burmese junta, there was a pervasive sense of discomfort. The fiercely nationalistic generals did not like the situation they found themselves in. Cornered by unilateral sanctions by the US – and to a lesser extent by the EU - the generals had no choice but to turn to China and the Russian Federation. No dictatorship is a monolith. A circle of more intelligent military officers began to seek various exits from the Dragon's den.

Because Aung San Suu Kyi was seen, rightly or wrongly, as 'rigid' in her opposition to the continued junta rule, the junta started identifying some of the 'influential' supporters of hers, both inside Burma and in the diaspora. Matthew Daley was aware of the emerging space, and so were a few of us in leading positions in the diaspora. In consultation with a group of leading dissidents in US and Canada, and with Daley's encouragement, I put myself up for the role of an interlocuter among the 'moderates' – for want of a better term – in the two main camps: the junta and our diasporic opposition.

Through Daley's intervention, the United States Institute for Peace arranged a 3-day intensive workshop for a group of Burmese dissidents in the US conducted by two US diplomats who were involved in various treaty negotiations including with the USSR and USA for nuclear arms reduction in Europe. We were given an overview of various types of political negotiations between adversaries.

The exposure to peaceful negotiations I had received on 3 different occasions focused on the psychological and technical matters – like different scenarios, worst and best options etc. Upon reflection I noticed that a crucial element for peace – empathy – was never deemed an important element for a successful peace effort.

There was also a contextual impediment for our – or my – peace efforts to bear any fruit. 'Talking to the enemy', openly or confidentially, was the red line for the Burmese opposition – without the public nod from Aung San Suu Kyi. Against this hostile political psychological climate in the Burmese opposition (Latt, 2024)[2], armed and non-violent, inside Burma and in diaspora, my efforts were doomed from the start.

I have not written about this 'peace initiative' to break the deadlock at the senior most leadership level of both the junta and the opposition. Suffice it to say, it failed for various reasons. The junta was less than genuine when it said it wanted to build trust and to work together for the good of the country through what is technically known as 'Track II', or un-official diplomacy without the license.

The main entity that my small team of Burmese dissident colleagues and I were engaging with was the military intelligence services then headed by the 3rd ranking general, General Khin Nyunt. In retrospect, my military counterparts were keener to neutralize my 'influential voice' and split Aung San Suu Kyi's international support base than to genuinely build up the so-called moderate voices from across the conflict line of the junta vs the opposition.

The junta apparently succeeded in their short-sighted mission. As Daley told a fellow exile of mine in Washington, "he (Zarni) had arrows stuck on his back." The arrows were fired by my own fellow dissidents, for marching ahead of the crowd.

Learning from and working with Johan Galtung[3]

No account of my journey as a peace activist will be complete without an acknowledgment of Galtung's influence on the way I approach the subject of 'peace'. Obviously, when we use the word 'peace' in reference to a given social reality, we are talking about the absence of peace.

In the summer of 2003, I first met Professor Galtung in the home of my adopted American sister Marilyn Langlois, at Richmond Point, by San Francisco Bay, a short drive from the headquarters of US oil giant Chevron, her late scientist father's employer. We both came from families – one Burmese and the other American – with ties to violence, corporations and/or militarism, which may help explain our shared concern for peace and our high regard for

Galtung, 'the father of peace studies'. [Marilyn's maternal aunt from Berkeley was Oppenheimer's secretary at the Manhattan Project in Los Alamos during World War II. My extended family in Mandalay have served in what has become a genocidal military in Burma over 3-generations since its inception under WWII Japan's Fascist patronage] (Zarni, 2020).[4]

Galtung exuded eternal optimism and bubbling energy, 'eternal sunshine', to put it poetically. Of a situation as dire and seemingly intractable as Palestine, Galtung would talk about his positive vision wherein all the Arabs and the Israelis can live in peace and equality. Not only was Galtung intellectually towering, but was also a physically towering figure, with characteristic disarming laughs and smiles.

We were in Rangoon together in the fall of 2005. It was during my short-lived, unsuccessful attempt at Track II mediation in my country of birth where we had reached a stalemate between Aung San Suu Kyi leadership and the ruling military regime. I arranged a one-on-one meeting for him to talk to the 3rd ranking Burmese general, who headed the country's military intelligence services, about the possibilities of peace from the TRANSCEND perspective.

The then British Ambassador Vicky Bowman accommodated the Galtungs in the ambassador's residence colonially named "Balmoral" across from the old War Office on Shwedagon Pagoda Road. I joined the meeting between Galtung and the senior member of the General Staff, and served as the interpreter between the two.

At her arrangement, Galtung was also meeting elsewhere in Yangon with the leaders of the country's peace NGOs, run by a group of national minority representatives.

My contacts in the Burmese military junta wanted to know if "the professor is our friend?"

But Galtung was no friend of any party in conflict, little did they know. He was there to help mediate the conflict. The generals were seriously disturbed that Galtung would talk to the ethnic equality rights advocates. His mission was to talk to everyone in the conflict. So, he naturally spent a day with those who wanted to rebuild the post-independence Burma of multiple ethnic nations as a 'federalist' entity where every group had equal representation and an equal say in the way the country was governed. Paying lip service to 'federalism', the junta viewed any version of Burma other than effectively 'unitary (military-controlled) state', as a formula for its disintegration. Ironically, it is the military's pursuit and defence of the unitary state, with itself as its guardian, which has become the main driver behind the raging multifront civil war in Burma, with no light at the end of the tunnel today.

Although 30-odd years senior to me in age and wisdom, I remember well how appreciative, eager and even respectful Galtung was in our interactions which involved him learning the specificities of Burma's conflicts, which he wished to help resolve. Like all great educators, Galtung was not a one-way street 'know-it-al' guru. Despite being feted internationally as the 'guru', he was a lifelong learner and was humble enough to know that he still needed to learn from others, which deeply impressed me.

Galtung made unparalleled intellectual and practical contributions to the advancement of our understanding of peace, its social objectives and the conditions for peace, in terms of our global understanding of such an elusive goal. The Norwegian Nobel Peace Committee's refusal to recognize Galtung's contributions to world peace and peace activism, or understanding of peace, was both disappointing and disgraceful. Just look at the list of the committee's ignominious choices for this most prestigious recognition: Henry Kissinger, Likud's Menachem Begin (whom Einstein called 'Terrorist', 'Fascist'), Aung San Suu Kyi, Abiy Ahmed, or Barak Obama (with the daily 'kill-list' over his White House breakfast table).

Johan's intellectual legacy is as 'the father of peace studies". Equally important to many of us around the world, he enabled us to see (just) peace not simply as a political objective, but as a value to live and act upon. It was this peace (and harmony) as a value or path of life that propelled me to start a second phase of my peace activism.

Multiculturalist Initiative as Peace Activism Act II

Natural calamities can trigger some kind of societal healing as storms, floods, earthquakes, etc. don't discriminate in their devastating impact on populations. Often the tsunami that struck the Sumatra Island of Indonesia in December 2004, among other places, and the subsequent end to the decades of conflicts in the province of Aceh is referred to as one such case. A class analysis can be made that the poor and the downtrodden are more likely to suffer from the ecological disasters than the rich and the powerful. In the spring of 2008 Burma was struck by a very powerful cyclone known as the Nargis. The junta chose the route to more conflicts and sufferings for the people by denying the international community's offer of desperately needed emergency aid to Burma's cyclone victims. Then and there, I decided that I couldn't continue to engage in any type of peace activism or advocacy in such a state where its principal leadership, *de facto* or *de jure*, put its own regime survival above the public welfare in such a dire situation.

Having removed myself from the Burma scenes, I re-devoted and re-focused my energy into re-building myself as a scholar of Asian Studies after a 3-year-visiting fellowship at Oxford University.

To be immersed again in Asian affairs, I relocated to Brunei in the winter of 2012. My academic assignment was to develop a new institute of Asian Studies at the University of Brunei Darussalam, with a research program on the South China Sea where Brunei is a claimant country in the territorial dispute with China.

Alas, my resumed academic career was not to be. The news of the organized violence against Muslim Rohingyas in Western Burma hit world news headlines in June 2012. My fellow Burmese activists inside Burma felt it was too personally risky for them to speak out about this mass violence made to appear 'communal' or horizontal. Their investigation on-the-ground revealed that the violence against Muslims, and Rohingyas in particular, was in fact orchestrated by the junta. Aung San Suu Kyi was not prepared to speak out against neither the mass violence against the Rohingya nor the frenzy of Islamophobia being whipped up by the country's most influential Buddhist Order. In April that year, she had already joined the military-controlled parliament as an MP, along with several dozen of her National League for Democracy members. She was single-minded about staying in the junta's good book as a partner for democratic reforms which the junta had promised.

My fellow dissidents inside knew that I would spring to action, had I known that the junta was behind the escalating Islamophobic violence in Western Myanmar, which had the potential to spread to other parts of Burma where there are substantial pockets of Burmese Muslims. So they started feeding me independently verified stories of death and destruction against Rohingya people, the most vulnerable and most destitute among the country's minority groups, already existing only with the humanitarian assistance provided by UN agencies such as the World Food Program.

While the INGOs such as the International Crisis Group and Amnesty International were characterizing the violence in Western Burma as 'communal', repeating the junta's official line, I started to use the sociological and legal frameworks of genocide, based on my own historical analysis of the violence against Rohingya in Western Myanmar. While undertaking a 3-year joint study (Zarni & Cowley, 2014) of the conditions of Rohingyas, with my researcher colleague and wife Natalie Brinham I was screaming genocide in all my public media appearances and writings, to the disapproval of Bruneian authorities. Brunei was more interested in cultivating commercial ties in the energy sector with the Burmese junta, the main culprit behind the waves of Muslim persecution in Burma, than it was to stand up for the Muslims of Burma. Finally, I was openly gagged from speaking out against my native country's Rohinga genocide, which in turn compelled me to resign publicly, as academic censorship (Htwe, 2013) is my professional red line. I left Brunei for Malaysia, before the 1st anniversary of my employment contract.

For the next 3 years, in Malaysia's supportive institutional setting at the Universiti Malaya in Kuala Lumpur, I spent considerable time and energy fundraising, outreach and developing a week-long multiculturalist education program, with the help of a Muslim activist resource centre on the outskirt of Bangkok and the Documentation Centre – Cambodia, the principal archive that supported the Khmer Rouge Tribunal from its start to close.

My peace education initiative rested on several pillars designed to help cultivate: 1) **empathy** among the participants for cultural, religious and racial or ethnic Others; 2) **understanding** of existing internal criminal and humanitarian law and the judicial processes that attempt to hold perpetrators of atrocity crimes (such as senior members of the Pol Pot regime who were on trial in Cambodia); 3) **historical understanding** of Rohingya identity, history, existence, as well as racist and state-sponsored criminalization, dehumanization and persecution; and 4) **rudimentary social scientific knowledge of genocide and crimes** against humanity. Importantly and necessarily, my educational program – so-named genocide sensitivity training or alternatively, multiculturalist initiative – devoted considerable time brainstorming ideas to confront this cardinal question – What needs to be done?

Over 3 years, the program brought about 120 Burmese activists, artists, writers, musicians and clergy from different faith communities including Buddhist, Hindu, Muslim and Christian, to Thailand and Cambodia for a week-long stay. Our daily contact averaged 10-12 hours. In Cambodia, we would visit mass graves, and the Khmer Rouge tribunal where the participants were briefed on relevant aspects of international law, judicial procedure, etc. by teams of lawyers representing defence, prosecution and civil party (victims).

The program was very worthwhile for me and the participants. However, if genocide education or sensitivity training aimed at preventing the genocide had gone from the slow-burning nature to a Rwanda-like full-blown death and destruction scenario, albeit on a numerically smaller scale – which took place in August and September 2017 – my peace education program failed to achieve its mission.

I am completing this writing in the midst of Israel's genocide in the occupied Palestine both generally and in Gaza. The Gaza Health Ministry released the figures for the Palestinians -- "direct kill" – by Israeli Defence Forces – as 44,000 in 400+ days. I have been dismayed by the categorical failures of Holocaust Memorial Museums which dot western capitals and cities across Europe, USA and Canada – most specifically Auschwitz, The Jewish Museum of Berlin, and the United States Holocaust Memorial Museum and, above all, Yad Vashem, or The World Holocaust Remembrance Center. The educators and the administrators of these educational institutions have dismally failed to practice what they preach: the universal pledge of Never Again! I remember feeling outraged by the US Holocaust Memorial Museum and the Auschwitz-Birkenau Museum (the official Polish museum and a UNESCO World Heritage-labelled institution of global importance) issuing a very strong statement condemning the Palestinian resistance which struck its occupier communities in Israel on 7 October while completely choosing to remain silent about Israel's almost-sixty years of semi-genocidal blockage of Gaza and the near total annexation of the West Bank and East Jerusalem.

If the genocide education by these world-class, extremely well-endowed institutions does not reflect any ounce of conscience and universal empathy I don't really have high hopes that peace education – typically carried out on shoe-string budgets by lone if dedicated educator-activists – will have a meaningful impact on the deeply troubled war on the brink of ecological mass extinction and of a Third World War. You can't have racists of all stripes and colours running these influential organizations and expect to build a world based on the universal principle and value of PEACE for all.

If "Never again!" means *never again for all*, peace must also mean *peace for all.*

That said, I draw a number of honest observations from both the grassroots informal education for peace – which the multiculturalist education initiative definitely was about – and the earlier peace efforts designed to push Burma's politics into the framework of transcending and transforming the violent, Zero sum game into a process of fostering peace both as a substantive goal and an organizing value for an ethnically and religiously heterogeneous society in Burma.

Thirty-six years after I started out an activist as a young Burmese student at the University of California, supporting the democratic movement in Burma, I find my birth country plunges progressively deeper into the abyss of human sufferings, the ever-expanding scope and sites of all-around civil war and the ongoing genocide against Rohingya people, despite all efforts for peace and reconciliation by so many individuals, Burmese and our foreign supporters.

Conclusion

I have gleaned 4 conclusions from my years as a peace educator, advocate and activist that I consider most crucial in doing peace:

- No peace activism or advocacy or education can succeed without aiming to foster a capacity to put oneself in others' shoes, irrespective of the conventional labels or categories – such as perpetrators or victimizers/victims, the oppressor/the oppressed. As Fanon so perceptively pointed out fostering peace and resolution requires dismantling these diametrically opposing poles.

- The 'reality tours' of conflicts, wars, and toxic pre-genocidal situations, as well as poverty (which in Galtung's pioneering terms is in and of itself the result of 'the structural violence' in organized social order) are essential for transformative peace education or activism. Here I draw insights from an epistemologically Buddhist perspective. Enlightenment or Education has to result in the fundamental transformation of the Knower-Learner in the process of peace education.

- Peace education or activism needs to appreciate the very real structural impediments and power differentials that are at work against any individual education program or activist initiative. Specifically, political states and capitalist economic organizations known as corporations have been known to conspire against the welfare of human communities, since Adam Smith in the mid-18th century. This eternal union of Power-Money has not shown any signs of divorce over the last 400 years since the British East India Company was established as the royally chartered vulture-like economic organization.

- Peace education and activism must shed its elitist, academic liberal garb and seek to educate average Joe – and Jane – on the street. Peace education is essentially different from the education of 'purely' academic or technological subjects, say, biology, chemistry, computer engineering or advanced math in that it is aimed at transforming the hearts and minds of the largest segments of a society in conflict. As such, peace education/activism entails disseminating its substantive and analytical ideas and instilling in people peace as a value – not simply a political objective.

Endnotes

1) For the historical and analytical overview of this particular phase of international Burma activism see Zarni, M. (2000).

2) A young Burmese scholar-activist colleague of mine Sai Latt offers a fresh social psychological analysis of the signature obstacle in making peace and seeking dialogue in Burma's increasingly intractable civil war – now in its 8th

decade. See: Latt, S. (2024, November 21).

3) Please see my tribute to Johan Galtung here: Zarni, M. (2024, March 4). *"America? I love the republic, but I hate the Empire": A Personal Tribute to Johan Galtung (24 Oct. 1930 – 17 Feb. 2024), the Man for Just Peace.* FORSEA. https://forsea.co/a-personal-tribute-to-johan-galtung/

4) I have published a reflective essay specifically on the program. See Zarni, M. (2020).

References

Htwe, N.T. (2013, January 14). *Myanmar activist [TRANSCEND member], professor resigns over Brunei University 'censorship'*. TRANSCEND. https://www.transcend.org/tms/2013/01/myanmar-activist-transcend-member-professor-resigns-over-brunei-university-censorship/

Latt, S. (2024, November 21) *What the Miss Grand International incident reveals about Myanmar's political psychology.* Frontier Myanmar. https://www.frontiermyanmar.net/en/what-the-miss-grand-international-incident-reveals-about-myanmars-political-psychology/

Zarni, M. (2000). Resistance and cybercommunities: The internet and the Free Burma Movement. In De Vaney, A., Gance, S. & Ma, Y. (Eds.), *Technology and Resistance: Digital communications and new coalitions around the world* (pp. 71-88). Peter Lang.

Zarni, M. (2012). *Growing up a proud racist in Burma.* E-International Relations. https://www.e-ir.info/2012/09/12/growing-up-a-proud-racist-in-burma/

Zarni, M. (2020). State and hate in Myanmar. One lone educator's resistance through public pedagogy. In Verma, R. & Apple, M. (Eds.), *Disrupting hate in education: Teacher activists, democracy, and global pedagogies of interruption.* Routledge.

Zarni, M. & Cowley, A. (2014). The slow-burning genocide of Myanmar's Rohingya. *Pacific Rim Law and Policy Journal, 23,* 3: 683-754. https://digital-commons.law.uw.edu/wilj/vol23/iss3/8

Chapter 26
Learning to be Free in Gaza

Amal Amara Takkash

I have faced 'the other' since birth - the same 'other' fleeing massacres in Europe, who I now find myself escaping, seeking safety abroad. For this 'other', security has meant erasing my identity, my sovereignty. This reveals that our Nakba is inextricably linked to the broader arc of human history. They were a people escaping horrific atrocities in Europe, only to then commit genocide on our land. We have no choice but to resist and defend ourselves, to do whatever it takes to survive.

I was born in Jaffa in 1946, two years before the Nakba. The youngest of 12 children, born to Ibrahim and Zaher Abu Amara. Our family's home was set among the beautiful orange orchards that provided our livelihood.

In 1948, the invasion of Jaffa marked the beginning of a campaign of terror that shattered the peace and freedom we previously knew. The Zionist militia forces killed or expelled the city's population of approximately 80,000 people, they aimed to empty all the cities of Palestine. The fall of Jaffa is considered one of the biggest catastrophes of the Nakba. Our once happy family life was suddenly shattered as we were forcibly expelled from the paradise we had called home for generations. Many family members died or were injured during our harrowing journey, an escape from a living hell. Fleeing as planes dropped bombs and bullets rained down, we kept moving until we reached the Egyptian border near the Suez Canal at an area called El Qantara. Exhausted and destitute, we sought refuge in the detention camps and tents set up for the influx of Palestinian refugees escaping from the northern cities and villages of Palestine.

The term 'refugee' becomes all too common. Within the camps, there is a severe lack of basic rights and freedoms. No work is permitted, and movement is restricted solely to the camp confines. Education is non-existent, with only detention centers and barracks provided. Even critical human aid is prohibited, and the camps are under constant surveillance and guard. When the borders and checkpoints were closed, accessing food and water became impossible. As a toddler in the refugee camps, I developed night blindness due to severe malnutrition. I recall holding onto the tent ropes just to navigate the camp in the evenings, as we initially feared I was going blind. Being slowed down and unable to see, I was struck with a chilling sense of terror. Our fight for survival was a brutal ordeal, but through this trauma, we learned a profound lesson: that human life is the most precious possession of all.

In the early days of living in the refugee camps, our family taught us valuable lessons. I will never forget when my mother tried to beautify our tent by putting up shelves to display a vase of flowers. Her first attempt failed, as there were no walls to support the shelves. My father and siblings gathered empty boxes and other materials and successfully installed shelves in the corner of our tent. During this period of deprivation - tents, hunger, and estrangement - we clung to our mother. She taught us patience, resilience, and resistance, nurturing our hopes of returning to the paradise we had been viciously driven from.

In that desolate, depressing environment, my father found time to educate and inspire us. I recall how he taught us to connect with nature and recognize our role within the surrounding ecosystem. He taught us to start seeds and plant them. I was overjoyed when the seeds began to grow roots, just like the Palestinian children who are planted and rooted in our land.

I will always treasure those days with my family - the closeness we felt, and the care they took to relieve our fears and entertain us. They told us stories, sang us lullabies to ease our minds during the air raids, and we dreamed of returning to the fields of Jaffa. Our parents and older siblings taught us traditional Palestinian songs about the seasons, festivals, and Ramadan. I was captivated by these songs - those soothing, traditional songs allowed me an escape from poverty and hunger. A place where I could live out my dreams through music and play.

Amidst this challenging intersection in my development, true heroes emerged to rescue us from our dire situation. A group of volunteer Palestinian teachers set up a makeshift school in the tents, despite having no supplies or books - only the lessons and songs they had committed to memory. Each morning before classes, they would assemble the students to sing the powerful anthem "Aidon" ("We're Returning" by Harun Hashim Rashid), affirming their determination to return home.

> *We will return and these borders will be broken.*
> *Those forts and barricades will come down.*
> *The fragrant fields and the fertile green coastline.*
> *What our forefathers built. Our land our land.* (Rashid, 2010)

My generation owes much to the selfless, young adults who volunteered to teach us, even before organizations like UNRWA were established or schools were accessible. They shared their knowledge orally, for we had no books or paper. We called it the 'school of the refugee tents' or 'family school' - a community effort to educate the children. And in those tent schools, the song "We Will Return" would ring out with heartfelt longing for our homes.

The refugee school taught us to love our country, life, and freedom. We learned to fight for our rights and to uphold justice, without transgressing or abusing. Our motto was, "Religion for God, the Nation, for Everyone". Our dream remained deeply rooted in our hearts and minds. We dedicated our lives to returning to our beloved homeland, building a loving and forgiving community of people from diverse backgrounds, religions, and ethnicities. I remember my mother and grandmother telling us stories about the harmony that once reigned in our hometowns, where Muslims, Christians, and Jews lived in peace and happiness. Our kind Jewish neighbors did not have tanks or bombs – no killing, no massacres. I dream of reclaiming that joyful life.

We learned the vital importance of unity and supporting one another, especially the less fortunate. We were all students, growing and learning together. We clung to the few resources available to us: education and resistance. Though uprooted, we defiantly held our ground, resolving to return home.

My family endured three years in these camps before being relocated to a limited border area in Gaza following a truce.

Image 1: Amal, bottom left with mother (center) and siblings in Gaza refugee camp

Through it all, we were taught to stand tall, to never feel lesser than those with homes and land. We learned the inherent value of each human being, and the power of education and perseverance in the face of adversity.

Moving from the microcosm of the refugee camps, our diaspora began in the city of Gaza. Growing up in Gaza as refugees of the Nakba, we progressed from a makeshift tent school to the UNRWA schools in Gaza. As my family faced these trying circumstances together, we had to make significant sacrifices. My older brothers stopped attending school and instead worked to support us financially. My oldest sister, a talented seamstress and traditional cross-stitch artist from Jaffa, also took on small jobs to contribute. Meanwhile, my mother's role was to stretch our limited resources as far as possible, carefully recycling and repurposing every scrap of clothing or food we had. Nothing went to waste. With the family working tirelessly to get by, my father had the added challenge of feeding us, keeping us safe, and finding adequate housing.

I grew up following an agenda designed to separate us from our roots and homeland and make us forget. But the opposite occurred. We did not forget the fear and terror we felt. Instead, we were filled with a deep nostalgia for the land and dignified life we had lost to the misery of diaspora. Their aim was to erase our very existence, to privilege the stronger over us. Despite their efforts, we endured, we did not die. On occasion, we would take trips to the northern Gaza border, where we could see our distant homes and fields, but we were forbidden from returning. We gazed at the bountiful trees, hungry and thirsty, trapped behind barbed wire which separated the Gaza Strip from the northern coast of Palestine.

After I finished high school in Gaza, we moved to the bustling city of Cairo, Egypt, where my brother and I could attend university. United as a family, we supported one another. My older siblings who were now scattered across the Arab world, found employment, and the remittances they sent back allowed us younger siblings to complete our college education. Despite the upheaval, my parents stood by us, providing a sense of safety and ensuring we could have a stable environment to attend school.

The word 'refugee' became a stain that was stamped upon us. Wherever we went, that label defined us. Whenever we had to fill out a form, our identity was ripped away again - government entities would mark our identity as 'Unknown' whenever we wrote 'Palestinian'. This was in the 1960s, a time of freedom and civil rights movements around the world. While equality and freedoms were expanding for others, ours were being stripped away and denied.

As young adults, we asked the urgent question: "What is to be done?" The answer was clear - we must return to our country! The chant shifted from "We Will Return" to the more resolute (Fida'i) "We Will Sacrifice".

Studying in Cairo allowed me the opportunity to connect with peers from the West Bank, which had been separated from the Gaza Strip, they lived under Jordanian rule while we in Gaza were under Egyptian control. We bonded over our struggle and displacement.

Engaging with the international student movement of the 1960s, which called for independence, freedom, and equality across Africa, Vietnam, and South America, further inspired us. Witnessing these countries gain their independence and support each other, especially the liberation of Algeria, encouraged us to continue our own revolution and organize our ranks. The lesson was clear: military power alone cannot extinguish the rightful struggle for freedom of an occupied people.

We began forming political groups that grew into larger parties. After the Nakba, when we lost our home and all we possessed, we learned to hold fast to our resolve and strengthen it. When the Naksa happened in 1967, we were not shaken by these disasters, we stood firm and absorbed the shocks. We strengthened our commitment to our land.

The formation of the PLO as the sole representative of the Palestinian people finally ended our marginalization. However, we soon realized our cause was unique - we were not facing colonialism from a great empire, but rather a Zionist movement supported by these empires, seeking to replace our people and expel us from our land. We welcomed immigrants fleeing the West, unaware of the plans being hatched for our displacement and elimination.

During my time at Ain Shams University in Cairo, the 1967 Arab-Israeli war broke out, resulting in the loss of Gaza and the West Bank to the Israeli occupation. We became determined more than ever to reclaim what had been taken by force. The world's liberation movements supported and recognized the PLO, urging us to share our story globally after the mainstream media remained silent about our plight. I felt compelled to open a dialogue and educate others about our legitimate rights to return and of self-determination. With my peers I organized an exhibition and seminars at the university to showcase Palestinian culture, traditions, and our deep roots in the land - countering the Israeli narrative that portrayed us as ignorant and backward. This was my introduction to public advocacy; I was inspired to continue this crucial work.

After university I moved to Kuwait to work as a teacher. Though geographically distant from my homeland I remained deeply connected to my Palestinian identity. We educated successive generations about our experience. We cultivated a generation that recognized the significance of a unified homeland for an enduring nation, which would accept nothing less than freedom for its people and land.

With my colleagues I explored a wide range of intellectual concepts, studying the works of Marx and Engels as well as socialist and capitalist theories. We grappled with our unique national experiences - countries torn apart, borders redrawn. We recognized the circumstances of our nations, which were fractured and had their borders redrawn by the West through the Sykes-Picot Agreement and Balfour Declaration after the Ottoman Empire's defeat in World War I. Rejecting subordination to any superpower, we steadfastly believed in the Arab identity, its values, and its endangered civilization. I put these convictions into action, participating in the establishment of the Palestinian Students Union in Kuwait, the Palestinian Teachers Union, and the Palestinian Red Crescent.

In the early 1970s, we organized the first international Palestinian symposium in Kuwait to promote dialogue. The symposium was overseen by the writers Ghassan Kanafani and Bassam Abu Sharif. This allowed us to present our narrative to the world, after the Zionist media had suppressed it and appropriated some of the symbols of our cultural heritage during a period of historical neglect.

The tragic assassinations of Ghassan and his young niece, as well as the attempt on Bassam's life in Beirut, marked a significant turning point in my life. This incident underscored the dangerous power of words and dialogue, and reinforced the vital importance of demanding rights, loyalty, and continuity. I made a solemn promise to myself and my colleagues to carry on Ghassan's unfinished work. The sadness was profound.

In all this sadness, life still goes on and there are happy moments to be found. While in Kuwait, I reconnected with my Palestinian friend from university, Ali, and we got married. He was from the village of Ashdod.

In 1948, his father was killed by Zionist gangs in Ashdod when he was an infant, and yet he did not seek revenge. Later in 1956, as a young boy he narrowly escaped being killed when he and his siblings and other family members were lined up against a wall in the garden of their home in Khan Yunis by Israeli military and shot at with a barrage of bullets. His beloved eldest brother was killed, while the rest of them were wounded. Another brother, who later became a teacher, was so severely wounded he was left permanently disabled. Despite experiencing such savagery and violence at many stages of his life, he still called for forgiveness. Despite all these personal losses, after the Oslo Accords he was willing to work with the other side to establish peace and economic opportunities for Palestinians in their homeland.

I learned that the shooting can stop, but the pain remains deep in the soul. Still, we continue our journey towards a secure future for ourselves and our children - a future that has yet to fully materialize. Following the Sabra and Shatila massacre in Lebanon, we were able to assist our Palestinian brethren in their struggle through the organizations we created. We realized the significance of being self-reliant, working together, and maintaining strong family connections in the diaspora.

The devastation persisted as the conflict between Iraq and Kuwait forcibly displaced half a million Palestinians, scattering them across Australia, Canada, and America, severing them from their roots.

We went to America, farther from our homeland than ever before. My husband and I earned our master's degrees from Xavier University in Cincinnati, Ohio. There, we met a translator at the university who helped us immensely, and we came to know one of our children's schoolteachers, both of whom became family friends. We are Palestinian and they are Jewish, but we did not let this difference divide us. We talked, exchanged ideas, found common ground, and grew as friends together. We confirmed that human relations do not have to be subject to religion or race and that hatred between Palestinians and Israelis was formed as a result of the violent occupation.

When the Oslo Peace Accords took place we were very excited; I was hopeful that we would finally reunite with family after decades of bitter separation. Separated from loved ones by borders and barriers, I was unable to be with my sister when she passed away, nor could my brothers join me when our mother died.

We returned to Cairo in preparation to enter Gaza after many years of living abroad as noncitizens. My husband and I were eager to live and work with our people for a better future for us and our neighbors. At this time, our daily life became directly connected to politics. How can one expect neighborly love while simultaneously harming and dispossessing that neighbor? The answer came to me from Japan. In Cairo, I met with the Nomura Center for Lifelong Education team for the first time, during a conference on coexistence.

"Life Long Integrated Education as Creator of the Future 1 & 2," by Mrs. Nomura, has been a guiding force in inspiring me to design educational programs for children, families, and society (Nomura, 1996, 2002). I discovered ideas that can be used to create programs focused on freedom, justice, human dignity, and peace. These concepts can be simplified and communicated effectively to the general public. English professor Hassan Sarsour of Gaza translated the book into Arabic. I have written a review and personal interpretation of the work. Gamal elBanna, an influential figure in Arab culture, published this work in Cairo.

I hope we can maximize the benefits of this valuable reference. Guided by Mrs. Nomura's Continuous Integrated Education theory, I established the Gaza-based Dar il-Hikma Center. Along with volunteers from the community I designed programs to help our children preserve their threatened Palestinian identity. Confronting the challenging circumstances, I engaged community members in programs that instilled a sense of purpose and acceptance in children. People actively participated, allowing us to sow seeds of hope for peace, despite the ongoing siege, destruction, and fear.

I heard children sing mournful songs about imprisonment, captors, and martyrs. As they played near the seashore, they made graves adorned with beautiful seashells, olive leaves, and the Palestinian flag. For this reason, the first stage of the program I developed was to reflect hope for peace in 1997.

As an alumnus of Al-Zaytoun Elementary School, I began working with the current students, sharing the collection of Palestinian culture I had documented – including songs of the moon, sun, sea, rainbow, and themes of peace and freedom. Traditional songs and games offered a brief respite from the wounds of oppression and occupation, filling them and me with happiness.

Through the "Who Am I, and The World Around Me" programs, I guided children to see themselves within the broader contexts of history and geography. These programs sought to preserve the children's cultural heritage and identity, while also cultivating their self-esteem and character as integrated parts of global society. Ultimately, the programs empowered the children to recognize their important, meaningful place and role in the world, no matter how small it may have seemed.

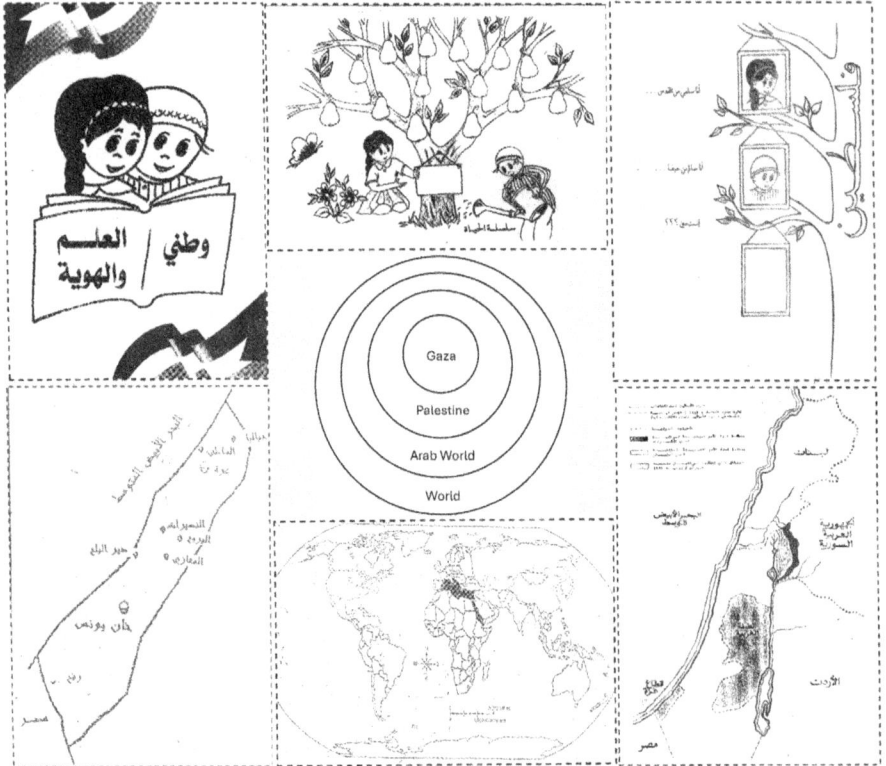

Image 2: Amal Amara Takkash

The above images depict Salma and Salem - two Palestinian children whose very names, meaning "Peace", symbolize the program's mission. The images show the children exploring their identity and connection to their hometowns, as well as the themes of cultural heritage, human rights, and global interconnectedness.

Global civilization is a tapestry woven from the diverse threads of human societies and cultures. Just as the body is made up of various components, it cannot be complete without each essential piece. In the same way that a single drop of water is essential to the vastness of the sea, the individual elements are integral to the greater civilization.

"Life is Beautiful", another program we worked on was making of traditional paper kites. The different generations shared and learned with each other. The older generation still remembers the names and different shapes of kites. This activity was deeply meaningful to me because my husband and I secured a temporary visa that allowed my older brother, Mohamed Ali, to briefly return to Gaza. He eagerly shared cherished memories about our childhood in Jaffa with the children. He taught them about the history and traditions of kite-making, regaling them with tales of the kite-flying competitions he used to participate in as a youth.

With the assistance of the Ministry of Youth and Sports, I organized the first traditional Palestinian hand-crafted kite festival in Gaza, the festivals were called Sunrise Kite festival, Kites Without Borders, Kites not Rockets.

We invited the Mayor of Haifa, Ameram Mitsna to come to the Gaza Governance, he was the military ruler of Gaza before the peace agreement. The children offered their kites as a peace offering. He invited us and our children to spend a day in Haifa. This was the beginning of dialogue reflected in the peace and good intentions of the kites presented: one of the Palestinian flag and another representing the Israeli flag. The mayor said that before they used to shoot down kites that were made to look like the Palestinian flag and now, he is accepting it as a gift. This was the first of the educational achievements, to take the Palestinian children towards co-existence, and for them to start to see the blue sky again.

With support from the Nomura Center, I expanded the Dar il-Hikma Cultural Center into the Jabalia refugee camp. With teachers, nurses, civil servants, journalists and other professional volunteers, we worked tirelessly with young mothers, families, and children to reconnect what was severed during the wars.

In 2022 we launched a program to support young Palestinian journalists. We held a competition across Gaza's schools, seeking talented students with an interest in media and reporting. The top candidates were then trained and mentored over several months at Dar il-Hikma. Finally, the young journalists began producing their own reports, sharing stories about life and traditions in Gaza. The young journalists documented historic areas such as the old city bakery and the fisherman's wharf. These locations have been tragically destroyed, however, what their cameras recorded remains for us as unforgettable memories, documenting historic areas in Gaza.

Cycles of aggression persist, as we retreat only to eventually return and start anew. From the aggression of 2001, to 2008, 2012, 2014, and 2021, the pattern repeats. Now, we face the greatest genocide of our people, which began in October 2023, as well as the destruction of all life. As we were feeling hopeful, peace slipped further away. Even so, within the darkness and depravity there is always a ray of light, as evident from a story that was relayed to me from Gaza by Dar il Hikma manger Aisha, about the Qarasyah jam. The center took great pride in reviving our cultural heritage through Palestinian cuisine. One key initiative was cultivating a rare, regional variety of prune (Qarasyah) and making jam that we sought to market internationally. The warehouse was destroyed during the onslaught on the north of Gaza, but remarkably the jars of jam were recovered undamaged and provided sustenance to the local neighborhood, saving many families from starvation.

Humanity's greatest achievement is our enduring capacity to create, innovate, and thrive in the arts and sciences. Human civilization was forged through the collective pursuit of knowledge and learning, evolving from the mastery of fundamental skills like hunting, fire-making, and trade. Conquering empires have understood that controlling a population requires suppressing its education and cultural identity. This often begins with the systematic destruction of libraries, museums, and other repositories of knowledge and heritage, as evidenced by the burning of the Library of Alexandria, the Baghdad Library, the destruction of Palestinian archives and libraries, and the looting of the Baghdad Museum. Endless wars have devastated humanity's linguistic and cultural treasures, robbing us of beautiful languages and cherished traditions. The rise of the war machine, coupled with insatiable greed, has accelerated this destruction.

As UNESCO has warned, we now face a stark choice: coexist peacefully or perish together. As concerned citizens, we must take responsibility for finding a way forward – a future free from conflict and devastation. Ultimately, the most precious resource we possess is the human beings who have shaped our shared past and present through their labor and ingenuity. Our perceptions of war and peace originate in the mind, ultimately shaping our reality. It is for this reason that integrated peace education is, in my view, essential.

Each community should be empowered to document their own history in their own words. Furthermore, rather than relying solely on abstract methods we should always aim to be universally applicable and to give a voice to the oppressed. Rather than relying on individual efforts, we should build institutions that can disseminate ideas of peace, education, and coexistence. As a group committed to promoting a culture of peace, we must develop effective mechanisms to spread this message. This includes leveraging educational curricula and various community awareness initiatives to help people benefit from the lessons of global human history.

Each year, Dar il-Hikma commemorates the events of World War II leading up to the atomic bombings of Hiroshima and Nagasaki. Students at Al-Zaytoun Schools in Gaza have written a short play titled "Birds of Hiroshima," which explores a path toward peace and security. Documentaries can powerfully depict humanity's dark history of slavery, colonialism, and the resulting destruction and suffering endured by people and cultures. These difficult topics could also be explored through more accessible mediums like children's animations and stories, helping educate younger generations about these important historical realities. Sharing our pain may remind us of past wounds, but it also brings us closer together. By acknowledging our struggles, we can liberate ourselves from the past and gain valuable lessons for the future. Much of our knowledge about the Nazi genocide of the Jewish people, comes from our exposure to World War II films. In continuation of this, we must come together to share the stories of the Nakba and the Holocaust, as both peoples have endured historical injustice and ongoing suffering. I urge us all to learn from these tragedies and strive for liberation. The world's unjust silence has allowed a continuous, never-ending horror to plague the Palestinian people. As two peoples, we must learn from history to avoid cancelling each other out. We must engage in respectful dialogue to stand united against racism and learn to coexist. The path forward is a single state that guarantees equality and the rights of all its citizens. By educating the privileged youth about historic exploitation and slavery, we can liberate them from the weight of that dark past and inspire them to think and act more justly and peacefully.

From the current painful experience, I see the need for more non-profit grass-roots committees such as the Nomura Center aimed at promoting global education and intercultural understanding to 1) Raise awareness about the importance of human diversity; 2) Develop programs to bridge divides between different regions by celebrating the rich cultural heritage of all nations; 3) Encourage freedom of belief and peaceful coexistence; 4) Highlight the dual-edged nature of science and technology – while advancing medicine, they have also enabled the creation of devastating weapons of war; and 5) Implement comprehensive programs to safeguard the environment and preserve the natural ecosystem – on land, the oceans, and in outer space.

I propose a new ethical oath to be taken by children. "I take an oath, that I will preserve human life wherever I go, and I will be a good shepherd to the earth", just as doctors take the Hippocratic Oath. This ethical pledge can be applied across all schools and disciplines. We have applied this concept at Dar il Hikma and have a workshop every year for the children. "I am the child: (name). My fingerprints attest that I will be an honest citizen of my homeland, Palestine, and the world".

Reliving horrific childhood memories with a new generation, I am confronted by the grim reality of weapons of mass destruction, which threaten to annihilate us all. We must halt the ongoing war of extermination and expansion, which threatens to annex larger sections of the Middle East. Concerned parties worldwide – both institutions and individuals – should coordinate efforts to awaken the global conscience.

Tragically, our children once more are denied access to education and schools, as this ongoing conflict continues to devastate their futures. Yet the chain of life continues uninterrupted, our daughters and sons once again return to carry the trust and deliver the message, just as we did in our own childhoods. Equipped with pens and the experiences gained from their families and the previous wars, they head to the tents, their hearts filled with treasures they need to share. Not out of duty, but voluntarily, they go forth to seek education and rise up. The future remains uncertain. Will the victims of this vicious cycle of genocide and profound trauma be able to forgive and forget? Thousands of young people have been left with life-altering disabilities, requiring extensive rehabilitation. Will they be outraged by the world's silence? While I cannot predict the outcome, perhaps the next generation will uncover solutions that are beyond our current vision.

Through perseverance and resilience, I weathered life's challenges, facing them head-on and emerging stronger. Guided by my faith, I sought to build connections, even with former adversaries. The fragility of life, when confronted with mortality, instilled in me a profound appreciation for its value. Inspired by this perspective, I designed programs to live life to the fullest, knowing that history will continue to unfold.

I am immensely proud of you, my sons and daughters. Continue to work on the peace education programs, incorporating the "Learn to be free" slogan which was initiated by our center. Encourage the children to engage in respectful dialogue and share their stories, even in this unjust world that often remains idle. Emphasize that through education, they can become whatever they aspire to be. The only way towards peace is through dialogue and finding common ground as humans. Just as the descendants of enslaved populations and oppressors must join in building a more equitable world, so too can the Jewish and Palestinian youth rise together towards a future free from violence. As a member of a displaced people, I have a story to share – one of many from my community. Each of us holds experiences worth telling to those interested in peace education. I am proud of my Palestinian heritage, both past and present, and I have faith that future generations will carry on the message of love and peace that has long been denied us. Peace education is the key to healing the planet and creating a better, more secure future for all children and future generations.

The author wishes to warmly thank her daughter Diana Takkash for professional collaboration and meaningful translation of this chapter.

References

Nomura, Y. (1996). *Lifelong integrated education as a creator of the future, volume 1. Principles of Nomura lifelong integrated education.* Trentham Books.

Nomura, Y. (2002). *Lifelong integrated education as a creator of the future, volume 2. Principles of Nomura lifelong integrated education.* Trentham Books.

Rashid, H.H. (2010). *Anthems of return.* Dār Majdalawi.

Chapter 27

Nurturing a Culture of Peace: A Shared Journey in Peace Education

Toh Swee-Hin & Virginia Cawagas

From Pathways to Confluence

As educators raised in different Southeast Asian societies, Malaysia and the Philippines, our paths crossed in Hiroshima. In 1986, the UN International Year of Peace, Hiroshima was the venue of the Triennial Conference of the World Council of Curriculum and Instruction (WCCI). The Conference was most moving and inspirational. The *'hibakushas'*, the surviving victims of the atomic bombs dropped on Hiroshima and Nagasaki in 1945, courageously recalled their stories of pain, loss, and grief to appeal to delegates from diverse regions to join the movement for nuclear disarmament and in the wider context, to prevent all wars.

During this first encounter we were reaffirmed in our common vision of a world that values and upholds not just nonviolence, but also peace rooted in compassion, human rights, respect, solidarity, love and justice for all beings. We began to learn and understand our separate pathways which gently met and interconnected in a confluence of a shared journey in peace education across the oceans and mountains, in the villages and cities, from university and school spaces to institutions and civil society movements, across the global South and Global North. Here our reflections on six decades of peace education 'work' can only be partial and selective, but hopefully sufficient to clarify our visions, theory, and praxis as peace educators and social activists.

A journey of a Thousand Miles
Begins with a Single Step

Virginia: As a high school teacher and then principal in a Catholic school run by one of the most socially progressive congregations, the Columban Fathers, I lived through the era of martial law imposed by then President Ferdinand Marcos. Political dissent, protest and armed insurgency grew against the Marcos dictatorship. I encouraged parents of my young students to join in creating a peaceful school community where academic 'excellence' was not the sole gauge of 'success'.

Then came the empowering and historical moment in Philippine political history, when after the assassination of opposition leader, Ninoy Aquino, the nonviolent EDSA people power revolution finally overthrew the US-supported Marcos dictatorship. As Executive Secretary of the Catholic Educational Association of the Philippines (CEAP), I participated in challenging the electoral fraud and joined the millions in the streets of Manila to form nonviolent barricades against the tanks and soldiers of Marcos. The EDSA experience taught me that educating for peace cannot be limited to 'cognitive' knowledge and understanding. I needed to join minds, hands, heart, and spirit with other peoples and take personal and social action to overcome violence and injustices.

EDSA did bring about a return to 'liberal parliamentary democracy' and re-opened a democratic space for civil society and socially progressive citizens and grassroots movements to transform society from authoritarianism, repression, and inequalities into democratic participation upholding human rights and social justice. However, four decades later, I share the view of many peacebuilders, peace educators, and social activists that the post-EDSA governments had largely failed to address the root causes of structural injustices, militarization, unsustainable development, and human rights violations. This context of EDSA's limited 'success' and continuing challenges has shaped my ongoing work in peace education in the Philippines as reflected later in my shared journey with Toh Swee-Hin.

I had expanded my web of peace education beyond the Philippines before

EDSA. My first meeting at the International Institute on Peace Education (IIPE) in New York in 1983 welcomed me to a global community of peace educators including the inspirational pioneers, Betty Reardon, Bob Zuber, Pat Mische and others. I felt encouraged and interconnected with educators worldwide sharing similar values, commitment and precious lessons on participatory and critical peace pedagogies.

In the Philippines, my contribution to the birth and growth of peace education in formal schools started from introducing an alternative Filipino educational paradigm highlighting peace education and values education for Philippine classrooms. I edited the first World Council for Curriculum and Instruction (WCCI) publication documenting inspiring lessons on nonviolent action from the 1986 People Power (Floresca-Cawagas, 1987).

After EDSA and stepping down as Executive Secretary of the CEAP, I was moved by the confluence of my work with the educational vision and praxis of Toh Swee-Hin to acknowledge the vital need to transform values education into a socially critical peace education. In this evolving journey towards a peace education paradigm that goes beyond individual and interpersonal peacebuilding toward national, international, and global perspectives, I was also led to reclaim from my Catholic faith the often neglected social teachings of the Church. As reflected in the liberation theology movement, authentic belief in one's faith or religion demands not just following rituals and doctrines, no matter how inspiring and 'true', but importantly principled practice of those beliefs and values to transform ourselves and our world.

Swee-Hin: A theme in Virginia's early journey that resonates with my own small steps in educating for a culture of peace is that critical awareness and commitment to act arises not just within formal learning spaces like schools and classrooms. Rather, an openness to wider societal events and most crucially direct participation in social movements helped develop my critical understanding of and catalyzed energies to resolve the root causes of   problems and conflicts affecting humanity and Mother Earth.

My schooling in Malaysia formed a colonial and neo-colonial citizenship identity which upheld the 'superiority' of 'Western civilization' and justified the racism perpetrated on indigenous peoples through the colonial project. My formal undergraduate studies in Australia focused on the sciences where

I learned virtually nothing about the painful realities of Australian history stained by two centuries of colonial oppression and dispossession. Nevertheless, it was inspirational to learn from the informal teach-ins and the huge marches of the anti-Vietnam War movement that arose in Australian campuses. Joining these events raised my critical awareness of the suffering, destruction, injustice, and folly of an unequal war waged by a superpower in the name of 'democracy' and 'anti-Communism'. This marked my first step into disarmament education as an indispensable dimension of peace education.

Another awakening came in the 70s during my graduate studies in the University of Alberta in Canada when my friends and I stood outside stores, persuading customers not to buy South African products, in solidarity with the anti-apartheid movement in South Africa. We felt it important to respond to the call for support from South African peoples struggling for justice and human rights. We remained hopeful that change would come, but we never imagined apartheid would be dismantled less than two decades later.

Working with colleagues in the Australian Peace Education and Research Association and other international education networks, I began to appreciate that 'peace' is necessarily a holistic concept. My earlier focus was on development education. Thus for me it was vital for a paradigm of peace education to clarify the multiple interconnections of social justice and unequal development with themes of militarization, human rights, environment, and intercultural understanding. When neo-conservative groups began to mount vociferous campaigns against peace education, it reminded us that peace-building is never a smooth journey (Toh, 1988a).

In 1980 I returned to Australia to begin my work to develop a graduate program in 'Peace and Development Education'. The development education underpinnings of this program exposed students to concepts, theories, analysis, issues, and problems of structural violence leading to global hunger, poverty, injustices, North-South inequalities, and an alternative PEACE oriented paradigm of development based on principles of participation, equity, appropriateness (e.g. technology, values), conscientization, and ecological sustainability. At the University of New England, I connected with other educators across diverse disciplines to commence one of the earliest Peace Studies majors in Australian campuses.

Like Virgina, my formation as a peace educator was much enriched through the international community and networks of peace education. In 1986 I participated in my first International Peace Research Association (IPRA) conference in Brighton, UK. There I met Robin Burns, convenor of the Peace Education Commission (PEC) within IPRA and peace educators from diverse regions, including Robert Aspeslagh. Robin and Robert co-edited the influential anthology *Three Decades of Peace Education around the World* (Burns & Aspeslagh, 1996; Toh & Cawagas, 1996). This PEC gathering as well as many others in the 90s, provided profound insights on how peace education is being envisioned and practised worldwide in different political, economic, social, and cultural contexts.

Another international network which facilitated my journey in peace education was the World Council of Curriculum and Instruction (WCCI) which encouraged mutual learning spaces in which educators for peace, multiculturalism, human rights, social justice, and environmental sustainability shared their lessons and challenges. It was, as Virginia recounted, at the 1986 Hiroshima Conference of WCCI that we met in person. From there on, our pathways confluenced into a river that has flowed for some 38 years across many Global South and Global North societies, meandering with the currents, replenished by rains, challenged by rocks of apathy, indifference or hostilities, inspired by countless courageous and dedicated peacebuilders and peace educators to advocate what may be called peace education by 'many other names'.

Signposts in the Philippines toward a Holistic Framework

Many of the most significant moments and signposts in our shared journey in educating for peace have been found in the Philippines, where we initially collaborated with others especially in Mindanao. Though named "the island of promise," Mindanao has tragically suffered from multiple conflicts including internal armed violence, cultural divisions, social injustices, human rights violations, and environmental plunder. Although massively resource rich, it has remained the poorest region as its wealth flowed to the politically dominant northern and central islands. It was in 1986, shortly after the historic non-violent people power 'EDSA' revolution ending decades of repression, that my (**Swee-Hin**) participation in Philippine peace education began. The post-martial law era opened up critical democratic spaces for civil society, to emerge from years of suppression.

Envisioning a Holistic Framework

On that first visit, by chance, I (Swee-Hin) stood in for Lourdes Quisumbing, Secretary of Education, to speak at a conference launching the first Peace Studies Centre in the Philippines at Xavier University. Virginia and I developed a framework for peace education for the conference. We proposed two major goals for peace education. First, it seeks to raise critical awareness and understanding of the root causes of all forms of conflicts and violence from micro to macro-levels. Second, based on this understanding and on appropriate values, we need to be empowered to take action for transformation, to change our realities from a culture of violence to a culture of peace. The framework had to be holistic and relevant to understanding the complex realities and root causes of violence and conflicts in the Philippines (Toh & Floresca-Cawagas, 1987). At that initial conference in Mindanao, Bishop Fernando Capalla, then one of the outspoken priests committed to peace and justice in the Philippines, firmly stated that all the themes and issues in the flower metaphor framework that I introduced were indeed most relevant. It was a joyful moment of affirmation.

This framework identified six interrelated dimensions and themes of issues and problems that underpin all forms of violence and conflicts, now often referred as the 6 petal-flower or flower metaphor. The framework is still based on six themes: dismantling a culture of war; living with justice and compassion; promoting human rights and responsibilities; building intercultural respect, reconciliation, and solidarity; living in harmony with the earth; and especially relevant to the Philippine context, cultivating or nurturing inner peace.

Furthermore, a holistic framework for peace education needs to be guided by pedagogical principles, as how we educate is equally important as the cognitive knowledge and understanding. These principles include *holism, dialogue, values formation,* and *critical empowerment. Holism* recognizes the interconnections and interdependencies of all the six themes and the role played by all forms of education. *Dialogue* rejects a banking model of education as Freire (1998) has critiqued but rather, a participatory and creative process of education and learning drawing on the lived experiences and realities of learners, enhancing socio-emotional learning, and using a wide range of creative pedagogies. *Values formation* emphasizes the need to motivate learners to understand and practice the values of peacebuilding. *Critical empowerment* ensures that learning is not merely cognitive understanding; learning needs to be translated into action for personal and social transformation (Cawagas, 2006).

The limited prevailing values education models in the Philippines led us to write the first two books in peace education there where we offered a holistic framework in peace education (Toh & Floresca-Cawagas, 1987; 1990).

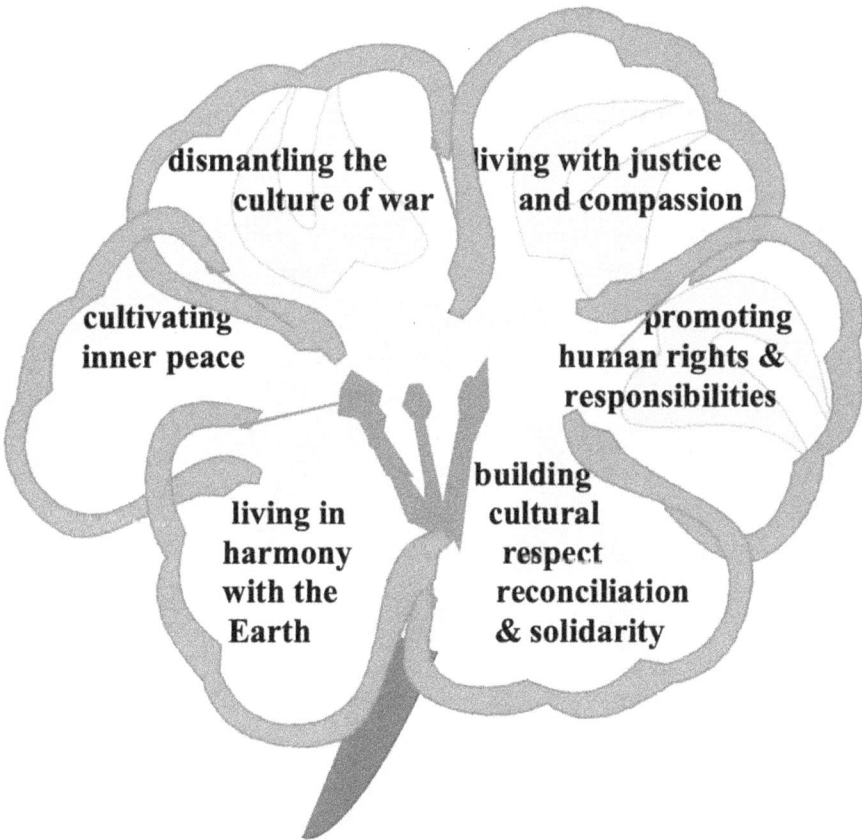

Image 1: A Holistic Framework of Educating for a Culture of Peace
(Swee-Hin Toh & Virginia Cawagas)

Planting seeds in Mindanao

After the initial Mindanao Conference, our holistic framework of peace education gained the attention of Notre Dame University (NDU) in Cotabato City, in the middle of the zone of long-standing armed conflict between the secessionist Moro National Liberation Front and the Philippine Government. The first Philippine graduate studies program in 'Peace and Development Education' for the MA (Education) and Doctor of Education (EdD.) degrees was implemented here. Twelve courses focused on the overall framework, and specific facets of a holistic concept of peace education (Toh, Floresca-Cawagas, & Durante, 1993). As Visiting Professors twice a year we taught in intensive on-campus courses at NDU followed by online learning. After several NDU faculty completed their graduate courses, the University was able gradually to integrate a core cross-faculty undergraduate Peace Education course.

Candidates continuously analyzed core issues and problems of peacelessness and conflict in terms of their connections to macro structures and realities. The motto "think globally, act locally" was made concrete in the Philippines and regional Mindanao contexts. Individual and social values that surfaced as views and perspectives were critically examined, and their implications for building a peaceful Philippines and world creatively painted. These educational outcomes, which are necessary for dialogue and conscientization, were produced by a consistent practice of participatory and creative pedagogies. Class members sang, acted, danced, laughed, cried, and critically challenged each other's as well as our views as teachers in ways which traditional schooling and even teacher training had suppressed. What helped considerably here, however, is the basic cultural predispositions of Filipinos to singing, dancing, acting and community performing, and to feeling the real joy accompanying such human expressions.

Through these experiences of creatively presenting the suffering of the poor, mock trials concerning human rights violations, and effects of cultural marginalization, the educator's role becomes much more of helping critical synthesis and reflection. It facilitates the students to assert initially their own worldviews for cooperative and constructive dialogue; raising any omissions of realities; enables students to surface and process personal biases and fears, hopes and dreams; assists students in drawing micro-macro and local-national-global connections and dynamics, and motivates learners to create their personal commitment to peacebuilding.

One helpful pedagogical strategy was to include field trips in the courses. Meeting marginalized peoples in their context enabled students to understand the impacts of more sustainable agriculture while maintaining indigenous culture, the destruction of sacred land from a massive energy project and the need for an urgent nonviolent resolution of the ongoing insurgency problem.

From its inception, the NDU peace education program has been conceptualized to reach out from the university into nonformal education among local communities and the wider Philippine society. Thus transformation in peace education, whilst vital at the educational level, is also concerned with social, political, economic, and cultural peacebuilding. Workshops have been conducted with community parishioners and members of development and church NGOs. The graduate courses have also resulted in the Centre for Peace Education coordinating petition campaigns to lobby for more peace-oriented policies and programs, such as 'freedom from debt', a logging ban on the rapidly vanishing Philippine forests, and solidarity for the schoolteachers on hunger strike against authoritarian DECS policies.

A most memorable nonformal educational opportunity occurred in December 1989, at the height of an attempted military coup against President Cory Aquino. With other core team members we spent three days in an infantry brigade camp of the Armed forces of the Philippines. Initially confronted by tense soldiers clutching their weapons and naturally suspicious of 'peace and justice' advocates, we encouraged the battle-hardened men to reflect on peace issues and problems, challenged them to be critical, even about official policies. As they began to appreciate the pedagogical processes of active teaching and learning, they were able to penetrate through their formal, dogmatic socialization in the military to consider possible alternatives for a peaceful Philippines that would be less militarized, more just, and ecologically sustainable. We remember vividly the clarity which some soldiers, because of their marginalized social backgrounds, analyzed structural violence; the creativity of their songs, dances, and dramas depicting the conditions of peacelessness in their country. We were able to repeat a workshop at regional headquarters, although this time attended by more junior officers who appeared more ideologically resistant to the peace paradigm.

Other networking occurred with governmental bodies like the National Peace Commission and the Office of Presidential Adviser on the Peace Process or NGOs concerned with specific issues of peace and development. We were also invited by the Catholic Relief Services and Mennonite Central Committee's Mindanao Peacebuilding Institute to design and conduct a Peace Education workshop for educators and peacebuilders in the Asian region. We collaborated frequently with interfaith dialogue groups for peace in Mindanao, notably the Silsilah Dialogue Movement, an organisation dedicated to interfaith dialogue between Christians and Muslims founded by a dedicated Italian priest, Fr. Sebastiano D'Ambra (2008), an MA and EdD graduate of the NDU program. I (Swee-Hin) contributed to the International Institute on Peace Education (IIPE) and Zamboanga de Ateneo University community-based peace education institute to share insights of Mindanaon educators with voices from Moro, Christian and indigenous peoples. And we conducted workshops for the Canadian-initiated Philippine Development Assistance Program (PDAP) in 2003 to promote peace education and peacebuilding programs relevant to local governance.

In recognition of the pioneering work of NDU in peace education, the Peace Education Center received an Aurora Aragon Peace Award in 1989. NDU continued to promote peace education by organizing the First Mindanao Congress for Peace Educators (2000). I (Swee-Hin) helped draft the resulting Cotabato Declaration on Education for a Culture of Peace.

Reflecting on the NDU experience in peace education, a number of key lessons were learned: a holistic concept of peace needs to underpin any peace education program; authentically practicing collaboration and horizontality so that both North and South partners equitably share knowledge, skills, creative energies, and risks in a spirit of mutual respect, and active linking of academic programs and learning with community contexts. Nearly four decades later, changes in administrative leadership have shifted the original vision and work of the NDU Peace Education program towards peacebuilding advocacy with less priority on peace education. Such changes do happen in the institutional life of any transformative educational initiative, but the legacy of NDU's pioneering effort to promote education for a culture of peace lives on through numerous other programs and projects catalyzed in Mindanao and elsewhere in the Philippines.

Outreaching Across the Islands

As awareness grew beyond Mindanao of the NDU peace education programs, we were also welcomed by universities, colleges, schools, NGOs and civil society organizations in other parts of the Philippines to share concepts, lessons and pedagogies in integrating the flower-petal framework of peace education and to dialogue with them on their own models. In 2008 then Philippine President Gloria Macapagal Arroyo signed E.O. 570: Institutionalizing Peace Education in Basic Education and Teacher Education. This helped increase institutional acceptance of peace education. Nearly two decades later, the challenge remains to mainstream this in the educational system.

We wrote resource books, modules and textbooks for classrooms, especially for the private schools (Floresca-Cawagas & Toh, 2012). This series in elementary social studies systematically integrates values and principles of peace education in both content and pedagogy. In 2024 we reunited with peace educators in Cotabato City to facilitate a workshop on Education for a Culture of Peace hosted by the Philippine Society for Peace & Development and Cotabato State University for teachers, academics and police and military personnel. The Society is seeking to mobilize alumni of peace education programs in the Philippines to enhance energies and renew commitment to education for a culture of peace, especially given the recent political changes in policies which are enabling citizens' voices to speak more assertively for democracy, human rights, and nonviolence after the era of violent 'war on drugs'.

A Peace Paradigm of Global Education at the University of Alberta

Our commitment to peace education has also been nurtured in North regions, including Australia, Canada, Japan, South Korea. We deeply appreciate the collaboration and solidarity of Global North-based peace educators. At the University of Alberta, we agreed that a holistic framework of peace education developed for the Philippines was equally relevant to North societies and their role in the world order impacting so heavily on violence and conflicts within the Global South and at international levels.

Peace education in Canada generally did not receive the same level of mainstream openness or interest then. Since Global Education was being promoted as a part of Canadian foreign and educational policy, we took the opportunity to develop a global education curriculum in which a peace paradigm is integral. Our Global Education courses for student teachers and for graduate students included all the themes in our *flower* framework. On the theme of *dismantling a culture of war,* we helped to raise critical consciousness of the root causes of war and other forms of physical violence and their nonviolent resolution (Reardon & Cabezudo, 2001; Toh & Cawagas, 2008). We recall intense workshops with Alberta schoolteachers and students held after 9/11 and collaboration with teachers in conflict resolution education and resolution, including the Safe and Caring Schools project of the Alberta Teachers Association. We continue in our retirement from academia to join campaigns to end conflicts such as Israel's genocidal war on Gaza and the Ukraine-Russia war that is bringing the world closer to nuclear destruction. In our courses, we emphasized that uprooting violence and cultivating peace calls on all peoples, including those in the Global North, to promote *living with justice and compassion.* Our students demonstrated their praxis in building a culture of peace by joining us in campaigns against racism and environmental destruction by mining corporations, and to defend the human rights of migrant workers and First Nations peoples in Canada and the Global South.

Engaging with UNESCO

Our shared journey in peace education from Global South to Global North contexts have also involved a long-standing engagement with UNESCO. I (**Swee-Hin**) was first initiated into UNESCO's vision and goal in 1994, when I served as a UNESCO 'expert' at the 2nd UNESCO International Forum on a Culture of Peace attended by several hundred delegates from governments and UNESCO agencies as well as NGOs (OPAPP, 1995). It was motivating to see government representatives engage in dialogue with members of civil society who challenged dominant policies of development and political orders that increased militarized conflicts and marginalization of poor communities. As rapporteur, I presented to President Ramos of the Philippines, the Forum's recommendations calling for UNESCO, member-states, and all peoples to continue the task of building and educating for a culture of peace. I was also a resource person in the UNESCO Culture of Peace Forums in Maputo (Mozambique) and Sintra (Portugal).

By the late 90s, I (Swee-Hin) served as a member of the UNESCO Feasibility Study to establish the Asia-Pacific Centre of Education for International Understanding (APCEIU) hosted by South Korea in 2000. The study affirmed the vision and mission of APCEIU not just as EIU, but EIU toward a Culture of Peace, and hence setting APCEIU's agenda from its birth as promoting in essence, education for a culture of peace (Toh et al, 1998; Toh, 2002).

At a regional level, we have facilitated APCEIU training workshops and designed curriculum manuals for hundreds of teachers, administrators and teacher educators in the Asia-Pacific region and later also globally (Kim 2002; Toh & Floresca-Cawagas, 2003; Cawagas, 2004). At the inter-governmental level, the commitment of UNESCO educators to promote a culture of peace has provided us with invaluable learning and action spaces to engage with government leaders, civil servants and civil society representatives, such as my (Virginia) workshop in Beijing involving North Korean, South Korean, and Chinese educators, and my (Swee-Hin) participation in numerous UNESCO Bangkok programs and curriculum projects.

One vital component of our training course with APCEIU included a field trip to the Demilitarized Zone (DMZ) between North and South Korea, thereby giving participants a direct cognitive understanding and socio-emotional learning about the militarized and non-peace tensions between the two Koreas and the need to reach a just peace settlement through diplomacy and peace talks. The DMZ had also an ecological retreat practising organic farming, ecological conservation and campaigning for peace between the two Koreas. Hence, such direct experiential learning in this field trip helped to immeasurably educate and motivate the participants to envision themselves as peacebuilders in their own contexts after the workshop.

Importantly, in our courses, participants are engaged in understanding and contrasting the dominant neoliberal paradigm of GCED and an alternative critical paradigm. We emphasize the need to challenge and transform the neoliberal GCED paradigm based on producing 'global citizens' with so-called 21st century competencies or skills but who do not question the corporate-led globalization underpinning Global North domination over Global South countries thus maintaining structural violence in the unequal global and national economic systems (Sant et al., 2018; Toh et al., 2018).

Multi-Faith Centre: Interfaith Dialogue for a Culture of Peace

In 2003, we were given the opportunity to start a Multi-Faith Centre (MFC) in Griffith University in Australia with the vision and mission of promoting interfaith dialogue toward a culture of peace. During our peace education journey in Mindanao, we witnessed the dedicated and risk-taking efforts of faith and religious leaders, notably Christian and Muslim, to engage in dialogue to build trust, reconciliation, and harmony among their faith or religious communities (Gardiola, 2003).

The challenging work of the Multi-Faith Centre was most relevant and timely. Worldwide, representatives of diverse faiths, religions, and spiritual traditions have been increasingly meeting to promote inter-faith, inter-religious or ecumenical dialogue so pivotal in developing greater active harmony of peoples within and across societies (Braybrooke, 1998; Toh, 2010). From dialogue and respect can come a process of reconciliation and healing of distrust, bitterness, and enmity as reflected in the activities and programs of numerous local and national faith and interfaith groups and international organizations such as Religions for Peace and the Parliament of the World's Religions. Through dialogue, members of diverse faiths are also recognizing that they all have many common values and ethical principles for guiding relationships among all peoples and cultures and hence are motivated to cooperate in resolving common societal and global problems of peacelessness (Cornille, 2013; Toh, 2020).

We organized forums, dialogues, conferences, prayer gatherings, celebration of festivals and meditations with the common theme of building a culture of peace. The Multi-Faith Centre gathered many faiths and inter-faith communities and social institutions or agencies to critically reflect on different peace-related themes that concern all Australians of whatever faith or culture. Our vision and hope was that these interfaith dialogue activities would lead various faith communities and social and cultural sectors to join their minds, hearts and spirit in common social action to build a more peaceful, just, compassionate and sustainable Australia and world.

The Multi-Faith Centre, while located in Australia, also sought links with related institutions and networks in the Asia-Pacific region and across the world. Such linkages have involved key universities with programs in faith and inter-faith dialogue studies, as well as inter-faith dialogue NGOs and networks for youth, women, and faith leaders. One major MFC conference in 2005 was an International Symposium on "Cultivating Wisdom, Harvesting Peace: Educating for a Culture of Peace through Values, Virtues and Spirituality of Diverse Cultures, Faiths, and Civilizations" (Toh & Cawagas, 2006). In 2008, an Asia-Pacific Symposium on Women and a Culture of Peace co-sponsored by Believing Women for a Culture of Peace highlighted the unique contributions that women of diverse faith communities are making to promote interfaith dialogue and intra-faith transformation for building peace. I (**Swee-Hin**) had opportunities to join Asia-Pacific intergovernmental interfaith meetings, an interfaith mission to Cairo and the Vatican and Religions for Peace and Parliament of the World's Religions conferences.

The MFC has also collaborated with teachers in the local Edmund Rice Catholic Schools to produce a curriculum module on how to integrate interfaith perspectives for peace education in curricula and school-community relationships (Cawagas, Toh & Garrone, 2007). The project was expanded to the national level for a revised curriculum for Edmund Rice schools ("With Head, Heart, Hands and Feet: A Framework for Educating for Justice and Peace").

In sum, our journey with the Multi-Faith Centre provided another meaningful signpost for promoting peace education by many other names, here through interfaith dialogue for a culture of peace. While the Centre for Interfaith Dialogue & Culture, which succeeded the Multi-Faith Centre, was closed in 2020, the MFC's legacy remains in the local community as various faith and religious communities continue to dialogue and cooperate in a spirit of harmony and peace. However, we must acknowledge that interfaith dialogue for a culture of peace is not free of tensions and obstacles, since faith or religious institutions can and do hold beliefs that contradict principles and practices in building various dimensions of peace, such as in human rights (e.g., gender identities, reproductive rights, exclusivist discrimination, apostasy). Hence, many advocates agree that interfaith dialogue needs to be accompanied by intra-faith dialogue, in which faiths self-critically examine their theologies and institutional practices and are willing to transform them to be consistent with their core values and principles.

Peace Education in The University for Peace

The University for Peace is located at Costa Rica. As a UN mandated university, it has a special obligation "to provide humanity with an international institution of higher education for peace with the aim of promoting among all human beings the spirit of understanding, tolerance and peaceful coexistence, to stimulate cooperation among peoples and to help lessen obstacles and threats to world peace and progress, in keeping with the noble aspirations proclaimed in the Charter of the United Nations".

Around 2004, we became Visiting Professors at UPEACE. Costa Rica is one of the minority of countries without a military and is well known for its environmental protection policies. Our courses over 2009-2016 included Peace Education, International Peace Studies and Gender Studies and supervising graduate students. The flower framework of peace education was again the template for the program enrolling over 200 peace educators from Southeast and South Asia, South Korea, Japan, and Africa.

Our UPEACE experience was especially meaningful in giving us the opportunity to collaborate with so many youth peacebuilders worldwide with diverse experiences in selected fields related to a culture of peace. The critical understanding and knowledge of multiple themes of peace was accompanied with critical pedagogies challenging students to promote personal and social action for building peace. In one memorable session, when the students were carrying placards and voicing slogans in a mock peace demonstration, the UPEACE security officer nervously followed us and the students as he 'believed' it was a real political action that may need his intervention! The Costa Rican context of not having a military was thought provoking for the students used to living in countries with militaries financed by disproportionately large budgets and in some cases, committing human rights violations.

Costa Rica's 'green' sustainable development policies of protecting its forests was also questioned by our students for continuing to deny indigenous peoples their rights to reclaim their ancestral lands exploited for cattle ranching and profitable eco-tourism.

There were real tensions and contradictions in the UPEACE institutional environment, for example some United States students complained that their country is unfairly critiqued for militaristic foreign policies and dominating the world politically and economically, appropriately challenged by social justice, feminist and anti-racism students and faculty. Critiques of the neo-liberal economic paradigm and support for globalization from below movements challenging transnational corporations for their unjust and unsustainable policies were sometimes questioned. Nonetheless, UPEACE provided a democratic space for dialogue among peacebuilders who would then return to their countries or join the international community of agencies and NGOs to practice their peacebuilding and peace education knowledge and capacities.

The University for Peace MA programme in Peace Education graduated two educators from Cyprus who have set up their own Center for a Culture of Peace. Four MA students conducted their internship project through a Peace Education workshop for 200 junior army officers in their camp in the Philippines. Other peace education alumni returned to their countries to establish NGOs such as PEACE Momo in South Korea, which trains teachers and civil society activists, and the Standing Together to Enable Peace (STEP) Trust in India, seeking to build a free, just, non-violent, sustainable, equal and mindful society through education, advocacy and action for teachers, youth and children. Junior professors from Rwanda, Uganda, Kenya, Nigeria and the Democratic Republic of Congo who came to UPEACE for their MA took a curriculum development course with me (Virginia) and designed a curriculum based on the flower model. Together with other faculty, we developed curriculum modules on peace education (Cawagas, Toh & Kakar, 2010). UPEACE experience reminded us that a holistic peace education framework or paradigm can be more readily adapted or adopted in other regions and communities.

A Shared Journey flowing on...

Our shared journey in peace education began in Mindanao in the Philippines. Nearly four decades on, as we look back on the signposts and turns, on steps forward but also backwards, there is still considerable work to be done in fulfilling the vision and mission of peace education. However, through our various efforts across Global North and Global South contexts as well as encounters with innumerable people and communities, we can take heart and be hopeful that educating for a culture of peace is challenging the forces of violence, injustices, greed, discriminations, and unsustainability and in the call of the World Social Forum, that "another world is possible! "

In 2016, we revisited the Philippines for a joyful and inspirational reunion with educators, older and younger, from formal, nonformal and informal institutions and spaces, to share memories, lessons, experiences, achievements, challenges and hopes in educating for a culture of peace. Stories from this gathering were compiled in an anthology (Toh, Cawagas, & Galace, 2017).

The stories renewed our hope and inspiration that after three decades, peace education in the Philippines has, despite obstacles and challenges, continued to grow and spread more leaves, seeds, flowers and fruits. As one educator said, "the fire is still burning!" The stories themselves speak of accomplishments and fulfilment of goals and purposes while faced with uncertainties on the then forthcoming Presidential elections. By 2017, the new Administration had raised political and social controversies and indeed even more challenges for peace education, including designing effective strategies to catalyze critical perspectives on the "war on drugs" campaign, the proposed restoration of the death penalty, and an increased public expression of gender insensitivity and sexism. Under the present Bongbong Marcos Jr Government, peace education must continue to overcome structural injustices, the power of political dynasties, systemic corruption, the climate crisis, and resolving the West Philippine Sea/South China conflict with China without increased militarized cooptation into the US-led containment of China. Moreover, globally, the challenges facing peace education are now even more substantive, as witnessed by ongoing wars of destruction and killing; continuing structural violence in an unjust global economy ruled by TNCs and the Global North states, and the climate crisis that demands decisive actions of climate justice rather than the dominant paradigm of climate action .

As we continue to flow in our shared journey of peace education, we share a few reflections with readers:

Virginia: I believe that the world is a huge classroom and the process of life is education. This means an endless journey to make the world more just and caring through personal example, and through continuing reflections, in solidarity with all those who have faith in life. A journey's end is only a beginning. In my eyes, mind, heart, hands and spirit, *peace educators* are **dreamers**. Should we not dare to dream of a world where we hear laughter of children rather than screams of pain and horror? Should we not have faith in the ability of human communities to overcome difficulties and transcend seemingly insurmountable tensions and dream of a common vision of a new relationship of trust, respect and caring? *Peace educators are also* **sowers**, *not just mentors or champions but sowers of seeds.* Moreover, with each new wave of creative designing and implementation, we can see how peace educators are seizing new opportunities for praxis and advocacy but still learning from the best practices of earlier generations of peace educators.

Peace educators are *also* '**teachers**', embodying virtues and values to reflect someone who is wise yet humble, firm yet gentle, complex yet simple, serious yet playful, authoritative and knowledgeable but not authoritarian. Likewise, in critical pedagogy and critical reflective teaching, our learners need trusting and creative spaces to surface and re-examine their values, assumptions, biases, hopes, fears and dreams in the light of the vision of a culture of peace. As teachers we need to see ourselves as active subjects within the structures, and power relationships within our institutions, and self-empowered to seek transformations for a better world through our teaching and role modelling.

Finally, *Peace educators are* **healers** promoting reconciliation, but also demanding truth and justice. How can there be healing if the truth of what happened is not revealed? I believe that only when structures and institutions are also and equally transformed to become more attentive to and concerned with the basic needs of billions of marginalized citizens can life be truly celebrated. Only if we feel in communion not only with our "God", however envisioned, but in communion with every being and every part of Gaia, can life become truly peaceful.

Swee-Hin: Our shared journey began with a Chinese proverb about taking the first step, if any journey is to be accomplished. Several small steps have been made, hopefully bringing us closer to the vision of a more peaceful and just world. Many more will need to be walked, but as with many friends in the peace education community, hopefulness is a necessary virtue, a source of energy to continue the often slow journey. In receiving the 2000 UNESCO Prize for Peace Education, I am deeply grateful for the inspirational collaboration and solidarity of countless peace educators worldwide. The challenges of educating and building a peaceful world for humanity and Mother Earth remain critical and huge with ongoing wars threatening to widen and erupt in WW3; the deepening climate crisis; social and economic injustices rooted in a profit-maximizing corporate-led globalization; gross human rights violations; increasing racism and extremism; and the rise of neo-facism. In Australia, a protest song became well known by telling the moving story of the Gurindji people's historic struggle for indigenous land rights, justice and cultural survival. Entitled *"From Little Things Big Things Grow"*, perhaps this song can be a meaningful metaphor for the seeding, nurturing, and growing of peace education within a common humanity and mother earth. For me, another experience which continually inspires a sense of hope is reflected during a journey to grow peace education in the Philippines. I recalled rounding a bend on a mountain road in South Cotabato in Mindanao and suddenly before our eyes, nestling amidst bamboo-lined hills, lies the magical Lake Sebu. In this ancestral domain of the gentle *T'boli* people, we met the kind womenfolk who showed us one of their ancient tribal traditions. Patiently, quietly, and skillfully, they weave numerous multicoloured threads into the spiritually inspired *t'nalak* tapestry designs which are indeed a precious gift to the Filipino multicultural society. As peace educators, let us all attempt to learn from them and to cultivate that same degree of patience, commitment, and humility as we try to gently weave a culture of peace within ourselves, in our communities, throughout the nation and around Mother Earth.

References

Abura, M., Bickmore, K., Brantmeier, E. J., Cawagas, V., Cremin, H., Gerstner, N.L., Joo, C., Kartha, R., Kester, K., McInerney, W. W., Seo, R., Toh, S.H. & Tongnan, X. (2024). Pedagogies of peace and coexistence in a more-than-human world: An intergenerational dialogue on educational peacebuilding and climate action around the globe. In Wiseman, A., Anderson, E., Damaschke-Deitrick, L., Galegher, E., Dzotsenidze, N. & Park, M. (Eds.), *Handbook on comparative education* (459-480). Edward Elgar Publishers.

Andreopoulos, G.J. & Claude, R.P. (Eds.). (1997). *Human rights education for the twenty-first century*. University of Pennsylvania Press.

Bello, W. (2004). *Deglobalization: Ideas for a new world economy*. Fernwood Publishing.

Braybrooke, M. (1998). *Faith and interfaith in a global age*. CoNexus Press.

Brecher, J., Costello, J., & Smith, B. (2002). *Globalization from below*. SouthEnd.

Broome, R. (2002). *Aboriginal Australians*. Allen & Unwin.

Bull, L. (2000). Walking with peace education: An indigenous journey. *International Journal of Curriculum and Instruction* 2(1): 65-84.

Burns, R. & Aspeslagh, R. (Eds.). (1996). *Three decades of peace education around the world*. Garland.

Cawagas, V., (Ed.). (2004). *Learning to live together: Teacher's resource book on education for international understanding toward a culture of peace*, Vol. 1, 13-31. UNESCO Asia-Pacific Centre of Education for International Understanding (APCEIU).

Cawagas, V. (2006). Pedagogical principles in educating for a culture of peace. In Toh, S.H. & Cawagas, V.F. (Eds.), *Cultivating wisdom, harvesting peace: Educating for a culture of peace through values, virtues & spirituality of diverse cultures, faiths & civilizations*. Multi-Faith Centre, Griffith University.

Cawagas, V. & Toh, S.H. (2003). A Journey towards peace in the mountains of Ichon. *Sangsaeng* Autumn, 33-37.

Cawagas, V.F. & Toh, S.H. (Eds.). (2005). *Our nation our world. Grade 1-6. 2nd ed.* SIBS Publishing.

Cawagas, V.F., Toh, S.H. & Garrone, B. (Eds.). (2007). *Many faiths one humanity. An educational resource for integrating interfaith perspectives in educating for a culture of peace.* Multi-Faith Centre, Griffith University & Edmund Rice Education.

Cawagas, V., Toh, S.H., & Kakar, N. (Eds.). (2010). *Peace education for civil society. Curriculum manual for South Asia and Southeast Asia.* University for Peace.

Cornille, C. (Ed.) (2013). *The Wiley-Blackwell companion to inter-religious dialogue.* Wiley-Blackwell.

Coumans, C. (2002). *The successful struggle against submarine tailings disposal in Marinduque, Philippines.* [Conference presentation.] https://miningwatch.ca/sites/default/files/marinduque_std_struggle_0.pdf

D'ambra, S. (2008). *Call to a dream.* Silsilah Dialogue Movement.

Dawson, A. (2024). *Environmentalism from below.* Haymarket Books.

First Mindanao Congress for Peace Educators. (2000). Cotabato declaration on education for a culture of peace. *International Journal of Curriculum and Instruction.* 2(1): 121-125.

Floresca-Cawagas, V. (1987). *Active non-violence in action: the Philippine experience.* World Council for Curriculum and Instruction, Philippines Chapter.

Floresca-Cawagas, V.F. & Toh, S.H. (Eds.). (2012) *Our nation our world. Grade 1-6 revised ed.* SIBS Publishing.

Freire, P. (1998). Pedagogy of freedom, ethics, democracy, and civic courage. Rowman & Littlefield.

Gardiola, M. (2003). *Walk for peace: Communities building zones of peace.* http://www.comutiversity.org.ph/peace_and_development.htm

Graveline, F. J. (1998). *Circle works, Transforming Eurocentric consciousness.* Fernwood Publishing.

Kim, M. (2002). Holism, dialogue, and critical empowerment: A pedagogy for peace. *Sangsaeng* Autumn, 22-23.

Knudtson, P. & Suzuki, D. (Eds.). (1992). *Wisdom of the elders.* Stoddart.

Mander, J. & Tauli-Corpuz, V. (Eds.). (2006). *Paradigm wars: Indigenous peoples' resistance to globalization.* Sierra Club Books.

Matriano, E. & Toh, S.H. (2013). Multicultural education, global education: Synergies for a peaceful world. In Lowman, R.L. (Ed.), *Internationalizing multiculturalism: Expanding professional competencies in a globalized world* (pp. 255–288). American Psychological Association. https://doi.org10.1037/14044-010

Nhat Hanh, T. (1991). *Peace is every step.* Bantam.

OPAPP. (1995). 2nd UNESCO International Forum for a Culture of Peace. OPAPP.

Philippine-Canada Local Government Support Program. (2003). *Walking the path of peace. Resource kit.* LGSP.

Reardon, B. & Cabezudo, A. (2002). *Learning to abolish war: Teaching toward a culture of peace.* Hague Appeal for Peace.

Sant, E. et al. (2018). *Global citizenship education: A critical introduction to key concepts and debates.* Bloomsbury Publishing.

Shiva, V. & K. (2020). *Oneness vs. the 1%.* Chelsea Green Publishing.

Sleeter, C.E. & McLaren, P.L. (1995). *Multicultural education, critical pedagogy, and the politics of difference.* SUNY Press.

Toh, S. H. (1988). Neo-conservatives and controversies in Australian peace education: Some critical reflections and a counter-strategy. In Alger, C. & Stohl, M. (Eds.), *A Just peace through transformation* (211-232). Westview.

Toh, S. H. (2002). Education for international understanding: A river from the mountain. *Sangsaeng* Autumn, 33-37.

Toh, S.H. (2010). Enhancing the dialogue and alliance of civilizations: Perspectives from peace education. *International Journal of Curriculum and Instruction.* 7(1): 3-23.

Toh, S.H. (2020). Peace, pacifism, and religion. In Edsforth, R. (Ed.), *A cultural history of peace in the modern age* (83-104). Bloomsbury Publishing.

Toh, S. H. (2023). Renewing our commitment to build a culture of peace through education. *Sangsaeng* No. 60, 8-10.

Toh, S.H. & Floresca-Cawagas, V. (1987). *Peace education: A framework for the Philippines.* Phoenix Publishing House.

Toh, S.H. & Floresca-Cawagas V. (1990). *Peaceful theory and practice in values education.* Phoenix.

Toh, S. H., & Floresca-Cawagas, V. (1993). From the mountains to the seas: Educating for a peaceful Philippines. In Haavelsrud, M. (Ed.), *Disarming: Discourse on violence and peace* (33-69). Arena.

Toh, S. H., & Floresca Cawagas, V. (1996). Toward a better world? A paradigmatic analysis, of development education resources from the World Bank. In Burns, R. J. & Aspeslagh, R. (Eds.), *Three decades of peace education around the world* (175-210). Garland.

Toh S.H. & Cawagas, V.F. (Eds.). (2006). *Cultivating wisdom, harvesting peace: Educating for a culture of peace through values, virtues & spirituality of diverse cultures, faiths & civilizations.* Multi-Faith Centre, Griffith University.

Toh, S.H. & Cawagas, V.F. (2008). Institutionalization of nonviolence. In Kurtz, L. (Ed.), *Encyclopedia of violence, peace, and conflict,* 2nd ed (1013-1026). Academic Press.

Toh, S.H. & Cawagas, V.F. (2010). Peace education, ESD and the Earth Charter: Interconnections and synergies. *Journal of Education for Sustainable Development.* 4(2): 167-180.

Toh, S.H., Cawagas, V.F. & Nario-Galace, J. (Eds.). (2017). *Three decades of peace education in the Philippines.* Peace Education Center, Miriam College & World Council for Curriculum and Instruction.

Toh, S. H., Floresca-Cawagas, V., & Durante, O. (1993). Building a peace education program: Critical reflections on the Notre Dame University experience in the Philippines. In Bjerstedt, A. (Ed.), *Peace education: Global perspectives* (111-146). Almqvist & Wiksell International.

Toh, S.H., Gundara, J., Kang, S. & Kim, H. (1998). *Feasibility study on the establishment of a Regional Center of Education for International Understanding (RCEIU)*. UNESCO.

Toh, S.H., Lee, F.D., Abesamis, G.M. & Esteban, C. (2018). *Preparing teachers for global citizenship education*. UNESCO.

Toh, S.H., Shaw, G. & Padilla, D. (2017). *Global citizenship education: A guide for policymakers*. Asia-Pacific Centre of Education for International Understanding (APCEIU).

Chapter 28
Successful Failure
My Journey as a Peace Educator

Werner Wintersteiner

"It's easy to write your memoirs
when you have a bad memory."
 -*Arthur Schnitzler, Austrian poet* (1993)

I am very grateful to the editors of this volume for the opportunity to reflect retrospectively on my work as a peace educator. However, when you review episodes in your own life and think about what happened and why, it is easy to run the risk of presenting developments that simply happened as the causal consequence of your own decisions and retrospectively giving many things a meaning that they may never have had. Everything that happens by chance, triggered by external factors or unconscious inner drives is then quickly presented as the result of conscious decisions. In doing so, however, we arrogate to ourselves a decision-making power over our own lives that we cannot have. It is also easy to succumb to the temptation to emphasize only oneself and one's own achievements, which were only possible thanks to a suitable environment and cooperation with many others. Even if you are aware of these dangers at the outset, you are by no means immune to succumbing to them. But readers have been warned.

I will trace some of the lines of development of my peace education work here, which precludes a purely chronological presentation, because many activities took place in parallel and the same or similar topics have occupied me for years or even decades. I will also mention the people who were very important to me at certain stages. It goes without saying that private and family encounters, circumstances and experiences (which are not discussed here) also flow into my work.

1. In the Beginning There Was Resistance

As a child of the 1968 movement – albeit somewhat younger than those actually active in 1968 – I early identified with the idea of resistance; as a pupil against a teaching staff that I (arrogantly enough) considered boring and incompetent; against a society that seemed alien and hostile to me – the only place of retreat for me was the pop music of the 1960s, which contributed a great deal to my politicization; as a student of German and French who opposed the 'system', including the university system in my home town of Vienna, and who helped to offer alternative, self-organized courses as well as being a member of a radical left-wing student group on a Marxist basis. Although I now distance myself from my dogmatism then, I did acquire a social science foundation by studying the Marxist classics, which broadened my horizons considerably. Even later, as a young teacher, resistance was an attitude that I felt was forced upon me rather than an independent option: due to my political activities as a student, I initially had difficulties getting a job as a teacher at all, but eventually I was able to assert myself. However, there were repeated attempts at censorship during my twelve years as a teacher. That was not pleasant, but it was also instructive: just as I experienced my commitment to peace as resistance, I quickly learned to understand peace as a program of resistance against the prevailing 'war system' (Betty Reardon).

2. Peace Activism and Peace Education

My interest in peace issues was not initially focused on peace education. My 'initiation' (still as a child) was my horror at the murder of Patrice Lumumba in the newly independent Congo, then the Vietnam War, as well as my concern about the conflict between Israel and Palestine; the Cold War was also constantly present. In the 1980s, it was all about Malvinas/Falkland, and above all about the growing threat of nuclear war – a constant theme. My own peace education work began at this time. During these years, starting with 'nuclear pacifism', I slowly developed an overall 'radical pacifist' position.

During this time, I saw myself as a 'teacher-activist' – on the one hand, I founded a local peace group, and on the other, I addressed peace issues in school lessons and, as I was also active in further education, in seminars for colleagues who also taught German. As there was no suitable material available at the time, I started to develop my own. These were beginnings that benefited me in my later career in university teaching.

Since I moved to university in 1988 after 12 years at school, not only have my horizons broadened considerably, but I have also moved from the mode of a pure practitioner to the mode of a scientist (without giving up my practical activities, not always of a pedagogical nature). I came into contact with action research and it provided me with many impulses and opportunities to critically reflect on my own pedagogical work. However, my interest was always more focused on the philosophical and political foundations of pedagogical action and less on classical-empirical research.

I was soon able to apply the pedagogical concepts, ways of thinking and methods that I learned at university for my field, German didactics (especially literature teaching), to peace education. Above all, I drew a parallel between the unavailability with which every poem, every novel, every play, eludes a clear interpretation by the recipients, and the impossibility of prescribing a peaceful attitude. At the same time, I also examined my new main field of work, literary didactics, from the point of view of peace education. In the 1980s, there was already a lively discourse on this subject, particularly in the field of children's and young adult literature, which I was able to build on. My position at university gave me a lot of freedom to pursue my interests. I was soon active in two fields and moved in two very different academic scenes. At the same time, I always tried to combine both fields, most programmatically in my collection of essays on peace education, which revolved around language and literature (Wintersteiner, 2001). In recent years, in collaboration with the German didactics expert Sabine Zelger, I have succeeded in publishing several peace education publications as themed issues of the journal for German teachers *ide* (with a focus respectively on flight, global citizenship and peace). Some of my colleagues from the field of peace education were surprised that I was able to "play in two fields" at the same time, while others – from the field of German didactics – were amazed that I was also a peace educator. My 'secret' was very simple: for me, these were not so separate areas – I saw them more as two fields of discourse and practice that enriched each other. And finally, my colleague and PhD thesis mentor, Dietmar Larcher, was also active in both fields. In retrospect, I can also see how much my main task at university for many years, editing the German didactic journal *ide*, also shaped my peace education. It was about networking, and always about having a general overview of as many areas as possible as well as spotting new trends. In-depth empirical research was not one of my tasks and goals at the time.

In terms of content, in this early phase I mainly drew on pacifist literature and language criticism to criticize militarism and propagate a peace-loving attitude, but above all – in the sense of political education – to enable learners to develop a critical attitude towards public opinion and media reports. Undoubtedly, naïve ideas of a kind of educational peace propaganda were still present at the time. [1]

As if that were not enough, a third component was soon added: the strong regional and regional-historical reference, the so-called Alps-Adriatic region. You might think that this made everything even more complicated. On the contrary, I found it helpful – the regional reference was a welcome link in the chain that additionally connected language and literature didactics with peace education.

This gave my peace education a deep historical dimension – a critique of outdated narratives and the prevailing culture of remembrance, which had still not thoroughly dealt with the National Socialist era. The preferred method was (and still is) the confrontation with the narratives of marginalized groups and neighbouring countries, which often evaluate the same events in contrasting ways.

3. The Alps-Adriatic Region as a Starting Point and an Opportunity

The move from the capital Vienna to the small city of Villach in the province of Carinthia in 1976, after completing my studies, had a decisive impact on my life. And for several reasons: on the one hand, compared to Vienna, Carinthia was a politically 'developing country' at the time. If you wanted to become politically active in Vienna, you simply joined the appropriate organization. In Carinthia, you first had to set one up. At the beginning of the 1980s, I founded a local peace committee with friends (especially Hans Haider and Hermann Gamerith) and soon also a larger, transnational network (see below). We were therefore more challenged, but also had greater creative freedom.

Characteristic of Carinthia at the time was the conflict between the parties in the provincial government and the German national 'homeland associations' on the one hand and the Slovene-speaking minority, which was fighting for its rights to schooling, official language and bilingual place-name signs. The conflict reached a climax in the late 1970s and became a political focal point throughout Austria. In view of the fact that Yugoslavia acted as the protecting power of the Austrian Slovenes, the issue also had an international dimension. I was committed to the minority and, as a young teacher who was just starting to teach at a secondary school, I also tried to get my pupils interested in this topic. However, given the political climate at the time, I hardly succeeded. In this sense, my start in peace education was not very encouraging.

My peace activism, on the other hand, was able to celebrate certain successes at the beginning of the 1980s. At that time, there was a strong peace movement in Western Europe with the main aim of preventing NATO from stationing new nuclear weapons in Europe. As Austria is neutral and free of nuclear weapons, I wanted to make a specific contribution to this movement and developed the proposal of a nuclear weapons-free zone around Austria – for our own security as well as a contribution to general disarmament. This plan, known as the *Villach Proposal*, became the program of a part of the Austrian peace movement, the *Independent Peace Initiative Austria* (UFI), supported by people like Gerhard Jordan or Georg Breuer. More importantly, it became the basis for cooperation between the peace movements in northern Italy (where the US nuclear weapons base Aviano is located near the Austrian border), Yugoslavia (especially Slovenia) and Austria. This area, known as the Alps-Adriatic region, was largely part of the Austro-Hungarian Empire until 1918. It lies at the crossroads of the Romance, Slavic and Germanic cultures and is ethnically very mixed. The Alps-Adriatic region was the scene of all European wars in the 20th century and has – certainly a special feature – experienced major border changes every time. This history has left its mark, which is still strongly expressed today in minority conflicts, conflicting historical narratives and political exploitation of the existing divisions. Peace work and peace education in the region cannot help but include this historical dimension. The alternative guideline we have developed is that of an Alps-Adriatic peace region (Wintersteiner, 2012; Wintersteiner et al., 2020). The 2018 *Alps-Adriatic Peace Manifesto* in particular summarized decades of experience and gives direction to the work. The English version was didactically commented on by Betty Reardon (2020) and thus placed in a larger context. Also worth mentioning is the research project that investigated tourist-educational remembrance work on the First World War in the border triangle of Italy, Slovenia and Austria (Wohlmuther & Wintersteiner, 2018).

In addition to the content of my work, the organizational aspect was always essential. As part of the *Villach Peace Committee*, we founded a small information journal in 1986, *alpe-adria*, which mainly reported on political movements and educational initiatives in the border triangle of Italy, Yugoslavia and Austria. In the course of the process of independence of Slovenia and Croatia, new and favorable opportunities for cross-border (peace education) cooperation arose. We used the momentum created at that time to found the *Alps-Adriatic Alternative* association in 1990, an initiative of Doris Pollet-Kammerlander and myself. The association was based in Austria, but extended its work to all Alps-Adriatic countries.

However, the wars that broke out soon afterwards in the disintegrating Yugoslavia represented a serious setback for all hopes of peace and also plunged us Austrian activists into a crisis of meaning. Some of the war events took place right on our border (such as the short war in Slovenia) and also directly affected our friends and colleagues. Nevertheless, we tried to maintain our transnational peace work even during the war.

With *Alps-Adriatic-Alternative* as one of the supporting organizations, we succeeded in organizing one-week summer seminars in Slovenia and Croatia from 1991 onwards, where we brought together teachers and educators from Slovenia, Croatia, Italy and Austria. The topics were peace education in the face of the ongoing war, living together in the Alps-Adriatic region and encounters with the 'other' on the other side of the nearby border. These events provided the participants with many long-lasting impulses. (cf. Wintersteiner 1994) The activities continue to this day, with different focuses and sometimes different actors (Wintersteiner & Sturm, 2021).

Support for the Gorski kotar Peace School in Croatia played a special role. Gorski kotar was the only region in Croatia with a mixed Serbian-Croatian population where there was no war. A single man, Franjo Starčević, Croatian head of the small municipality of Mrkopalj, achieved this miracle through consistent commitment and after long negotiations. In 1992, in the midst of the war, he founded a 'peace school' to maintain peace in the long term. These were workshops where children from both ethnic groups came into contact with each other and literally learned peace. Soon children from other parts of the former Yugoslavia also came. Together with friends, I organized international support: donations, media publicity and, for a while, support from the Council of Europe. We also managed to establish numerous school contacts with Austria. The "peace hero" Franjo Starčević, who we often invited to speak to young people and teachers, made an impact through the power of his example, which he conveyed simply and yet full of passion (Otmačić, 2021).

In the 2000s, the political situation in Carinthia eased when the issue of bilingual place name signs, one of the biggest areas of conflict, was resolved for the first time. The decisive factor here was the understanding between the largest organization of Carinthian Slovenes and the German nationalist 'Kärntner Heimatdienst', which from then on stopped its anti-Slovenian propaganda. And since Slovenia's independence, transnational relations also improved. In this situation, activists from the minority and peace movement launched a cross-border civil society project with the programmatic title "Building the Peace Region Alps-Adriatic. Envisioning Future by Dealing with the Past. Promoting open and inclusive public discourse within Austria and Slovenia and between the countries." Wilfried Graf and Marjan Sturm, who also played a decisive role in reconciling the opposing organizations, provided the impetus. For three or four years, there were regular meetings of Austrians and Slovenians who openly discussed all the sensitive issues of our shared history of the 20th century without claiming to reach a common denominator – a very instructive experience for me (Brousek et al., 2020). This was followed by the launch of a peace education initiative, the project "Dialogic remembrance in educational practice" (Italy, Austria, Slovenia), in which I was also involved (https://dialogischeserinnern.at/).

4. Theory Work and the Link with Practice

Moving to university as a German teacher trainer offered me new opportunities to work. Gradually, I developed a different way of thinking, a more scientific approach to peace education and political activism. I developed a habitus as a scholar-practitioner.

Despite the variety of topics and concepts I have dealt with, perhaps three main strands of my theoretical work can be identified, without them constituting the totality of my research interests. The first two strands can be assigned to my qualification work, the dissertation and the habilitation, around which a number of other texts and activities are grouped; the third strand will be presented later.

Philosophical, Socio-psychological and Cultural-scientific Foundations

My dissertation, *Pedagogy of the Other*, written in the second half of the 1990s, was deliberately not a continuation of my practice, but I wanted to develop philosophical, political and pedagogical foundations for peace education. I looked at the concept of education for a culture of peace from various angles. This resulted in a theoretical work that was strongly based on Edgar Morin's anthropology and Emmanuel Lévinas' philosophy of the other. For me, his concept of alterity is the core of any philosophy of peace. In addition, the work has benefited a great deal from Johan Galtung, Zygmunt Bauman, Günther Anders and Betty Reardon. From the very extensive section on peace education and global education, I drew many initial foundations for my current work with global citizenship education. I still regard *Pedagogy of the Other* as my foundational work today (Wintersteiner, 1999; Vriens, 2005).

Multilingualism, Literature and Transculturality

I did not engage with postcolonial thinkers until later, in the 2006 publication *Poetics of Diversity*, my habilitation thesis. The title is a reference to a book by the poet and essayist Edouard Glissant from Martinique. To him I owe the most important concepts of this writing – creolization, the all-world (appropriate to Morin's Homeland Earth), archipelagic thinking, and rhizomatic identity. Drawing mainly on literary examples from the global North and the global South, I trace the power relations in the cultural sphere as they have become more acute, especially as a result of globalization. In a second volume, *Transcultural Literary Education*, I draw pedagogical conclusions from these findings. These two studies were the second major theoretical thrust that reoriented my thinking and helped me to broaden my horizons in the direction of the global South (Wintersteiner, 2006a, 2006b). Through this work, a merging of literary, didactic and peace education thinking, I was able to develop further cornerstones for my current focus, Global Citizenship Education.

Both strands of theory ultimately strengthened my concept of peace education as education for a culture of peace, as outlined above all by Betty Reardon. With my focus on language and literature, I was able to connect well with this.

5. The European and Global Dimension

Peace Institute Stadtschlaining as an Early Gateway to the World (1982-)

Since its founding by Gerald Mader in 1982, the Austrian Peace Center in the small town of Stadtschlaining was for me, a novice in peace studies, the most important gateway to the world of peace research and at the same time a tribune and meeting place for my own activities. The institute, which soon acquired a worldwide reputation as a forum and training center for peace, enabled me to make the acquaintance of many greats in our profession and to work on numerous initiatives, including the publication of a small series of educational material for peace educators in collaboration with Arno Truger. When the European University Center for Peace Studies was established in Schlaining for a time (1990-2013), I was also able to teach students from all over the world, especially in the subjects of peace education and the culture of peace. To this day, despite several changes of management, my contact with Schlaining has never been broken off.

European Youth Academy (1992-2000)

My most important activity in the 1990s, which also had the greatest impact on me, was the founding of the *European Youth Academy* (1992 to 2000). After the fall of the Iron Curtain, curiosity about the "others" and the desire to cooperate was very great throughout Europe, and it also affected the education authorities in Austria, who financed this academy. My colleague Bettina Gruber and I came up with the idea of allowing school classes from all over Europe, East and West, to work together virtually for a year and then offering them the opportunity to meet, learn together and exchange ideas in a week-long seminar in Villach (Austria). It was organized by the aforementioned association *Alps-Adriatic-Alternative*. Bettina, as managing director of the Villach office, also bore the main burden of running the Youth Academy, which was not only an international project but also a major local event. Working through the association was a prerequisite for success, as the bureaucratic operation of a university would have been more of an obstacle than an instrument for this pioneering educational project.

In terms of peace education, the Youth Academy was a particularly important experience, as it required a combination of international cooperation work, teacher training and educational work with young people. The feedback from the students and teachers was largely enthusiastic, and it also offered us and all the peace educators involved an incomparable wealth of experience, especially through the comparison of a good dozen learning cultures from different countries (cf. Bürger, Gruber & Wintersteiner, 2002). In 2000, when a right-wing nationalist government came to power in Austria, we lost all support. We not only had to stop the Youth Academy, but also dissolve the *Alps-Adriatic-Alternative*.

IPRA, PEC and JPE (2000-)

International contacts are a matter of course in peace education, as peace ultimately always means world peace. The *Institute for Peace Education* in Germany with Uli Jäger and Günther Gugel set the course for my development as a peace educator, and this collaboration continues to this day. Later, I had opportunities to work with many colleagues in many countries. Without going into detail, I would like to mention the International Peace Research Association (IPRA). I was a member of its Peace Education Commission (PEC) Council for many years, and also had the honor of being invited by Anita Wenden in 2000 to work on the concept development committee of the *Jour-*

nal of Peace Education (JPE). Since the founding of the journal in 2004, I have been a member of the scientific advisory board.

The Global Campaign for Peace Education (2000-)

An important event was my acquaintance with Argentinian peace educator Alicia Cabezudo and especially Betty Reardon from Teachers College, Columbia University. She quickly became my mentor and a good friend and actively supported most of my projects ever since. It was also she who invited me to the historic peace conference in The Hague in 1999 (*Hague Appeal for Peace*), where I got to know the entire international peace education scene. *The Global Campaign for Peace Education* (GCPE) network was founded there by Magnus Haavelsrud and Betty Reardon and I was able to be part of it from the very beginning. This exchange opened up new perspectives for me and enabled me to make new acquaintances, for which I am still grateful today. I also felt encouraged in my peace culture approach by the Campaign's cooperation with UNESCO, which developed the Culture of Peace program under its then director, Federico Mayor Zaragoza, and with the significant involvement of David Adams.

In 2005, a Fulbright Scholarship enabled me to work for a semester at the Peace Education Center of Teachers College, Columbia University. I used my stay at this center, founded by Betty Reardon and directed by Janet Gerson and Tony Jenkins, to study the recent history of peace education. I had just founded a peace education center at my university that same year.

EURED (2000-2006)

While the right-wing nationalist government in Austria meant the end for many initiatives, new funding opportunities arose at European level. This enabled me to launch the pan-European EURED project in 2000. EURED was the acronym for "Education for Europe as Peace Education", a working group of peace educators from six countries. We held workshops and an international conference at the University of Klagenfurt and published a balance of peace education in Europe (Wintersteiner, Spajić-Vrkaš & Teutsch, 2003). However, the most important result of several years of work was the curriculum 'Human Rights and Peace Education in Europe'. Our aim was to implement this curriculum in the form of a pan-European in-service teacher training course. This initially proved difficult, as the European institutions were able to provide funding for research, but had no legal basis for promoting its implementation in practice. Eventually, with the help of UNESCO and a number of sponsors, it was possible to offer a two-year course. The five seminars in different countries (Spain, Germany, Hungary, Italy and Austria) were also a very enriching learning experience for us, the international team. In many ways, this went beyond the comparable work with the teachers at the European Youth Academy. For this course was broader in terms of content and went into more depth theoretically.

EURED was a project that was realized parallel to the first phase of the *Global Campaign for Peace Education*. And Betty Reardon, who inspired the Global Campaign, also played a key role in the conception and implementation of EURED. And without Mireia Uranga Arakistain (Spain), Gabriele Eschig (Austrian UNESCO Commission), Diane Hendrick, Ursula Gamauf and Rüdiger Teutsch (all Austria), EURED would not have been possible. Unfortunately, after the successful conclusion of the pilot project in 2006, the window of opportunity closed again and all our attempts to secure a continuation came to nothing.

Looking back, however, I also see weaknesses in myself. Above all, I stubbornly clung to my idea that EURED had to be an international course. Although this stubbornness led to it actually being held, I completely underestimated the potential of the network. As a result, we lost those colleagues who did not want to teach on the course and we ignored requests to join the network. Last but not least, we missed out on possible project funding because we wanted to do implementation rather than research.

6. Institutionalization of Peace Education (2005-)

The Peace Center at the University of Klagenfurt

After my non-university organizational base (*Alps-Adriatic-Alternative*) broke away, I turned more strongly to the opportunities within the university. Completing my habilitation in 2003 also strengthened my position within the university.[2] In addition, there was a considerable number of committed colleagues at our university (one of the youngest in Austria at the time) who had similar concerns to mine. Here, a trio consisting of Helga Rabenstein (Romance philologist), Brigitte Hipfl (media scholar) and myself (German scholar and peace educator), supported by Dean Karl Stuhlpfarrer (historian) and Rector Günther Hödl (also a historian), succeeded in founding a new organizational unit, the University Peace Centre, "from below" in 2005. We deliberately chose the dual title "Center for Peace Research and Peace Education" in order to counteract the neglect of peace education by traditional peace research. This gave peace education a university home in Austria for the first time. Although the center was initially understaffed and never fully equipped, it was able to provide numerous impulses through a variety of collaborations. Bettina Gruber, my colleague from *Alps-Adriatic-Alternative*, who was very familiar with the peace scene, took over the co-directorship of the center which made it possible to get started quickly. We have her to thank for many initiatives, documented in the center yearbooks published from 2006 to 2016.[3] Even if our resources were not sufficient to establish a full course of study, we are still able to offer a certified additional course of study that is very popular.

Despite the recognition that the Peace Center received, it soon encountered increasing resistance from within the university. My efforts to unbundle my dual job – professor of German didactics and director of the Peace Center – and make it into a two-person position failed. The university's governing bodies even planned to dissolve the center. It was only in 2010 that Dean Verena Winiwarter was able to secure the Center's continued existence for a few years by clustering it with three non-university institutions, including the Peace Institute in Schlaining.

After my retirement in 2016, Hans Karl Peterlini, Director of the Institute of Educational Sciences, saved the Center from imminent closure by integrating it into his institute. As the holder of a UNESCO Chair for Global Citizenship Education, he has many opportunities for cooperation with the Center, which is now headed by Claudia Brunner, the first woman and second person in Austria to complete a habilitation in peace research.

As important as the institutionalization of peace education is, being affiliated with an institution is not a prerequisite for my personal work. My retirement in 2016 did not mean a break in my work. I have more opportunities for activity than I have time and energy for.

7. Global Citizenship Education – New Impulses for Peace Education

The Dynamics of a University Course

The three-year Master's course (further education) in Global Citizenship Education (GCED) at the University of Klagenfurt is a success story. It is a success that is due in large part to my partnership with Heidi Grobbauer, the director of the development NGO KommEnt, who played a key role in the concept and implementation of the course. The course has already been awarded two prizes.

This training program for teachers, teacher trainers and NGO leaders has been offered since 2012 and is already in its fourth round at the time of writing. The course, which is funded by two Austrian institutions, is very well received. The students deal with conceptual foundations as well as pedagogical theories and practices, and reflecting on their own practice is also an important component. Through the three-year study group, peer learning, an internship and a study trip, the course offers plenty of impetus to work on one's own habitus. In my opinion, this format is the best structure to enable truly transformative learning. But the course team itself, now led by UNESCO Chair Peterlini, also receives considerable impetus to continue developing the concept. Simultaneously, many other activities have been added and the network of trained educators is growing.

In Search of an Eco-social and Post-colonial Transformation

The five pillars of the university course – *postcolonialism* (metatheory), *cosmopolitanism* (social science foundations), *planetary thinking* (natural and social science approaches), *global and social justice* (ethical foundations), *learning and education as transformation* (educational science foundations) – are also a good basis for linking together global citizenship education and peace education.

We call it, according to a formulation by Betty Reardon and Alicia Cabezudo, "Peace Education for global citizenship" (Reardon & Cabezudo, 2002, p. 24; Wintersteiner, 2019). I see this as an important concretization of a pedagogy for a culture of peace.

With my intensive engagement with GCED, I have probably finally reached a third phase of theoretical work, which, although it builds on the *Pedagogy of the Other* and *the Poetics of Diversity*, goes well beyond them. It is above all post-colonial and ecological studies that also give my peace education new accents. The search for systemic concepts for a way out of the polycrisis is now in the foreground, which by no means rejects my previous point of reference, the culture of peace, but which seeks to embed it better. Inspired by Edgar Morin's work on *Homeland Earth*, which has been decisive for me since the 1990s, by Betty Reardon's critique of the war system, by the discourses on global citizenship (education), especially those of Vanessa Andreotti and Karen Pashby, and by the ecological discourse, which is increasingly incorporating critical, feminist and postcolonial elements (e.g. Dipesh Chakrabarty), I try to receive overall concepts for social transformation and make them fruitful for peace education. The impulses of Wilfried Graf and the work of Herbert Kelman, which combine social psychology, politics and culture, are also very important in this respect.[4]

At the same time, the current wars – above all Russia's attack on Ukraine and the Gaza war – have prompted me to take a closer look at pacifism and non-violence and to search for alternatives to an ever more threatening spiral of conflict escalation, armament and war mentality - a task that goes far beyond peace education, but is also highly relevant.

8. Overall Reflection

Working on Four Cornerstones

In retrospect, I am aware of certain patterns in my work, especially the combination of *peace theory, peace activism, peace education* and *organizational work*. Obviously, I have operated, not always fully consciously, in a square whose four corners I have always tried to balance: *structures – instruments – concepts – activities*. Often there were no suitable structures, neither university nor non-university, to systematically pursue peace education, hence my constant efforts to create such structures, be it NGOs, networks or university institutions: the Villach Peace Committee, Alps-Adriatic-Alternative, the University Peace Center, the Peace Cluster, and others. On this basis, I was concerned with the creation of suitable peace education instruments (courses and seminars) – primarily the Youth Academy, the Alps-Adriatic seminars, the EURED course, the GCED master's program.

A good part of my publications is dedicated to concepts, programs and experiences with peace education. My most important peace education activities as a teacher trainer have not so much taken place in schools and universities, but rather in the freer field of self-organized seminars, workshops or courses. This greater freedom allowed for a more appropriate didactics.

Undaunted Failure

But this freedom also came at a price. The structures kept breaking down, which meant that the instruments could no longer be used, the concepts proved to be outdated or unrealizable in official structures, and the activities had to be started all over again. So sooner or later, every success was bought with a failure. This shows how decisive the framework conditions are for peace education – the political climate, the policy itself, the institutions in which the work takes place.

In any case, this insight is a reason for modesty. What I have been able to do is not the result of my autonomous development, but was the use of room for manoeuvre that was created or narrowed again by occasions and impulses from outside. It takes enabling structures to make structures possible. Above all, I need people who support and encourage me, who challenge and criticize me, who work with me. I have mentioned a number of them here, but many others, unnamed, were also formative for me.

I can say that I have succeeded in some things, even if many of the things I have tried have come to nothing or have not lasted as long as I had hoped. I often didn't achieve what I was aiming for, but I did achieve other things that came my way. And so, inspired by Wilfried Graf, I adopted Stéphane Hessel's maxim: fail, fail again, fail better and better – that is the path to success.[5]

"Do not go gentle into that good night"

What next? Even if you shouldn't have too high hopes for new beginnings at over 70 years of age, I still hold with Dylan Thomas (2000, p. 100), whose poems my daughter once gave me as a present:

> *Do not go gentle into that good night,*
> *Old age should burn and rave at close of day;*
> *Rage, rage against the dying of the light.*

'Rage' is indeed called for, because 'dying of the light' does threaten human life on the entire planet, without the disunited human race being able to muster adequate countermeasures. The obstacles to learning that exist are also part of my recent peace education studies (Wintersteiner 2021). I hope that younger generations will overcome these obstacles. In any case, there is no room for resignation: "The clarity of a radical critical analysis surprisingly results in confidence. Such contradictory experiences underlie our actions in everyday life. That is what makes up our lives" (Meueler, 2004, p. 371).

Endnotes

1) At the same time, in the 1980s I was already striving for a self-reflective peace education and political education that was aware of the limits of its own effectiveness (see: Saxer & Wintersteiner, 1988).

2) A habilitation is in some countries, including Austria, the highest university degree, or the procedure by which it is achieved. One has to fulfill a university's set criteria of excellence in research, teaching, and further education including a habilitation thesis. The degree opens the road to a professorship, but there is no guarantee to get this position.

3) https://www.aau.at/erziehungswissenschaft-und-bildungsforschung/arbeitsbereiche/friedensforschung-und-friedensbildung/publikationen/jahrbuecher-friedenskultur/ [partially in English]

4) A step in this direction is also my book *Die Welt neu denken lernen* (2021). [Learning to rethink the world]

5)   https://www.radiofrance.fr/franceculture/stephane-hessel-un-media-teur-ne-2702966

References

Bürger, H., Gruber, B. & Wintersteiner, W. on behalf of the Federal Ministry for Education, Science and Culture, (Eds.). (2002). *Education for intercultural understanding. "The European Youth Academy" handbook*. StudienVerlag.

Brousek, J., Grafenauer, D., Wintersteiner, W. & Wutti, D. (Eds.). (2020). *SLO-VENIJA | ÖSTERREICH: Befreiendes Erinnern – Osvobajajoče spominjanje*. Drava.

Gruber, B. & Wintersteiner, W. (Eds.). (2014). *Learning peace – an integrative part of peacebuilding. Experiences from the Alps-Adriatic region*. Drava.

Meueler, E. (2004). Bildung für nachhaltige Entwicklung. Rückblick in ideol-ogiekritischer Absicht. In Steffens, G. & Weiß, E. (Eds.), *Jahrbuch für pädagogik 2004. Globalisierung und bildung* (361-373). Lang.

Otmačić, V. (2021). *Islands of peace in a sea of war*. [Conference paper]. Inter-national Conference "Nonviolence and Intercultural Dialogue", Oxford, 6-7 June 2020 (online). https://www.academia.edu/101935769/Islands_of_peace_in_a_sea_of_war_Valentina_Otmacic_2021

Reardon, B. A. & Cabezudo, A. (2002). *Learning to abolish war: Teaching toward a culture of peace*. = The Hague Appeal for Peace, Global Campaign for Peace Education.

Reardon, B. A. (2020). *The Alps-Adriatic Manifesto: New politics for a post COVID world*. Global Campaign for Peace Education. https://www.peace-ed-cam-paign.org/the-alps-adriatic-manifesto-new-politics-for-a-post-covid-world/

Saxer, R. & Wintersteiner, W. (1988). Von der unmöglichkeit politischer bil-dung in der schule und von ihrer notwendigkeit. *Informationen zur deutschdi-daktik (ide)* 2, 15-24.

Schnitzler, A. (1993). *Buch der sprüche und bedenken. Aphorismen und fragmente*. Fischer.

Thomas, D. (2000). *Selected poems.* Penguin Books.

Vriens, L. (2005). A fundamental study of the basic concepts of peace education. *Journal of Peace Education* 2 (2), 215-217.

Wintersteiner, W. (Ed.). (1994). *Das neue Europa wächst von unten. Friedenserziehung als Friedenskultur.* Drava

Wintersteiner, W. (1999). *Pädagogik des Anderen. Bausteine für eine Friedenspädagogik in der Postmoderne.* Münster. Agenda.

Wintersteiner, W. (2001). *'Hätten wir das Wort, wir bräuchten die Waffen nicht.' Erziehung für eine Kultur des Friedens.* StudienVerlag.

Wintersteiner, W. (2006a). *Poetik der Verschiedenheit. Literatur, bildung, globalisierung.* Drava. (extended new edition 2022).

Wintersteiner, W.(2006b). *Transkulturelle literarische bildung.* StudienVerlag.

Wintersteiner, W. (2012). 'Kärnten liegt am meer'. Vision einer friedensregion. In Petritsch, W., Graf, W. & Kramer, G. (Eds.), *Kärnten liegt am meer. Konfliktgeschichte/n über trauma, macht und identität* (524-545). Drava/Heyn.

Wintersteiner, W. (2019). Peace education for global citizenship. The genuine global dimension of Betty Reardon's concept of peace education. In Snauwaert, D.T. (Ed.), *Exploring Betty A. Reardon's perspective on peace education* (15-28). Springer.

Wintersteiner, W. (2021). *Die Welt neu denken lernen – Plädoyer für eine planetare politik.* Bielefeld: transcript.

Werner W., Beretta, C. & Miladinović Zalaznik, M. (Eds.). (2020). *Manifest l o Alpe-Adria. Stimmen für eine Europa-Region des Friedens und Wohlstands | Voci per una regione europea di pace e prosperità | Glasovi za evropsko regijo miru in blagostanja.* Löcker.

Werner W., Spajić-Vrkaš, V. & Teutsch, R. (Eds.). (2003). *Peace Education in Europe. Visions and experiences.* Waxmann.

Werner W. & Sturm, M. (2021). Visionen und wege – Zivilgesellschaftliche kooperationen im Alpen-Adria-Raum. In Anderwald, K., Hren, K. & Stainer-Hämmerle, K. (Eds.), *Kärntner Jahrbuch für Politik 2021 | Koroški politični zbornik 2021* (277-293). Mohorjeva / Hermagoras.

Wohlmuther, C. & Wintersteiner, W. (2018). *"Dort, wo unsere Großväter gegeneinander kämpften ..." Die ,Friedenswege' an der Frontlinie des Ersten Weltkriegs: Tourismus und Frieden im Alpen-Adria-Raum.* Drava.

Chapter 29
Further Journeys in Peace and Education

Robert Zuber

The offer to participate in this volume came at the 30th anniversary of the volume I edited in 1994 under the title "Journeys in Peace Education" with support from Åke Bjerstedt and the Department of Educational and Psychological Research at Lund University (Zuber, 1994). Åke's stewardship of Peace Education Reports was instrumental in keeping communities of scholarship and practice in relatively close contact as the field of peace education cut one or more of its teeth.

Four of the authors (myself included) who wrote for that earlier volume agreed to write for this one as well. I have stayed in touch with them as I have been able, especially Virginia Cawagas and Swee-Hin Toh who have been thoughtful, caring and committed comrades over many years. While I have drifted considerably from the peace education discipline, I've maintained (and created) commitments to both peacebuilding and progressive pedagogy in large measure due to Virginia and Swee-Hin's influences.

The 1994 authors have continued their unique journeys over the years. The wise and passionate Tena Montague is no longer with us, no longer able to jar her friends and audiences out of complacency on matters of race and gender, no longer able to push us to think harder and deeper about our gifts and responsibilities in a world which sometimes seems to be spinning out of control. I still miss her fertile and creative intellect and her kind and quirky family every day.

I have also lost touch with David Hicks and his 'futures' project but still recall the impact it had on me and surely many others drowning in the 'here and now' without a larger sense of the skills, capacities and traits of character we need to cultivate in order to meet fresh global challenges.

Robin Burns also wrote for that volume long ago and she kindly serves as one of the two primary instigators (along with Magnus Haavelsrud) of this current incarnation. My own participation in this project was motivated by the prospect of honoring both the two editors and a friend to many involved with both peace and pedagogy, the late Robert Aspeslagh. The irony here would be apparent to anyone who followed Robert's life and career closely (as Robin did), a life which overcame significant obstacles from childhood in part because of the creative and at times wonderfully contrarian way he chose to engage the world. In the end, he was more a painter than he had ever been a peace educator, but his influence on me and others represented in this project was considerable, and his name demands honoring in this context.

Perhaps like others, I have been surprised by how many of the values and issues highlighted in the earlier 'Journeys' have followed me throughout my life, including those diverse and sometimes quirky investments such as with Cameroon NGOs in crisis and helping to pastor a Harlem church in a crack cocaine-infested neighborhood. Quirky also has been the opportunity to sit in the UN Security Council, day after day, where my Global Action to Prevent War colleagues and I try to make sense of a largely dysfunctional, intensely political process that people worldwide expect more from. The 'through line' of all these investments has been the balance struck between addressing concrete human needs and critiquing a policy community that fails those needs far too often.

The persistence here of some of the language, values and investments from that earlier 'Journey' is less about my own stubbornness and more about an oft delayed and distracted 'growing into' values and aspirations from earlier stages. We sometimes forget that we aren't the people now we were 30 years ago. We've hopefully learned some things, 'grown into' some things, as we have surely failed to learn others. Such is the condition of imperfect people trying to apply a bit of thoughtful healing to this current incarnation of a human community consumed by threats both immediate and chronic.

As personal evolution takes a back seat to creeping mortality, I recalled a sports quotation that "you are what your record says you are." Indeed, while the door is not entirely shut on a generation which struggled to bring peace education and other progressive incarnations into focus, the remaining cracks continue to shrink in size. Clearly, I'm not in a position to offer salient critiques of current practices, positive or otherwise. It is possible, however, to reflect on those earlier principles which I have tried to 'grow into', to critique their contemporary relevance to social justice, environmental sustainability, gender equality and other pursuits.

In doing so, it seemed pertinent to repurpose text from that earlier 'Journey'. The laziness of this choice is offset by the value of scrutinizing earlier pronouncements, weeding out those which have turned out to be miscalculations at best or fantasies at worst. Despite having a professional and personal record with considerably more investments than successes, the tapestry of those investments has remained relatively stable. Perhaps not peace education per se, but certainly education as a social responsibility within and beyond schools and classrooms, of the pursuit of peace as much about social justice and environmental degradation as about weapons and power politics, and of traits of faith and character – especially gratitude -- that help sustain our struggle in times of distress. Part of this work surely involves offering guidance as requested to those at risk of losing their way as many of us were once in danger of losing our own.

Education Beyond Schooling

I came very early to believe that those in peace education should rethink their relationship with the schools in order to avoid potentially harmful consequences or unfounded expectations. We must continually remind ourselves that 'education' as a human activity is not the unique province of schools and their practices. As the formidable Lawrence Cremin made clear to his many Columbia students, education about the world, its cultures, processes and values, takes place in a variety of contexts, including families, the media, the churches, government agencies, scientific laboratories, even the streets. I have had some wonderful teachers in my life, the names of whom could fill these pages. However, much of what I cherish has come to me via teachers plying their wares in educationally rich contexts beyond school walls.

In schools, it is clear that what came to be known as the 'implicit curriculum' - the knowledge and values which exist as unstated assumptions of school life - exerts great influence over the lives and choices of students. However, classrooms which can have transformative effects on students requires curriculum inspired by teaching which promotes friendship, tells the truth about the world, magnifies occasions for age-appropriate, responsible interactions, provides spaces for active questioning and even disagreement, and opens doors into a world of creative risk. Needless to say, such teaching is infrequently encouraged in these cautious times and thus remains in relatively short supply.

We must also address what I believe is a significant drawback to school-based learning, setting students on a path to 'master' smaller and smaller pieces of the external world while knowing precious little about themselves. How will young people come to appreciate what makes them unique packages of strengths and limitations? How will they learn to assess what truly 'counts' in their lives? Among the skills that schools cultivate, addressing 'know thysel' inadequacies and self-deceptions are rarely among them. Over the course of a human life, credentials may well matter a great deal to material comfort and professional recognition, but I am convinced that character driven by the practice of honest self-awareness continues to matter more.

My interns at Global Action over a generation, well over 150 of them, seem largely obsessed with school and its responsibilities. School literally runs their lives while providing them in return with relatively safe, age-specific social contexts. Safety, of course, is an illusion, for them and for the rest of us. Indeed, increasingly, these young people display often unidentified anxiety over the state of the world writ large, but closer to home over struggles over jobs, income and mating. Indeed, for many of our fine young interns, their tenure at the UN has merely expanded their list of questions with no easy answers. It has also made them wonder if the UN and other large institutions actually crush more enthusiasm for change than they cultivate. Or more fairly that they modulate and even suppress the timeline for change considerably more than what so many youth in our world are now demanding.

Their frustration and anxiety have reminded me every day over a long life of the need to change how, what and where we 'teach', but also to fix what is broken in our politics, our international relations, our food systems, our ecology. Part of the bargain we make with children is that there is a point to all of our rules, our lessons, our precautions, our discipline. The hope, of course, is that they will inherit a world which may be over-heating, grossly unequal and excessively weaponized, but which still offers possibilities beyond an endless series of crises for which they may or may not be well prepared.

As much respect as I have for school teachers, I fear that the rest of us adults are simply not holding up our end of a larger education bargain. We have allowed education to become literally synonymous with schooling and then we have promoted the goals of such schooling as credentialling more than character building. We have become more concerned with test scores than creating an enveloping environment which reinforces core objectives of learning and life and helps students overcome anxiety related to complex changes such as those associated with rapid climate change and evolving digital technology.

We believe that, as an antidote to high anxiety, there is sanity in agency, in the ability to take specific action regarding the justice issues and related concerns which occupy many of our thoughts and lives. I know that in my own engagement with multiple concerns, despite legitimate criticism of Global Action's own pathways and priorities, has helped substitute and magnify real problems I can actually address for the problems running through my brain which often left me with few options beyond self-doubt, an over-fondness for Malbec, and sinus headaches.

At the UN, I often worry when I hear diplomats hawking 'education' - in some instances 'peace education' - as key to promoting cultures of peace and tolerance, of equity and access. How much of this, I wonder, is sincere appreciation for the role education writ large can play in helping youth overcome anxiety and embrace the world and its challenges? And how much is that tendency of officials to 'kick the can down the road', to assume that young people will somehow locate their agency for change in ways that privileged diplomats and officials often do not? Do officials not see that the lines connecting schooling and a sustainable peace are more crooked than straight?

Do they not grasp the extent to which school-based credentials are at least as likely to serve personal aspirations as societal ones?

The lines are crooked indeed, and we must learn to navigate them as we engage young people, lines characterized by truth telling without confounding youth with images and crises about which they can worry much but currently do little. It will be their world to manage soon enough. It is ours to manage now and we must commit to much more effectiveness in that regard. The last thing we should want is well-educated children growing up on a rapidly melting, increasingly lifeless planet run by people with little understanding of how their greed and grievance has compromised opportunities for billions.

The Peacebuilding Imperative

Much of our collective, if modest efforts on peace and security have evolved over years of combining a preoccupation with nuclear and other weapons of mass destruction with social, environmental and political deficits which make the stockpiling and modernization of such weapons virtually inevitable. Here we highlight abuses perpetuated against women, racial minorities and ethnic subcultures; an ecology which is increasingly vulgar and dangerous to all life forms, not merely our own; misuses of political and social power resulting in gross inequalities and violations of basic human rights; and a nation-state system which continues to seduce persons into allegiances largely archaic and servicing of narrow political interests.

These are only some of our current concerns, and we have gained some skill in our capacity to name specific abuses and aggressions perpetrated against people and communities by those in power often with no regard for the consequences of their actions. We have collectively done too little, however, to challenge the assumptions and prerogatives of power itself, most of which are not publicly accountable.

What we have delivered is regular presence (or annoyance) inside the United Nations over many years. The UN is an institution which thankfully highlights virtually every human threat and aspiration in its various conference rooms. But it has also forfeited considerable credibility through a combination of punchless, politically compromised resolutions and diplomats mandated to put more positive spins on national priorities than evidence can support. Much UN credibility loss has been directed towards the Security Council, a body which, like the UN as a whole, represents positions determined not around the Council oval but in national capitals. In the Council, there is coercive authority to impose sanctions or arms embargoes, authorize peacekeeping operations with robust mandates, and take other measures to protect and preserve peace and security. Only some of these measures have had their stated impact while others have even pulled targeted nations and communities in more precarious directions.

Fortunately, with input from a variety of member states and stakeholders (including ourselves), the UN created and sustained a mechanism to foster peacebuilding efforts in conflict and post-conflict situations minus the political drama of the Security Council. The Peacebuilding Commission (PBC), founded in 2005, has solidified an important niche in the UN's peace and security architecture, offering counsel to both its constituent bodies (General Assembly and Security Council) as well as to member states facing threats of conflict. The PBC serves as a comprehensive platform to help states assess and address the impact of social inequalities, sea level rise, forced migration, biodiversity loss, national debt burdens, racial/cultural tensions and more to prospects of violent outbreaks. Its sessions have over time become more holistic and prevention-minded; also more inclusive of diverse stakeholders from local NGOs to officials of development banks than the culture and working methods of the Security Council would normally permit.

The advantages of the PBC approach are both apparent and instructive. Too many of the world's peoples are now living on the edge. As I write, the focus of global concern rests on Gaza, Ukraine and Sudan, but also on our burning, melting, biodiversity-challenged planet, and our anxious, grievance laden populations willing to point the finger in anger at anyone but themselves. We simply cannot speak meaningfully about weapons without talking about motivations for their potential use, nor without assessing their massive costs as vast food, health, housing and protection concerns remain unaddressed. Similarly, we can't speak meaningfully about conflict prevention without also having contingency plans in place for how to build back and restore communities and societies if our conflict prevention efforts fall short.

All peacebuilding is tied to skills which the world possesses in abundance but which are often denied a place at the peace table. With inspiration from the PBC, we have made it a point not to prioritize talking to audiences made up of 'peace movement types' but to groups of business and finance students, of engineers, pastors and artists, of social workers and health professionals. As such, we have done our small part to expand circles of concern, to understand more about how expertise is assessed and conferred in multiple contexts, and to collaborate on ways to make such expertise available as needed, to build and rebuild when conflict or disaster looms. A world of people with skills similar to my own is, by definition, woefully deficient in keeping our societies viable in crisis. We can credibly advocate for better promise keeping in the development, humanitarian and peace sectors so long as we recognize that the 'keeping' in most instances will be done by others.

We must also remain clear about how tickets to participation are allocated, ensuring that we do not leave skills sidelined with much to accomplish and much to teach the rest of us. Indeed, one of the lessons of the UN's flailing efforts to fulfill the Sustainable Development Goals is that too much SDG direction remains in the hands of diplomats and technocrats and too little in the hands of local actors of diverse ages, genders and cultures, people with contexts and connections for healing and change. Through our association with local projects affiliated with Green Map (greenmap.org) as well as with a bevy of other local initiatives in most all global regions, it becomes clear every day that we in our UN bubble still have much to learn and consider, if we are to help make more responsive policy. This was clear to me in the 1990s and has remained constant through travels, discussions and events over 30 years: If the world were fairer, more welcoming of diverse local skills and talents, I would not have the job I have. Clearly there is talent and commitment in abundance in this world which the peacebuilding lens can help to both identify and incorporate. It is high time that we commit to more robust peace recruitment or, at a minimum, recognize the skills and capacities at local level that we leave on the table at our collective peril.

Gratitude as Fuel for Abundant Living

A concern that I have long held in relationship to our fields of inquiry is the ways in which our generally insufficient knowledge of the human condition impacts our priorities, ideas and actions. In our little slice of policy life, we are too-often content to sound the alarm about social justice and related concerns as though such knowledge can, by itself, motivate caring, transformational responses on the part of the hearers. It may do so if the metaphorical soil is sufficiently fertile, if trust in the messenger has been sufficiently established, and if the listeners are actually committed to practice what is being preached. But for most, alarms are likely to raise levels of anxiety as much as levels of engagement given what we know about crises swirling about our world to which most people can barely sustain attention, let alone cope.

Through our UN-based Global Action project we have made our position on this crystal clear if not always entirely convincing – that better policy requires better people. Here we refer to people who see and feel more deeply, people who are as committed to keeping promises as making them in the first place, people who can offer more practical solidarity with the needs and aspirations of others in this moment of excessive grievances and entitlements, people willing to demystify their privileged positions as an invitation to participation in more horizontal policy deliberations. We refer also to people willing to take risks for others within and beyond their circles of concern, people able to gratefully experience the wonder of this created order rather than always insisting on certainty which they then try much too hard to impose on others.

The formula for a life of dignity in times such as these remains diverse and multi-faceted. While insisting on certain, minimal standards of civilized behavior in keeping with international law and justice norms, we seek also to promote the pursuit of personal and community fulfillment, making more space for lives which are free to make culture, undertake ethical exploration, and engage in relationships characterized by fairness, gratitude, service and mutual support.

Sadly, in this suspicious and authoritarian moment, the narrowness of our enthusiasms tends to create more enemies than it can heal. Whatever else it may need, this world clearly needs no more enemies, no more divisions in the family of humanity. Indeed, such divisions appear to be multiplying rather than abating as human beings from Israel to Sudan and from Myanmar to DR Congo have chosen to inflict – and defend -- brutality in the name of some spurious national or ideological interest. We demonstrate over and over that we as a species are more clever than wise, more self-interested than compassionate, more ambitious than kind, more analytical than intuitive. If it is true that we are what we practice not what we pronounce, then our 'practice time' these days seems to be taken up finding more and more innovative if not overtly predatory ways to promote and defend personal interest.

Over the past few years, we have attempted to incarnate some of our concerns for character and gratitude in organizations and entities taking the lead in rethinking social relations and responsibilities. Of these, special mention accrues to Dr Robert Thomas at the Scheller School of Business at Georgia Tech University who has enabled his students to think through the personal and even business benefits of adopting 'servant leadership' modeling. Also valuable is the 'Inner Economy' model developed by Dr Lisa Berkley, one which seeks to recover the full panoply of oft-ignored human intelligences, including the emotional intelligence which often seems as an endangered species in our public, educational and policy institutions.

These and other colleagues present and past such as Professor Douglas Sloan of Columbia University have maintained that there is critical need for a different work in this often aggressive and self-interested world, a work which is in part about service and political engagement at community and policy levels but even more fundamentally about insight and imagination, about reinvesting in our overly-narrow perceptions and visions in and about the world. Sloan spoke often of the need to "unmask officialdom," as one means of distancing our minds from official half-truths and misinformation. He also spoke of the "excluded discourse" of art and faith characteristic of much of our education, discourse which leaves us valuing possession more than appreciation, certainty more than paradox, abstraction more than participation, status more than self-awareness, detachment more than vulnerability.

Such contributions serve as reminders that we often lack the vision, imagination and even courage to live in a different way. We continue to 'purchase the surfaces' and allow pretense to success or virtue to become hallmarks of our time. Such pretense can be as insidious as it is pervasive. Children ask if life has a chance. We distract them with personal technology and delusions of authority and control. Old people ask us to help make sense of a life transforming into death. We patronize their questions and detach ourselves from their realities. Students ask for truth. We provide them with conventional ideas about a world under strain and offer the illusion that learning and growing is what happens only in 'school'. Church members ask for guidance towards enlightenment and connection. We provide them with irrelevant and even dangerous theological formulas and dubious pathways to an imperfectly understood spiritual knowledge. All of this is pretense, born not of malice but of an impoverished perception. We don't see enough or know enough, we fail to creatively link the world we have to the world we want, and we no longer recognize the profound power of our chosen habits over so many of our thoughts and practices.

This leads to what has become for me a lifetime preoccupation, the 'intelligence' related to the path of faith, a path which I have deviated from far too often, but which remains a source of hope and meaning, of mindfulness and gratitude, for myself and many other families and communities.

I have had only one experience with 'church' which incarnated what I have understood to be the essence of community-based faith, and that was the now-defunct All Saints Church in East Harlem. For years and under duress from crushing poverty and an out-of-control drug trade a diverse community both taught and learned how to care for each other, how to honor each other, how to preserve, protect and build with precious little outside support. It was thus painfully ironic that their successes were undermined by gentrification and other economic predation from folks seeking their real estate, not their community.

Despite these ironies, I have known people living a faith which literally embarrasses my own, persons of diverse talents, skills and circumstances, persons who would likely be embarrassed themselves by the suggestion that their faith was a model for others. Indeed, some of the greatest models of successful, intentional, grateful living have been given to me from the unlikeliest of sources. Such, in our time, is the nature of the spiritually mature. For us, the mature are generally not the ones demonstrating exemplary skill and achievement based on some dubious assertion of 'merit'. They are, instead, the ones who can live with wisdom and gratitude within the paradoxes and limitations of their own circumstances. As often unidentified peacebuilders and peacemakers, they are the ones who do more, and care more, who understand more, and transform more, than their worldly credentials and assets would ever suggest. They are the ones who continually rise above themselves even if they do not always rise above the rest.

Over the years, we have come to know many such people and in more than a few instances have been moved and educated by their caring and competent impulses. They make clear that faith remains relevant to sustaining our practical commitments as educators, as peacebuilders, as nurturers of our under-exercised human intelligences, as purveyors of gratitude through difficult times. However one understands the pull of divinity, it surely must pull in the direction of mindfulness more than isolation, compassion more than indifference, wonder more than comfort. It must also pull us to abandon traits of character which diminish the best of us, which give us license to cast dispersion on others without confessing our own responsibility, or to use our powers of reason more to rationalize or explain away behavior after the fact than guide our intention before the fact.

In times such as those we now live through, we too easily claim to know what we stand against. Sometimes, we know what we stand for. Sadly, we don't always know who we stand with, nor the role of gratitude in persevering in our chosen mission and vision. As I tried to communicate 30 years ago, we are not grateful because the world is so just and peaceful, because our dreams are so noble, because our accomplishments are so distinguished, or because our needs and access are so privileged. We are grateful because of this place and opportunity given to us in which we have been invited to find ourselves and our communities of work and hope. We may not have the power to turn loaves and fishes into a banquet for thousands, but we can learn more about how to turn our bounty into picnics of justice, spreading our blankets, opening our baskets and inviting more of the world to sit with us.

As people of faith, as educators, as peacebuilders, we must be more honest about our motives, intentions and frustrations, but also keep operating in and through history, as though history matters. For us, despite discouragements, it must matter, not because we claim this to be the only reality, but because this is the only reality in which we know to struggle, know to heal, know to transform. This current incarnation of our world, this world which struggles to adapt to a persistent human onslaught, this world of people who confuse faith with authoritarian vengeance and swaps out healing gratitude for discordant grievance, this constitutes the sphere of our redemptive action. We need justice and sanity to happen here, even if we also choose to believe that it can also happen elsewhere, and we need to quickly demonstrate that we can rise to that challenge.

Concluding Remarks

As I reflect back on what could barely be called a 'career' of moving in and out of engagement with pedagogy, peacebuilding and faith-based service, I still find cause to believe in our common future. As friends of mine occasionally scold me, we have 'muddled through' before and we will likely do so again.

I'm inclined to believe this truth, but I've also seen first-hand threats and challenges from multiple vantage points, and I recognize that changes to our planet and its life forms are coming more quickly than we had originally anticipated. Are we able as a species to adapt and respond with urgency matching the scale of the threat? We are in more ways than we admit, creatures of habit in personal and institutional contexts, and those habits make it difficult to change course, even if we were sufficiently inclined to do so. Our patterns of response on a planet unwilling to honor our stubbornness can make the transformative task that much more difficult and leaves more of us shaking our heads at times in frustration and even discouragement at our collective prospects.

As my generation begins a slow 'fade to black', there are several tasks which still beckon such as those enumerated in this essay. We certainly must demonstrate that we can widen our circles of concern, helping more people and their skills find places of engagement at all levels where engagement matters. We have spent much energy trying to define what and who should be allowed inside those circles only to find ourselves trapped inside them. Breaking out allows fresh ideas, skills and stakeholders into the mix, and likely frees us to realize our full agency while restoring some of the sanity siphoned away through daily doses of the worst of our human condition.

We can do better, we know we can do better, but we are running out of time to prove it before our 'Journey' literally hits the rocks.

References

Zuber, R. (1994). Journeys in peace education: Critical reflection and personal witness. In Bjerstedt, Å. (Ed.), *Peace education reports no. 14*. Lund Univ. (Sweden). Malmo School of Education. https://files.eric.ed.gov/fulltext/ED384551.pdf

Chapter 30
Footprints In Wind

Corinne Kumar

We have entered the night to tell our tale
to listen to those who have not spoken.
we who have seen our children die in the morning deserve to be listened to:
we have looked on blankly as they have opened their wounds
Nothing really matters except, the grief of the children

their tears must be revered
their inner silence speaks louder than the spoken word
and all being and all life shouts out in outrage
we must not be rushed to our truths
whatever we failed to say is stored secretly in our minds
and all those processions of embittered crowds
have seen us lead them a thousand times
we can hear the story over and over and over again

our minds are muted beyond the sadness
there is nothing more we can fear.[1]
 - Mazisi Kunene (1982)

We live in violent times:
times in which our community and collective memories are dying;
times in which the many dreams are turning into never-ending nightmares,
times that are collapsing the many life visions into a single cosmology

times that have created its own universal truths-
equality, development, peace,
truths that are inherently discriminatory, even violent.
times that have created a development model that dispossesses the majority,
desacralizes nature, destroys cultures and civilizations, denigrates the women;
devalues the women;
time in which the wars bring a time of violent uncertainty, brutal wars:
wars for resources- oil, land, diamonds, minerals:
wars of occupation,
terrorism, going global and franchised to all, the world over;
times that are giving us new words; pre-emptive strike, collateral damage,
embedded journalism, enemy combatants, military tribunals, rendition:
new words:
words soaked in blood.
times in which the dominant political thinking,
institutions and instruments of justice are hardly able to redress the violence
that is escalating and intensifying,
times in which progress presupposes the genocide of the many; the gendercide
of women;
the violence taking newer and more contemporary forms, cybercrimes, manipu-
lation of the many by the few through Artificial Intelligence,
times in which human rights have come to mean the rights of the privileged, the
rights of the powerful and for the masses to have their freedoms, their human
rights, they must surrender the most fundamental human right of all,
the right to be human;
times in which the political spaces for the Other are diminishing, even closing.
Times that are destroying diversity as the world moves towards one science,
one notion of progress, one development model, one policy determining secure
living through wars militarization, and nuclearization;
the one single story, the one central mountain,
the world, it would seem, is at the end of its imagination.
who will deny that we need another imaginary?
Perhaps it is in this moment when existing systems of meaning fragment, that
we may search for new meanings;
Only the imagination stands between us and fear: fear makes us behave like
sheep when we should be dreaming like poets. (Kumar, 2005, pp. 183-184)[2]

So let me gather some stars and make a fire for you, and tell you a story[3]: It is a story of horror and hope; a story of the missing, the disappeared; a story so real, yet magical: a story from Lawrence Thornton (1991) in *Imagining Argentina*:

It is a story about the country under the dictators. The hero is a gentle person Carlos Rueda, an intense man who directs a children's theatre and is at home in the world of children. During the time of the dictators, Carlos discovers that he has an extraordinary gift. He realizes that he is the site, the locus, the vessel for a dream. He can narrate the fate of the missing. From all over Argentina, men and women come to his home and sitting in his garden, Carlos tells them stories: tales of torture, courage, death, stories about the missing, about the disappeared.

One day the regime arrests his wife Celia, for a courageous act of reporting. The world of Carlos collapses, till he realizes that he must keep her alive in his imagination. Only the imagination, says Carlos, stands between us and fear; fear makes us behave like sheep when we must dream like poets.

As the regime becomes more violent, it is the women who object. It is the women as wives, as mothers, as daughters who congregate in silence at the Plaza de Mayo. Silently, each carries a placard announcing or asking about the missing. The women walk quietly, sometimes holding hands.

It is not just an act of protest; it is a drama of caring; each listening to the other's story, each assuring the other through touch, weaving a sense of community.

The community grows as the men join them. All the while, through the window, the Generals watch them.

People realize that they cannot be indifferent observers, spectators, bystanders, even experts. The indifference of the watchers to the regime is not enough. One must be a witness. A witness is not a mere spectator s/he looks but s/he also listens. s/he remembers.

Everything must be remembered. Nothing must be forgotten. We must explore the new imaginary not as experts but as witnesses. We must retrieve history from memory. In remembering and retrieving memory we are invited to explore the new imaginary as spoken by different voices, in different languages, through different cultures and civilisations and through the many universalisms that underlie the political philosophies of our times. We need to imagine alternative perspectives for change: to craft visions that will evolve out of conversations across cultures and other traditions; conversations between cultures that challenge and transcend the totalitarianism of the western logos; conversations that are not mediated by the hegemony of the universal discourse. Offering critical and creative challenges to this dominant cosmology that determines the universals of our time, the dominant discourses of science and technology, of development and democracy; of poverty and privilege, of the colonization of our economic and political structures, of the militarisation of our minds and our imaginations.

At times, it would seem that the journey has been long. At other points, a story only recently begun. It was but yesterday that Vincente was smiling at my passionate articulation of the development paradigm. Theory far removed from the grime of engagement with the subjects of study. Only yesterday again, I am learning and deepening my own understanding of crime, reparation, justice, from the Gacaca, Truth and Reconciliation Commissions, from myriad movements small and large that put the survivors and those who did not survive, at the centre of finding just resolutions. Roads that took me to newer places and newer ideas, roads on which travelling itself was an education. My quest for changing the world around me led me to larger and larger worlds which were underwritten by the same organising principles of exploitation and oppression. The language differed - totalitarian, libertarian, democratic, autocratic, communist, socialist - but the song remained the same.

Peace studies were an early foray in my questing journey. It led to many things - the deepening of the anti-nuclear movement, the expansion of the feminist gaze and interpretation of the world - what was intuitively sensed grew richer in understanding through engagement with diverse movements and cultures, including but not limited to academia.

The horizon shrinks as my own time that I have walked this world seems increasingly limited. Even as wars of greater intensity are waged, wreaking destitution and misery on the weakest amongst us, and hope seems at an end, some small sparks of humane action rooted in empathy and fairness, keep alight the promise that what is human in us can never be completely extinguished. I know when the time comes for me to go, I leave a world that has great injustice written into its ways of being, into its way of seeing, but also a world where through resistance and persuasion new ways of convivial living are possible.

To all those who listen to the Song of the Wind:
In a different place, in a different time, Black Elk heard the Song of the Wind
I saw myself on the central mountain of the world,
the highest place, and I had a vision because I was seeing in
the sacred manner of the world, she said

Remember she said, she was seeing in the sacred manner of the world
And the sacred, central mountain was a mountain in her part of the world
'But' Black Elk continued to say: 'the central mountain is everywhere'

From my central mountain, the point where stillness
and movement are together, I invite you to listen to the wind;
more specially to the wind from the South: the South
as third world, as the civilizations of Asia, the Pacific, the
Arab world, Africa, Latin America; the South as the voices
and movements of peoples, wherever these movements exist;

the South as the visions and wisdoms of women:

the South as the discovering of new paradigms, which
challenge the existing theoretical concepts and categories
breaking the mind constructs, seeking a new language to
describe what it perceives, refusing the one, objective,
rational, scientific world view as the only world view:
the South as the discovery of other cosmologies, as the
recovery of other knowledges that have been hidden,
submerged, silenced. The South as an 'insurrection of these
subjugated knowledges'

The South as history; the South as mystery

The South as the finding of new political paradigms,

inventing new political patterns, creating alternative
political imaginations: the South as the revelation of each
civilization in its own idiom: the South as conversations
between civilizations:

The South then as new universalisms

And in our searching for new understandings of the South,
it promises to bring to the world new meanings, new moorings.

It invites us to create a new imaginary
to birth a new cosmology;
The South then as new political imaginary (Kumar, 2005, pp. 165-166)

In the mid 1980s, I was invited to a conference on Peace and Serenity in Tokyo, organised by Prof. Yoshikazu Sakamoto. Ivan Illich and I were speakers on a panel. After I had spoken in a manner that I believed was a fairly reasoned and cogent manner, I received a note from Ivan which said, "we need to talk. A walk perhaps?' Flattered and not knowing what to expect, we stepped out for a short walk. What came from Ivan was a barrage of words, the gist of which was how stupid I was, unthinking and one-sided and dreary my presentation was! My memory of my reaction is that of a goldfish gulping, for he told me that my world and its analysis was akin to the small bowl. Circumscribed and limited by smallness, he went on to tell me that I had to step beyond certitudes that circumscribe and seek and imagine alternatives. To find paths in the forest....

Many, many years later I was at a conference in Cuernavaca, Mexico. I went to call on Ivan. My friend Sylvia Marcos, a feminist professor, engaged with the Zapatistas, arranged that meeting. I gave Ivan my thanks for introducing me to alternatives to mainstream thinking and the narratives they construct. Danger lies in accepting the logic that is manifest through seemingly self-evident axioms. I learned to go beyond the binaries set in query and critique, to query set dialogues, to find the root of the root. A manner of seeing that changed the questions we asked, changed paradigms, prising the dialectic from embedded master narratives.

My wondering that started with Ferrer saw me work with institutions and help in founding a few others.

Two decades on the planet. Before me lay opportunities a good education afforded. At a conference on Development, where the speaker was particularly vapid, I stepped out for a cup of coffee. Picking up my coffee, I went and sat at a table where a gentleman with a grey beard was already seated, sipping his coffee. In conversation that followed, I told him that I was enrolled in a PhD program on development at the University. I still remember his resounding laugh, and the words he spoke – "what will you do after that? Perhaps write books which will sit in libraries, which we will read. And then what?" Embarrassment overcame me. He scribbled on a piece of paper the bus I should take to reach him in Anantapur, where he worked, telling me that if I wanted to understand him, to come.

That man was Vincente Ferrer, an Italian Catholic priest, who had worked with landless agricultural labourers in Manmad in Maharashtra. As thanks for his long years of work, he was externed by the government of Maharashtra. Kasu Brahmananda Reddy, the then Chef Minister of Andhra Pradesh invited him to work with the bonded labour issue in his state. Ferrer chose Anantapur, for it was amongst the poorest and most backward districts of the state.

My mother was reluctant to let me go to a village in an unknown, far-off place. To visit an old man with a grey beard to understand what he was doing. She could not fathom why, and truth to be told neither could I. Save for a piqued curiosity at the gentle derision he displayed to my empathy that was expressing itself through engagement with academia and ideas, probing reasons for what drove large segments of my society to impoverishment and kept them there.

After a long bus journey, I landed at his doorstep at 8:30 in the morning. The man in the grey beard sat at breakfast surrounded by volunteers and acolytes and he was speaking while people around him listened. He asked me to join him on his visit into the village. I went with him and did so every day following. The two days that I had told my mother I would be away for had stretched.

One day a woman approached Vincente. Her sari was draped in a manner covering her entirely, from her head to her toes. She was holding a baby in her arms, which she begged Vincente to take from her. The woman had leprosy and the world being what it was in the 70s shunned people with the disease. Their lives hadn't changed in millennia. Vincente looked at me and said, "take the child". I looked blank. My upbringing, acculturation had ingrained a sense of cleanliness and hygiene that instinctively prevented me from touching and physically engaging with all that was considered 'unclean'. Leave alone a person suffering a disease like leprosy. Vincente repeated, "take the child". And I did. We took her home.

In that moment, in a small way, I understood exclusion, of borders and barriers, of breaching them through the simple act of touch, of holding, of empathy, that vaporises the distinctions that disadvantages fortune, health or other circumstances place us in.

I had left home telling my mother I would be back in two days. Little knowing that I would stay there for over two years. In the process, bidding goodbye to the promise of mainstream careers and more importantly always finding consciously and unconsciously the paths less travelled. Or even traversing pathless lands. Vincente's laughter at my planned life set me free forever from living charted paths.

Transgressions, deliberate and inadvertent, are a part of our living, our lives. Redressal and its manner defines who we are and how we see our societies and ourselves. Throughout our long histories, there has been a blindness to what happens to half of us, the women. Their stories are sub-texts, appendages and footnotes to stories and histories. In modern times, ancient perceptions resulting in age old crimes finding newer and more efficient methods of perpetration, exacerbate the wrongs women suffer. When societies recognise these crimes and evils as they are, the approach to resolution remains steeped in the dominant paradigm. To truly feel, even before justice can be delivered, there has to be a feminisation of perception. Including the heart with the head. Replacing retribution in justice delivery with reparation. From which a reconciliation is possible, healing wounds. Healing individuals and communities. Understanding, through which those who inflict suffering can never do so again, for they have lived in the skin of the sufferer in the process of resolution.

Let me tell you another story:

This story began a long time ago:
with our grandmothers, then their grandmothers, and their grand grandmothers
stories that have been told over the ages over and over and over again!
her-stories, vibrant, verbal herstories of pain and suffering, of survival and
hope of tears and laughter.
And yet, always there was time for celebration, the song, the dance, the
image, the poem, the dream and always, always, the story.

> I would have liked to have told you the story
> of a nightingale who died
> I would have liked to tell you the story
> had they not slit my lips[4]
>   - Samih al-Qasim (1983)

Fragments of the story are beginning to be told through the slit lips, through
the silences.[5]
Women are finding their voices in their anguish, their anger making what
has been understood as private sorrows into public crimes.
Violence against women has been seen as personal violence, domestic problems, and therefore, individualized and privatized.
But these are crimes against half of humanity, these are violations of the
right to be human.

The frames that have defined the institutions and instruments of justice
have been drawn, blinded to and mindless of gender; and have been based
on the legitimated discrimination and degradation of women.
Women have been denied, dispossessed, de-valued, excluded, erased.
Women have been made invisible.

It is to this invisibility, to this disappearing of women- foeticide, infanticide,
dowry killings, rape, that we must speak,
Inviting the women to tell their stories,
In their idiom, in their tongue.

We invite you through the Courts of Women, they invite us to write new

pages in history, to break new ground to cross patriarchal lines that have
forbidden us to speak our truths: to break the silence that enshrouds the
violence. We must interrupt all that has invisibilised us, to re-tell history, to
reclaim the power of memory, the power of voice,
the Courts of Women invite us to write another history:
For we must remember: the ways we have survived, the seeds we have
kept, the medicinal herbs we have grown, the threads we have woven,
the knowledges written on our skins as we explore knowings deep in our
consciousness, truths that we know and must be known, stories that must
be told
we are the storytellers of our times.
The Courts of Women begin to speak truth to power, speaking to those who
use, misuse, abuse power, yet also, speaking truth to those who are power-
less- women, dalits, adivasis, marginalized and oppressed peoples, people
with no power,
the nameless, the faceless, the rightless.

The Courts of Women are a journey of the peripheries of power, where power
itself is being re-woven from the fabric of powerlessness. From the learning
and engagement with hearts and minds moved by the suffering around them
- people who worked, the comfort women from the wars of the 20th century,
from those who survived nuclear testing on far flung Pacific islands, losing
health and homes, to blockades that devastated health systems from Cuba to
Iraq, to the indigenous people run over by an idiom that trivialised millennia of what they considered sacred, ethnic cleansing in Cambodia, Rwanda,
Bosnia, racism across the globe - the list is endless! The Courts of Women was
construed as a space in which these crimes were perceived and articulated
through the eyes of women. Women as the primary site in which this oppression and resistance played out. It is constructed as a narrative where the
woman is the primary narrator from whose story we build the larger linkages
that make these specific crimes come to pass.

Our hinged lives turn and revolve around people and events. 1990 was a year
my life just didn't turn but literally came apart. My husband, partner, fellow
dreamer, my companion, left me. Tragically. My rooted work with the Centre
for Informal Education and Development Studies and Vimochana continued,
but larger events created predicaments that necessitated a move to North

Africa. I was invited by members of the board of an organisation whose president was Nelson Mandela, to work with them. I was there for twenty long years. Years in which I met amazing people - Madiba, Desmond Tutu, Fatima Meer, Winnie Mandela, Albertina Sisulu - women and men who held dreams and nurtured an engaged peace in the face of violence - mindless, sadistic, institutionalised and casual. An entire range, but they held to the notion that an embracing, engaging peace could liberate a land and its people from hate and prejudice.

Knowledge creation in modern times grows at a breathless pace. It goes in all conceivable directions and the underpinnings that propel research and discovery are diverse. From the logic of sheer capitalism to the idealism of libertarian free existence, all reasons drive the quest for creations to make life better either for profit of a few, or the selfless sacrifices made by many for the greater common good. Then there are keepers of ancient lore, knowledges that have recessed to the edges of consciousness, but thrive in small spaces restricted by prejudices that modernity brings with it, as the sole arbiter of what is 'logical', 'progressive'. Culling from the past that which can illuminate the present with understanding the diverse strands that make human thinking and evolution rooted in the innateness of fair and just, we engage with the present to build futures that can make violence in all its forms redundant. This engagement with the new and emerging, with the old and sustaining, we call, 'The Open University'.

The Open University is not just subversive, because we have found that paradigms that are erected shepherd even our resistance and understanding in pre-determined paths. Imagination to challenge these age-old wrongs in manners that question the logic that enables perpetration. That redressal cannot be through denying victimhood by state and society taking the place of the sufferer. That vengeance perpetuates all that is wrong from inception. That reparation and healing can come only through recognition of the primary source that makes the violence and crime possible. The Open University is that space that makes engagement of these ideas possible. It invites the experts and the wise, the student and the pilgrim, seekers in the quest to make a convivial world a possibility in our lifetimes, in our communities, in our societies, in our places of learning.

Chiapas has been a geographical location that has moved from Mexico to vivify imagination beyond boundaries that are cartographic, or didactic. The movement against a State, translated into questions that addressed the very roots of resistance of who the oppressors were, who the oppressed - through seeing with the heart rather than with the head. From the extreme resistance of armed revolution, the obverse of unjust governance to understanding the eternal cycles of life, livelihoods, land, ecology, environment, gender - of finding a way and sense to all of it. They challenged pre-set, pre-conceived notions of power, its exercisers and challengers, through three little words, "Asking, We Walk". There is an element of the nomadic, the most ancient of the hunter-gathering populace we all descend from. Travel light, carry no more than you need. It applies as much to ideologies as to the materiality of existence.

The Open University in its own way articulates the deep principles that lie in those three words.

Asking, We Walk

The threats to imagination that Artificial Intelligence poses by intruding upon all the faculties that make imagination possible. Manipulation that is subtle. Shepherding individuals as well as communities into silos of servitude, exploiting them for ends determined by corporations and states. Mazes whose walls are crafted from the vulnerabilities of our lives, from the exploitation of weaknesses and frailties that make us human.

We are human because centred in perception, an ability to see with the heart. It implies bringing to bear accumulated experiences, individual and collective, to sieve and sift with sensitivity what we see, hear, live. The head brings logic to the table. Logic and reason attempt to distance themselves from emotion so that decision making, courses of action that we take factor the most sensible way, but not always the most sensitive path. Machine learning is steeped in logic. Emotion can be imitated, but it cannot replace human empathy. A future where the head and heart are completely divorced stares at us. A fearful possibility that science led development is walking all of us somnambulists.

Cyber-crimes are imagined as the use of technology to conduct the conventional criminal activity. However the manner in which technology has breached homes small and big, our minds, our lives, are without defence against diffusion and manipulation by interests counter to our well-being.

So, what can I say about this journey that has been such an adventure, a song that I have sung to the sun, to the river, to the mountain, at bedsides, at battle grounds, in sites of births, at sites of goodbyes. Coalesced in me are despair and hope, as I mentioned in the beginning. I was not born with the insights that accrued to me in this quest, this vagabondage. I have been a spiritual seeker, a Marxist, a feminist, an activist, an itinerant scholar, student, teacher, a pilgrim.

On a pilgrimage in the world, in my time. Guided by stars at night and shadows in the day. In truly dark times, pathless lands lit by the lights of empathy and compassion, light all of us which we carry within us, but seldom ask for its illumination. Friends who became family and family who became more than friends, all who held me and carried me and continue to carry me, in my time that remains.

I started writing this piece on my days as a member of the International Peace Research Association and the Peace Education Commission. Peace was and is, a defining quest in my life. However, I have understood that there are many kinds of peace. This journey is an engagement in finding that peace that fulfils and animates our worlds.

different and together.

Endnotes

1) Mazisi Kunene, South African poet.

2) This passage, as well as several others in this chapter, are adapted from the author's 2005 essay: *South wind: Towards a new political imaginary* (approximately pp. 184-185).

3) This story is adapted from the author's 2005 essay: *South wind: Towards a new political imaginary* (pp. 165-166).

4) Samih al-Qasim, Palestinian poet.

5) The following 4-5 paragraphs are adapted from the author's 2005 essay: *South wind: Towards a new political imaginary* (p. 191).

References

al-Qasim, S. (1983). Slit lips and other poems. *Index on Censorship*, 12(6), 30-32. https://doi.org/10.1080/03064228308533636 (Original work published 1983)

Kumar, C. (2005). South wind: Towards a new political imaginary. In Waller, M.R. & Marcos, S. (Eds.), *Dialogue and difference: Feminisms challenge globalization* (165–199). Palgrave Macmillan.

Kunene, M. (1982). Congregation of the story-tellers at a funeral of Soweto children. In Kunene, M., *The ancestors & the sacred mountain: Poems*. Heinemann Educational.

Thornton, L. (1991). *Imagining Argentia*. Bantam.

Part VI: Looking Ahead

Chapter 31
Peace Education in a Pluriverse

Magnus Haavelsrud

Preamble: *Children don't come into this world knowing how to fight and to hate. They learn how to hate. They don't come into the world as racists. They can learn to be peace lovers. They can learn to embrace all people.* (Archbishop Tutu, 1999)[1]

In this chapter I aim to explore some concepts that might be suitable in any context when searching for pathways to peace. This search, I claim, depends upon finding out in each context about violence to be transformed and peace to be maintained. And as Archbishop Tutu points out, peace in its many aspects is learned. Ways and means to promote this learning, and a critique of the barriers not only to peace but to new learning and action, are part of the search.

Peace education has been considered a tool for developing a new universalism in which diversity and difference among contexts is recognized as important in learning and building peace. My exploration here begins with an examination of this new universalism – recently called the pluriverse (Escobar, 2019). Different contextual conditions are seen as important in the formation of worldviews, beliefs and values. In order for better communication to take place among different parts of the pluriverse, the next issue explored is communicative and cognitive justice, vital so that respect for all knowledge forms and traditions be achieved. In communications among contexts where there is strong inequality and even structural violence, I then consider the different consciousness of victims and perpetrators and the implications as well as ways for constructive dialogue in non-antagonistic conflicts. Consciousness-raising in its various forms leads me to examine the interdependence of structural and cultural perspectives – an interdependence that may form a synthesis in what has been called *cultural structures*. The remainder of my chapter explores the possible role of unbounded organizing. Finally, I connect these threads in the concept of a comprehensive peace education.

A New Universalism

Contextually rooted peace education goes back to the early days peace education was founded in the international peace research movement (see for instance Borrelli, 1972, 1993; Wulf, 1974).[2] d´Souza (1985) wrote that peace education is a tool in developing a new universalism from within and below. She called for a *new universalism* in which the oppressed peoples of the world participate in the transformation of their own societies - and even participate in the creation of a new world order! She writes about a *new universalism which respects the plurality of different societies, of their philosophies, their ideologies, traditions and cultures.* Her call resonates with Tortosa (2019, pp. 9-12) in his claim that *maldevelopment* is a result of what is intended to be development. Modernity has not grasped this concept of a new universalism and is rooted in "the idea that we all live in a single, now globalized world, and critically, the idea of science as the only reliable truth and harbinger of ´progress'"(Kothari et al., 2019, p. xxii).

The new universalism, however, searches for a world in unity – *but securely based in diversity.* Contrary to the so-called "rules-based" international order of today referred to in current political discourse, this search does not start with unity dictated from above, but from a diversity in constant creation from below. This evolving diversity can be greatly helped by an *evolving unity which supports an evolving diversity.* Unity and diversity depend upon each other and this *interdependence* can be an instrument for creating or developing more unity in diversity - or should it rather be called more diversity in unity? In analyzing this interdependence, it is necessary to consider how the life world is related to political, cultural and economic conditions at regional, national and world levels. Reality as experienced in the life world is in constant relation to realities outside the experiential world. *These relations* may be a most important set of contextual conditions to be accounted for both before and during peace education interventions. And ongoing evaluation of transformations achieved in a context is a valuable source for decisions on how to continue the process of peace education.

Contextual Conditions

A context is not an isolated unit. A most important characteristic of a context may be its *relations* to what is outside the everyday life in the here and now. Reality as experienced in the life world is in constant relation to realities outside including the life world of ´others´ as well as structural characteristics of institutions and governance in, for instance, politics, economy and culture.

The relations to what is outside the lived experiences in the life world context are significant for understanding how human beings are products of society and how society is a human product and also understood as an objective reality. Berger and Luckman (1984) discuss these processes as internalization, objectification and externalization. The human enterprise of constructing reality (externalization) is influenced by the role of knowledge, they claim. And this is exactly what peace education aims at! But a task in peace education is also to prevent internalization and attempts at forming the human being in support of structural violence.

I find the works of Pierre Bourdieu of great help when he explains how a person´s disposition to perceive and act (habitus) is influenced by the composition and volume of what is called symbolic and economic capital in his or her socialization. This explanation of how the human being internalizes contextual preferences is countered by the externalization of the human being when modifying or even revolutionizing contextual rules that have been influencing the formation of their habitus. This means that habitus and objective reality seeks harmony and that both may transform in the process of adapting to each other.

This *process* of harmony seeking, however, is often conflictual and may involve the three forms of direct, structural and cultural violence as discussed by Galtung (1996). It may be a challenging task to find nonviolent and peaceful methods of resistance by victims of violence. Perpetrators have all kinds of methods and resources at their disposal. In cases when nonviolent disobedience and non-cooperation on the part of the ruled is met with even more violence from the ruler it may turn into *violent* resistance/defense by the ruled. In any case violent struggles and disharmony carried out by both established power holders and opposing forces is part of the process of seeking harmony. The question is if this process leads to a harmony in which the privileges on the part of the ruler continue or whether the process leads to a reduction of inequalities as part of peace. This paper reflects on how peace education can contribute to conflict transformations in this process of harmony seeking by finding common ground of interest to both victims and perpetrators.

The weaker party may choose nonviolent ways of disobedience and non-cooperation in power struggles with rulers. Disassociation from the power of rulers may take the form of "silence which carries the message of power; it is the full stop between one category of discourse and another; it is the dislocation in the potential flow of discourse which is crucial to the specialization of any category", writes Bernstein (1996, p. 20). So gaining power by the marginalized means to remove or reduce the control of the powerful. It means stronger framing and classification in which ties to power are weakened. Realizing this, no wonder powerful rulers attend to communication technologies in creating obstacles for the ruled to withdraw in silence. Maybe withdrawal has become so difficult that disassociation and silence as a principle is outdated? If so, the *transcend method* (Galtung, 2000) is always available in seeking conflict transformations that may be in the interest of both ruler and ruled.

In peace education the purpose is transformation of violent cultures and structures towards a harmony built on peace. What is important is the realization that the human being in his or her cultural preferences may opt for harmony with structures of peace and oppose structures of violence. It is a question of challenging the status quo when habitus is strong enough to oppose structures of violence – whether that violence takes the form of bombs, occupations or indoctrination/propaganda. A combination of the three forms of direct, structural and cultural violence is quite common and history is full of examples of transformations that have taken place partly due to the contributions of strong individuals (notable examples are Mandela, Gandhi, Luther King etc …).

Communicative and Cognitive Justice

Communication among diverse parts of the pluriverse is essential for the continuous search for better understanding of the interdependencies among them. This communication needs sensitivity to what Pedro-Caranana et al. (2023) calls communicative justice. I regard *communicative justice* in the pluriverse as one condition for reaching what Visvanathan (1997) calls *cognitive justice:* all knowledge forms and knowledge traditions have a right to be *respected* not only in the culture where they originated but everywhere! Diversity developing from within and below contexts will strengthen the aim of safeguarding cognitive justice. In this view valid knowledge is not restricted to scientific knowledge produced by scientists, but *includes* knowledge from all livelihoods as expressed in the 10000 ethnicities that Elise Boulding (2000) wrote about. We are here talking about Indigenous Knowledge Systems (IKS) as discussed by Odora Hoppers (2002). The encounter and even possible integration of scientific knowledge with IKS becomes a most important task in the new universalism called the pluriverse. The meeting of knowledges produces new knowledge in which all cultures are invited to interact and contribute towards an evolving unity from below.

It is of utmost importance that everybody is *respected* as qualified to participate in ways of understanding contextual conditions - and to find out about the relations between conditions within a context and beyond it. Respect does not mean acceptance of all and oftentimes contradictory opinions. Respect implies, however, that all views are welcome in the search for a most valid analysis of contextual conditions. This means that worldviews, beliefs and values of any culture are important departure points for this analysis. Analysis of contextual conditions is therefore not the monopoly of outside the-context think tanks with their various metaphysics that might have few if any roots in contexts under study. Answers to what needs change – and what needs cultivation and maintenance – are to be found in respect of people´s identity rooted in their cultural traditions including worldviews and knowledge systems.

Let me give three examples where requirements of communicative and cognitive justice are lacking: 1) Recent history of colonization shows how wars, oppression, occupation, annexation and brutality in colonial practices was grounded in racism and dehumanization. The so-called 'savages' were marginalized – even killed – by the colonizers' so-called 'civilization'. 2) Nowadays, neoliberal market ideology creates universal standards imposed by hegemonic forces as evident in a recent tale told by Andes women in Latin America: Neoliberalism´s modern technologies and investors pose a constant danger to the traditional production of handicrafted garments and the skills, knowledge and meaningful ways of being, learning and knowing in which the garments are produced. This very culture might disappear along with the handicraft itself (Pedro-Caranana et al., 2023, ch 2). 3) The fact that we are all co-habitants in the pluriverse has not been learned by perpetrators who have carried out the recent brutality on an occupied people![3] When the perpetrator *also* is the occupier this example shows a grave breach of humanitarian law which requires an occupier to be the *protector* – not the *killer* - of the occupied.

Contrary to these three examples, communications *among* contexts in the pluriverse seeking unity in diversity are rooted in each culture´s self understanding. This within and below perspective is the starting point for communications among contexts as well as with external actors on - for instance national and international levels – including both governmental and civic actors.

Cultural Structures

In their discussion of *transformation by enlargement* Odora Hoppers and Richards (2012) view culture and structure in relation to each other and coin this relation as a *cultural structure.* When we consider the distinction between cultural and structural violence it may oftentimes be difficult to see the manifestation of each of these forms of violence as one may be entangled with the other. Then the concept of *cultural structure* may denote this interdependence.

Peace education has over the years contributed to the analysis of contextual conditions. How micro life worlds and macro structures influence each other is central when considering these relations. Borrelli (1972), for instance, based his interventions in the Neapolitan context in a socio-political analysis of the sub-proletarian reality in that city. He found that the feudal political system at that time was *interdependent* with the sub-proletarian clan culture. And his peace action interventions were based in his research that called for strengthening the sub-proletarian capacity to participate in structural changes. And an important part of that structure was exactly the clan culture that was being exploited in the political system of the city. Here we have an early example of cultural change through non-formal peace education aiming at structural change in a feudal system of governance (Haavelsrud, 2020, pp. 79-83).

Unbounded Organizing

Unbounded organizing began with Clodomir de Morais in Brazil in the 1960s with what he called Organization Workshops (OW) – later to be known as the *Large Group Capacitation Method*. The doctoral thesis of Gavin Andersson (2004) has traced its roots and its further enrichment in relation to Vygotskyian psychology including the Cultural Historical Activity Theory (CHAT). He has applied *unbounded organizing* in South African community development as cooperative action among large numbers of people (at least 80 and up to 1000). The main purpose of unbounded organizing is aligning across sectors to serve the common good (Andersson & Richards, 2015). De Morais complemented Freire´s work in that participants learned how to organize in large groups as compared to the cultural circles of less than a dozen participants that was Freire´s initial dialogue group. After the Brazilian coup in 1964 De Morais fled the country and conducted OW in FAO projects in several countries. The theory behind OW was fertilized in the work of the Labras in Chile when they:

> …introduced the work of Leont'ev, and most specifically his adage 'the object teaches'. Just as a football invites kicking, so do tools and materials, or plants, suggest activity.

> Leont'ev built on the achievement of Lev Vygotsky showing the linkage between mind and action, extending Vygotskian insights to the collective scale, looking at the activity and learning of large groups. Like Vygotsky he understood that mediational means affect the ways of acting on an object or towards an objective; worldviews, language, concepts, signs, tools and methods shape any action. (Richards & Andersson, 2022, paras. 25-26)

Consciousness

As noted in one of the examples above, some are both occupiers and perpetrators and inflict unspeakable violence directed at victims who go to sleep without knowing if and when a bomb shall be dropped – even upon your children! Even though there are pathways to peace in both the perpetrator context and in the victim context, the search for these pathways pose different challenges. We need the help of Paulo Freire in understanding the psychologies of both perpetrators and victims. He writes that the human being is *a subject whose historical task is to name and change the world*. Perpetrators disagree with this understanding when they dehumanize the other while praising themselves. The Tutsis in Rwanda were called cockroaches in radio programs in the genocide there. The Jews were seen as subhuman (Untermenschen) in Nazi Germany. An Israeli government figure talks of Palestinians as human animals. Dehumanization, writes Freire, shows a tendency to sadism because – referring to Erich Fromm - a basic characteristic of a sadistic person is to rule over and control the other by denying his or her freedom to be human.

Dehumanizing the other is contrary to treating the other as a subject. This task of recognizing the other as subjects aims at *widening and deepening consciousness* to make it possible to grasp the specific conditions in both the perpetrator and the oppressive context – as well as the relations between them.

Oppressed people have a great responsibility for their own liberation and emancipation, writes Freire. A condition might be for the oppressed to distance themselves from the oppressor – both physically and mentally – as the oppressor has a way of even forcing victims what to think of him/her. How to keep oppressors away by disassociation is well described and implemented by both Paulo Freire and Clodomir de Morais in their work in northeastern Brazil. Gandhi taught us about how to disobey and not cooperate with oppressors. Modern surveillance technologies may be a serious obstacle to disassociation by oppressed people from oppressors nowadays. Assuming that Orwellian society has not creeped into too many of the 10000 ethnicities, the power of cultural change may still be in the hands of people beyond the controls of outside rulers.

Even though the ruler may be in a position to impose both physical and structural violence, he or she may have difficulties in imposing his or her preferences in cultural violence. One way towards structural change is via cultural change as the two are interdependent in that changes in one cause change in the other. Reflecting and acting upon the relationship between physical, structural and cultural violence as it is manifested in the life world may indicate how cultural change may contribute to reduction in the other forms of violence (Galtung, 1996, 2000).

Concluding Remarks: Future Directions for Peace Education

As my aim in this chapter has been to identify ways and means to understand conditions for peace learning *in any kind of context* I have selected the search lights of communicative and cognitive justice, cultural structures, unbounded organizing and consciousness. Research has shown the importance of formal, informal and non-formal learning in political socialization (Haavelsrud, 2010, ch. 1). Informal learning takes place in the home and in the community. Non-formal sources of learning include mass and social media, religion and voluntary organizations. How the three relate to each other is of great significance in any part of the pluriverse.

When formal education does not allow for freedom of expression, peace education has to rely on informal and non-formal education. Boulding (1999) views the participation and influence of children upon parents and other adults as an important practice ground for making history. She found children to carry with them the potential for intuition and imagination so important for going beyond cognitive reasoning. She finds it very important that parents and adults take children seriously and listen to them (which is now a requirement in the Convention on the rights of the child). There is, however, a great variety of families in the thousands of ethnicities around the world. This variety in primary socialization is of great significance as noted also in the research by Basil Bernstein and Pierre Bourdieu when they both show how habitus and codes, respectively, are formed according to various social strata in modern societies. Recognizing indigenous knowledge systems, family life also varies according to livelihoods rather than according to social strata in modern societies.

Recognizing this pluriversal variety it seems that the building of a global civic culture for peace has to start with recognizing the family unit as a basic holder of knowledge. In the ongoing dialogue in building a global civic culture no existing culture may remain the same after the variety of modern and indigenous knowledge systems meet in exchange under the requirement of communicative and cognitive justice.

The alternative to box and even disciplinary thinking is transdisciplinarity. Integration of knowledge privileged by modernity and indigenous knowledge systems may find their place even in the academy (Soudien, 2019). But this integration depends upon the premise that everyday life as experienced and perceived by learners in context is up front in both pedagogy and research. Reardon (2021) has rendered a valuable contribution to such integration in her discussion of ways and means in what she calls a *comprehensive peace education*. She sees the confrontation with real life challenges as a source of knowledge in peace education. This view invites all contexts and livelihoods to reflect and act in interplay allowing visions, preferences and policies to emerge aiming at transforming reality. And evaluating changes of what has been obtained leads to a new confrontation with reality, she writes. These reflection and action cycles are grounded in the life experiences of all human beings in any part of the pluriverse. This cosmopolitan paradigm invites all human beings to work on the common task of searching for pathways to peace in their part of the pluriverse as they are confronting their realities and coming up with solutions to the way forward.

Endnotes

1) Tutu (1999). Archbishop Tutu also expressed his admiration for young people who contributed to the passing of anti-apartheid laws in the US Congress in this recording.

2) See also a dialogue about peace education among Adam Curle, Paulo Freire and Johan Galtung in Haavelsrud ed. (1975) and IPRA/PEC Newsletters *Archive UBIT/A-0303 on Peace Education*. Trondheim: Norwegian University of Science and Technology.

3) See: The 179-page report from Human Rights Watch: *Extermination and Acts of Genocide* and the 296-page report from Amnesty International on Israel's genocide against Palestinians entitled 'You Feel Like You Are Subhuman': Israel's Genocide Against Palestinians in Gaza, both published in December, 2024. In November 2024 the International Criminal Court ordered the arrest of the prime minister and defense minister of Israel for criminal acts against humanity and war crimes. In January 2024 The International Criminal Court wrote that it can be argued that Israel commits genocide in Gaza. An apartheid state exerts violence on all citizens – even the privileged - because *de jure* dehumanization makes even the peaceful complicit in various forms of physical, structural and cultural violence. It should not come as a surprise that peace education priority in an apartheid state is to get rid of it.

References

Andersson, G. & Richards, H. (2015). *Unbounded organizing in community.* Dignity Press.

Andersson, G. M. (2004). *Unbounded governance: a study of popular development organization.* Milton Keynes: Open University.

Bernstein, B. B. (1996). *Pedagogy, symbolic control and identity: theory, research, critique.* Taylor & Francis.

Borrelli, M. (1972). *Socio-political analysis of the sub-proletarian reality of Naples and lines of intervention for the workers of the center 1972/1973.* Available in Archive on Peace Education www.arkivportalen.no A-0303, Norwegian University of Science and Technology.

Borrelli, M. (1993). The context of peace education in the peripheries of Europe. In Haavelsrud, M. (Ed.), *Disarming: Discourse on violence and peace.* Arena.

Boulding, E. (2000). *Cultures of peace The hidden side of history.* Syracuse University Press.

D´Souza, C. K. (1985). *The reality, the rhetoric: The need for a new political culture.*

Unpublished manuscript for the UNESCO Teacher´s Handbook on Disarmament Education, Archive A-0303 on Peace Education in www.arkivportalen. no, Norwegian University of Science and Technology Library and UNESCO archives.

Escobar, A. (2018). *Designs for the pluriverse: Radical interdependence, autonomy, and the making of worlds*. Duke University Press.

Escobar, A. (2019). Civilizational transitions. In Kothari, A., Salleh, A., Escobar, A., Demaria, F. & Acosta, A. (Eds.), *Pluriverse: A post-development dictionary*. Tulika Books.

Galtung, J. (1996). *Peace by peaceful means: peace and conflict, development and civilization*. International Peace Research Institute/Sage Publications.

Galtung, J. (2000). *Conflict transformation by peaceful means (the Transcend Method): Participants' manual, trainers' manual*. United Nations.

Haavelsrud, M. (Ed.). (1975). *Education for peace: reflection and action*. IPC Science and Technology Press.

Haavelsrud, M. (2010). *Education in developments: Volume 2*. Shaker Publishing BV.

Haavelsrud, M. (2020). *Education in developments: Volume 3*. Arena.

Kothari, A., Salleh, A., Escobar, A., Demaria, F. & Acosta, A. (2019). Introduction. In Kothari, A., Salleh, A., Escobar, A., Demaria, F. & Acosta, A. (Eds.), *Pluriverse: A post-development dictionary*. Tulika Books.

Odora Hoppers, C. (2002). *Indigenous knowledge and the integration of knowledge systems: towards a philosophy of articulation*. New Africa Books.

Odora Hoppers, C. & Richards, H. (2012). *Rethinking thinking: Modernity's "other" and the transformation of the university*. University of South Africa.

Pedro-Caranana, J., Herrera-Huérfano, E. & Aalmanza, J.O. (Eds). (2023). *Communicative justice in the pluriverse: An international dialogue*. Routledge.

Reardon, B. (2021). *Comprehensive peace education: Educating for global responsibility*. Peace Knowledge Press.

Richards, H. & Andersson, G. (2022). *Why the world needs unbounded organizing.* Unbounded Academy. https://www.unboundedacademy.org.

Soudien, C. (2019). Testing transgressive thinking: The 'Learning through Enlargement' Initiative at UNISA. In Jansen, J. D. (Ed.), *Decolonisation in universities: The politics of knowledge.* Wits University Press.

Tortosa, J. M. (2019). Maldevelopment. In Kothari, A., Salleh, A., Escobar, A., Demaria, F. & Acosta, A. (Eds.), *Pluriverse: A post-development dictionary.* Tulika Books.

Tutu D. (1999). Recording of founding panel of the Global Campaign for Peace Education, Hague Appeal for Peace. Archive UBIT/A-0303 on Peace Education. Trondheim: Norwegian University of Science and Technology.

Visvanathan, S. (1997). *A carnival for science: essays on science, technology and development.* Oxford University Press.

Wulf, C. E. (1974). *Handbook on peace education.* International Peace Research Association.

Epilogue

Robin Burns

I believe it would be arrogant to attempt to summarise the varied chapters here. They represent so many contexts, approaches, experiences and actions that are all part of the work which can perhaps fall under the label 'peace education' in its many forms. As argued in many chapters, it is an expanding concept that involves the promotion of human rights, justice, conflict transformation, cognitive justice, empathy and connection not just with our communities, with the 'other' but also with nature. So in this final chapter I want to present the work of two of the members of PEC who were formative for my attempted understanding, the late Sanàa Osseiran, from Lebanon, and Corinne Kumar, of India. I have chosen these because Sanàa worked for peace in the Middle East during one of the periods of exceptional violence involving her homeland, Lebanon. And while issues underlying the ongoing conflicts in the Middle East are also found in the situation in India, and Africa where Corinne has worked from a base in Morocco (as in many other contributors' contexts), her balanced assessment of where we stand is, I believe, a hopeful challenge for future directions in peace work.

Sanàa Osseiran was the IPRA representative to UNESCO. Not long before her untimely death, she was concurrently directing two projects in collaboration with UNESCO. One was training trainers in conflict resolution in Lebanon, as part of UNESCO's Culture of Peace Action Programme in cooperation with International Alert. The other was a United Nations World project for cultural development, under the title "Cultural symbiosis in Al-Andalus". The latter was to provide curriculum materials about a period on the Iberian Peninsula when there were stretches of peace between the Muslim rulers and the Christian and Jewish co-inhabitants. (Recently checking this, I found 2024 comments in Wikipedia suggesting this peaceful co-existence is now disputed by some historians). She also published a handbook of teaching and resource material on conflict resolution, education for human rights, peace and democracy that was published by UNESCO. This work was shared with several members of IPRA / PEC and with Lebanese educators. Sanàa was involved in the 1990 UNESCO International Conference on peace-building and Development in Lebanon, a significant and unique event as a collaboration between a UN agency and an academic non-governmental organisation (IPRA) in dealing with a conflict area. Sanàa authored the final report of the conference, while Magnus Haavelsrud, Robert Aspeslagh and Celina Garcia, all found in this volume, were involved with it (Osseiran, 1990). It was hailed as a future example of coordination between international and national NGOs to work with the UN system. In his report to IPRA from the conference, Haavelsrud considers the possibilities for finding political rather than violent solutions by bringing NGOs together.

In her contribution to the 1996 Burns & Aspeslagh anthology she posed as a first question: "Can people subjectively involved in a conflict talk about peace education? Does the perception of the futility of violence emerge from within the antagonistic parties, from outside, or from the combined efforts of both? Do the causes of these wars emanate only from local elements, or are they likened to extraneous factors?" (Osseiran, 1996, p. 237). These are questions that contributors here have also asked, pointing over and over again to the combination of factors. Haavelsrud brings these issues together in his discussion of contexts in the pluriverse.

As a former journalist, it is therefore not surprising that Sanàa wrote of the role of the media as an "indirect educator", her examples indicating how reports of changes in the Middle East situation affected opinions towards the different parties. In turn, the media context reflects both historical and current information, beliefs and perceptions due to the circumstances in different contexts, e.g. the experience of the French with Algerians leading to projecting those images onto Muslim Arabs; attitudes of Americans and Japanese in the study were likewise tainted by local/national issues and by the stage of the war in Lebanon (Osseiran, 1996, pp. 238-239).

Her conclusion is that:

> Peace education should be the task of each curious and courageous hu-
> man being, curious enough to probe further into information given to
> him or her, and courageous enough to criticise the standard views about
> a given culture or a given situation...Moreover it is crucial to relate the
> economic and strategic interests to local realities, and to question why
> these particular countries, or certain other countries in the world, are go-
> ing through these wars. Once an overall picture is constructed, the nec-
> essary links are connected, and contacts and encounters are encouraged,
> then perhaps peace education can be in a position to resist violence. (Os-
> seiran, 1996, pp. 247-248)

Following this challenge, I think it is appropriate to repeat these lines from
Corinne Kumar's chapter:

> The horizon shrinks as my own time that I have walked this world seems
> increasingly limited. Even as wars of greater intensity are waged, wreak-
> ing destitution and misery on the weakest amongst us, and hope seems
> at an end, some small sparks of humane action rooted in empathy and
> fairness, keep alight the promise that what is human in us can never be
> completely extinguished. I know when the time comes for me to go, I
> leave a world that has great injustice written into its ways of being, into
> its way of seeing, but also a world where through resistance and persua-
> sion new ways of convivial living are possible.

> So, what can I say about this journey that has been such an adventure, a
> song that I have sung to the sun, to the river, to the mountain, at bedsides,
> at battle grounds, in sites of births, at sites of goodbyes. Coalesced in me
> are despair and hope, as I mentioned in the beginning. I was not born
> with the insights that accrued to me in this quest, this vagabondage. I
> have been a spiritual seeker, a Marxist, a feminist, an activist, an itinerant
> scholar, student, teacher, a pilgrim.

> On a pilgrimage in the world, in my time. Guided by stars at night and
> shadows in the day. In truly dark times, pathless lands lit by the lights of
> empathy and compassion, light all of us which we carry within us, but
> seldom ask for its illumination. Friends who became family and family

who became more than friends, all who held me and carried me and continue to carry me, in my time that remains.

I started writing this piece on my days as a member of the International Peace Research Association and the Peace Education Commission. Peace was and is, a defining quest in my life. However, I have understood that there are many kinds of peace. This journey is an engagement in finding that peace that fulfils and animates our worlds. Different and together. (Chapter 30)

We invite you, the reader, to join us and participate in that journey.

References

Osseiran, S. (1990). *Peace-building and development in Lebanon. A report.* IPRA and UNESCO.

Osseiran, S. (1996). Peace education as protest and resistance against marginalization and eurocentrism: peace education in a violent context: the Middle East Wars as a caste study. In Burns, R.J. & Aspeslagh, R. (1996). *Three decades of peace education around the world* (237-251). Garland.

Appendices

A Global Strategy of Communication and Consciousness Raising in Various Local Settings[1]

Introduction

Our purpose is to help change world reality, recognizing ourselves as subjects whose vocation it is to change reality, i.e., the exploitative system in which we are all partaking. This purpose, however, puts us in a dilemma, for we must find ways in which to survive in a system while at the same time asking to transform it. In this regard we must accept and reject at the same time. Our purpose is to find a strategy for action in which the right balance is struck between acceptance and rejection.

The characteristics of the new world system we have in mind when deciding on the strategy include the following: participation in decision making at all levels; social justice, i.e. the realization of human rights; elimination of violence, both direct and structural; ecological balance; and economic well-being. We believe that these values can only be achieved in a world in which political power is decentralized to people in their real contexts, so that each grouping of people should become economically and culturally self-reliant and politically independent.

The following strategy, then, purports to be a global strategy for communicators located in the four major categories of the present imperialistic system. These categories are:

1. The centre of the industrialized nation
2. The periphery of the industrialized nation
3. The centre of the non-industrialized nation

4. The periphery of the non-industrialized nation.

It assumes different degrees of overt acceptance and rejection of the system, which is to be changed, and it assumes that individuals in each of the four categories have a task to fulfill in breaking down the system and creating a new one. It assumes also, however, that everybody involved in the strategy, regardless of overt acceptance and rejection, covertly feels that his/her loyalty is to the poor and oppressed and to the new world order, and not to the present exploitative system.

General Strategy

A general strategy of consciousness raising in the present world should comprise a set of simultaneous and complementary actions taking place in all areas of the structure of imperialism. In some but not necessarily all cases, these actions will be linked by direct cooperation between one area and another. This requires that we identify potential points of linkage and established criteria for complementarity.

A specific diagnosis must be made of the following factors for each area: substructures and processes to be changed; the potential agents of change; obvious and potential obstacles to change. This diagnosis must include the psychological as well as the structural aspects of societies concerned.

In addition to this diagnosis an analysis has to be made of the most appropriate processes for conscientization and the most effective channels of communication. These should be determined mainly by the specific content of the message, the substance of the action, and the values and perceptions of those whom we want to engage or reach.

Five ground rules of the general strategy are as follows.

First, action should be of a wide variety, so as to take advantage of every opportunity, and to provide for a flexible approach capable of adapting to changes in specific circumstances, for example change of government, economic trauma, natural catastrophe, etc. The communication process should not be centralized. The plan should be in all possible directions, inputs should come from all areas and single-source dependency should be avoided, in order to lessen the risk of repression and cultural imperialism. In other words, the mechanics and processes should be not only as effective as possible but also consistent with the goal-value attuned to a "global movement," not "world organization".

Second, each person in the communication project should think of herself as an agent of change, and also as a resource and potential model of the new values. How can we make ourselves more effective agents? How can our lives demonstrate the desirability and viability of the new value system? These are crucial questions for strategy planning. An example would be changing our own work situations to non-hierarchical organisations, thus providing a concrete model of a new set of human relations. As persons we should also solidify our individual contacts through concrete actions of cooperation and bearing witness, even if only symbolical, to solidarity with the peripheries. We must think of all areas of our personal lives, families, social relations as well as political and professional environments, as possible areas of consciousness raising.

Third, all actions should be judged on their potential to change the structures. In the short range, actions that affect substructures may be constructive, but complementary actions in other substructures must be undertaken as well to synergize efforts towards the longer range total change of the macrostructure.

Fourth, actions are to be judged by their ability to change emotional structures in human relations. Whereas the eco-political structures are more readily visible, and therefore specific actions more easily planned, the socio-emotional structures are to a large extent "invisible", as they are seen by almost none outside the dominated groups. They are perhaps the most insidious aspects of Western cultural imperialism, as can be realized through our experience with racism and sexism, and our struggles (both internal and external) in communication.

The prototype of the structure to be dismantled here is the Male Market Manager (MMM), who himself requires liberation from his burdens of authority and suppression of those human attributes which do not fit the model. Such a liberation process can be planned by polarizing the attributes valued by the model and those devalued (i.e., female, accommodating, service oriented, etc.). The MMM needs to move from theoretical to concrete, from logical, sequential analysis to intuitive thinking, emphasizing discontinuity and contradiction; to see dependency as sometimes humanely integrating and independence as sometimes alienating; to accommodate changing reality in present and future contexts, rather than holding to static structures, be they the conservative elements of the present or ideologically prescribed future contexts. He/she must move from ambitious, conforming and competitive modes of behavior to creative and solidarity affirming behavior. We must recognize that there is a bit of the MMM in all of us.

Fifth, to undertake actions, we need to be aware of objective conditions, affective reactions, and the mental change which may come from the action. These mental changes may lead to change in praxis and ultimately to change in the objective reality from which the action started. To engage persons in the change process we must take into account that the specific political position of any individual is the result of contradictory forces in his/her context as perceived by the individual. This perception is conditioned by the external imposition of "what constitutes truth" on one side and by the psychic constitution of the individual on the other side. The psychic constitution is in return influenced by the social structure on the micro and macro levels. A global strategy for consciousness raising must, therefore, take this into account. This means that a dialectical relationship must exist between the contradictions. This dialectic is best achieved through dialogical media in which the objective contradictions and the perceptions of these are gradually exposed to the participants in the learning process. In practical terms this means on one side that shocking exposé of contradictions can counteract the conscientization process. On the other side, it could mean that one-sided attention to the psychic constitution of the individual would also counteract the process. Consequently, the right balance must come through active participation in dialogue.

In planning the general strategy, we must determine which new points of linkage must be joined and which old points must be broken. For the first part we believe a set of constructive cooperative links between and among Peripheries must be set up reinforcing the potential strength coming from recognition of their common interests and dissipating their competition and antagonism that is imposed by the exploitative division of peripheries originated in the Centre of the Centre. Another important new link should be established between the Periphery of the Centre and the Periphery of the Periphery. Each needs to become aware of the ways in which they are commonly manipulated by the Centre and find points on which co-operative efforts could result in moving the structures toward greater symmetry and equity.

Another important potential link is between those pockets of the Centre now moving toward the new value system, for example, the International Peace Research Association (IPRA), and the Peripheries. This is most essential for purposes of security (in some cases legitimation) and for access to resources and communication channels (media and established educational structures). Likewise, the present links between Centres which reinforce their interests as opposed to the Peripheries must be broken. The strategists must seek modes of dispelling their fears of the new value system, i.e., counter-penetration of ideas.

In determining which actions are to be taken in which sphere, two factors must be considered, power (resources) and mobility. What needs to be moved where and who has the greatest capacity to move it?

Conclusion

The consciousness-raising mechanism here may be set into motion by confrontation of alternative theories and conflicting value structures, by recognizing and dealing with emotional reality and nonverbal communication, by the necessity to provide concrete human experiences to illustrate intellectual abstractions. The tensions exposed in such a process are in many respects those with which we have struggled during these past days at Västerhaninge.

This GLOBAL STRATEGY represents for the Consciousness-Raising Group a conversion of those tensions into a new form of energy, a positive force through which each of us can maximize our potentialities and catalyze each other within the context of a political and emotional community working together to realize the new values. We value our individual experiences which come together in our mutual conscientization as a group, and we appreciate the catalytic force provided by IPRA in bringing all of us together in this Seminar.

Endnotes

1) Originally published in the IPRA Newsletter available in archive on peace education https://arkivportalen.no/entity/no-NTNU_arkiv000000037626 and also included as chapter 3 in: Burns, R. J. & Aspeslagh, R. (Eds.). (1996). *Three decades of peace education around the world: An anthology.* Garland.

Appendix 2
Bylaws of PEC

1. The Peace Education Commission (PEC) is established to conduct the education activities of IPRA.

2. The purposes of PEC are to facilitate international cooperation between educators, peace researchers and activists toward more effective and widespread peace education, to engage in activities that will facilitate education about the causes of war and injustices as well as conditions for peace and justice. To this end PEC shall undertake, sponsor or support educational projects within schools as well as out of school through close cooperation between researchers and educators at all levels, and where appropriate, with other peace organisations, especially research and education agencies.

3. PEC will engage in various activities, such as:

- organizing courses and conferences on peace education;

- assisting and initiating peace education activities in different countries and in other international organizations, where interest exists among educators, activists, community leaders and scholars;

- encouraging publication of articles on peace education in research, educational and scholarly journals;

- directing the attention of researchers to aspects of peace education that might require further investigation and cooperating with them in research;

- undertake, sponsor and support educational materials development, as well as teaching learning methods required by peace education.

4. PEC shall review its activities at the IPRA General Conference held biannually.

5. A Council shall be elected to assist in carrying out the activities of PEC, and to advise and assist the Executive Committee of PEC. The PEC Council shall consist of not more than 15 members, at least eight of which are practicing or experienced educators. Members shall serve two years. The PEC Council shall represent as far as possible the different geographical regions of the world. Members of the Council shall be elected by the IPRA General conference. A quorum is 10 members.

6. The Executive Committee shall consist of not more than five members in addition to the Executive Secretary. The committee members are elected from the PEC Council members at the IPRA General Conference.

7. An Executive Secretary of PEC shall be elected for two years by the plenary of the IPRA General Conference. The Executive Secretary is responsible for the conduct of day-to-day activities of PEC. He or she will consult with the PEC Executive Committee as far as practical and shall represent PEC in the name of the Executive Committee. The Secretary shall not serve more than two terms.

Full text of the Last Nobel Peace Prize Nomination to Johan Galtung in 2024: The Time has Long Since Come.[1]

Now the world is arming itself. Armament, more military equipment and more modern military technology are seen as necessary to prevent war. Within this mindset, war rages, destroying all meaningful, creative work for millions of people. Warnings and constructive signals are being sent out by the UN system, from NGOs and others. Alfred Nobel also saw the prevention of war differently. He wanted to stimulate disarmament, not armament, with his prize. Inspired by Bertha von Suttner (Peace Prize 1905) and other peace activists, he saw the possibility of new ways of acting. Active peace work can promote the fraternity of nations and prevent war and be peace-making in major or minor conflicts, Nobel believed. Therefore, he wanted to stimulate peace advocates, people who creatively and systematically work to understand how conflicts can be transformed into dynamic and non-violent cooperation on real problems.

The Norwegian Nobel Committee can use its signal power to award a Peace Prize to Johan Galtung, one of the most worthy candidates ever proposed for the prize. The Nobel Committee unfortunately failed to award the Peace Prize to Mahatma Gandhi, one of history's most innovative peace advocates, who fought against British imperialism through nonviolence and civil disobedience. Now the committee still has a chance to award the prize to 93-year-old Johan Galtung, an innovator like Gandhi, a theorist and peace practitioner who has dedicated his entire life to this work. It is no exaggeration to say that he started modern peace studies and, through tireless work for half a century, contributed to making this study a respected academic discipline in universities all over the world. Almost all good conflict resolution work in our time – by diplomats and negotiators of all kinds – is influenced by Galtung's work and methods and the tradition he represents. Here are reasons why he is a worthy and important winner in 2024:

Building New Knowledge about Peace, Conflict and Violence. Broad-based Dissemination and Application of Knowledge

Nobel wanted to stimulate science that brings humanity forward, and the four prizes awarded in Sweden reward outstanding science. For the Peace Prize, the will placed the greatest emphasis on practical work for peace and disarmament. But Galtung has also created a broad and easily understandable theoretical and methodological basis for practical peace work. The research has been inspired across disciplines: Galtung's thoughts on the prevention of violence at different levels are inspired by medicine, social research, psychology, pedagogy, mathematics and linguistics - and, as the cosmopolitan he is, by world religions and what he calls "deep cultures".

Fundamentally, it is to understand conflicts as something natural in human interaction, and violence as the smoke signal that signals a conflict in which all parties are about to lose. In order to resolve a conflict, it must be reshaped, 'transformed' into a win-win situation by peaceful means. Being able to talk meaningfully with each other is important in this work, and a skill that can make everyday life better for everyone. Inspired by the African term 'sabona' – Zulu for 'I see you' – his conflict theory is adapted for both children and adults who practice developing skills in conflict transformation. And by spreading such skills among the population, it can also become more natural to use the skills in more or less serious, national and international conflicts. Galtung instilled that in conflicts we must be prepared not to find the truth, but truths. The first commandment in mediation is to spend time gaining knowledge about the parties in a conflict, their culture, history, despair, needs and demands. Knowledge is a prerequisite for empathy for both parties, which in turn is a prerequisite for awakening the necessary trust before any proposals for a solution are brought to the table.

Understanding Inequality as a Basis for Conflict, and Nuanced Interpretation of the Concept of Violence

The enormous poverty in large parts of the world is a source of despair and conflict and has made development aid important in international politics. Here too, Galtung has been involved in terms of theory. It is not about development in the singular, which means that the Western world creates the whole world in its image, but developments, in the plural. Development must take place from the standpoint and premises of individual societies. Dialogue and respect for "the other" are among the means for peace. Galtung has also created the fruitful concept of "structural violence", where social and political institutions prevent people from having their basic needs met. "Cultural violence" can also contribute to this. War is the extreme form of "direct violence". Structural and cultural violence can create an environment of deep insecurity that increases the risk of direct violent conflict, ultimately leading to war and civil war. In war, everyone loses, while knowledge of how conflicts can be transformed can lead to win-win situations and the prevention or cessation of violence.

Conflict Transformation as Practical Peace Work

Galtung's 'Transcend method' shows the way to how the theory can work in practice. The UN's 'Disaster management training programme' uses a practical manual written by Galtung, and the method has been tested in numerous intra- and international conflicts. He has authored more than a hundred books and mediated in more than fifty conflicts internationally. Pedagogically designed training courses are held in many places in the world, at universities and under the auspices of institutions and voluntary organisations. Future conflict solvers get to try their hand at intense group work where creativity is challenged in the work of bridge building. The challenges do not end because one party 'wins' or a temporary compromise is reached.

The Peacemaker

Nobel had a peace policy idea, and wanted to use the prize for "peacemakers" who "...have worked most or best for the fraternization of nations and the abolition or reduction of standing armies and ...spread peace congresses." Galtung has worked for peace throughout his career. Around 1960, he established Europe's first Institute for Peace Research, PRIO, which still exists in Oslo. Before he was given the world's first professorship in peace research, he was involved in discussions about nonviolence and peace brigades. Later, he lived his international life, always as a sought-after professor and lecturer on peace and conflict resolution, and eventually also as a conflict resolution actor and leader of the Transcend network. Universities around the world, including in Tromsø, offer studies in Peace and Conflict Resolution, rooted in Galtung's work. Disarmament, or "reduction of standing armies," has always been an advocate. Galtung has been a sharp and vocal critic of extensive and costly armaments, imperial power and military blocs. His criticism is based on the facts, not on the basis of person or country, but with a position in the West, his criticism of US military violence has earned him many opponents. Nevertheless, his analyses are highly valued precisely in the USA, where numerous universities have invited him to guest professorships and lectures. He is a true cosmopolitan, who has lived and worked in many countries. In the "Mémorial" museum for World War II in Caen, France, there is a large department for the Culture of Peace, created by Galtung at the invitation of the museum.

The Tireless Work - Through Now 70 Years

Johan Galtung first wrote about his intention to research peace in 1951. The years in between include a great deal of work to create meeting places, conferences and organizations. He helped found the International Peace Research Association (IPRA), which in the 1980s received a UNESCO prize for peace education. IPRA's Peace Education Commission was founded in the early 1970s and has published the Journal of Peace Education since 2004. Galtung participated in the launch of the Global Campaign on Peace Education, a campaign that was nominated for the 2021 Peace Prize. This is just to name a few of his peace-related achievements.

Galtung's research and teaching have inspired generations of peace researchers and peace workers around the world. He has been nominated for the prize several times before. Here we would just like to mention that at the nomination in 2008, the written nomination was supported by 73 members of parliament, jurists at international legal institutions, then and former professors of social sciences and heads of peace institutes. This nomination also provided several examples of successful practical conflict resolution through the Transcend method. Galtung's theories express and provide an epistemological basis for cultural and structural violence prevention work, a type of peace work that the Nobel Committee has highlighted on a number of occasions as a worthy basis for a peace prize.

We believe that Johan Galtung fulfills the ideas that were the basis for the Nobel Peace Prize. The time is ripe for the person Galtung to be awarded the prize in 2024. With his person, the committee will also highlight current peace-related work around the world. More people will be able to open their eyes to the fact that conflicts can be transformed into peaceful coexistence.

Endnotes

1) This is a translation from Norwegian of the 2024 nomination for the Nobel Peace Prize submitted by professor of history Randi Rønning Balsvik and co-authored by Balsvik, Magnus Haavelsrud, Vidar Vambheim and Klaus Melf. Similar nomination texts were submitted in 2022 and 2023. Knut Holtedahl was also part of the nominating group in 2022 – he died 15th July, 2022.

Appendix 4
Peaceful Anti-Nuclear Campaign Actions in India

S.P. Uduyakumar

(spuduyakumar@gmail.com)

- Relay hunger strike – every single day 10 am to 5 pm,

- Inviting prominent political, religious or cultural leaders for day-long hunger strikes,

- Meeting officials and submitting memorandums,

- Handing over memorandums to statues,

- Dumping memorandums in a river,

- Feeding donkeys the memorandums,

- Dialogue with government officials, scientists and others,

- Setting up an expert team,

- Organizing seminars on nonviolence, democracy, development etc.,

- Organizing massive conferences,

- Organizing all party meets,

- Having political leaders meet with the Chief Minister, Prime Minister etc.,

- Inviting supporters from all over the country for solidarity public meetings, hunger strikes,

- Reaching out to nearby villagers and youth with outside volunteers and campaigners,

- District-wide teach-ins,

- State-wide agitations,

- Nation-wide campaigns,

- Sending back voter identity cards,

- Boycotting elections,

- Supporting a specific party/candidate in the elections,

- Asking the local MPs and others to resign and facilitate by-elections,

- Observing Independence Day as Black Day,

- Refusing to accept government schemes,

- Refusing to let government officials into our villages,

- Laying siege in front of the nuclear plant entrance,

- Preventing workers from entering the workplace,

- Laying siege to harbours,

- Laying siege to the State Assembly,

- Blocking trains,

- Blocking roads,

- Organizing continuous agitations of various types for a week/month,

- Burning national flags of visiting international leaders' countries,

- Burning effigies of visiting leaders,

- Bandh (shut down) all over the district/state (future plan),

- Agitations in distant towns and villages,

- Bike rally through neighboring villages and towns,

- Rallies to nearby towns and villages and agitations in those places,

- Congregating in a particular village and rallying to a nearby village or town,

- Commemorating national and international leaders' births and deaths,

- Remembering activists' deaths and sacrifices,

- Ringing Church/Temple bells and congregating people,

- All night religious vigils,

- Organizing yagnas (rituals) and special poojas (prayers),

- Prayer meetings,

- Hindu bhajans (singing) and Muslim prayer at Lourdes Church,

- Candle light processions,

- Celebrations such as "Asserting Freedom, Celebrating Resistance,"

- Celebrating religious festivals,

- Celebrating cultural festivals

- Composing and singing struggle songs,

- Poetry recitals,

- Guarding the village entrances,

- Guarding the struggle leaders' residence,

- Collecting signatures on petitions,

- Writing letters to embassies,

- Writing letters to human rights organizations,

- Writing letters to international organizations,

- Floating letters on the sea,

- Sending 'Thank You' letters to international supporters,

- Collecting info through RTI petitions,

- Publishing booklets with RTI replies,

- Non-cooperation movement,

- Refusing to let rooms and houses to nuclear plant workers,

- Refusing to sell food stuff to nuclear plant workers,

- Congregating on the sea,

- Singing and dancing on the beach,

- Marching on the seashore,

- Human chain on the seashore,

- Boycotting fishing,

- Jal-satyagraha (striking in neck-deep waters),

- Burying ourselves in the sand,

- Living in cemeteries,

- Shaving heads off,

- Wearing black shirts and/or black ribbons,

- Deserting the village temporarily,

- Burying 'time/history capsules' all over the state,

- Women canvassing support in villages and towns,

- Women leaders travelling to distant places all over the country,

- Women speakers speaking in public meetings and campaigns,

- Women breaking alcohol bottles and driving away bootleggers,

- Women abstaining from sex and pregnancy to convince their menfolk,

- Women meeting District Collector and submitting memorandums,

- Women holding press meet,

- Sending children on marches and rallies,

- Children writing thousands of postcards to authorities,

- Children meeting District Collector and submitting memorandums,

- Children submitting memorandum to the Chief Minister at the Secretariat,

- Children visiting foreign embassies and submitting memorandums,

- Children holding press meet,

- Children boycotting school,

- Youth organizing cultural programs,

- Youth organizing colleagues in neighboring villages,

- Youth guarding the village, roads etc.,

- Empowering women with newspaper and book reading during hunger strikes,

- Publishing Newsletters,

- Publishing handbills, pamphlets, booklets, books,

- Organizing photo exhibitions,

- Painting walls with specific protest messages,

- Pasting posters,

- Email campaigns,

- SMS campaigns,

- Social Media campaigns and canvassing,

- Forming social media friends' circles,

- Internet-based streamlining, live telecast, documentaries etc.,

- TV interviews,

- Radio interviews,

- Magazine interviews,

- Regular Press Releases and Updates,

- Filing cases with the High Court,

- Filing cases with the Supreme Court,

- Filing cases with the National Green Tribunal,

- Using court appearances of prisoners for campaigns,

- Legal education campaigns,

- Organizing blood donation campaigns,

- Organizing food donations,

- Serving meals for campaigners,

- Replacing round bulbs with CFL bulbs

- Supporting 'New Energy' schemes,

- Promoting solar panels,

- Promoting windmills, etc.

Authors' Biographical Notes

Zvi Bekerman (Israel), PhD, is a recently retired professor from the Seymour Fox School of Education at the Hebrew University of Jerusalem. During his tenure, he specialized in the anthropology of education, focusing on informal, integrated bilingual, civic, and multicultural education, with a particular emphasis on child learning processes. His extensive research has explored diverse educational settings, from informal environments to formal institutional frameworks. Bekerman's current research interests include studying learning dynamics within ultra-orthodox Yeshivas and exploring the pedagogical applications of artificial intelligence.

Amada Benavides de Pérez (Colombia). Graduated in Education with a specialization in Social Sciences and a master's in international relations. Consultant on the issues of borders, border development and integration; security and peace; youth; human rights, culture of peace, peace education and human rights education. She is the Founder of Schools of Peace Foundation and president since 2003. For her extensive international involvement see endnote 1 in her chapter.

Robin Burns (Australia), has worked, studied and published in psychology, social anthropology, comparative education, women's studies, and public health. Between her first Master's degree and returning to academia for her PhD on development education, she spent 3 years in the Australian Diplomatic Service. She followed Robert Aspeslagh as executive secretary of the Peace Education Commission and became the first female president of the Australian and New Zealand Comparative and International Education Society. Her last major research projects investigated the issues for scientists working in remote areas and took her to a summer on an Antarctic station.

Virginia Cawagas (The Philippines/Canada) was a Professor in Peace Education at the UN mandated University for Peace in Costa Rica, an Adjunct Professor of Education at the University of Alberta, a teacher and principal in several Philippine schools, and Executive Secretary of the Catholic Educational Association of the Philippines. She has extensive teaching and curriculum development experiences in diverse societies in education for peace, human rights, gender equality, global citizenship and critical multiculturalism. Her social activism spans the Philippines' EDSA People Power Revolution against martial law and solidarity campaigns for Indigenous Peoples, women, migrant workers, refugees, disarmament and interfaith dialogue.

Giuseppe Desideri is a Doctor of Philosophy, and is qualified and has worked in law, education, pedagogy and public administration. He served as National President of the Italian Association of Catholic Primary School Teachers (2010 – 2023). He is Rector of the Libera Università Popolare Maria Badaloni in Rome, President of the AIMC Foundation, and General Secretary of the World Union of Catholic Teachers. Author of numerous publications in pedagogy and didactics, he is a member of the scientific coordination committee of the "Centro Polispecialistico Pedagógico Paulo Freire" in Rome and President of the Foundation Casa dello Scugnizzo, (a multi-functional social assistance foundation) established in Naples by Mario Borrelli.

Diana Francis (UK), PhD, is an author, peace activist, nonviolence trainer and mediator, former President of the International Fellowship of Reconciliation (IFoR), Vice-President of the Movement for the Abolition of War (MAWE), and founding member of Rethinking Security.

Ela Gandhi (South Africa), a social worker and political activist, served two terms in the South African Parliament representing the ANC. Presently works in an honorary capacity as Chairperson of Gandhi Development Trust and Phoenix Settlement Trust and is a co-President of Religions for Peace International. She is a recipient of several local and international awards and 4 honorary doctorates from two South African Universities, a British University and an Indian University.

Celina Garcia (Costa Rica). Many years ago my life changed when a friend mentioned IPRA. Not knowingly, something missing in me as a human being, was finally fulfilled. After years of travelling internationally due to my husband's job, I returned to Costa Rica, my country of origin, and opened *Fundacion CEPPA* (Center for Peace Studies), a small foundation based on Quaker-inspired programs *Alternative to Violence Project (AVP)* used mostly in prisons, and *Creative Conflict Resolution*, a process that involves using empathy, collaboration, and creative thinking to resolve disagreements, mostly used in schools. We have trained some 26,000 adults and children in Costa Rica and several other countries. [Celina is a former executive secretary of the Peace Education Commission (eds)].

Magnus Haavelsrud (Norway). Professor emeritus at the Norwegian University of Science and Technology. He took part in the creation of the Peace Education Commission of the International Peace Research Association and served as its first Executive Secretary 1975-79. He worked with Betty Reardon in the School Program of the Institute for World Order in New York and served as the Carl-von-Ossietzky Guest Professor of the German Council for Peace and Conflict Research. He was distinguished fellow of the South African Research Chair in Development Education 2008-18. His writings on peace include studies in political socialization and educational sociology. Co-founder (with Betty Reardon) of the Global Campaign for Peace Education and since 2023 member of the Campaign´s Steering Committee. Co-founder (with Anita Wenden et al.) of the *Journal of Peace Education* serving on its Editorial Board 2004 - 2023.

Catherine Odora Hoppers (Uganda/Sweden) is an extensively published scholar, and international policy specialist across international development domains especially education, North-South questions, disarmament, peace and human security, and indigenous knowledge systems. She is the Ambassador for Non-Violence in Durban University of Technology (South Africa), and in 2015 she was given the Nelson Mandela Distinguished Africanist Award by H.E Thabo Mbeki for her promotion of indigenous knowledge systems. She got the "Woman of the Year" award and was named as a "Leading Educationist" and was honored in the Gallery of Leadership by the University of South Africa (Pretoria). She now holds a Canadian Research Chair Tier 1 in Pluralistic Societies - Transdisciplinarity, Cognitive Justice and Education in the University of Calgary, Canada, to introduce elements of her work in the SARCHI Chair to the academy in Canada.

Yumiko Kaneko (Japan). Mrs Kaneko is the Director General of the Nomura Center for Lifelong Integrated Education (Public Interest Incorporated Foundation). She has been involved with the Center for some decades since young adult illness led her to reflect and search for answers. She has embraced the integrated, holistic approach of the Center and supports Nomura Centers overseas.

Soon-Won Kang (S. Korea) is Professor emeritus at Hanshin University. During her 35 years' professorship at Hanshin University, she taught education for peace, human rights, global citizenship and international understanding, and democratization based on sociology of education and lifelong learning. As a coordinator of the Peace Education team at the Social Education Institute of Korean Christian Academy, 1995-1998, she developed and expanded Korean peace education through UNESCO, teacher education and academics. Her peace education research is focused on comparing peace education in divided societies such as Korea, Northern Ireland and Cyprus.

Soonjung Kwon (S. Korea) is an assistant professor, Carter School for Peace and Conflict Resolution at George Mason University Korea, working in education policy, school culture and change, and specializing in school violence, peace, human rights, global citizenship education and education for SDGs. At the Educational Policy Institute, Seoul Metropolitan Office of Education, she worked on related areas and on policy guides to promote students' human rights and a peaceful school culture. Active as a committee member in both the local NGO *Conflict & Dialogue* and academic Societies, she has also translated the *Encyclopedia of Peace Education* into Korean.

Mustafa Köylü (Türkiye) was born in Amasya, Türkiye in 1962. He received his BA degree in Religious Studies (1985) and an MA degree in Psychology of Religion (1989) from Ondokuz Mayıs University. He received a D. Miss. from the United Theological Seminary, Dayton, OH, USA. in 1997 and a PhD. from Ondokuz Mayıs University in Religious Education in 2002. Between 2016 and 2021, he worked as dean of Kyrgyzstan Turkish Manas University, Faculty of Theology. He currently continues to work as a professor at Ondokuz Mayıs University, Faculty of Theology. He has more than 20 published books in Turkish. He continues his work mainly on religion and values education, peace education, comparative religious education and religious communication.

Corinne Kumar (India). Corinne Kumar has dedicated her life to working for human rights and advocating alternate models of development. She founded the World Courts of Women in 1992 and continues as the coordinator. For more than 20 years she served as Secretary General of El Taller, an international NGO committed to working with civil society organizations to address issues of poverty, underdevelopment and women's rights. She was a founding member of the Centre for Informal Development Studies, of the Asian Women's Human Rights Council and of Vimochana, an NGO in Bangalore, India concerned with domestic violence, dowry-related deaths and workplace sexual harassment. Editor of Asking We Walk: The South as a New Political Imaginary, she has also published numerous journal articles. Ms Kumar has been a valued member of the Peace Education Commission.

Syed Sikander Mehdi (Pakistan), PhD. Educated at Dhaka University, Bangladesh and Australian National University, Canberra, former Professor Syed Sikander Mehdi is a leading Pakistani peace scholar. He pioneered the introduction of courses on peace studies in the public and private universities of Pakistan. He taught International Relations at Karachi University for over 30 years, and also courses on peace at the University of Jaume 1, Castellon, Spain, and the University of Innsbruck, Austria. He was a visiting research fellow at the International Peace Research Institute, Oslo, Henry Stimson Centre, Washington D.C., and Kyoto Museum for World Peace, Ritsumeikan University, Japan. Publications include peace and culture of peace, violence and nonviolence, nuclear weapons and human insecurity, forced migration issues, and museums for peace.

George Mutalemwa (Tanzania), PhD. Director and Co-founder of the Africa Peace and Development Network and former Executive Secretary of the Association of Catholic Universities and Higher Institutes of Africa and Madagascar (ACUHIAM). Professor Mutaalemwa has been Acting Deputy Vice-Chancellor for Academic Affairs at St. Augustine University of Tanzania (SAUT). He was the Founding Editor-in-Chief of the *Journal of Sociology and Development,* and his scholarly publications include *Peace Studies for Sustain-*

able Development in Africa: Conflicts and Peace Oriented Conflict Resolution and *Peace as Nonviolence: Topics in African Peace Studies.* He is a Council member of the International Peace Research Association (IPRA) and the African Good Governance Network (AGGN).

Mazim Qumsiyeh (Palestine). Prof. Qumsiyeh is founder and volunteer director of the Palestine Institute for Biodiversity and Sustainability, Bethlehem University (palestinenature.org). He published over 250 scientific papers, over 30 book chapters, hundreds of articles, and several books including *Sharing the Land of Canaan* and *Popular Resistance in Palestine.* He previously served on the faculties of the University of Tennessee, Duke, and Yale Universities. Since returning to Palestine in 2008 he and his wife have started a number of institutions and projects. In 2014, they founded and run (as full-time volunteers) the Palestine Institute for Biodiversity and Sustainability (PIBS) at Bethlehem University. His publications cover topics ranging from cultural heritage to human rights to biodiversity conservation to cancer. Currently leading the effort to produce the new National Biodiversity Strategy and Action Plan for Palestine. He serves on the board of a number of Palestinian youth and service organizations and oversees many projects related to sustainability of human and natural communities. He is laureate of the Paul K. Feyerabend Foundation award, the Takreem award, Peaceseeker of the year award, and was nominated for the Nobel Peace Prize 2025.

Robin Richardson (UK) was the first director of the World Studies Project, 1973-79, and in that capacity had several contacts with IPRA's peace education commission (PEC). In the 1980s he was an adviser or inspector in local education authorities in England, and was then director of the Runnymede Trust. In the period 2002-2012 he worked as an equalities consultant for the government's Department for Children, Schools and Families. Latterly he has compiled a personal website at www.patience-and-passion.org.

Hillel Schenker (Israel) has been the Israeli Co-Editor of the *Palestine-Israel Journal* (www.pij.org) based in East Jerusalem, the only joint Israeli-Palestinian publication, since 2002. From 1977 to 1990 he was one of the editors of *New Outlook,* the Tel Aviv-based Middle East Monthly in the spirit of Martin Buber's philosophy of dialogue. Schenker has written for *The Guardian, The Nation, Los Angeles Times, L.A. Weekly, Ha'aretz, The Jerusalem Post, The Jerusalem*

Report, The Times of Israel and commented on the BBC, CNN, i24 and other print and electronic media. He is currently completing an activist memoir whose working title is "From Utopia to Dystopia? Eye-Witness in Israel-Palestine".

Alexander Sergunin (b. Russian Federation, 1960) is Professor of International Relations at the St. Petersburg State University and Higher School of Economics (Moscow). He has a PhD (History), Moscow State University (1985) and Habilitation (Political Science), St. Petersburg State University (1994). He teaches International Relations Theory (including Peace Research School) and Conflict Resolution. He had numerous research projects with the former Copenhagen Peace Research Institute, Stockholm International Peace Research Institute, Peace Research Institute Oslo, Schleswig Holstein Institute for Peace Studies (Kiel), United States Institute of Peace, etc. His research focus is conflict prevention and resolution, confidence — and security-building measures, arms control regimes in regions such as Europe, Arctic, Asia-Pacific region and US-Russian bilateral relations.

Yurii Sheliazhenko (Ukraine) is a peace scholar and human rights defender. He holds a PhD in jurisprudence. He is active in local and international peace networks, such as Ukrainian Pacifist Movement, European Bureau for Conscientious Objection, International Peace Bureau, War Resisters' International, World BEYOND War. He also maintains the peace education project Free Civilians School of Pacifism. Regardless of his unequivocal and systematic condemnation of the Russian army's attacks on Ukraine, the Ukrainian authorities are prosecuting him for his pacifist appeals and defence of the right to conscientious objection to military mobilization.

Dale T. Snauwaert (US), PhD, is Professor of Philosophy of Education and Peace Studies, Director of the Graduate Certificate Program in the Foundations of Peace Education and the Undergraduate Minor in Peace Studies at The University of Toledo. He is the Founding Editor of *In Factis Pax: Online Journal of Peace Education and Social Justice*. He is the author of the recent book *Teaching Peace as a Matter of Justice: Toward a Pedagogy of Moral Reasoning* as well as *Exploring Betty A. Reardon's Perspective on Peace; Reclaimative Post-Conflict Justice*, with Janet Gerson *Betty A. Reardon: A Pioneer in Education for Peace and Human Rights;* and *Betty A. Reardon: Key Texts in Gender and Peace*, with Betty Reardon.

Crain Soudien (South Africa) is a sociologist and an emeritus professor in Education and African Studies at the University of Cape Town, an Honorary Professor at Nelson Mandela University, a Distinguished Visiting Professor at the University of Johannesburg and the President of Cornerstone Institute. A former Deputy Vice-Chancellor at the University of Cape Town and a former Chief Executive Officer at the Human Sciences Research Council, he is a fellow of the International Academy of Education, the African Academy of Science, a Senior Fellow of NORRAG, Geneva Graduate Institute, a member of the Academy of Science of South Africa, and a Chen Yidan Visiting Global Fellow at Harvard University. He has published extensively in the areas of education, culture, history and social difference.

Amal Amara Takkash (Palestine). Amal is a dedicated educator, advocate for social justice, and a champion of Palestinian cultural heritage. Born in Jaffa, Palestine, she spent her formative years in Gaza before her family moved to Egypt, where she completed her education. Amal's career includes teaching and curriculum development in Kuwait, followed by graduate studies in the United States. She later returned to Egypt and eventually settled in Gaza. With a profound passion for children's literature, Amal gathers and publishes traditional Palestinian songs and games for children. In 1996 and with the support of Nomura Center for Lifelong Integrated Education, she founded Dar il Hikma Cultural Center in Gaza, focusing on peace education through music, play, and storytelling. In her free time, Amal finds joy in nature walks, keeping her family entertained with social media trends, creating recipes by combining Palestinian dishes with international cuisine, and snuggling with her cat and a good book.

Toh Swee-Hin (S.H.Toh) (Malaysia/Canada) is Professor Emeritus, University of Alberta (Canada) and formerly Distinguished Professor, University for Peace in Costa Rica and Director, Multi-Faith Centre, Griffith University (Australia) promoting interfaith dialogue toward a culture of peace. His vision and action for peace encompasses formal institutions and grassroots movements to educate for peace, disarmament, human rights, social-economic justice, intercultural understanding, sustainable development, interfaith dialogue and global citizenship in the Global South and North as well as in UNESCO and local and international networks. His work for peace and non-violence was recognised with the 2000 UNESCO Prize for Peace Education.

S.P. Udayakumar (India). As a secondary English teacher in Tigrai Provice of Ethiopia he learnt of UNESCO and established UNESCO Clubs in schools there. This led to initiating peace activities in Ethiopia after discovering IPRA and PEC. Successive PEC executive secretaries encouraged him in his work and to pursue post-graduate study in the US which culminated in three years as Johan Galtung's assistant during doctoral studies at the University of Hawai'i. Since return to India he has become a committed anti-nuclear activist and is currently the Coordinator of the People's Movement Against Nuclear Energy (PMANE).

Werner Wintersteiner (Austria), PhD, is a retired professor from Klagenfurt University, Austria. Specialized in German didactics and teacher training, he is also a peace researcher and peace educator. He was the founding director of the "Centre for Peace Research and Peace Education" at Klagenfurt University and still serves as a member of the team of the Master's programme Global Citizenship Education (GCED). He is also a board member of the Herbert C. Kelman Institute for Interactive Conflict Transformation, Vienna/Jerusalem. His research fields include peace education and global citizenship education; peace, conflict and memory politics; culture and peace; the Alps-Adriatic region; literature and peace; literature education.

Christoph Wulf (Germany), Dr. phil., is Professor of Anthropology and Education at Freie Universität Berlin. His books have been translated into twenty languages. He was founding secretary of the Education Commission of the International Peace Research Association, president of the Network Educational Science Amsterdam, and initiator and chairman of the Commission on Pedagogical Anthropology, German Society for Educational Science. He received an honorary professorship from the University of Bucharest and continues to enjoy visiting professorships and research visits around the world. Main research interests: Historical-cultural anthropology, pedagogical anthropology, aesthetic and intercultural education, performativity and ritual, diversity and emotion, mimesis and imagination; peace and cultural education; Anthropocene research.

Kazuyo Yamane (Japan), PhD (Peace Studies), University of Bradford. She was an Associate Professor of Peace Studies from 2011 to 2016 and a former vice director of the Kyoto Museum for World Peace, Ritsumeikan University;

Visiting Researcher of Ritsumeikan University; Expert Advisor to the Kyoto Museum for World Peace; a Senior Advisor to the International Network of Museums for Peace (INMP); an editorial member of INMP Newsletter and Muse Newsletter of "the Japanese Citizens' Network of Museums for Peace", and Author of *Grassroots Museums for Peace in Japan: Unknown Efforts for Peace and Reconciliation*, etc.

Maung (Mr) Zarni (Burma/Myanmar). Exiled in UK, Maung Zarni is a leading scholar of Rohingya genocide and a well-known peace and rights activists. He is a non-resident fellow with the (Genocide) Documentation Center – Cambodia, co-founder of Southeast Asian activists and scholars organisation FORSEA, and Burmese coordinator of the Free Rohingya Coalition. He pioneered using InfoTech in the 1990s for building the Free Burma Coalition, an international human rights movement. He has a BSc (chemistry, University of Mandalay,1985), an MA (education, University of California, Davis, 1991) and a PhD (curriculum and instruction, University of Wisconsin, Madison, 1998). Undertakings include teaching and research in the USA, UK, Thailand, Malaysia, and Brunei. His most recent honour is his nomination for the 2024 Nobel Peace Prize.

Robert (Bob) Zuber (US) PhD, is director of UN-based Global Action to Prevent War and Armed Conflict. He directs a team of researchers, advocates and interns monitoring all facets of the UN's work on peace and security. He is a consultant, adviser or board member to non-profit and educational organizations including Green Map System, the Martin Luther King Jr. Center in Cameroon, Global Connections Television, and Women in International Security. With degrees in philosophy, theology, psychology and education from Yale and Columbia Universities, he has written and spoken extensively and organized seminars and conferences in over 30 countries on topics from atrocity crime prevention and combating illicit small arms to the full participation of women in peace policies and processes.

Acknowledgments

Our sincere thanks are offered to all the contributors to this volume. It has been a pleasure to work with you and to learn of your involvement in a variety of contexts and learning situations, so many of you over decades, as the search for peace continues.

Palestinian journalist Aisha Zakzouk has generously given permission for us to use for the book cover her delightful photo of children with traditional handmade kites at the annual Dar il-Hikma (Nomura Center) Palestine kite festival in Gaza 2023.

We would also like to thank friends and colleagues for their interest and suggestions, prompting us to look for further input from diverse contexts.

To Tony Jenkins, who offered to publish this with Peace Knowledge Press, our warmest gratitude. Your patience, care and encouragement has been outstanding. Every best wish with your work with the Press.

Finally, thank you to our four-footed friends Mandy the cat and Rino the dog for their patience with their humans during the production.

Robin Burns and Magnus Haaveslrud, editors

www.ingramcontent.com/pod-product-compliance
Lightning Source LLC
Chambersburg PA
CBHW031114020426
42333CB00012B/89